The Fabergé
IMPERIAL
EASTER
EGGS

Detail of Fifteenth Anniversary egg, 1911

The Fabergé IMPERIAL EASTER EGGS

Tatiana Fabergé

Lynette G. Proler

Valentin V. Skurlov

CHRISTIE'S

Christie's would like to thank Elena and Victor Ilyukhin and Crédit du Rhône, Geneva, for their encouragement and support on this book.

First published by Christie, Manson and Woods Ltd, 1997
8 King Street, St James's, London SW1 6QT

All rights reserved. No part of this publication may be reproduced, stored in
a retrieval system or transmitted, in any form or by any means, electronic, mechanical or
otherwise, without the prior written permission of the publisher.

British Library Cataloguing-in-Publication Data
A catalogue record for this book is available from the British Library

ISBN 0-90343-248-X

© 1997 Tatiana Fabergé, Lynette G. Proler, Valentin V. Skurlov

Editor: Cathy Muscat
Designers: Martin Richards, Simon Bell
Printed and bound in Great Britain by P.J. Reproductions Ltd, London

Contents

Foreword by Alexis de Tiesenhausen	6
Preface	7
The Imperial Easter Eggs: an updated and corrected list	10

PART 1

1	The First Imperial Easter Egg	15
2	The House of Fabergé	21
3	The Imperial Family	35
4	The Imperial Easter Eggs	44
5	The 1902 Exhibition: Baron von Dervis Mansion	52
6	The Austerity Years: The Russo-Japanese War 1904-1905	58
7	A Discovery: The Last Imperial Easter Eggs, 1917	61
8	After the Revolution	64
9	The Kelkh Easter Eggs	70
10	Undocumented Easter Eggs	78
11	The Kremlin Collection by Tatiana Muntian	82

PART 2

Catalogue Raisonné of the Imperial Easter Eggs	91
The Original Fabergé Invoices Translated	236

PART 3

Appendices

I	Description from a Fabergé album of the Imperial Easter eggs presented to Alexandra Fedorovna between 1907 and 1916	250
II	Newspaper accounts of the 1902 exhibition at the von Dervis mansion	251
III	Descriptions of Imperial Easter eggs from inventories: Gatchina Palace (1891), the Winter Palace (1909)	253
IV	Documents certifying transfer of confiscated treasures from the Anichkov Palace to the Moscow Kremlin Armoury (1917) and their later transfer to the Sovnarkom (1922)	255
V	Correspondence, certificates and inventories relating to the transfer of museum treasures from the Foreign Exchange Fund of the Narkomfin, the Moscow Jewellers' Community and other sources, to the Moscow Kremlin Armoury	257
VI	Information on the sales of Imperial Easter eggs from the Moscow Kremlin Armoury in 1930 and 1933	262

Notes	263
Select Bibliography	267
Index	268
Photographic credits	271
Acknowledgements	272

Foreword

Some might ask: 'Why another book on Fabergé Imperial eggs with so many already written on the subject?' Such was my reaction when I first heard of the project. Reading the manuscript, however, completely changed my mind.

For more than sixty years, Fabergé scholars have been deprived access to the Russian archives which, until recently, were closed and dispersed, preventing proper research and evaluation of the House of Fabergé's success. Would a book on Cartier, for example, be conceivable without access to the company archives in Paris? The wealth of information unveiled in this book by the authors is, therefore, totally unparalleled. Not only have they located almost all the invoices for the Imperial Easter eggs created by the Fabergé firm but, after many years of uncertainty and conjecture, they have finally established the correct chronology of the eggs between 1885 and 1917, discovering 'en passant' various other related and previously unknown facts. We now know, for instance, that in 1904 and 1905, eggs were not delivered to the Imperial family due to the political crisis Russia was suffering both at home and abroad. Furthermore, we finally learn the circumstances surrounding the creation, in 1885, of the first egg, which was delivered to Tsar Alexander III for his wife, the Empress Maria Fedorovna.

We also learn more about what happened to such works of art under the Bolshevik regime, when museum curators and art experts were confronted by the dilemma between their duties as curators and the demand of the Soviet government to sell priceless works of art to the West – including, of course, Fabergé's Imperial commissions. Opposed to the sale of some of the Imperial eggs abroad, the director of the Armoury Museum had discretely argued, for example, that such an action would then 'make it impossible to set up a Marxist Leninist Exhibition'!

This policy of selling Russian treasures abroad has resulted in certain paradoxes to which Russia alone has the key. How did the museums manage to retain, for example, such masterpieces as the Romanov Tercentary egg, the Trans-Siberian Railway egg or the Alexander III Equestrian egg, each a powerful expression of Imperial Russian nationalism? It might be argued that the sombre style of the Steel Military egg made it difficult to sell, but what about the others? Not only is each individual egg an amazing 'tour de force', but they all celebrate the Romanov dynasty and achievements under the Tsars – ideas in clear opposition to the basic concepts of the new communist regime. Yet despite all the political and cultural dogma advocated by Lenin and Stalin, Russia has succeeded in retaining possibly the most fascinating and historically important of the Fabergé Imperial eggs.

Alexis de Tiesenhausen
*Head of Christie's Russian Department
in Europe and America*

Preface

Imperial Russia has always seemed romantic to the outside world, with the famed splendours of its lavish Court, its magnificent palaces and its gold-domed churches. It was here that Tsars Alexander III and Nicholas II reigned at the end of the 19th and the beginning of the 20th centuries. Like their predecessors who had endowed Russia with sumptuous palaces filled with art, they too encouraged and inspired designers and craftsmen to create the most exquisite works of art, including the Imperial Easter eggs made by Carl Fabergé.

The excitement that these beautiful objects elicited when they appeared on the Western market shortly after the Russian Revolution was partially due to the fact that they had previously been seen by only a few members of the Russian Imperial family, for they had been given as personal gifts. Indeed, a long-time employee of the House of Fabergé, H.C. Bainbridge, noted in his memoirs that he had worked for the firm for many years before he learned, purely by chance, that Carl Fabergé was making intricately jewelled Easter eggs for the Tsar.[1]

It was in trying times that these treasures began to leave Russia and to be purchased by Western collectors. In 1934, the first Imperial Easter egg that Fabergé made, the white enamelled and gold Hen egg, realized only £85 at Christie's in London, while the more elaborate eggs sold for between £500 and several thousand dollars. Since then, of course, prices have rocketed. The most recent Imperial Easter egg to come on the market, the Winter egg, which had been sold in 1949 for $4,760, fetched the world record price for an Imperial Easter egg of SFr 7,263,500 ($5.6 million) when sold at Christie's, Geneva, in November 1994.

Only a few Fabergé exhibitions have been organized in Europe and the United States since the 1960s, where the Imperial Easter eggs inevitably took centre stage. They caused a sensation whenever they were displayed and held viewers spellbound. While much information has been published about them, they have never yet been fully and accurately catalogued. A noted author on the subject of Fabergé writes that '... earlier speculative datings of eggs have been somewhat thrown into disarray due to findings in the Imperial archives'.[2] This is putting it mildly indeed. The old structure has not just been shaken, but has entirely crumbled, giving way to a new and authoritative one.

Many theories and myths about the eggs have been perpetuated over the decades, and the standard information has often been based on conjecture and hazy tradition rather than documented fact. For instance, it has been claimed that the Imperial Mosaic Easter egg in the collection of Her Majesty Queen Elizabeth II was originally purchased by King George V from Emanuel Snowman's firm, Wartski, in 1934. However, the authors have discovered an invoice in the Royal Archives that shows that Cameo Corner of New Oxford Street sold the egg to King George V in 1933.[3] But how could A. Kenneth Snowman, as late as 1993, write '... I do not, in all honesty, believe that there is much really fresh to be said on the subject [of

Fabergé] at this late stage' in the knowledge that material in the Russian archives was already beginning to reveal new and enlightening documentation?[4]

Notwithstanding Snowman's statement, one of the central problems facing previous researchers and authors has been that of determining the correct sequence of the years in which the Imperial Easter eggs were made, as well as the first year in which an Easter egg was created by Fabergé for the Tsar. As long ago as April 1934, Franz Birbaum, the firm's chief designer, wrote to Carl Fabergé's son, Eugène, that it would be interesting to compile a comprehensive descriptive list of the Imperial Easter eggs,[5] but nothing was done about this. The possibility became more remote as, over the years, the men and women involved in creating the eggs died, many of them facing very difficult times after their escape from Russia.

Because access to the archives in Russia was prohibited, it is understandable that erroneous and imprecise information about the Imperial Easter eggs was perpetuated year after year, publication after publication. And yet, inaccuracies on the Imperial Easter eggs still persist. For example, in the catalogue accompanying the 1996 Fabergé in America exhibition, the number of Imperial Easter eggs is incorrectly reported to be 56, and it is also asserted that the first Easter egg was produced in 1884,[6] whereas we now know that 1885 is the correct date. Another recent source likewise has attempted to date the first Imperial Easter egg to 1884, and has suggested that Fabergé produced the first Imperial Easter egg on his own, without an explicit order from the Cabinet.[7]

After the 1917 Revolution the archives were sealed and kept under lock and key for over seventy years until *glasnost* made it possible to search the bookshelves and files. Many of the documents and photographs in this book are taken from these archives, and have never before been published.

We believed that a thorough search of the various dusty shelves and files in Russia would yield Fabergé's invoices, which would give details of the transactions and payments from the Tsar for the eggs. Our belief proved correct and, as a result, we are now able to present invoices for 40 of the 50 Imperial eggs created by Fabergé, thus establishing, among other things, the prices paid for them and the dates of their manufacture and presentation. These transactions are confirmed by account books from His Imperial Majesty's Cabinet, and a statement by N. Petrov, Chief of the Cabinet, which gives the dates and prices of another two eggs. Added to this is the information assembled from correspondence between Alexandra Fedorovna's Secretariat and His Imperial Majesty's Cabinet concerning payments made to Fabergé in 1912 and 1914-1916. An exciting bonus was our recent discovery of photographs of two of Carl Fabergé's original watercolours, both dated 1917, together with correspondence relating to them. The two additional Imperial Easter eggs they represent have not been included in the total count of 50 eggs, as the documentation is not conclusive as to whether these eggs were completed.

Our researches have enabled us to establish for the first time the correct chronology of the famous Imperial Easter eggs created by the House of Fabergé, based on authentic documents and reliable archival material. We have been able to demonstrate that the first Imperial Easter egg was definitely made in 1885. Equally important, we have been able to prove that Tsar Alexander III was directly involved in the execution and ordering of the first Imperial Easter egg, and that Fabergé received suggestions on the design of these eggs through His Imperial Majesty's Cabinet. We have also been able to correct some traditional misnomers: for example, the egg previously called the Cuckoo egg was known at Fabergé's as the Cockerel egg, and the Orange Tree egg was called the Bay Tree egg.

The information gathered from the archives has resulted in the elimination from the corpus of several Easter eggs that have previously been catalogued as Imperial. The mythical figure of 56 eggs keeps cropping up and it is now clear that it includes some eggs that are not Imperial. A summary and review of these undocumented Easter eggs can be found in Chapter 10.

We have also discovered documents disclosing the sad fate of some of the Imperial Easter eggs during the period of sales in the 1930s to finance the Soviet administration. A number of eggs were sold from the collection of the Moscow Kremlin Armoury. Only ten of the Imperial Easter eggs remain in Moscow today, and for many years it was forbidden even to mention the shameful fact that most of these unique treasures had been sold. Today, the Moscow Kremlin Armoury, which houses within its walls a priceless treasure trove formerly belonging to the Russian Tsars, acknowledges the great importance of the Imperial Easter eggs by stating that 'the pride of the Kremlin collection... are undoubtedly the Imperial Easter eggs'.[8]

In addition to providing essential information for museum curatorial staff and Fabergé experts in their scholarly activities, we trust that, through the inherent beauty of the Imperial eggs and the remarkable historical background against which they were created and subsequently dispersed, this long-awaited volume will provide interesting and pleasurable reading. We hope that these pages will evoke some of the spirit of the time and place, and will form a fitting tribute to Carl Fabergé to commemorate the 150th anniversary of his birth.

Notes

1. In the 19th century, the Russian calendar followed the old-style Julian calendar which lagged 12 days behind the Gregorian calendar used in the West. In the letters and documents presented throughout this book, the Russian dating system has been adhered to. Easter dates from 1895 to 1916 are taken from the St Petersburg encyclopedia Brockhaus and Efron.

2. The catalogue raisonné section features relevant excerpts from the Fabergé invoices. Full translations of the original invoices and a summarized pictorial chronology of the Imperial Easter eggs appear in a separate section at the back of the book.

3. The majority of the images of the Imperial Easter eggs and their surprises have been enlarged so that their beautifully intricate details can be fully examined and appreciated. The actual measurements can be found in the detailed description that accompanies each egg listed in the catalogue raisonné section.

The Imperial Easter eggs: an updated and corrected list

Sequential N° of Eggs	Year Presented and Empress MF = Maria Fedorovna AF = Alexandra Fedorovna	Name of egg	Corrections to Previous Literature
1.	1885/MF	Hen egg	von Habsburg and Lopato had suggested 1884 as date for Hen egg
2.	1886/MF	Hen egg with sapphire pendant (missing)	
3.	1887/MF	Blue Serpent Clock egg	
4.	1888/MF	Cherub egg with chariot (missing)	
5.	1889/MF	Nécessaire egg (missing)	
6.	1890/MF	Danish Palaces egg	Previously dated 1895
7.	1891/MF	Memory of Azov egg	
8.	1892/MF	Diamond Trellis egg	
9.	1893/MF	Caucasus egg	
10.	1894/MF	Renaissance egg	
11.	1895/MF	Twelve Monograms egg	Previously dated 1892. All earlier authorities assign Danish Palaces egg to 1895 (it belongs in fact to 1890)
12.	1895/AF	Rosebud egg	
13.	1896/MF	Alexander III egg (missing)	
14.	1896/AF	Revolving Miniatures egg	
15.	1897/MF	Mauve Enamel egg (missing)	Earlier authorities assign Pelican egg to 1897 (it belongs in fact to 1898)
16.	1897/AF	Coronation egg	
17.	1898/MF	Pelican egg	Previously dated 1897
18.	1898/AF	Lilies of the Valley egg	Previously thought to have been made for MF
19.	1899/MF	Pansy egg	Empress not previously identified
20.	1899/AF	Bouquet of Lilies Clock egg	Empress not previously identified
21.	1900/MF	Cockerel egg	Previously named the Cuckoo egg and thought to have been made for AF
22.	1900/AF	Trans-Siberian Railway egg	
23.	1901/MF	Gatchina Palace egg	Previously dated 1902
24.	1901/AF	Basket of Wild Flowers egg	Previously thought to be non-Imperial
25.	1902/MF	Empire Nephrite egg (missing)	
26.	1902/AF	Clover egg	
27.	1903/MF	Danish Jubilee egg (missing)	Previously dated 1888 or 1906 and thought to have been made for AF
28.	1903/AF	Peter the Great egg	
	1904	No eggs made this year	Alexander III Commemorative egg or Moscow Kremlin egg previously assigned to this year
	1905	No eggs made this year	Colonnade egg previously assigned to this year
29.	1906/MF	Swan egg	Previously thought to have been made for AF

Sequential N° of Eggs	Year Presented and Empress MF = Maria Fedorovna AF = Alexandra Fedorovna	Name of Egg	Corrections to Previous Literature
30.	1906/AF	Moscow Kremlin egg	Previously dated 1904
31.	1907/MF	Cradle with Garlands egg	Previously dated 1905 or 1910; thought to have been made for AF. Previously named Love Trophy egg
32.	1907/AF	Rose Trellis egg	
33.	1908/MF	Peacock egg	
34.	1908/AF	Alexander Palace egg	
35.	1909/MF	Alexander III Commemorative egg (missing)	
36.	1909/AF	Standard egg	
37.	1910/MF	Alexander III Equestrian egg	
38.	1910/AF	Colonnade egg	Previously dated 1905
39.	1911/MF	Bay Tree egg	Previously named Orange Tree egg
40.	1911/AF	Fifteenth Anniversary egg	
41.	1912/MF	Napoleonic egg	
42.	1912/AF	Tsarevich egg	
43.	1913/MF	Winter egg	
44.	1913/AF	Romanov Tercentenary egg	
45.	1914/MF	Grisaille egg	Previously named Catherine the Great egg
46.	1914/AF	Mosaic egg	
47.	1915/MF	Red Cross egg with Imperial Portraits	
48.	1915/AF	Red Cross egg with Triptych	
49.	1916/MF	Order of St George egg	
50.	1916/AF	Steel Military egg	

The Last Imperial Easter Eggs (possibly never completed)

	1917/MF	Karelian Birch egg	Never identified in prior publications
	1917/AF	Blue Tsarevich Constellation egg	Prior publications concentrated on Twilight egg now known to be non-Imperial

Undocumented Eggs with Previous Imperial Attributions

	1889	Resurrection egg
	1885 or 1891	Blue Striped Enamel egg
	1899	Spring Flowers egg
	1913	Nicholas II Equestrian egg
	1917	Twilight egg

Reflections of Glory
The creations of a master craftsman

ABOVE: *Hen egg, 1885, The* FORBES *Magazine Collection. This is the first Imperial Easter egg made by Carl Fabergé for Tsar Alexander* III

PRECEDING PAGES: *Anichkov Palace, St Petersburg, and His Imperial Majesty's Cabinet (building with columns pictured on the left)*

1

The First Imperial Easter Egg

The discovery in the Russian archives of the following letter was cause for great excitement. This was the breakthrough needed to resolve two of the major questions that previous historians had debated for over fifty years – namely, in which year was the first Imperial Easter egg made by Fabergé, and was the Tsar involved in its design?

This letter was written on 1 February 1885 by Tsar Alexander III, called Sasha by his family, to his brother Grand Duke Vladimir Alexandrovich, asking him to speak personally to Carl Fabergé about the design of the surprise concealed inside an Easter egg.

> *This could be very nice indeed. I would suggest replacing the last present by a small pendant egg of some precious stone. Please speak to Fabergé about this, I would be very grateful to you... Sasha.* [9]

This letter definitively verifies 1885 as the year of manufacture and delivery of the first of the Imperial Easter eggs, designed by Carl Fabergé for Tsar Alexander III to present to his wife, the Empress Maria Fedorovna, on the occasion of the twentieth anniversary of their betrothal.

This was the beginning of a tradition that was to last thirty-two years. The House of Fabergé produced exquisite Easter eggs first for Tsar Alexander III until his death in 1894, and then for his son and heir, Nicholas II, who carried on the legacy, presenting an annual Easter egg not only to his wife, Alexandra Fedorovna, but also to his mother, the Dowager Empress Maria Fedorovna.

One month after Alexander's letter, Grand Duke Vladimir, enjoying his involvement in this secret project, sent the now famous Easter egg to the Tsar, together with a letter written in mock-pompous, archaic style:

Grand Duke Vladimir Alexandrovich (1847–1909)

*Tsar Alexander III
(1845–1894)*

*The Empress Maria
Fedorovna (1857–1905)*

21 March 1885

I send you herewith, dear Sasha, an egg made according to your wishes by the jeweller Fabergé. In my opinion, the article is a complete success and can even be said to be praiseworthy for its fine and intricate workmanship. In accordance with your wishes, the ring was replaced by an expensive ruby pendant egg, the stone of impeccable quality. If Minny (the Empress Maria Fedorovna) should wish to wear the little egg separately – this symbol of autocracy, all honour to it – the case contains a thin chain for the purpose. I attach hereto a brief, and probably unclear, set of instructions on how this complicated article should be handled in order to extract the treasure contained therein. First, turn the top half to the left and remove it. Second, repeat this operation with the yolk. Third, having grasped the hen in your hands, press under its crop, and at the same time, after seizing the beak with your fingernails, lift it up, which will cause the bird to split into two. Fourth, you must take out the crown, base forward, and having grasped each half with four fingers, you must bend them both back so that a diamond rim remains, with the aforementioned symbol of autocracy; the rim should be pressed at its base, at the end where a little joint-pin protrudes. The rim is then folded back, and the ruby treasure can

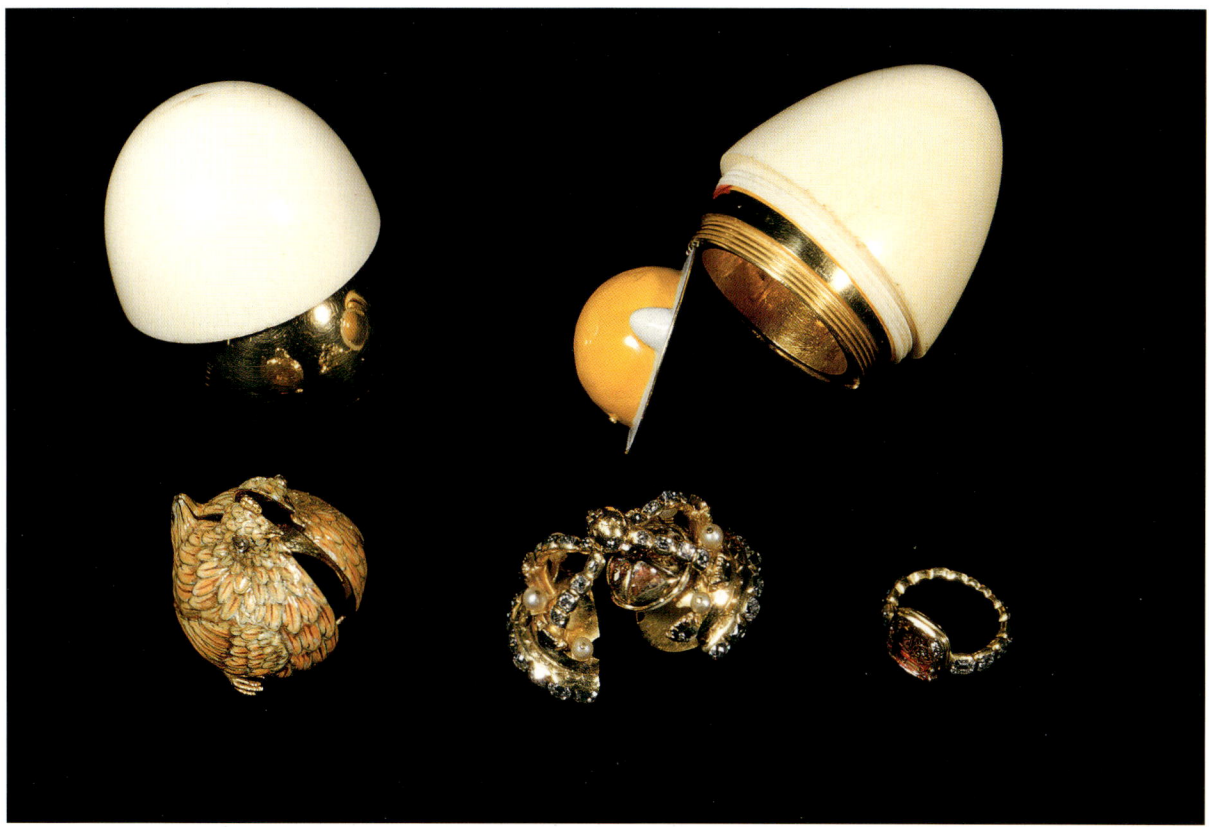

This royal jewelled and enamelled Danish gold Easter egg (early 18th century) probably inspired the first Imperial Easter egg. (Chronological collection of the Queen of Denmark)

then be unhooked. Altogether, this object in the totality of its various component parts calls for the most delicate handling. I have tried to be as clear as possible, and submit to your indulgent judgement the extent to which I have succeeded.

Man, irrespective of the social position to which fate has called him, is by nature a cadger, and I therefore end my missive with an immodest request: if you find that you have any little eggs left over from last year, could you very kindly spare them for me, as my allowance from the treasury is insufficient and does not correspond to the number of people I have to embrace at Easter. And for this my immodesty I apologize most profoundly. [10]

The Tsar was delighted with the Easter egg, but seemed worried about the Empress's reception of his gift, and wrote to his brother the very same day.

Gatchina, 21 March 1885

I am very grateful to you, dear Vladimir, for the trouble you have taken in placing the order and for the execution of the order itself, which could not have been more successful: the workmanship is really very fine and exquisite. Your instructions for the delicate handling of the object are so explicit that I was able to carry them out easily and with complete success. I do hope that the egg will have the desired effect on its future owner [the Empress Maria Fedorovna].

On my return to St Petersburg I shall send you any glass eggs that may be left over...

Your brother, Sasha. [11]

What had inspired the Tsar in 1885 to present his wife with this golden gift at Easter time? The answer lay in the fact that Easter is the most important celebration of the Russian Church year, as significant as Christmas is in the West. The following extract from a letter written by the Empress Maria Fedorovna to her mother, Queen Louise of Denmark, gives a good idea of the spirit that prevailed on those occasions.

Livadia, Wednesday evening, 16 April 1886

Easter night with the marvellous, solemn service in our lovely little church was magnificent. It began with a procession in which we all walked round the church, each holding a lighted candle and preceded by the choir chanting the Easter hymn Christ is Risen *most beautifully...* [12]

The centuries-old Russian tradition of bringing hand-dyed eggs to church to be blessed during the Easter midnight service, and then presenting them to family and friends, evolved over the centuries into the exchange of valuable Easter presents among members of St Petersburg society.

Every year the Imperial family's attendance at the Easter midnight church service was recorded in the St Petersburg newspaper, *Novoie Vremia*, as in this entry on 9 April 1914:

6 April: Their Majesties sojourn in the Crimea.

Their Majesties the Emperor and the Empress Alexandra Fedorovna and their august children attended the Easter midnight service and liturgy at the Church of the Livadia Palace, to which Grand Duke Konstantin Konstantinovich, Grand Duchess Elisaveta Mavrikievna and Grand Duke Dimitrii Konstantinovich were also invited.

The service held on Holy Easter night at the Church of the Anichkov Palace was attended by Her Imperial Majesty Empress Maria Fedorovna... On Easter Sunday about 600 people came to pay their respects, all of whom kissed Her Imperial Majesty's hand and received from her a china egg. On the following day another 600 people came to pay their respects. [13]

Accounts such as these underscore the significance of Easter in the Russian Orthodox Church. The solemnity of Good Friday was followed by celebrations after the Saturday midnight service, when aristocratic families gathered at huge banquets to end their fast, presenting Easter eggs to their families and friends.

Tsars Alexander III and Nicholas II continued that ritual. In all, the House of Fabergé created 50 Imperial Easter eggs, 30 for Maria Fedorovna and 20 for Alexandra Fedorovna, elegant treasures so perfectly crafted that they elevated the jeweller's art to sublime heights.

Anichkov Palace, St Petersburg

On the Champ de Mars, in front of the Winter Palace before the beginning of the 1904 parade. Left to right: Grand Duke Dmitri Constantinovich (1860–1919), Prince Felix Yusupov Count Sumarokov Elston (1856–1928) and Grand Duke Vladimir Alexandrovich (1847–1909)

From left to right: Empress Maria Fedorovna (1847–1928), her mother Queen Louise of Denmark (1817–1899) and her sister the Princess of Wales (1844–1925)

2

The House of Fabergé

The four-storey House of Fabergé at 24, Bolshaia Morskaia, St Petersburg, housed the main workshops and sales room, an art studio, a library and Fabergé's own apartments.

The Fabergé family originated in France, but were forced to flee their native land in the 17th century because of the religious persecution suffered by Huguenots (Protestants) in a predominantly Catholic country. During the early 19th century the family settled in Russia. Gustav Fabergé, born in 1814, was a goldsmith's apprentice in St Petersburg and opened his own modest jewellery shop there in 1842 at 12, Bolshaia Morskaia. His eldest son, Peter Carl (or Carl Gustavovich to use the Russian formula), was born on 30 May 1846. Gustav wanted him to have all the education and training he would need to succeed in life, and when Carl was 18, he sent him out of Russia to explore the world, exposing him to the very best Europe had to offer and apprenticing him to several respected goldsmiths in Frankfurt, Paris and London. In 1860, Gustav retired to Dresden, leaving the firm in the hands of capable managers. In 1872, at the age of 26, Carl returned to St Petersburg an accomplished goldsmith ready to take the destiny of the House of Fabergé into his own hands. Over the course of the next decade his expertise and proficiency as a jeweller elevated him to the ranks of the most renowned jewellers throughout Russia and Europe.

The year 1882 was the pivotal point in Carl's career because four separate events occurred that set the House of Fabergé on course to its zenith. First, Carl was left in charge of the entire firm by the death of Hiskias Pendin, Gustav's trusted work master and Carl's mentor and teacher. Then Carl's younger brother, Agathon, a most talented designer, joined the firm and gave it new impetus with his creative ideas. Carl, who was a Merchant of the Second Guild, which allowed him to employ more than sixteen workers and to train apprentices, was then awarded the title of Master, which allowed him to use his own hallmark, not only that of the firm. His reputation was high enough to exempt him from having to take the technically

The Fabergé family

```
Gustav Fabergé    =    Charlotte Jungstedt
  (1814–1893)            (1825–?)
```

- Peter Carl Fabergé (1846–1920) = Augusta Julia Jacobs (1852–1925)
- Agathon (1862–1895)

Children of Peter Carl Fabergé and Augusta Julia Jacobs:
- Eugène (1874–1960)
- Agathon Carl (1876–1951)
  = (1) Lydia Treuberg (1875–1944)
  = (2) Maria Borzova (1889–1973)
- Alexander (1877–1952)
  = (1) Johanna Tamermann (1882–1930)
  = (2) Nina Belichova (1889–1973)
- Nikolai (1881–1883)
- Nikolai Leopold (Nicholas) (1884–1939)
  = Marion Tattershall

Grandchildren:
- Agathon (1898–1966)
- Peter (1901–1970) = Xenia Strecker (1897–1972)
- Theodore (1904–1971) = Tatiana Cheremeteff (1901–1983)
  - Tatiana (b. 1930)
- Igor Carl (1906–1982)
- Rurik (1908–1978)
- Oleg Agathonovitch (1923–1993) = Sirrka-Liisa Korkman (b. 1916)
- Alexander (1912–1988)
- Irina (1925–1988)

LEFT: *Bust of Carl Fabergé by Joseph Limburg*

BELOW: *Carl Fabergé at work*

Carl Fabergé's library in his apartments at 24, Bolshaia Morskaia, St Petersburg

demanding three-day examination jewellers were required to take to demonstrate their mastery of goldsmithery and the most difficult elements of jewellery-making which included stone-setting, engraving, welding and chasing. And finally, having been entrusted by the Hermitage Museum with the task of repairing and restoring its collections of precious objects for a number of years, Carl was invited in 1882 to participate in the Moscow Pan-Russian Exhibition. It was at this event that the Imperial couple became acquainted with the House of Fabergé and were captivated by the beautiful display of jewels and *objets de luxe*.

Over the next few years honours and fame were deservedly showered on the House of Fabergé, and in 1885 Tsar Alexander III not only gave Carl Fabergé the order to design and execute the first Imperial Easter egg, but also bestowed upon him the sought-after title of Supplier to the Court of His Imperial Majesty. In 1890, he received the title of Valuer to the Office of His Imperial Majesty, and was made an honorary hereditary citizen. Fabergé's *objets de luxe* had transformed and redefined the meaning of elegance in a world of extravagant splendour.

The House of Fabergé became the largest jewellery firm in Russia, employing around 500 craftsmen and designers. In 1900, at the peak of the firm's success, Carl Fabergé commissioned the architect Carl Schmidt to design and erect a four-storey building in St Petersburg, at a cost of 416,000 roubles. It was located on Bolshaia Morskaia, one of the city's most fashionable and desirable locations, and housed most of the main workshops, including those of Mikhail Perkhin, Henrik Wigström,

The House of Fabergé's main sales room

Eugène Fabergé (1874–1960)

Albert Holmström and August Hollming. The large main sales room was on the ground floor, and the building included an art studio for the designers and sculptors and a large library. On the top floor was Carl Fabergé's own luxurious apartment, 'arranged with his own famous taste'.[14]

Princes, pashas and potentates, emirs and emperors, billionaires and barons, kings and queens of Europe, all crossed the threshold of the House of Fabergé seeking a suitable gift, something extraordinarily beautiful for an anniversary, a christening or a wedding. In those circles hardly any personal event could be celebrated without a surprise from the House of Fabergé. Franz Petrovich Birbaum, who worked for the firm as a draughtsman and senior designer, wrote in his memoirs in 1919:

> *The Grand Dukes and the Grand Duchesses enjoyed visiting the shop personally, and spent a lot of time choosing their purchases. All the aristocracy of St Petersburg, persons of title, rank and wealth, could be seen there every afternoon between four and five o' clock, and the shop was particularly crowded during Holy Week, when everybody was hurrying to buy the traditional Easter eggs...*[15]

The demand for these exquisite small treasures was so great that Carl Fabergé opened branches in Moscow in 1887, Odessa in 1900, London in 1903 and Kiev in 1905, bringing into the firm his brilliant and talented brother, Agathon, and later his four sons, Eugène, Agathon, Alexander and Nicholas.

Birbaum wrote in his memoirs about Agathon, Carl Fabergé's brother:

> *His surviving designs bear witness to his unremitting application and never-ending search: ten and even more variations of the same motif can often be found, and*

Gustav Fabergé (seated in bath chair) with his son, Agathon, standing behind him. On the left are his niece and nephew, Wilhelmina Koschke and her brother Fedia, and on the right, his two male nurses

however simple an object might be, he would consider it in all its aspects and would not proceed to its manufacture until he had considered it in all its possibilities and had calculated all its effects... he seldom limited himself to a drawing, but preferred to mould a wax model and to apply the appropriate gems to it in order to bring out the beauty of each stone: large stones might lie about for weeks awaiting drawings of their settings... Equal attention was naturally paid to execution, and not infrequently an article was rejected because of a minute fault and was thrown back into the crucible. [16]

Carl Fabergé was blessed with sons of enormous talent. His eldest son, Eugène, joined the House of Fabergé in 1894 after studying goldsmithery and jewellery design at the Academy of Hanau in Germany. He collaborated with his father on new designs and projects and was an integral part of the firm. In his father's absence, objects had to pass Eugène's inspection before being given the stamp of approval and allowed

Students and rector of the Baron von Steiglitz School of Technical Drawing, c. 1890. Seated on the far right is E.E. Jacobson, who was employed by Fabergé

1911 advertisement for the shop in Odessa

to be sold on the shop floor. Eugène and his brother, Agathon, co-managed the St Petersburg shop together with their father. Their brother, Alexander, an artist, studied at the Baron von Steiglitz School of Technical Drawing in St Petersburg and later at Cacheux in Geneva. He designed jewellery and was one of the managers of the Moscow branch. Nicholas, the youngest son, also an artist and jewellery designer, joined the London branch at the beginning of 1906. The House of Fabergé was indeed a family enterprise.

In 1900, the House of Fabergé was invited to exhibit jewellery at the Paris Universal Exhibition, where they were awarded the Grand Prix and Carl Fabergé was recognized as *maître* by the jewellers of Paris. In addition, he was decorated with the order of the Legion of Honour, the most prestigious of French awards.[17] His sons, Eugène and Agathon, also received awards, and the firm's head workmaster, Mikhail Perkhin, received a bronze memorial medal. The report of the Commissioner General of the Russian Section of the Universal Exhibition contained a special note to the effect that 'the House of Fabergé occupied a place of honour among the jewellers, having obtained many orders and sold practically everything that had been brought'.[18]

Even though several of the Imperial Easter eggs had been exhibited for the first time in Paris, they had never been shown in Russia, and so, in 1902, a charity event was organized under the patronage of the Empress Alexandra Fedorovna at the Baron von Dervis mansion in St Petersburg. (There is a more detailed description of this event in Chapter 5.)

It was clear to all who met him that Carl Fabergé was not an ordinary man. He was simple and direct, and given to few words. Although he employed over 500 men and women at the House of Fabergé, he had a way of distilling the hubbub around him into creative energy, focusing on the immediate moment and the activity at hand. His greatness and genius never overshadowed his human side, and he was known to be tolerant, sensitive and gentle. During the most dangerous period of the first Revolution in 1905, he insisted not only that his workmen remain safely at home, but also that they should continue to receive their wages.

Like many individuals blessed with extraordinary talents and intellect, Carl Fabergé was known to have at least one interesting idiosyncrasy. He resisted giving advance notice to his family and craftsmen when the need arose for him to travel, even to far-away countries. He would suddenly put on his hat and walk out of the front door, refusing to take any luggage with him. He bought all his clothes and

Advertisement for the shop in Moscow

Carl Fabergé, his wife Augusta and their son, Eugène, in Lausanne, 1920

toiletries as he travelled. One day Fabergé arrived at the Negresco Hotel in Nice without any luggage, and the doorman denied him entrance. Fortunately, one of the Russian Grand Dukes who was just leaving recognized him and called out a greeting. Of course, Fabergé was then ushered most apologetically into the hotel.

To Fabergé, his craftsmen constituted the very heart and soul of his firm. Being an accomplished goldsmith himself, with the coveted title of master, Carl oversaw and took an active part in the many complicated stages of production in the various workshops attached to his firm. Henry Charles Bainbridge, the manager of the London branch, wrote in 1934:

> *They lived, worked, ate and slept as it is man's desire to do these things. They wanted for nothing. The very thing which the Soviet was devised to inaugurate was already flourishing in Russia when the new regime came into being. Flourishing on a small scale, no doubt, but highly organized and intensive. A system under which every man was given full opportunity to express himself, and took it, for his own benefit and that of those working with him; simple to a degree but capable of unlimited expansion.* [19]

The identities of only a few of the designers of the Imperial eggs are known. Alma Theresia Pihl designed the Winter and Mosaic eggs, and the undelivered egg of 1917 for the Empress Alexandra Fedorovna was designed by Alexander Ivashev and Carl Fabergé himself.[20] While Carl Fabergé was without doubt the mastermind behind the creation of most of the eggs, Birbaum indicated that he was responsible for the design of more than half of them. Perhaps one day we will discover which ones if the Fabergé archives referred to in a meeting of the Petrokommuna (the post-revolutionary municipal authority of Petrograd) held in March 1919 are ever found. In the minutes of that meeting, the Bolsheviks asserted that 'the masters fled, after hiding their documents and instruments'.

Carl Fabergé's genius lay partly in his ability to convey his artistic ideas to his craftsmen. His wonderful sense of humour gave life to the whimsical hardstone carvings of mischievous monkeys and well-fed, merry mice, all combined, of course, with virtuoso craftsmanship. He loved a joke and never missed an opportunity to play one on a friend, and his friends felt obliged to reciprocate. One such incident revolved around a mock complaint of Fabergé's that a friend of his had sent him caviar for Christmas for twenty years. He suggested there were things other than caviar in Russia – camels, for instance. And sure enough, the friend's next Christmas gift was a camel, led by a resplendently dressed Kalmuck right up to the front door of Carl's jewellery shop.[21] The animal was then presented to Prince Wyazemski's nearby private zoo.

Unfortunately, the tides of fortune began to turn for the House of Fabergé with the advent of the First World War. Among the millions of soldiers sent to the front were many of its workmen. Sadly, Derbyshev, Fabergé's most talented hardstone sculptor, was killed at the beginning of the war. The disasters Russia suffered in the war helped to turn popular feeling against the Tsar and the Imperial family. While the gaiety and extravagance of the Edwardian era was at its height, political unrest in Russia was bubbling just beneath the surface. The Tsars failed to contain this seething cauldron, and in 1917, through agitation and propaganda, the Bolsheviks incited the masses to rebel against the Romanovs and everything that was associated with them. The House of Fabergé was nationalized by the Bolsheviks in 1918 and Carl Fabergé prepared to leave St Petersburg. He had already obtained a *laissez-passer* from the Imperial German Consulate General on 14 September 1918. On 24 September 1918 he applied for a diplomatic passport from Commissar Iossilevich and left several days later on what proved to be the last diplomatic train to Riga, not realizing that he would never be able to return to his beloved Russia again. The revolution in Latvia, which started on 18 November 1918, forced Carl Fabergé, now in his seventies, his life threatened once more, to flee to the relative safety of Bad Homburg and then later to Wiesbaden.

Carl's sons, Agathon and Alexander, were imprisoned by the Bolsheviks. Agathon was released to evaluate the jewels and gemstones confiscated from the Imperial family, wealthy aristocrats and merchants, only to be jailed again when the Bolsheviks found it difficult to sell these gemstones at the prices he had quoted. He remained in prison for another year, during which time he nearly died.

A letter has survived in which Agathon Fabergé wrote to his brother Eugène after his release from prison, describing the appalling conditions he was forced to endure. In reading his letter, we must bear in mind that his correspondence was being censored by the Bolsheviks and that he still faced the possibility of further imprisonment, or even execution. Normally, Agathon would have written to his brother in Russian, but instead wrote in German, hoping the censors would not fully comprehend and would allow his letter to be sent. His reference to being forced to take a rest obviously alludes to his imprisonment.

Carl Fabergé shortly before his death in 1920

27 December, 1920

For the past year and a half I have been obliged, against my will, to take a rest, and am now free. During that time, I had a severe attack of typhoid fever and barely managed to survive it. For three months in the hospital I was lying in utter filth – from the beginning of January to late March of this year. I am healthy now, but rather nervous and work at the Postal Museum. [22]

Augusta Fabergé (1852-1925)

Agathon finally escaped from Russia to Finland in 1927. Alexander, who had also been jailed, was freed with the help of Nina Belishova, who succeeded in bribing his guards. He and Nina eventually settled in Paris. Carl's wife, Augusta Bogdanovna, and Eugène avoided capture and certain death in Russia by crossing the border into Finland towards the end of December 1918, travelling by sleigh and on foot in darkness through snow-covered woods.

The stress of separation and worry about the fate of the rest of his family took their toll on Carl Fabergé, causing him to fall seriously ill in Wiesbaden. Eugène managed to reach him there, and in June 1920 accompanied him to Switzerland, where part of his family had already taken refuge. Carl never recovered from the shock of the tragedy that had befallen Russia, the Imperial Family and the House of Fabergé. In exile, Carl, who had always been so very active, kept repeating 'this is no longer a life worth living'.[23] Carl Fabergé died in Lausanne, Switzerland, on 24 September 1920, aged 74 and those who knew him said that he died from a broken heart.

C. Fabergé

Supplier to the Imperial Court

Gold, Diamonds and Silver Artifacts

St Petersburg, Morskaia 24, Moscow, Kuznetskii Most 4, Odessa, de Ribas 31

The House of Fabergé was founded in St Petersburg in 1842 by Mr G. Fabergé and was subsequently transferred to its present owner, honorary citizen Carl Gustavovich Fabergé. The Moscow branch of the firm has been in existence since 1887, and the Odessa branch since 1901. The firm also has an area at the Nijnii Novgorod Fair.

The House of Fabergé has been granted the honour of acting as Supplier to the Court of Their Imperial Majesties and all the Members of the Imperial Family, and also to a number of foreign Crowned Heads.

The firm's factory currently represents one of the largest establishments of its kind in the Empire.

The articles produced by the firm have won the following awards: a gold medal at the All Russian Exhibition in Moscow in 1882; a gold medal in Nuremberg in 1885; a diploma of honour for articles shown hors concours at the Northern Exhibition in Copenhagen in 1888; a State emblem of the double-headed eagle at the All Russian Arts and Industry Fair in Nijnii-Novgorod in 1896; and appointment as Court Jewellers to His Majesty the King of Sweden and Norway for exhibits hors concours in Stockholm in 1887; when Mr C.G. Fabergé was a member of the jury at the World Exhibition in Paris in 1900, he was awarded the order of the Legion of Honour.

The firm offers an enormous choice of articles of the most up-to-date design:

A) in gold, with or without precious stones, such as: earrings, bracelets, brooches, pendants, chains for ladies and gentlemen, rings, necklaces, opera glasses, cigarette cases, medals, etc.

B) in silver: bratinas, vases, jardinières, glass-holders, tea and coffee services, writing sets, platters, carafes, plain and chased tableware, samovars, inkstands, blotters, desk clocks and various gift items.

We accept orders for the above-mentioned objects, as well as prizes for societies organizing racing and jumping events, and we send out-of-town customers designs, estimates and illustrated price-lists on request.

All our articles are made of high-quality materials, and special attention is paid to their artistic execution; every article, even if its cost is no more than a rouble, is fashioned with due care and precision.

The first-class artists who work for the firm provide it with a rare variety of exquisite designs which can compete with the most outstanding products of Russian and foreign firms operating in the same area.

The firm's large turnover enables it to sell its wares at very reasonable prices, which are kept as low as is commensurate with maintaining the high quality of the work.

Fabergé advertisement in the Russian Jewellers' Directory

The Odessa branch of the House of Fabergé

Fabergé stand at the Nijni Novgorod Fair

The Moscow branch of the House of Fabergé

Craftsmen of the House of Fabergé

HEAD WORKMASTERS

Hiskias Maununpoika Pendin (1823–1881)
He apparently started his apprenticeship with an optician in St Petersburg in 1833 when he was only 10 years old. He became a jeweller in 1840 and worked for Gustav Fabergé. He was the mentor and inspiring teacher of Carl Fabergé.

Erik August Kollin (1836–1901)
He studied goldsmithery with Alexander Palmén at Tammisaari. From 1858, he began working in St Petersburg with August Holmström at Gustav Fabergé's workshop. Kollin became master goldsmith in 1868, had his own workshop on Kazanska Street and worked exclusively for Fabergé. He was head workmaster from 1870 until 1886, when Perkhin replaced him. His widow took over his workshop after his death in 1901.

Mikhail Evlampievich Perkhin (1860–1903)
He was born in the village of Okulovskaia, Shuiskii near Petrozavodsk. On 24 January 1884, he registered as a goldsmith's apprentice with the St Petersburg Craft Council. It is thought that he studied in Kollin's workshop. In 1895, he became a merchant of the 2nd Guild and an honorary citizen. He became Fabergé's head workmaster in 1886 and had his own workshop at 11, Bolshaia Morskaia until 1900, when he moved to Fabergé's new premises at 24, Bolshaia Morskaia. His workshops produced about half of the Imperial Easter eggs, as well as some of the firm's best pieces.

Mikhail Perkhin (1860–1903)

Henrik Emanuel Wigström (1862–1923)
He lived in St Petersburg from 1878 and joined a goldsmith's workshop where he underwent his apprenticeship. In 1884, he began working for Mikhail Perkhin. Perkhin and his wife were godparents to Wigström's children. When Perkhin died in 1903 he became head workmaster. Perkhin bequeathed his workshop to Wigström because he wanted the renown it had acquired to be maintained. Wigström returned to Finland after the Revolution.

Henrik Wigström (1862–1923)

August Wilhelm Holmström (1829–1903)
He underwent his apprenticeship in St Petersburg with the jeweller Herold in 1850 and was promoted to master in 1857. In the same year he was elected chief workmaster of the House of Fabergé and in 1858 he bought his own workshop, which undertook work exclusively for Fabergé. The 1892 Diamond Trellis egg bears his mark. The copies of the Imperial regalia – miniatures on a scale of 1:10 – which were shown at the 1900 Paris exhibition, were also executed in Holmström's workshop.

Holmström's daughter, Fanny, married workmaster Knut Oscar Pihl, and his granddaughter, Alma Theresia Pihl, worked as a designer.

August Holmström (1829–1903)

Albert Woldemar Holmström (1876–1925)
He was the son of August Holmström and was apprentice to his father. After his father's death in 1903, he took over his workshop with the help of Lauri Ryynanen, their experienced workmaster. Albert produced the Winter and the Mosaic eggs, both designed by his niece, Alma Theresia Pihl.

Georg Stein (1870–1954)
He was a goldsmith who worked for the House of Fabergé. He executed the miniature gold coach for the Coronation egg.

STONE CARVERS AND SCULPTORS

Albert Holmström (1876–1925)

Karl Feodorovich Woerffel (1847–c. 1918)
He was a merchant of the First Guild and one of the founders of the Gem-Carving Company, Russkiye Samotsvety.

Piotr Derbyshev (birth-date unknown–1915)
He studied at the Ekaterinburg School of Art and Industry. He walked all the way from Ekaterinburg to St Petersburg on foot. He became one of the best stone carvers, but was drafted into the army during the First World War and was killed in action.

Piotr Mikhailovich Kremlev (birth-date and date of death unknown)
Like Derbyshev, he studied in the Ekaterinburg School of Art and Industry. In 1915, he became the head of the stone carving factory of the House of Fabergé in St Petersburg. His workshop was located at 44, Angliskii Prospekt.

Karl Woerffel (1847–c.1918)

MINIATURISTS AND DESIGNERS

Franz Petrovich (François) Birbaum (1872–1947)
Swiss by birth, Birbaum was chief workmaster (artist-designer and artist-miniaturist) from 1893 to 1918. In his memoirs, he indicated that he was responsible for designing over half of the Imperial Easter eggs. From 1918–20, he worked as designer at the Peterhof gem-carving factory. In 1920, he fled Russia and returned to Switzerland.

Alma Theresia Pihl (1888–1976)
The daughter of Knut Oscar Pihl and Fanny F. Holmström, she worked in her uncle's workshop as a designer. Her most famous creations were the Winter egg and the Mosaic egg.

Konstantin Yakovlevich Krizhitski (birth-date unknown–1911)
He painted the exquisite miniatures for the Caucasus and Danish Palaces eggs.

Franz Birbaum (left) with Eugène Fabergé taken in Switzerland, c.1930

Johannes Zehngraf (1857–1908)
He was a Danish miniaturist who studied in Denmark and Germany. He carried out orders for all the royal families of Europe. Zehngraf was the chief miniaturist for Fabergé and decorated the Lilies of the Valley egg.

Vassilii Zuiev (1870–c.1917)

Vassilii Ivanovich Zuiev (1870–c. 1917)
He graduated from the Baron von Steiglitz School of Technical Drawing in 1895. He was Drawing Master at the Imperial Lyceum. In 1903, Nicholas II saw his work at an exhibition at the Steiglitz Institute, and thereafter Zuiev was appointed official Court miniaturist. After 1904, most of the Imperial Easter eggs were decorated with his miniatures. His works include the Fifteenth Anniversary egg.

Alexander Ivanovich Ivashev (birth-date and date of death unknown)
He was responsible for the design, with Carl Fabergé, of the 1917 Blue Tsarevich Constellation egg, which was never completed. He worked for the House of Fabergé from 1895 to 1918.

Gustav Shkilter (1874–1954)
He worked for the House of Fabergé and taught modelling at the Baron von Steiglitz School of Technical Drawing. He designed the 1916 Steel Military egg which was made in the Putilov Steel plant renowned for its high-quality steel production.

ENAMELLERS

Alexander Fedorovich Petrov (birth-date and date of death unknown)
He was an enameller for the House of Fabergé in St Petersburg from 1895 until 1904, and the father of Nikolai and Dmitrii, who took over from him in 1904.

Gustav Shkilter (1874–1954)

Nikolai Alexandrovich Petrov
(birth-date and date of death unknown)
He was chief enameller of the House of Fabergé between 1895 and 1917. He and his brother, Dmitrii, owned their own workshop. Both had studied in their father's enamelling workshop.

Dmitrii Alexandrovich Petrov
(birth-date and date of death unknown)
He worked exclusively for the House of Fabergé. Little else is known about his history and contributions.

Peter Nikolaievich Popov
(birth-date and date of death unknown)
He was an enameller employed at the workshop of the Petrov brothers from 1893 to 1917.

Members of Carl Fabergé's workshop: N.A. Petrov, enameller (far right); E.E. Jacobson, designer (2nd from right); Franz Birbaum, designer (3rd from right)

Nicholas II *Alexandra Fedorovna*

The Imperial Family

ALEXANDER II = MARIA ALEXANDROVNA
(1818–1881)   née Princess of Hesse
Tsar 1855   and the Rhine
           (1824–1880)

Alexandra	Nicholas	**ALEXANDER III** =	MARIA FEDOROVNA	Vladimir	Alexei	Maria	Sergei	Pavel
(1842–1849)	(1843–1865)	(1845–1894) Tsar 1881	née Princess Dagmar of Denmark (1847–1928)	(1847–1909)	(1850–1908)	(1853–1920)	(1857–1905)	(1860–1919)

NICHOLAS II =	ALEXANDRA FEDOROVNA	Alexander	George	Xenia	Michael	Olga
(1868–1918) Tsar 1896	née Alix of Hesse and the Rhine (1872–1918)	(1869–1870)	(1871–1899)	(1875–1960)	(1878–1918)	(1882–1960)

Olga	Tatiana	Maria	Anastasia	**ALEXEI**
(1895–1918)	(1897–1918)	(1899–1918)	(1901–1918)	(1904–1918)

3

The Imperial Family

Endeavours to bring Russia out of the past into a more enlightened age began with Peter the Great in the 18th century. He was the first Tsar to travel outside of Russia and was so impressed by what he saw in Western Europe that he resolved to transform his country into a modern state. Among his greatest achievements was the foundation in 1703 of the city of St Petersburg, which he made his Western-style capital. He and his daughter, Elisabeth, who reigned from 1741 to 1761, laid the foundations for several Imperial Palaces in the beautiful 800-acre royal enclave of Tsarskoie Selo (Tsar's Village), 15 miles south of St Petersburg. These palaces include Peterhof, the summer palace on the Gulf of Finland, and the thousand-room Winter Palace in St Petersburg, the official residence of the reigning Tsar, where thousands of resplendently dressed guests were entertained at brilliant balls and elaborate state and ceremonial functions.

A century and half later Alexander II inherited the Winter Palace. The Imperial apartments and state rooms were filled with treasures collected by Catherine the Great in the 18th century. The floors were covered with parquet made of exotic woods with elaborate designs. The columns and walls were inlaid with exquisite semi-precious stones, including malachite, jasper, lapis lazuli, and marble of many hues. The ceilings, which were decorated in high relief and covered with gold leaf, supported festooned chandeliers, their crystals shimmering from the hundreds of twinkling candles. The effect was dazzling, especially during Court events.

It was to this palace, on 28 February 1881, that Alexander II was brought, mortally wounded, his body shattered by a bomb thrown by a nihilist. It is ironic that the revolutionaries killed one of the greatest reformers in the history of Russia, who had abolished serfdom and was preparing to give Russia the long-awaited constitution that would have transformed it into a modern European state.

Alexander II was succeeded by his second son, Grand Duke Alexander, who ruled as Alexander III. He had not been prepared to rule, for his older brother, the Tsarevich Nicholas, had been trained as the next in line to the throne; however, he had contracted tuberculosis. Nicholas had been engaged to Princess Dagmar, daughter of the King of Denmark, and on his death-bed in 1865 he joined together the hands of the princess and his brother Alexander, and expressed his desire that they should marry. Thus Alexander came to the throne having inherited not only Nicholas' title, but also his bride-to-be.

Alexander III, traumatized by the assassination of his father and his sudden ascent to the throne, retreated with his family to the seclusion and relative safety of the Gatchina Palace. He was thoroughly convinced of the merits of autocracy and did not see the necessity of changing the political system. He abandoned any further reform proposals. The Tsar was a stern ruler, devoutly religious and not given to many extravagances. Throughout his reign, he was plagued with bouts of depression. Except for occasional bursts of spirited liveliness when he entertained his guests with performances on his trombone, he lived in solitude away from the bustle of Court activity, seeking refuge in his religion.

His somewhat rough appearance and informal manners did not conform to the standard expected at other courts. Queen Victoria, for example, remarked that he was a sovereign whom she did not look upon as a gentleman.[24] He in turn was hostile to, and distrusted, everything British and German, his reaction stemming from Britain's role in the Crimean War. In fact, promoting the Pan-Russian movement was part of Alexander's political agenda.

The Tsarevich Alexander Alexandrovich married the Princess Dagmar on 10 November 1866 and moved into the Anichkov Palace. After her conversion to the Russian Orthodox faith, she became known as Her Imperial Majesty Maria Fedorovna. The new Emperor and Empress made their home in the somewhat cramped suites of the magnificent but spartanly decorated Gatchina Palace, some

The Winter Palace on the banks of the River Neva, St Petersburg

Tsar Nicholas II c. 1900

thirty miles south of the capital, raising their five children in the relative security of the countryside. They returned to the Anichkov Palace for the Easter celebrations and the winter social season of royal balls and masquerades. The Empress enjoyed the exotic magnificence of the St Petersburg Court. In the year of their marriage, the wife of the American Minister wrote that the Empress 'wore the Russian court dress... of dark blue velvet very heavily embroidered with gold... I saw on her neck a sapphire as large as a hen's egg'.[25] The dark-haired Empress delighted in parties and balls: 'I danced and danced. I let myself be carried away.'[26] Balls and galas abounded in St Petersburg society and it was not unusual for the nobility to attend three or more a week.

Although Tsar Alexander III's stature was formidable, his heir the Tsarevich Nicholas, born in 1868, grew to be a slight though handsome young man. He was more extroverted than his father, and possessed a gentle charm. Nicholas was given an excellent education and, in accordance with his Imperial rank, did his service in the Guards. The gentlemen Guards' reputation for hard-drinking and rowdy behaviour was deservedly earned. The Tsarevich threw himself into the fellowship and fraternity life of drinking, military inspections, and dark-eyed singing gypsies.

> *Each day we drill twice... the dinners are very merry... after meals, the officers play billiards, skittles, cards or dominoes... we got stewed... tasted six sorts of Port and got a bit soused... we wallowed in the grass and drank... felt owlish... the officers carried me out.*[27]

Nicholas was introduced to, and then fell in love with the talented and petite Polish ballerina, Mathilde Kshesinskaia. She was a favourite with Nicholas and his cousins, and was showered with jewels and gifts from the House of Fabergé. Nicholas gave her a magnificent art nouveau-style mansion, where the romance flourished until his betrothal in 1894 to Alexandra (Alix), Princess of Hesse and the Rhine. Ironically, many years later, this same mansion, looted and occupied by Lenin during the Revolution, became Bolshevik headquarters, where the decision was made regarding Nicholas II's ultimate fate.

In 1882, the Pan-Russian Exhibition took place in Moscow under the royal patronage of Tsar Alexander III. This is when the beautiful display of jewels created by the House of Fabergé must have drawn the Tsar's attention. The House of Fabergé received high praise from the press and was awarded the coveted gold medal. Within a short time, the Tsar and other members of the Imperial family were purchasing exquisite jewels and objects from the House of Fabergé, which led in 1885 to the

LEFT: *Empress Alexandra Fedorovna (1872–1918)*

RIGHT: *Tsar Nicholas II (1868–1918)*

Grand Duke Sergei Alexandrovich (1857–1905)

commission of a special Easter egg for the Tsar's wife Maria Fedorovna. In that same year, the Tsar bestowed upon Carl Fabergé the ultimate honour, awarding the House of Fabergé the title of Supplier to the Court of His Imperial Majesty.

The decades prior to the new century were a time of peace and tranquillity for the Imperial family. Daily life and routines changed little over the years. Winters were spent in St Petersburg, followed by a long comfortable train journey to the Crimea, where they stayed at their favourite palace, Livadia. In May or June, they travelled north to Peterhof, on the Baltic, where Nicholas and Alexandra had first met in 1884, cruising for several weeks along the coast of Finland aboard the sleek 128-metre-long royal yacht, *Standard*. In August, they hunted from their Imperial lodge at Spala, in Poland, then retraced their steps to Livadia, returning to Tsarskoie Selo in November.

As the Imperial family was related to most of the royal houses in Europe, these sojourns were occasions for meetings and large family gatherings. In fact, towards the end of the 19th century, the five reigning monarchs of Russia, Greece, Great Britain, Denmark and Norway were all first cousins, as the result of strict adherence to the custom of inter-marriage between the royal houses. Alexandra and Dagmar, daughters of King Christian IX of Denmark, were married to the future monarchs of England and Russia, and even though there was no love lost between Alexander III and Queen Victoria, they did not allow this to get in the way when it came to arranging dynastic marriages.

It was the wedding, in 1884, of Elizabeth of Hesse and the Rhine, Queen Victoria's granddaughter, to Grand Duke Sergei, Alexander III's brother, that brought her sister Alix, the beautiful, tall, blonde, blue-eyed German princess, to St Petersburg. Nicholas fell in love with her at first sight. He was sixteen, she was twelve. They were infatuated with each other and scratched their names with her diamond ring on a glass window pane of a small Imperial summer house on the Peterhof grounds. Nicholas presented her with a diamond brooch, which the princess returned to him the next evening at the children's ball in the Anichkov Palace. Princess Alix had been brought up by her English grandmother, Queen Victoria, and was everything an impeccably English princess should be, in taste, language and morality. But their marriage was not to take place until much later, and Nicholas was forbidden to see her. He wrote in his diary:

> *My dream is one day to marry Alix H. Have loved her for a long time, but even more deeply and strongly since 1889, when she spent 6 weeks of the winter in Petersburg. Have fought my feeling for a long time, trying to deceive myself with the impossibility of my cherished dream coming true...* [28]

He refused to accept marriage to any other candidate put forward by his father. Nicholas' patience was finally rewarded, when in 1894, ten years after he had first met his beautiful Princess Alix, permission was given to an ecstatic Nicholas to make a proposal of marriage.

His father was very ill and near death as a result of injuries sustained in a train wreck in 1888. The following is an account of the Emperor's valiant efforts to save his family and all those aboard the train.

> *On 29 October, 1888 the long Imperial train was travelling fast towards Kharkov. About one o'clock the train was approaching the small town of Borki... the Imperial family was having lunch in the dining-car. Suddenly the train lurched violently twice and everybody fell on the floor. Within a second or two the dining-car was torn open and the heavy iron roof caved in just a few inches above the passengers' heads. The explosion had sliced off the wheels and the floor of the car. The Emperor was the first to crawl out from under the roof. This done, he held it up so that his wife, children, and the others were able to get out of the wreckage. It was truly a Herculean effort on Alexander's part, and, though nobody knew it at the time, it was to cost him dear... the Empress Maria forgot all about herself... she was heroic, helping the doctor with a real nurse's zeal... There were 281 casualties, 21 of them fatal... many members of the household were either dead or crippled for life. Kamchatka, the Tsar's favourite dog, was crushed by a piece of the fallen roof.* [29]

With his father's death rapidly approaching, the gentle and reluctant Nicholas was about to accede to the throne. There had never been an unmarried Tsar on the throne of Russia, and the Imperial family decided Nicholas should marry without delay. To give him moral support, he was allowed to take the German princess for his wife.

Alexander III died on 1 November 1894. His funeral was followed several weeks later by the wedding of Nicholas and Alexandra in the Winter Palace chapel on 26 November. The lengthy rituals for the two State occasions were draining and emotional. Alix remarked, 'our marriage seemed to me a mere continuation of the services for the dead, with this difference, that now I wore a white dress instead of a black one'. The new Empress was thrust at the age of 22 into the exalted position of consort to the autocratic ruler of the Russian Empire, unable to communicate in the native language of her new land, without friends and with no knowledge of the intrigues and inner workings of the Imperial Court.

Tsar Nicholas II and the Empress Alexandra at the Vladimir Palace

It was a difficult and lonely existence for Alexandra. The new Emperor was quite preoccupied with the overwhelming burdens and responsibilities of running the country, while his grieving mother vied for his attention. The Dowager Empress was determined not to relinquish her central role. She invoked the seldom-used Romanov house-rule whereby, as mother of the Emperor, she took precedence over her daughter-in-law. The astonishingly youthful Dowager Empress, in a magnificent gown, diamonds blazing, stunned even the Court as she proudly walked on the arm of her son, while Alexandra followed meekly behind, escorted by one of the Grand Dukes. Even at her own coronation, Empress Alexandra Fedorovna's carriage was preceded by that of her mother-in-law.

On the day of their coronation (9 May) at the Kremlin in Moscow, where all Europe's royalty and thousands of peasants had gathered to glimpse the new Tsar and Tsarina, Nicholas II wrote in his diary:

By 12 an entire gang of princes had gathered, with whom we sat down to lunch. At 2.30 the procession began to move. I was riding on Norma, Mama was sitting in the first gold carriage and Alix in the second, also alone. [30]

Following the hastily arranged wedding, the new Emperor and Empress moved into a small suite of rooms at the Anichkov Palace in St Petersburg, the home of the Dowager Empress. Apartments at the Winter Palace were renovated for them, but it was to Tsarskoie Selo that the Emperor chose to bring his bride. The Alexander Palace, just 500 yards away from the much larger Catherine Palace, was to be their country home and principal residence until the end of their lives. Alexandra Fedorovna remained true to her Victorian English upbringing, creating a cosy, chintz-filled haven for Nicholas and their family.

The new Emperor and Empress each received two million roubles a year for their personal expenses. Nicholas II continued his father's tradition of presenting an

The Imperial Family, Tsarskoie Selo, 1892

The coronation procession of Nicholas II (1896)

annual Easter egg to his wife, as well as one to his mother, the Dowager Empress. He paid for the eggs bought from Fabergé from his personal funds, although there was one case, in 1895, soon after their marriage, when he paid only half the cost of the egg intended for his mother. Nicholas regarded the Easter present as a family gift, with the expenses to be halved with his wife. He wrote on Fabergé's bill, 'the underlined items to be shared between the Empress Alexandra Fedorovna and myself', and among the underlined items was 'blue enamel Louis XVI egg, cost 4500 roubles, $^1/_2$ share, 2250 roubles'.[31]

Apparently, however, a few heated words on the subject were exchanged with the thrifty Alexandra Fedorovna, and all the subsequent eggs for his mother were paid for from his own funds. The Empress' German and English upbringing was to be reckoned with after all.

It was through the family relationships of the Romanovs that the fame of the House of Fabergé spread. The Imperial family presented visiting royalty and heads of state with gifts designed by the House of Fabergé. The Dowager Empress also delighted in receiving these luxurious gifts. Her sister, Queen Alexandra of Great Britain, owned a large group of Fabergé's hardstone carvings, given to her by her husband, King Edward VII, modelled on her favourite animals at Sandringham House in Norfolk.

Fabergé's *objets de luxe* were expensive. Even the least expensive items, such as the miniature pendant Easter egg, hidden inside the 1890 egg, cost 60 roubles, an amount equal to two years' salary for the average tradesman.

When Tsar Alexander II came to the throne in 1855 he already had far-reaching reforms in mind, and in 1861, put into effect his plan for the emancipation of the serfs, thus freeing hundreds of millions of mostly illiterate peasants. This did not change the harshness of their lives, except for a selected few, and it destabilized most

Nicholas II with members of the royal Siamese family during his travels in the Far East c. 1890

of the others. In later years, Tsars Alexander III and Nicholas II did not heed the warnings of discontent and failed to make the necessary social changes. At the turn of the century, Russia was going through the industrial revolution that Great Britain and America had experienced several decades earlier. Many of the freed serfs flooded the capital, St Petersburg, as well as other cities, to work in factories, but thousands continued to live in poverty. Without their family structure close to them, they were easily swayed by revolutionary ideas. A time bomb was ticking away, and the seeds of anarchy were sown.

In the first few years of the 20th century, extremists were stirring up the population against the Tsar and plotting his downfall. The difficulties the Tsar and Tsarina faced were compounded by the fact that none of their four beautiful daughters could inherit the throne. In the event of the Emperor's death, and without an heir, the Imperial line would end. Their elation and joy at the birth of their son and heir, Alexis, in 1904, soon turned to gloom. Within months, Alexis had developed severe bleeding, the first signs of the fatal genetic disease haemophilia that afflicted several male descendants of Queen Victoria. When conventional medicine failed, Alexandra, in desperation, put her trust in Grigorii Rasputin, a Siberian peasant monk, whose healing powers she believed would save her dying son. Rasputin's influence over the Tsarina and her family increased to the point where the Empress was urging her husband to heed Rasputin's advice on internal government policy.

Although Maria Fedorovna did not share her daughter-in-law's views on Rasputin, there were many at her court who had long outlived their usefulness but could not be dismissed. Mademoiselle Sidonie de L'Escaille, the Empress' Belgian *dame de compagnie*, was at court for so long that nobody could remember a time when she was not old.[32] On 25 May 1906, the Empress wrote to Mademoiselle de L'Escaille of her mounting anxiety:

You are right to wonder at the speeches, so violent and full of hate, that were delivered at the beautiful Tauride Palace, but nothing else could be expected after the socialist and democratic, etc., elections, which indeed are not really representative of the country...Well, let us hope that something good will come of it – but for the time being it does not look like it. The assassinations unfortunately continue with the same success and the same rage, and they have the effrontery to demand that all those criminals should be set free, thinking that this will stop. What an illusion, to believe that these people who are worse than wild beasts could have any feelings of gratitude: they are simply brutes and rogues who have no other goal but assassinations and stirring up revolution. What sorrow and sadness to have to witness all this disintegration and downfall. But we must not lose courage, but always put our hope in God who will, I hope, take pity on us and help us to survive this terrible crisis. [35]

Nicholas II and Alexandra Fedorovna dressed in costumes from the reign of the first Romanovs, at the 1903 Winter Ball held at the Winter Palace

The crisis to which she referred had been brought about by a series of events, including the Russo-Japanese War of 1904–5 (see Chapter 6) which had shocked the nation. This war had been followed by general strikes in which millions of workers participated, by mutiny in the army, and by the 1905 march on the Winter Palace which left many hundreds dead, shot down by the Tsar's own troops. All these things contributed to the collapse of the Russian Empire.

The Emperor and Empress, shaken by all these events and fearing for their lives, took refuge with their family at Tsarskoie Selo. But there was yet another blow with the outbreak in 1914 of the First World War, which took the lives of millions of Russian soldiers. The confidence and affection shown to Rasputin by the Empress gave rise to scandalous rumours in St Petersburg that drove the Imperial family further into seclusion. War with Germany only deepened the distrust of the Russian people for their German-born Empress. The reverence that the people had always shown towards their Tsar waned, and it was not difficult to turn their loyalties around. On 13 March 1917, St Petersburg, renamed Petrograd, was in the hands of the revolutionaries, and two days later Tsar Nicholas II abdicated. By 22 March, the Imperial family was under house-arrest, and in April 1918, the revolutionaries moved them first to Tobolsk and then to Ekaterinburg, in Siberia. On 17 July, by order of Lenin, just after midnight, the Tsar, his family, and their faithful retainers were awakened from their sleep, brought downstairs into the basement and brutally slaughtered. Within a few short months, 17 of the Romanovs had been mercilessly slain, including Tsar Nicholas II's brother, Grand Duke Michael, heir to the Romanov throne, Grand Duchess Elisabeth, sister of the Empress, and eight of the Grand Dukes and Princes of Imperial lineage. Imperial Russia had ceased to exist.

4

The Imperial Easter Eggs

'*Carl Fabergé had the privilege of inventing and providing the Tsars Alexander III and Nicholas II with artistic Easter eggs... he produced 50 of them altogether.*'[34]

This note, written by Eugène Fabergé, confirms the authors' conclusion that only 50 Imperial Easter eggs were made by the House of Fabergé. It must be deduced, then, that the additional four or more eggs identified as Imperial in various books devoted to this subject, as recently as 1996,[35] either are not Imperial or have been produced by goldsmiths other than the House of Fabergé.

Much has been written over the years identifying some of the Easter eggs as having belonged to the Tsarevichs. But the authors have found no archival evidence to support these claims and believe that there were never any Easter eggs presented by either Tsars Alexander III or Nicholas II to their sons and heirs.

The first Imperial Easter egg was commissioned in 1885 by the Emperor Alexander III to be given at Easter to his wife, the Empress Maria Fedorovna. The Empress' delight with her gift initiated this yearly tradition which continued until the October Revolution of 1917 and the tragic end of the Romanov dynasty.

The design and manufacture of the Easter eggs was usually left to the discretion of Fabergé and his designers and workmasters. Franz Birbaum writes in his memoirs that 'the designs for Easter eggs were not submitted for approval, and Fabergé was given complete freedom in design and execution'.[36] However, the Tsar was obviously interested and involved. He consulted with Fabergé, sometimes directly and sometimes through His Majesty's Cabinet, as can be seen in the case of the second egg, the Hen with Sapphire Pendant, given to the Empress as a surprise gift in 1886.

Each Imperial Easter egg took almost a year to complete, sometimes longer.

Display cabinet with Easter eggs in the Maple drawing-room of the Alexander Palace

Work usually began soon after Easter and was hardly finished by Holy Week of the following year; the days just before delivery were anxious for everyone who worried that something might happen to these fragile objects at the last moment. The masters did not leave their working places until the Fabergés returned from Tsarskoie Selo, in case an emergency arose. [37]

The Imperial Easter eggs were made in the greatest of secrecy. They were rarely spoken of within the House of Fabergé, and the craftsmen and specialists chosen to manufacture them kept their part of the bargain, remaining silent all year while labouring to bring these fragile and exquisite creations to life.

Carl Fabergé's son, Eugène, was occasionally awarded the privilege of personally delivering the Easter egg. In a letter written in 1934 to H.C. Bainbridge he describes one of his journeys:

As the Tsar then dwelled at the Livadia Castle near Yalta... I was ordered by my father to carry it [the 1912 Tsarevich egg] personally to His Majesty. So I made this voyage through all Russia... The eve before the same Easter my father had to deliver, in the Tsar's name, the other egg, destined to Empress Maria Fedorovna, who remained in St Petersburg. [38]

Tsar Nicholas II at his desk

Every year Fabergé changed the theme of each egg, reflecting the previous year's important events and achievements celebrated by the Imperial household. But what inspired Carl Fabergé to create as many as seven eggs with the themes of birds for

Maria Fedorovna, including a hen in 1885, another hen in 1886, a pelican in 1898, a cockerel in 1900, a swan in 1906 and a songbird in 1911? Was it Carl Fabergé or Maria Fedorovna who had such a penchant for birds? It was well known that Fabergé was very fond of birds. Apparently, he even taught a starling to whistle a melody from Gounod's opera, *Faust*.

The Easter eggs made for Alexandra Fedorovna over a 16-year period cost an average 10,000 roubles each. It took many highly skilled craftsmen – designers, gem cutters, gem setters, engravers, enamellers, polishers – working together for a year or more to create each masterpiece. George Stein, who had perfect vision and worked without a magnifying glass, laboured for 15 months, 16 hours a day, to fabricate the gold replica of the Coronation carriage, the surprise inside the 1897 Coronation egg.

It is always difficult to try to give present-day equivalents for past monetary values, but in reviewing several factors, including the wages paid to certain salaried individuals in Russia during the same period, and the rate of inflation over an extended period of time, it is clear that the Tsar's expenditure on annual Easter presents, was significant. In 1885, for example, a general in the Russian army earned 6,000 roubles a year, whilst a colonel earned 1,500 roubles. The average annual income of a Fabergé craftsman was 1,400 roubles, although George Stein was lured over to the House of Fabergé from Kortman after being offered the princely sum of five roubles per day, instead of the usual three, working 300 days a year for an annual salary of 1,500 roubles. How significant the Tsar's purchases for Easter were can now be determined. On the basis of the exchange rate of 10 roubles to the pound sterling which prevailed from the late 1890s until the First World War, the Tsar would have paid the House of Fabergé the following amounts if he had recently purchased either of these two Easter eggs [39]:

1889 Nécessaire egg – original cost 1,900 roubles – £76,000
(lowest amount paid by the Tsar for a Fabergé Easter egg)

1913 Winter egg – original cost 24,600 roubles – £984,000
(highest amount paid by the Tsar for a Fabergé Easter egg)

In the dusty archives kept in Russia, newly discovered invoices and documents that have provided the detailed knowledge about pricing have also given answers to many of the other questions surrounding the eggs. Of the 50 Imperial Easter eggs known to have been made by the House of Fabergé, 42 have been identified in various museums and collections around the world. Thirty eggs were made for the Empress Maria Fedorovna, and all eight of the missing Imperial Easter eggs belonged to her. Three of the eggs (1888, 1889 and 1902) were transferred to the Kremlin from the Anichkov Palace. These three, along with the five others that disappeared during the looting and pillaging of the Anichkov and Gatchina Palaces by the Bolsheviks, have yet to be found. Hope still exists that these eight Imperial Easter eggs are stored in private collections, though it is more likely that they were either destroyed or else they are in the hands of unsuspecting individuals who do not realize that the objects they possess were once owned by an Empress of Russia.

All 20 of the Easter eggs presented to the Empress Alexandra Fedorovna by her husband Nicholas II survived the Revolution. Fortunately, her palaces were guarded long enough for the confiscated treasures to be crated up and taken by train to the Kremlin in Moscow. There in the 1930s they were sold for a fraction of their value to individuals and dealers from the West, eventually finding their way into private collections and museums.

СТОЛИЦА и УСАДЬБА

ЖУРНАЛЪ КРАСИВОЙ ЖИЗНИ

№ 55.   ЖУРНАЛЪ ВЫХОДИТЪ СЪ 15 ДЕКАБРЯ 1913 ГОДА.   1 АПРѢЛЯ 1916 ГОДА. ПЕТРОГРАДЪ.

ПАСХАЛЬНЫЯ ЯЙЦА —
ПОДАРКИ ГОСУДАРЯ ИМПЕРАТОРА ГОСУДАРЫНѢ ИМПЕРАТРИЦѢ АЛЕКСАНДРѢ ѲЕОДОРОВНѢ.

Яйцо въ память 200-лѣтія С.-Петербурга изъ золота съ бриліантами (въ стилѣ Régence). Снаружи съ двухъ сторонъ виды на слоновой кости домика Петра Великаго и Зимняго Дворца и портреты-миніатюры Петра Великаго и Государя Императора Николая II. Посредствомъ механизма поднимается памятникъ Петра Великаго, сдѣланный изъ золота и помѣщенный на скалѣ изъ сапфира. Внутренность крышки прозрачной эмали — изображаетъ восходящее солнце.

TOWN AND COUNTRY

A JOURNAL FOR GRACIOUS LIVING

No. 55   First issue : 15 December 1913   1 April 1916
                                                Petrograd

EASTER EGGS

Presented by the Tsar Emperor to the Empress Alexandra Fedorovna

Gold and diamond Regency style egg, commemorating the bicentenary of the founding of St Petersburg. On two sides of the exterior are paintings on ivory of Peter the Great's little house and of the Winter Palace and miniature portraits of Peter the Great and the Emperor Nicholas II. A mechanical device lifts up a model of the Peter the Great monument, made of gold and fixed to a sapphire rock. The interior of the transparent enamel lid represents the rising sun.

Egg commemorating the tercentenary of the rule of the House of Romanov, gold on a white enamel background, with gold eagles, crowns and caps of the Romanov epoch and miniature portraits, painted on ivory by the artist V.I. Zuiev, of all the ruling members of the Romanov House. The egg rests on a three-sided Imperial eagle which in turn is fixed on to the Romanov coat-of-arms shield of purpurine and enamel.

The egg contains a globe consisting of two northern hemispheres on which the seas are made of steel and the land, with mountains in relief, of different-coloured gold. One hemisphere represents Russia at the time when Tsar Mikhail Fedorovich Romanov came to the throne, and the other, Russia at the time of the tercentenary celebrations.

Egg representing the Temple of Love, Louis XVI style, of gold, pink and white enamel and pale-green translucent jadeite. Four amourettes are seated around the pediment and a cherub stands on top of the egg, with its clockwork mechanism and revolving dial-plate. A pair of doves flies between the temple columns, wreathed in garlands of different-coloured gold and platinum.

Egg and pedestal of rock crystal, pierced by a rod bearing six double frames with twelve views, painted on ivory, of palaces in which Her Majesty spent her life. The tip of the rod on which the frames with the views revolve is surmounted by a large, pointed cabochon emerald of rare beauty. Under the egg is the monogram A with the Royal Crown of Hesse, and lower down, the monogram A θ with the Imperial Crown of enamelled gold and diamonds.

Egg commemorating Their Majesties' visit to Moscow during the Easter celebrations. The style of the egg is reminiscent of the Uspenski Cathedral and some architectural features of the Moscow Kremlin. The festively-lit interior of the Uspenski Cathedral, with its famous decorations and icons, may be seen through the windows, and a musical mechanism plays the Cheruvim chant. The pediment is made of Siberian alabaster, the architectural part of different-coloured gold, the egg itself of white enamel and the dome of polished gold. This egg is made without any precious stones whatsoever, and all its merit lies in its artistic fashioning and delicate representation of the architectural features of the Uspenski Cathedral.

This egg, commemorating the fifteenth anniversary of the reign of the Tsar Emperor Nicholas II, is made of gold covered with translucent white enamel, with garlands of green enamel and diamonds. The exterior bears some exquisite miniatures, wonderfully painted on ivory by the artist V.I. Zuiev, representing such outstanding events in the reign of the Tsar Emperor as:

OPPOSITE AND OVERLEAF: *pages from the original* Town and Country *journal published in 1916 featuring the Easter eggs presented to the Empress Alexandra Fedorovna by Tsar Nicholas II*

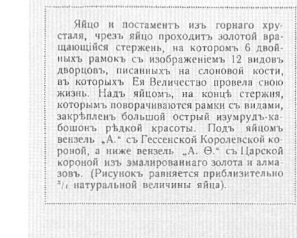

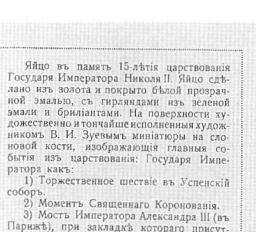

Яйцо въ память 300-лѣтія царствованія дома Романовыхъ, золотое съ бѣлымъ эмалевымъ фономъ, съ двуглавыми орлами, коронами и шапками Романовской эпохи и портретными миніатюрами (писанными на слоновой кости художникомъ В. И. Зуевымъ), всѣхъ царствовавшихъ представителей Дома Романовыхъ. Яйцо покоится на трехсторонемъ Государственномъ орлѣ, который въ свою очередь утвержденъ на Романовскомъ щитѣ изъ пурпурина съ эмалью.

Внутри яйца помѣщается земной шаръ, состоящій изъ 2-хъ сѣверныхъ полушарій, гдѣ моря сдѣланы изъ стали, а земля съ рельефными горами — изъ разноцвѣтнаго золота. На одной половинѣ изображена Россія во время восшествія на престолъ царя Михаила Ѳеодоровича Романова, а на другой — Россія ко дню 300-лѣтняго юбилея.

Яйцо и постаментъ изъ горнаго хрусталя, чрезъ яйцо проходитъ золотой вращающійся стержень, на которомъ 6 двойныхъ рамокъ съ изображеніемъ 12 видовъ дворцовъ, писанныхъ на слоновой кости, въ которыхъ Ея Величество провела свою жизнь. Надъ яйцомъ, на конецъ стержня, которымъ поворачиваются рамки съ видами, закрѣпленъ большой острый изумрудъ-кабошонъ рѣдкой красоты. Подъ яйцомъ вензель „А." съ Гессенской Королевской короной, а ниже вензель „А. Ѳ." съ Царской короной изъ эмалированнаго золота и алмазовъ. (Рисунокъ равняется приблизительно ²/₁ натуральной величины яйца).

Перетягивать поясъ указанія включивши воскресные стерженекѣ группъ и портретовъ особенно воспроизвести. Законъ 30 марта 1911 года.

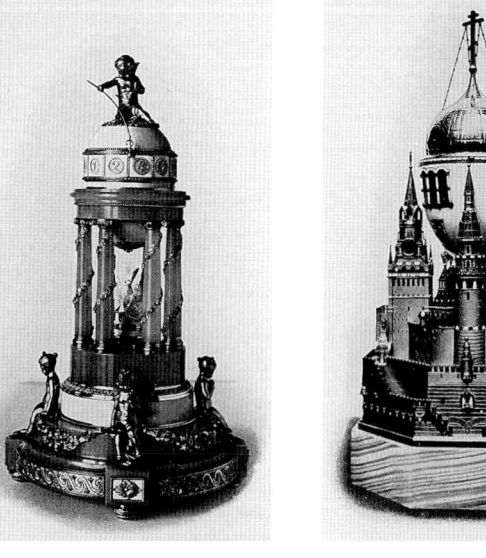

Яйцо, изображающее храмъ любви, въ стилѣ Людовика XVI — изъ золота, розовой и бѣлой эмали и блѣдно-зеленаго просвѣчивающаго жадеита. Вокругъ постамента сидятъ 4 женскія аморетки. На яйцѣ часовымъ механизмомъ и вертящимся циферблатомъ золотой амурчикъ. Между колоннами храма — пара голубковъ. Гирлянды изъ разноцвѣтнаго золота и платины.

Яйцо въ память посѣщенія Ихъ Величествами Москвы во время Пасхальныхъ праздниковъ. Яйцо своимъ стилемъ напоминаетъ Успенскій соборъ и архитектурныя особенности московскаго Кремля. Чрезъ окно видна празднично освѣщенная внутренность Успенскаго собора съ его знаменитыми украшеніями и иконами. Музыкальный механизмъ внутри играетъ херувимскую пѣснь.

Постаментъ изъ сибирскаго алебастра, архитектура — разноцвѣтнаго золота, само яйцо изъ бѣлой эмали, куполъ — изъ полированнаго золота. Полное отсутствіе драгоцѣнныхъ камней у этого яйца. Все достоинство — въ художественномъ отдѣлкѣ и тонкомъ выполненіи архитектурныхъ мотивовъ Успенскаго собора.

Яйцо въ память 15-лѣтія царствованія Государя Императора Николая II. Яйцо сдѣлано изъ золота и покрыто бѣлой прозрачной эмалью, съ гирляндами изъ зеленой эмали и бриліантами. На поверхности художественно и тончайше исполненныя художникомъ В. И. Зуевымъ миніатюры на слоновой кости, изображающія главныя событія изъ царствованія Государя Императора какъ:
1) Торжественное шествіе въ Успенскій соборъ.
2) Моментъ Священнаго Коронованія.
3) Мостъ Императора Александра III (въ Парижѣ), при закладкѣ которого присутствовалъ Его Императорское Величество.
4) Домъ въ Гаагѣ, гдѣ происходила 1-ая мирная конференція. Huis in't Bosch.
5) Торжественный пріемъ Членовъ 1-ой Государственной Думы въ Зимнемъ Дворцѣ.
6) Музей Императора Александра III.
7) Открытіе памятника Петра Великаго въ Ригѣ.
8) Открытіе памятника 200-лѣтія Полтавской битвы (въ Полтавѣ).
9) Перенесеніе мощей преподобнаго Серафима Саровскаго и портреты Императорской семьи.

На обоихъ концахъ — плоскіе спеціально граненые бриліанты, подъ которыми помѣщены: вензель Государыни Императрицы — „А. Ѳ." съ короной, и годъ „1909".

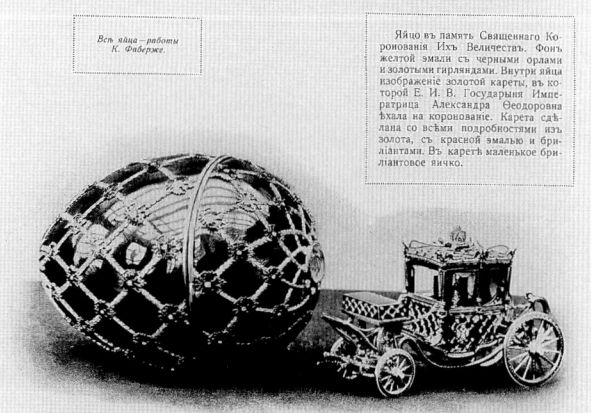

Яйцо въ стилѣ Ренесансъ, изъ горнаго хрусталя съ украшеніями изъ разноцвѣтной эмали; орлы и дельфины изъ чистаго синяго ляписъ-лазури. Внутри Императорская яхта „Штандартъ", изъ золота и платины, съ подробнѣйшимъ исполненіемъ всѣхъ снастей, съ трапами, пушками, вертящимся рулемъ и т. д.

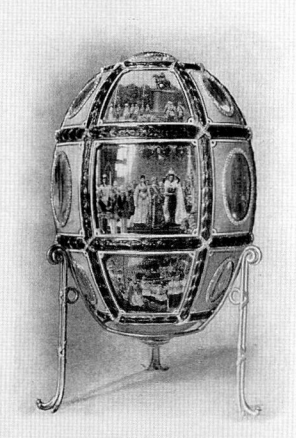

Всѣ яйца — работы К. Фаберже.

Яйцо въ память Священнаго Коронованія Ихъ Величествъ. Фонъ желтой эмали съ черными орлами и золотыми гирляндами. Внутри яйца изображеніе золотой кареты, въ которой Е. И. В. Государыня Императрица Александра Ѳеодоровна ѣхала на коронацію. Карета сдѣлана со всѣми подробностями изъ золота, съ красной эмалью и бриліантами. Въ каретѣ маленькое бриліантовое яичко.

Яйцо въ память открытія Великаго Сибирскаго Желѣзнаго Пути. Яйцо въ русскомъ стилѣ съ Государственнымъ орломъ наверху, покоится на трехъ Романовскихъ грифонахъ изъ золота и на постаментѣ изъ бѣлаго оникса. Вокругъ яйца гравирована точная карта Сибирскаго Пути отъ С. Петербурга до Владивостока. Внутри яйца находится сложенный въ три раза поѣздъ Сибирской желѣзной дороги, представляющій его фотографически-точную копію. Поѣздъ сдѣланъ изъ золота; миніатюрный локомотивъ снабженъ механизмомъ, позволяющимъ двигать поѣздъ. Къ концу поѣзда прицѣпленъ вагонъ-церковь. Рисунокъ равняется приблизительно ⁷/₁₀ натуральной величины яйца.

50

1. *The solemn procession to the Uspenski Cathedral.*
2. *The moment of the Holy Coronation.*
3. *The Alexander III Bridge in Paris, the foundation of which was attended by His Imperial Majesty.*
4. *The house in The Hague (Hous in't Bosch) where the first peace conference was held.*
5. *The Ceremonial Reception for the members of the First State Duma at the Winter Palace.*
6. *The Emperor Alexander III Museum.*
7. *Inauguration of the Peter the Great monument in Riga.*
8. *Inauguration of the monument marking the bicentenary of the Battle of Poltava (in Poltava).*
9. *Transfer of the relics of Saint Seraphim of Sarov and portraits of the Imperial Family.*

At both ends of the egg are flat, specially-ground diamonds covering the Empress's monogram AΘ with a crown and the year 1909.

Egg commemorating the Holy Coronation of Their Majesties, on a background of yellow enamel, with black eagles and gold garlands containing a model of the gold carriage in which Her Imperial Majesty, the Empress Alexandra Fedorovna, drove to the coronation. The carriage is fashioned, down to the last detail, of gold with red enamel and diamonds, and contains a small diamond pendant egg.

Renaissance-style egg, of rock crystal with different-coloured enamel decoration; eagles and dolphins of pure blue lapis lazuli. The egg contains a gold and platinum model of the Imperial yacht 'Standard', with detailed representation of all the rigging, trap-doors, cannons, revolving steering-wheel, etc.

Egg commemorating the inauguration of the Great Siberian Railway, fashioned in Russian style, surmounted by an Imperial eagle and resting on three gold Romanov griffins and a white onyx pediment. A detailed map of the Siberian Railway from St Petersburg to Vladivostok is engraved round the middle of the egg, which contains a photographically accurate replica of a train of the Railway, folded into three parts. The train is made of gold and the miniature engine is fitted with a traction mechanism. A church-carriage is attached to the end of the train.

5

The 1902 Exhibition

Baron von Dervis Mansion

An exhibition of Fabergé objects belonging to members of the Imperial family was opened on 9 March 1902 at the Baron von Dervis mansion in St Petersburg and closed on 15 March. This important event was the first and only opportunity for the Russian public to see the Imperial Easter eggs, for those were always kept in the private Imperial apartments, access to which was reserved exclusively for the Imperial couple and their children.

The exhibition was a charity event organized under the patronage of Empress Alexandra Fedorovna and featured Artistic Objects and Miniatures by Fabergé. Both the Empress and Baroness von Dervis belonged to the Imperial Ladies' Patriotic Society, and the proceeds of the event were intended to aid the Society's schools.

Translation of advertisement for the 1902 von Dervis exhibition

> **EXHIBITION**
>
> FABERGÉ ARTIFACTS, ANTIQUE MINIATURES AND SNUFFBOXES
> *belonging to members of the Imperial family and private persons held at the von Dervis mansion (English Embankment, 28) in aid of schools under the august patronage of Her Majesty the Empress Alexandra Fedorovna and the Imperial Ladies' Patriotic Society*
>
> WILL CLOSE
> on Friday, 15 March, at 4 p.m.
>
> *The exhibition is open from 11 a.m. until 6 p.m.
> Until 4 p.m. on Friday 15 March   Entrance Price: 1 roub. 10 kop.*

The von Dervis family arrived in Russia from Germany after one of their ancestors received an invitation from Tsar Peter III (1728–1762) to act as a legal consultant in St Petersburg. Pavel Grigorievich, a railroad magnate, became one of the richest men in Russia. In 1854 he purchased a mansion in St Petersburg at 28, English Embankment. While he continued to live and develop his business in Russia, his concern over the poor health of his family motivated him to build a beautiful villa in Nice. His wife, Vera Nikolaievna, and children lived there. The Baron's philanthropic efforts in Nice included establishing several orphanages, schools, and a Russian Orthodox Church.

Despite von Dervis' efforts to provide a mild climate and the best medical care for his family, in 1881 his beloved daughter, Varvara, died at the age of 16. Tragedy struck once more. When the train carrying her coffin arrived at the station, he suffered a fatal heart attack.

Portrait of Baron Pavel Pavlovich von Dervis (1870–1943)

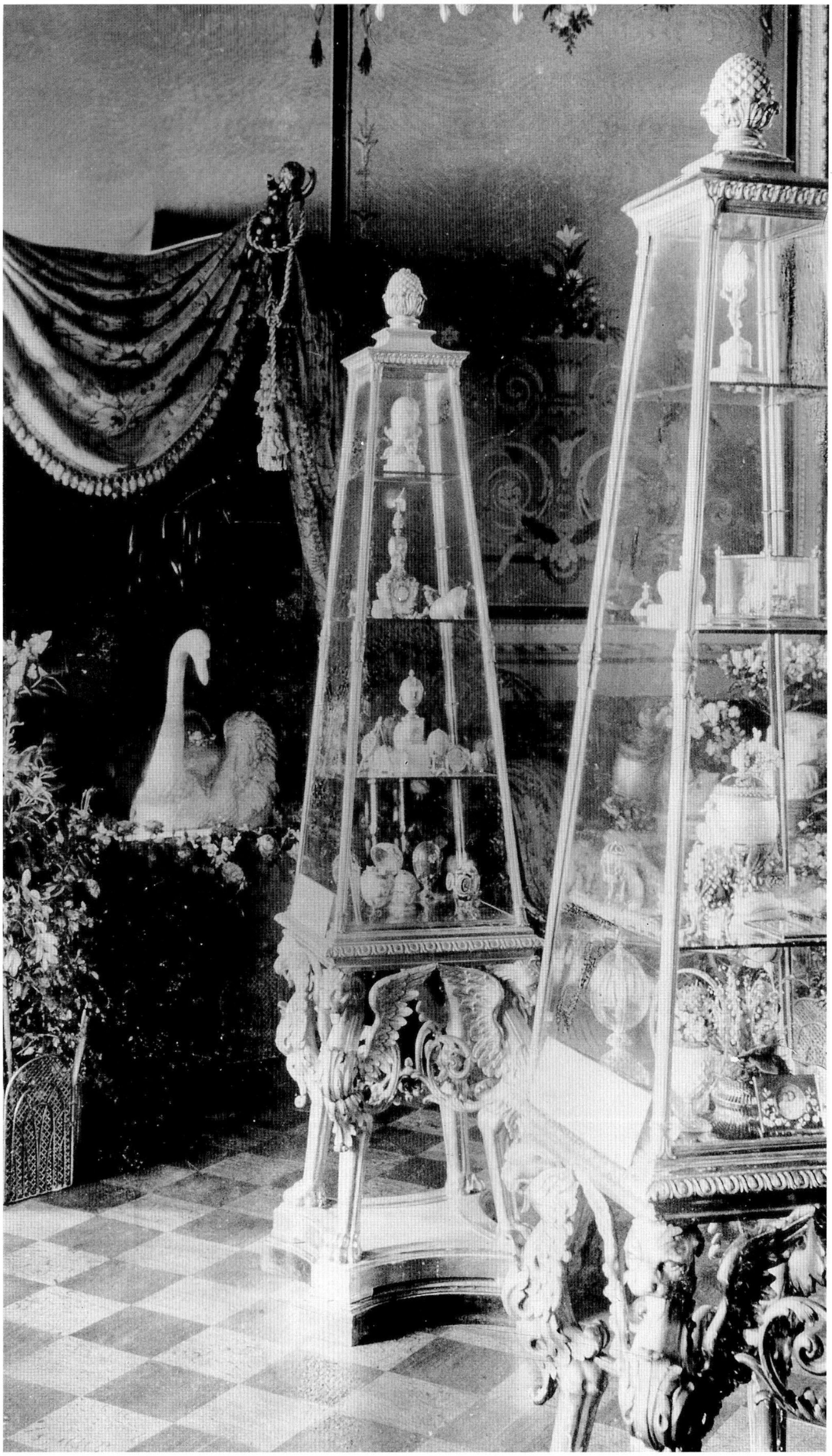

LEFT: *Vitrine displaying Easter eggs presented to the Empress Maria Fedorovna. Among the exhibits, the following Easter eggs can be distinguished:*
Top shelf: Diamond Trellis egg (8). Third shelf down: frame surprise of Pansy egg (19), left; Blue Serpent Clock egg (3), centre. Bottom shelf, left to right: Gatchina Palace egg (23); Renaissance egg (10); Pansy egg (19); Caucasus egg (9).

There are several eggs in this cabinet which cannot be identified and it is probable that they are among the missing Imperial eggs.

RIGHT: *Vitrine displaying Easter eggs presented to the Empress Alexandra Fedorovna. Among the eggs visible in this photograph are: Second shelf down: State Carriage surprise from Coronation egg inside bevelled glass case (16). Third shelf, left to right: Bouquet of Lilies Clock egg (20); Rosebud egg (12), in front, partially concealed; Trans-Siberian Railway egg with train surprise in front (22); Coronation egg (16), at the back, partially concealed; Lilies of the Valley egg (18), right-hand corner.*
Bottom shelf: Revolving Miniatures egg (14), left; Basket of Wild Flowers egg (24), right.

55

The Baron's widow, Vera Nikolaievna, and her children returned to their mansion in St Petersburg. Vera Nikolaievna concentrated on educating her youngest son, Pavel Pavlovich, born in Nice 17 April 1870, and continued the humanitarian endeavours promoted by her husband. She opened several girls' orphanages and set up soup kitchens for the poor. Her charitable achievements were renowned.

Vera Nikolaievna's eldest son, Sergei Pavlovich, who was born in 1864, was a talented and serious musician. He studied at the Moscow Conservatory. Sergei married and lived next door to his mother at 34, English Embankment. Pavel was raised in this cultured atmosphere exposed to music, theatre, languages, and art, but his love of horses predominated. In 1890 he joined a cavalry regiment. While still in the army, he built an enormous stud farm on his mother's estate. Pavel lived the life of a 'gentleman farmer', eventually owning 2,500 magnificent thoroughbreds.

In 1889, Vera Nikolaievna made the decision to completely remodel her mansion at 28, English Embankment. As the family owned a number of properties along the English Embankment, she decided to move next door to number 34. Her enormous wealth enabled her to employ St Petersburg's most successful architect, Alexander Fedorovich Krasovskii. His new design for the mansion reflected the elaborate Florentine style so fashionable in St Petersburg at that time. When the construction was complete, Vera Nikolaievna allowed her wonderful new mansion to be opened to the public, hosting the now famous 1902 exhibition, which was installed in the sumptuous Gold Drawing Room.

The exhibition room at the von Dervis mansion, St Petersburg, 1902

A recent photograph of the von Dervis exhibition room.

Vera Nikolaievna died on 25 February 1903, less than one year after the exhibition. The mansion was sold shortly thereafter. The mansion at number 34 was also sold, and Sergei and his wife moved to Paris. But, with the advent of the First World War and the beginning of the Revolution, the aristocracy and wealthy industrialists were to face unbelievable hardships. Pavel, who had barely managed to survive the starvation, persecution and mass purges during the Revolutionary and Stalinist years, was faced once again with insurmountable obstacles when, in 1941, the Nazis invaded Russia. Baron Pavel Pavlovich died of starvation in February 1943.[40]

6

The Austerity Years

The Russo-Japanese War 1904–1905

The discovery of invoices from the House of Fabergé identifying 40 of the 50 Easter eggs was invaluable in establishing the correct chronology of the eggs, but left a two-year gap, 1904 and 1905, in which Easter eggs were not presented. The all-important events celebrated by the Imperial family, which Fabergé would normally incorporate and glorify in the designs of the Imperial Easter eggs, would have to wait, for in 1904 Russia was at war for the first time in thirty years.

In 1903 the Tsar and Empress visited Moscow. This was regarded by all to be a significant occasion, as it was their first visit to the ancient capital since their coronation in 1896. As usual, Fabergé designed an Easter egg to commemorate this auspicious event (the Moscow Kremlin egg, 30), even going so far as to mark the date '1904' on it, the year in which it was to have been presented to the Empress. But in January 1904 the Japanese launched an attack against Russia, and the Tsar may have suggested postponing the delivery of the Easter egg.

Tsar Nicholas II had been ill-advised by his ministers to invade Manchuria in the belief that Japan would be unable to mount a defence against this assault. The ministers had underestimated Japan's military might, and in an unforeseen turn of events, Japan attacked Russia. The Russian army and navy suffered terrible defeats, with great loss of life. Although the Tsar must have been stunned by this devastating news, he reacted in his usual laconic and unperturbed manner:

26 January 1904

... received a telegram from Alexeiev [Chief of Staff, Mikhail Alexeiev] *with the news that that night Japanese torpedo boats had carried out an attack against the 'Tsarevich', 'Palladia', etc. which were at anchor, and put holes in them.* [41]

The war dealt a tremendous blow to Russian society and the general mood that gripped the country is reflected in the diaries of S.R. Mintslov:

31 March 1904

It is rumoured everywhere that the 'Petropavlovsk' has been sunk. What Easter celebrations and what Easter presents can there be while Russian sailors are perishing! [42]

Franz Birbaum recalls in his memoirs that during times of armed conflict the House of Fabergé either did not make any Easter eggs, or made less expensive, simpler ones. One of the reasons for this was the drafting of master craftsmen for active military service which left the firm short-staffed and unable to fulfil Imperial commissions.

The ordeal of war was tempered momentarily with the approaching birth of a royal child. To the absolute delight of the Tsar and Empress, a son and heir, the Tsarevich Alexei Nicholaievich, was born in 1904. Despite the lack of staff, Carl Fabergé set about designing an important Easter egg to celebrate the Imperial family's happy event. The result was a splendid blue enamel Easter egg in the shape of a cradle (Cradle with Garlands egg, 31) in which the Tsarevich's first portrait was concealed.

Revolution, however, was also in the air. Dangerous uprisings, strikes, riots and full-scale battles were occurring in the cities. This was no time for the Russian Court to be indulging in luxuries, and the Imperial family was afraid of publicity concerning their expenditures. A public outburst occurred when it was alleged that the Admiral General, Grand Duke Alexei Alexandrovich, Nicholas II's uncle, had frivolously spent funds set aside for the modernization of the navy on diamonds for the prima ballerina, Elisabeth Baletta. Some pithy observations on this controversy are recorded by Mintslov:

31 January 1904

Funny and absurd rumours are spreading among our townsfolk. The following is an example that has come to my ears:

Grand Duke Aleksei, a sailor, gave his mistress, the French actress Baletta... a small silver model of a ship with little diamond nails. This is the form in which this event spread among the people – passed around with dissatisfaction, head-shaking, oohs and ahs, and of course in low voices: Why should we expect any good from them? all that money going to waste! Aleksei Alexandrovich has given his mistress, that Frenchwoman, a silver ship, and spends whole days sailing in it with her! [43]

As the war continues, Mintslov chronicles the mounting disillusionment with the Imperial family.

7 February 1905

Grand Duke Vladimir, Maria Fedorovna and Trepov say that they have received and continue to receive letters announcing that they have been condemned to death. No members of the Imperial family appear in the streets, whereas only recently you were bound to come across one of them if you went along the Nevskii or the Morskaia. [44]

The invoices prepared by the House of Fabergé during these difficult times show that the Imperial family curbed their spending. The amounts received were quite insignificant compared to previous expenditures. They were probably payments for jewellery and other objects and did not include disbursements for Easter eggs, on which the Tsar had been spending 16,000 roubles each year. In 1904, the House of Fabergé received only 8,543 roubles [45] from the Emperor, and in 1905 a lesser amount of 4,052 roubles and 50 kopeks. [46]

Then in early 1905, tragedy struck when Grand Duke Sergei Alexandrovich, whose wife was the sister of the Empress Alexandra, was killed by terrorists in the Kremlin. His assasination came as a severe shock to the Imperial family. It was the first time in Russian history that a member of the Romanov House had been murdered within the ancient citadel. Perhaps it was because of this tragic event and the fact that the Grand Duke was buried in the Kremlin Tchudovo monastery that Fabergé decided to postpone the presentation of the Moscow Kremlin egg until 1906.

The war abroad and the increasing unrest at home were the muted chimes of the death knell for the Imperial family and the Russian Empire. Otto-Gustav Jarke, the Managing Director of Fabergé's Moscow factory, wrote to his partner, Allan Bowe, during the uprisings, describing the serious and dangerous situation that they were having to face.

20 December, 1905 / 2 January, 1906

Dear Mr Bowe,

The terrible events here hardly bear writing about, but please believe me that everything you may hear about them in London is true and even worse, and that some really awful things have happened... On Sunday morning, at the corner of Sofika, a gun battery was stationed with a detachment of soldiers... Oh, God! If you could have seen it! Heaps of people were shot like rabbits, it was horrible – all those wounded, in pools of blood! At half past one, I wanted to leave the shop and go out into the street, when suddenly, there was a crack, and a bullet whizzed past my ear and knocked a piece of plaster from our shop wall, so I was unable to go out. An enormous number of people have been hit by stray bullets. The revolutionaries fought with desperate, death-defying courage, and the soldiers also battled valiantly, advancing directly into the range of fire. I tried to keep the soldiers in our neighbourhood. Our people are out of danger, thank God!

... The people were terribly excited, firing cannons. A fine situation! Things are now gradually going back to normal, but no one is allowed to go out of doors after 9 o'clock at night, they 'will be fired upon' if they do: that is how the order reads, and that is how it is carried out. Anyone, man or woman, who appears in the street after 6 p.m. is liable to be searched, and if he or she is found to be carrying a revolver, they are shot with that selfsame weapon... We manage to get home by 5 p.m. The telephone is still not working, as Dubassov changed the line so that the revolutionaries could not use it... I have received a telegram from Odessa, telling me that everything is quiet there... As for our people, their stocks must be practically all sold, since we have been selling at our normal prices, while all the others have been quite knocked out.

... Thank God that I distributed all the goods and money among different places, so that everything turned out all right. [47]

It was not until after the war, at Easter time in 1906, that the Imperial family indulged themselves once again, and took delivery of two Easter eggs, the Swan egg (29) and the Moscow Kremlin egg (30).

7

A Discovery

The Last Imperial Easter Eggs, 1917

The House of Fabergé continued to function for a short while after the Revolution in 1917. The political situation in the country was confused, but the experience of the revolutionary activity of 1905 gave grounds for hope that stability would again be restored. Carl Fabergé had begun to design and create, as he had done for the past 31 years, the usual two Imperial Easter eggs to be presented to the Empresses in 1917.

In a document dated late in 1916, Carl Fabergé asks for his best workmasters to be exempted from the draft, saying that he will be unable to fulfil 'an order from His Imperial Majesty now being executed for a large Easter egg of white quartz and nephrite of exceptionally artistic workmanship'.[48] It is clear he is referring to the egg mentioned in the letter below by Franz Birbaum.

This letter, which is in the archives belonging to Tatiana Fabergé, has not previously been published. It was written by Birbaum to Eugène Fabergé in August 1922 and sheds light on the fate of the last Fabergé Imperial Easter eggs. Birbaum writes as follows:

> *With regard to the orders of which you write, it is of course difficult to reconstitute anything without documentation. One thing I remember for certain is the order of an egg for the Tsar by Ivashev and Carl Gustavovich. This, you may remember, is an egg of dark blue glass incrusted with the constellation of the day of the Tsarevich's birth. The egg is supported by silver cherubs and clouds of opaque rock crystal. Unless I am mistaken, the egg contained a clock with a revolving face. The execution of this egg was interrupted by the war. The cherubs and the clouds were finished, but the egg itself with its incrustation and the pedestal were not finished. Where all this has disappeared to I have no idea, and when I visited the House after the raid, I found*

Drawing of the Blue Tsarevich Constellation egg – one of the two Imperial Easter eggs designed in 1917, but apparently never completed

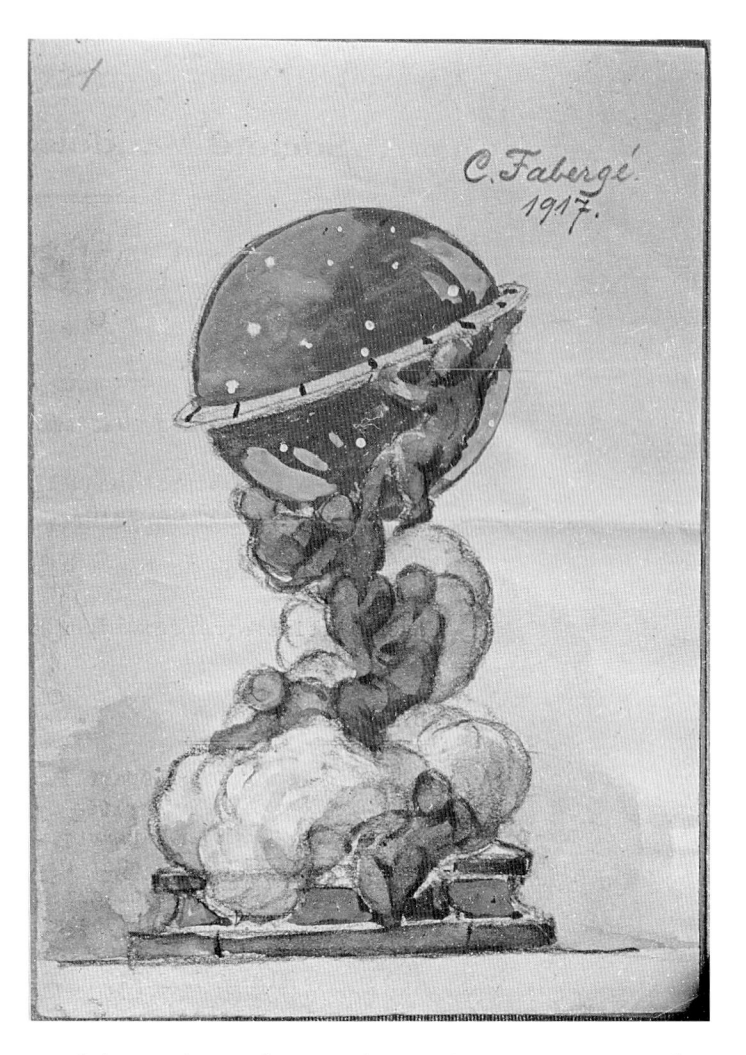

> *no trace of this article. Another egg referred to by Wigström must be the simple wooden one with slight mounting which was to have been presented in 1917 but which Kerensky* (leader of the Provisional Government) *did not allow to be delivered to the Tsar. It is quite possible that these were orders to Carl Gustavovich with miniatures by Zuiev, but as I did not design them I cannot say anything about them.* [49]

As can be seen, Birbaum believes the 1917 Easter eggs were never completed, but as Henrik Wigström was the head workmaster and Birbaum admits that Ivashev and Fabergé were the designers, Birbaum's observations may not be fully accurate.

> *The eggs prepared for Easter 1917 were never finished; a certain person unknown to me suggested that I should finish them and sell them to him, but the firm did not accept the offer.* [50]

Apparently, Wigström had written from Finland asking Eugène Fabergé to pay for work on two Easter eggs for 1917.[51] The drawing of the egg mentioned in Birbaum's letter is known.[52] It bears the date 1917 and the signature C. Fabergé, and indeed depicts cherubs supporting an egg-shaped celestial body.

The reference to the wooden egg is very exciting. In a box of old photographic glass negatives belonging to Tatiana Fabergé there appeared among several other interesting negatives one that contained what appeared to be two drawings of Easter eggs, both dated 1917 and signed by Carl Fabergé. The first one was immediately recognizable from Birbaum's description as the Blue Tsarevich Constellation egg, the second matched Wigström's description of a simple wooden egg, which was probably

Drawing of the Karelian Birch egg – one of the two Imperial Easter eggs designed in 1917, but apparently never completed

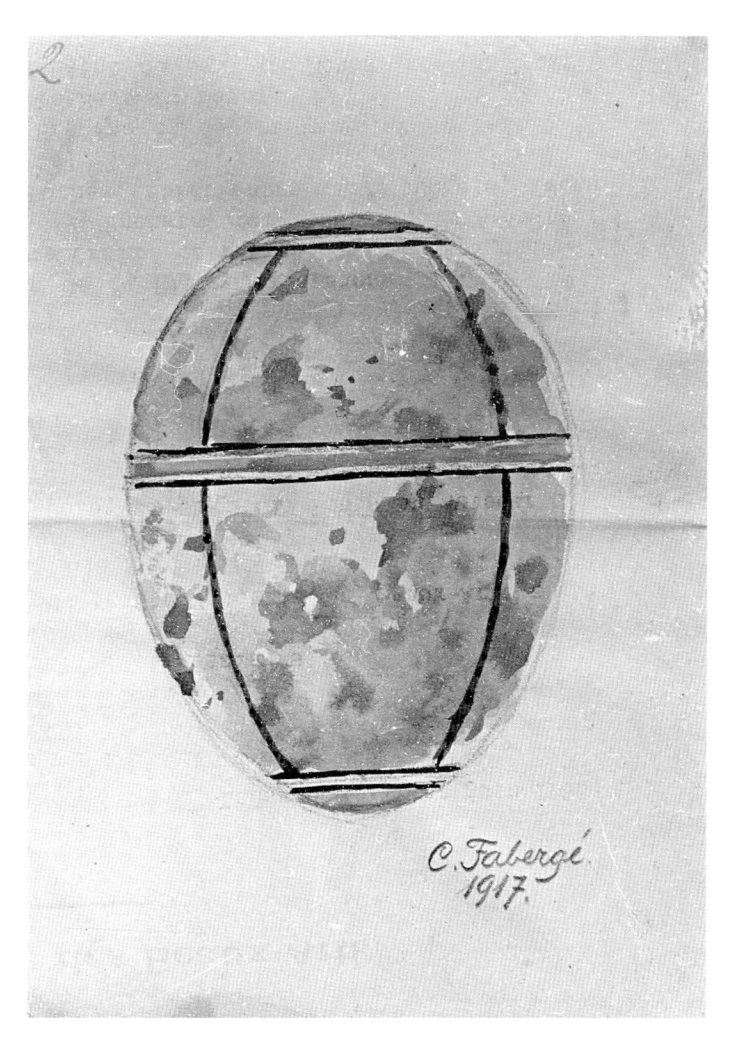

made of Karelian birch. The drawing clearly shows that the shell of the egg was designed in two halves which could be opened to reveal a surprise.

A most intriguing notation in an inventory listing of treasures that was confiscated from Grand Duke Vladimir Alexandrovich's Palace only five days after the October Revolution included the following description of item No. 561:

> *Wooden egg in gold setting, inside an elephant, mechanical, silver and gold, with rose-cut diamonds. Fabergé.* [53]

The above egg contained as a surprise a silver and gold mechanical elephant, which may have represented the Danish Elephant Order, a favourite design of the Danish born Empress Maria Fedorovna. It is quite likely that of the two Easter eggs designed by Fabergé for 1917, this was the one destined to be presented to her.

By March of that same year, the Imperial family was already under house arrest by the Provisional Government. The Empress Maria Fedorovna, was by this time in Crimea. It is conceivable, therefore, that the Karelian Birch Easter egg could have been taken instead to the Palace of her late brother-in-law, Grand Duke Vladimir Alexandrovich, where his widow, Maria Pavlovna, was in residence.

This would be an appropriate ending to the sad fate of the Romanov dynasty. The fascinating history of the Easter eggs began in 1885 with the involvement of Grand Duke Vladimir Alexandrovich, Tsar Alexander III's brother, and here, perhaps, it ends at his palace in 1917.

8

After the Revolution

*I*n the early months of the Revolution, Russia was in great turmoil. Immediately following the October Revolution Lenin's government confiscated and nationalized all Imperial property. The palaces and country estates belonging to the Imperial family, the aristocracy and wealthy merchants were all under attack. All of Russia's cultural heritage was plundered by mobs storming the palaces. Hordes of people swarmed the poorly protected buildings. Their owners fled for their lives and crazed throngs tore apart the palaces, carting away everything they could carry and destroying the rest. It was not just looting, it was total destruction. The exquisite crystal chandeliers and walls of malachite in the Winter Palace were smashed to pieces, the large rare porcelain vases shattered, and the elegant silk furnishings torn down and burned.

Agathon Fabergé's country estate was among the houses ravaged. The 1919 report by the Department for Preservation of Art and Antique Objects noted that:

... this wonderful house has been completely destroyed... In fact, nothing turns out to be left: absolutely everything has been taken... everything has been turned upside down, broken, fabric and leather cut off the pieces of furniture that remained...

In the early hours of the morning of 17 September 1917, a 40-wagon train pulled into Moscow. It was loaded with the trove of treasures from the Anichkov Palace, residence of the Dowager Empress Maria Fedorovna which had been plundered by the Bolsheviks. Eighty-four crates filled with unbelievable riches, including most of the Imperial Easter eggs, were delivered to the Moscow Kremlin Armoury for storage. The Empress' other residence, the Gatchina Palace, was looted by General

Yudenich's troops in 1919. The writer, Kuprin, witnessed soldiers and officers hauling whatever they could out of the Palace. During the ransacking of the two palaces, eight of the Imperial Easter eggs disappeared without a trace.

The missing Imperial Easter eggs are those made in the years 1886, 1888, 1889, 1896, 1897, 1902, 1903 and 1909, and they all belonged to the Empress Maria Fedorovna.

All of the eight unrecovered eggs are now known to us only by their recently discovered invoices which give a brief description of their appearance and the materials used, the year in which they were made, and the prices paid for them by the Tsar. In addition to this, we are fortunate enough to be able to identify two of the missing eggs, dating from 1903 and 1909, through photographs from the archives of Tatiana Fabergé. The inventory of the Moscow Kremlin Armoury for 1922 mentions over 40 eggs, including unattributable ones such as the Flask egg, proving that by no means had all of the Imperial eggs been transferred from Petrograd to Moscow.

Fortunately, because her palaces were guarded and kept intact, all 20 of the Imperial Easter eggs belonging to the Empress Alexandra Fedorovna are accounted for and are now in museums and private collections.

The 1916 Order of St George egg was the last of all the Imperial Easter eggs to be presented to Maria Fedorovna. The Dowager Empress had travelled to Kiev supervising the Red Cross activities in the south [54] before moving on to the Romanov estates in the Crimea. It is possible that Fabergé had delivered the Imperial egg to her there. In spite of a house search by Bolshevik sailors (who missed her jewellery cases), the Dowager Empress succeeded in taking this egg, along with her other valuables, when she finally agreed to be evacuated from Yalta to England aboard the battleship HMS *Marlborough* in April 1919.

Gatchina Palace

Display of the Imperial regalia which was inventoried and valued in the early 1920s. Agathon Fabergé (standing second from left), being an expert on gemstones, was released from prison to participate in the valuation

During the perilous first years of the Revolution, the crates containing the Easter eggs remained unopened in the Kremlin Armoury store rooms, guarded by Kremlin staff. The museum curators and other experts were directed to inventory and evaluate the hoard of treasures, with the objective of selling them off for hard currency to finance the new regime. It was during this period that Agathon Fabergé, an expert in gemstones imprisoned by the Bolsheviks, was released (from 1921 to 1923) to carry out the task of valuing the Russian Crown Jewels and the mounds of jewellery confiscated from the aristocracy during the Revolution. He was imprisoned again upon completing the valuation, but finally escaped from Russia in 1928.

Although many important antiques and works of art were sold in 1927, the curators at the Kremlin were able to delay the sale of the Fabergé Imperial Easter eggs until 1930. At this time, they were ordered to be delivered to Antikvariat, the new government bureau established by Lenin in 1921, to sell State treasures to the West. In 1930 and 1933, fourteen of the Imperial Easter eggs were officially sold by Antikvariat. All sales of the Imperial Easter eggs were effected in the Soviet Union, and Antikvariat sent none of them to auction houses. Although several eggs were ultimately sold by Christie's and Sotheby's, they arrived there through other channels.

Given that only ten Imperial Easter eggs remain in Russia, that the Dowager Empress carried one egg with her when she escaped to England, that eight eggs went missing after the outbreak of the Revolution and fourteen were sold by Antikvariat, it can be surmised that the remaining 17 eggs made their way to the West by unauthorized means.

Unfortunately, the official sales receipts do not record any of the names of the individuals to whom they were sold, although it is well known that the American industrialist, Armand Hammer, one of the first Americans to do business with the fledgling Soviet Government, lived in Russia for almost a decade and sold a number of Imperial Easter eggs to collectors in the West. He did not operate as a private collector exporting art, however, but probably worked as an agent for the Soviet government selling works of art to provide Stalin hard currency for his Five Year Plan (1928-1932). In 1932 Hammer returned to the West with an immense hoard of Imperial Russian treasures, including a number of Imperial Easter eggs, ostensibly traded to him by the Soviet Government as compensation for concessions nationalized by the new regime.[55] He set up business and heavily promoted and marketed the sale of these riches. He displayed and sold these beautiful jewelled objects in his New York gallery, at various World Fairs, and at the New York department store of Lord and Taylor. Mrs Matilda Geddings Gray saw Hammer's display at the Chicago World Fair in 1933 and subsequently purchased four Imperial Easter eggs from him, one of which she gave to her niece for her first wedding anniversary. In his astonishingly candid book, Carl Blumay, Hammer's publicity director for 25 years, wrote:

> *According to Armand, "buyers turned out in droves. Our success in St Louis led to sales in eight other stores, culminating in a huge sale at Lord and Taylor in New York at the beginning of 1933. I trotted out my Fabergé collection and sold thirteen diamond-studded Fabergé eggs...".*'[56]

It appears that there was one other major dealer buying and selling Fabergé Imperial Easter eggs – Emanuel Snowman. His son, A. K. Snowman, has identified nine Imperial eggs which he believes his father acquired in Russia between the years 1925 and 1939.[57] None of these eggs were listed in the official sales invoices from the Moscow Kremlin Armoury. One can only imagine the state of disarray in Russia at that time, which made it possible for officials, and even petty bureaucrats, to have access to the Imperial family's accumulation of riches. The appetite for the Romanov treasures was insatiable among many dealers who acquired jewels and objects in exchange for a small percentage of their value. For example, in England Queen Mary's well known passion for collecting was unsurpassed when it came to bargaining for the possessions of her exiled and impoverished Russian relatives.

Diplomats Ambassador Herbette of France and Ambassador Davies of the United States (husband of Marjorie Merriweather Post), who were assigned to Russia shortly after the Revolution, were among those who had the foresight to bring with them out of Russia treasures, including several of the Imperial Easter eggs, that had previously belonged to the Romanovs.

A photograph of a gathering of the Bolshevik committee organised to value and partially dispose of the Imperial regalia and other works of art

1. *Bay Tree egg (1911)*
2. *Moscow Kremlin egg (1906)*
3. *Romanov Tercentenary egg (1913)*
4. *Trans-Siberian Railway egg (1900)*
5. *Fifteenth Anniversary egg (1911)*
6. *Steel Military egg (1916)*
7. *Mosaic egg (1914)*
8. *Standard egg (1909)*
9. *Winter egg (1913)*
10. *Pelican egg (1898)*
11. *Peacock egg (1908)*
12. *Revolving Miniatures egg (1896)*

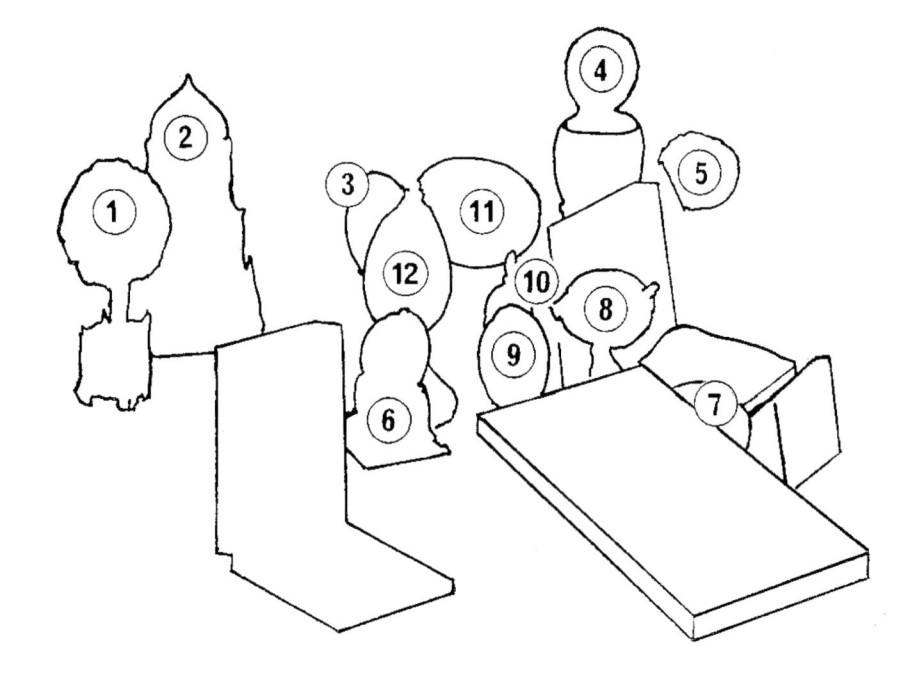

This chart is an attempt by the authors to identify the route through which the Imperial Easter eggs passed from the Soviets to their first owners. What exactly transpired during those early years will probably never come to light.

Year/Empress*	Name of Easter Egg	Amount/Year Sold by Antikvariat (Price in roubles)	Acquired By
1885/MF	Hen egg	1500 r. 1930	Armand Hammer**
1886/MF	Hen egg with Sapphire Pendant	Missing	
1887/MF	Blue Serpent Clock egg		
1888/MF	Cherub egg with Chariot	Missing	
1889/MF	Nécessaire egg	Missing	
1890/MF	Danish Palaces egg		
1891/MF	Memory of Azov egg		Moscow Kremlin Armoury
1892/MF	Diamond Trellis egg		
1893/MF	Caucasus egg	5000 r. 1930	Armand Hammer
1894/MF	Renaissance egg	1500 r. 1930	Armand Hammer
1895/MF	Twelve Monograms egg		
1895/AF	Rosebud egg		Emanuel Snowman***
1896/MF	Alexander III egg	Missing	
1896/AF	Revolving Miniatures egg	8000 r. 1930	Armand Hammer
1897/MF	Mauve Enamel egg	Missing	
1897/AF	Coronation egg		Emanuel Snowman
1898/MF	Pelican egg	1000 r. 1930	Armand Hammer
1898/AF	Lilies of the Valley egg		Emanuel Snowman
1899/MF	Pansy egg	7500 r. 1930	Armand Hammer
1899/AF	Bouquet of Lilies Clock egg		Moscow Kremlin Armoury
1900/MF	Cockerel egg		Emanuel Snowman
1900/AF	Trans-Siberian Railway egg		Moscow Kremlin Armoury
1901/MF	Gatchina Palace egg		Alexander Polovtsov
1901/AF	Basket of Wild Flowers egg	2000 r. 1933	Armand Hammer
1902/MF	Empire Nephrite egg	Missing	
1902/AF	Clover egg		Moscow Kremlin Armoury
1903/MF	Danish Jubilee egg	Missing	
1903/AF	Peter the Great egg	4000 r. 1933	Armand Hammer
1904	No eggs made this year		
1905	No eggs made this year		
1906/MF	Swan egg		Emanuel Snowman
1906/AF	Moscow Kremlin egg		Moscow Kremlin Armoury
1907/MF	Cradle with Garlands egg		
1907/AF	Rose Trellis egg		Alexander Polovtsov
1908/MF	Peacock egg		Emanuel Snowman
1908/AF	Alexander Palace egg		Moscow Kremlin Armoury
1909/MF	Alexander III Commemorative egg	Missing	
1909/AF	Standard egg		Moscow Kremlin Armoury
1910/MF	Alexander III Equestrian egg		Moscow Kremlin Armoury
1910/AF	Colonnade egg		Emanuel Snowman
1911/MF	Bay Tree egg		Emanuel Snowman
1911/AF	Fifteenth Anniversary egg		
1912/MF	Napoleonic egg	5000 r. 1930	Armand Hammer
1912/AF	Tsarevich egg	8000 r. 1930	Armand Hammer
1913/MF	Winter egg		Emanuel Snowman
1913/AF	Romanov Tercentenary egg		Moscow Kremlin Armoury
1914/MF	Grisaille egg	8000 r. 1930	Armand Hammer
1914/AF	Mosaic egg	5000 r. 1933	Armand Hammer
1915/MF	Red Cross egg with Imperial Portraits	500 r. 1930	Armand Hammer
1915/AF	Red Cross egg with Triptych	500 r. 1930	Armand Hammer
1916/MF	Order of St George egg		
1916/AF	Steel Military egg		Moscow Kremlin Armoury
1930	11 eggs sold for a total of 46,000 roubles		
1933	3 eggs sold for a total of 11,000 roubles		

* MF = The Empress Maria Federovna   * AF = The Empress Alexandra Federovna
**If, as he indicates, Armand Hammer sold 13 eggs, it is almost certain they were among those eggs officially sold by Antikvariat.
***A.K. Snowman believes his father acquired nine eggs in Russia.

9

The Kelkh Easter Eggs

The name Kelkh is outstanding among the celebrated collectors of Carl Fabergé's masterpieces at the turn of the century, but very little has previously been published about the family. Acquiring precious objects from the House of Fabergé was evidence of newly earned wealth and status, admitting industrialists and financiers into a world previously reserved for monarchs and titled aristocrats. Alexander and Varvara Kelkh sought that prestige, commissioning from the House of Fabergé seven extraordinary Easter eggs which rivalled in importance and beauty those given to Empress Alexandra Fedorovna by her husband Tsar Nicholas II. In fact, over the years, the Kelkh Easter eggs have on several occasions been identified and sold as Imperial. [58]

Varvara Petrovna Bazanova belonged to a prominent and affluent Muscovite merchant family. Her grandfather, Ivan Bazanov, founded several companies in Siberia in the 1860s in partnership with Yakov Nemchinov and Mikhail Sibiriakov. Their vast holdings included gold mines, railways, and shipping companies, and the Bazanovs and Sibiriakovs held the largest percentage of shares in these enterprises. Upon her father's death, Varvara and her mother, Yulia Ivanovna, inherited the family fortune, with Yulia continuing to manage the Bazanov family interests, and founded a new company in 1904 with Konstantin Sibiriakov. Yulia Bazanova owned several mansions with the most fashionable addresses in Moscow, one of them still known today as Bazanov House. She was a charitable and generous woman who supported many local organizations.

It was a common practice for marriages to be arranged between the sons and daughters of wealthy industrialists and members of the aristocracy who brought little else than their titles with them to the union. This was the case when the heiress Bazanova married the nobleman Nikolai Ferdinandovich Kelkh in 1892.

Early photograph of six of the Kelkh Easter eggs acquired by A La Vieille Russie in Paris c. 1920 together with the Nobel Ice egg (see page 81)

Nikolai, born in 1860, was the son of State Counsellor Ferdinand Kasparovich Kelkh, a German Lutheran school inspector who had been granted the status of hereditary nobleman for his many years of service.

Nikolai had a brother, Alexander, and two sisters, Anna and Amalia. The wedding of Varvara and Nikolai Kelkh took place in the Alexandrovskaia Church of the Alexandrovsky Military School, where Nikolai probably received his military training. The charitable leanings of Varvara's family then spread to the Kelkh family as Nikolai contributed the enormous sum of 250,000 roubles for the construction of a hospital in Irkutsk.

Two years later Varvara was already a widow, and in 1894, married Nikolai's younger brother, Alexander Kelkh, in all probability to retain the title belonging to the Kelkh family. It is known that two daughters were born to them, one of whom died in 1916 and the other married a diplomat who was posted to Japan. Varvara and Alexander lived separately, Varvara in Moscow at 60, Mokhovaia and Alexander, who was in military service in St Petersburg at 53, Bolshaia Morskaia.[59] Varvara Kelkh maintained her financial independence throughout her married life, keeping real

71

Kelkh Hen egg (1898)

estate and securities, as well as other assets she and Alexander acquired, solely in her name. In 1896, the couple purchased a mansion in St Petersburg at 28, Sergeievskaia for the princely sum of 300,000 roubles. The Bazanov money paid for the house, and the title was placed in Varvara Petrovna's name. Several of St Petersburg's leading architects worked on remodelling and redecorating the mansion, including Carl Carlovich Schmidt, who had designed Carl Fabergé's own country house in Osinovaia Roshcha, as well as the renowned House of Fabergé on Bolshaia Morskaia.

In 1898 Varvara moved to St Petersburg, but did not live in the house with Alexander until 1900. It was in that same year, 1898, that the Kelkhs commissioned the first Easter egg from the House of Fabergé (the red enamel Hen egg, now in the FORBES Magazine collection), as well as ordering a superb silver Gothic table service. Following the tradition established by the Tsar, the wealthy Kelkhs commissioned Carl Fabergé to create for them more impressive Easter eggs every year, perhaps trying to outshine the Imperial family.

It is not exactly clear what brought the Kelkhs to Fabergé. It is possible that their interest was prompted by Carl Schmidt, who was related to the Fabergés, and it is not inconceivable that business contacts existed between the two firms, with the Bazanov companies supplying gold and minerals to the Fabergé workshops. However, it is

Kelkh Twelve Panel egg
(1899)

Kelkh Pine Cone egg
(1900)

73

Kelkh Apple Blossom egg (1901)

clear that although the Kelkh family commissioned the Easter eggs, Alexander's own financial situation precluded him from personally placing an order for such truly royal luxuries, and it was Varvara who paid for these expensive Easter gifts.

While Varvara Kelkh is famous today for her collection of Easter eggs, a little known fact is that she was renowned at the time for her outstanding collection of gemstones. The famous blue diamond that once had belonged to Carl Fabergé was in her private collection.[60] The stone was originally destined to be purchased by Tsar Nicholas II as a gift for the Tsarevich's tenth birthday in 1914, but was deemed too frivolous a purchase by the ever prudent Empress. In 1901, Alexander Kelkh

Kelkh Rocaille egg (1902)

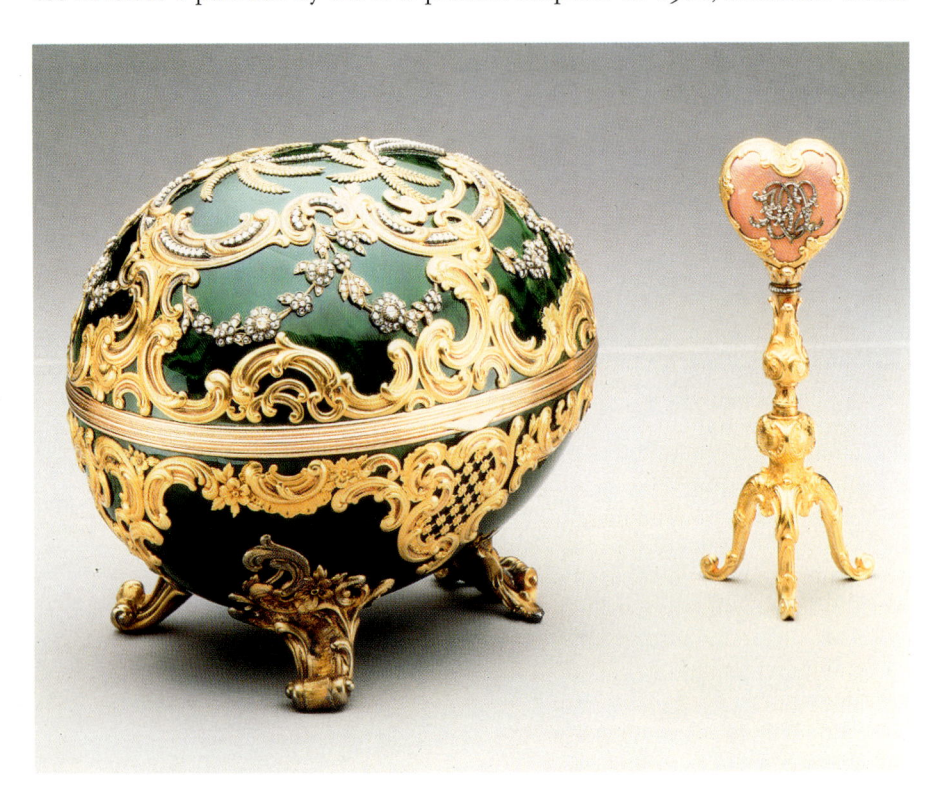

74

Kelkh Bonbonnière egg (1903)

left the army, with the rank of retired lieutenant, to become fully involved in the many Bazanov businesses. He became President of the Board of Directors of the Siberian and Lena-Vitim Steamship Line and of the Promyshlennosty Company when it was formed in 1904. Varvara Kelkh's name was invariably mentioned in the *Almanac of All St Petersburg* as a member of various philanthropic societies. These included the All Russia Red Cross Ladies Committee, the Russian Photographic Society, and the Imperial Russian Musical Society which were patronized by Empress Alexandra Fedorovna, Dowager Empress Maria Fedorovna, and other members of the Imperial family.

The Bazanov and Kelkh families prospered during the years leading up to 1904 and a second house was purchased for 200,000 roubles, in the name of A.F. Kelkh, at 13, Glinka Street in St Petersburg. But this seems to be the last year of their financial success and the end of stability for the Kelkh family. The political shocks suffered in Russia during the outbreak of the Russo-Japanese War in 1904 and the outbreak of the first revolution the following year destabilized the economy, causing their previously healthy enterprises to falter.

The years following the Russo-Japanese War were devastating for the Kelkh family. Varvara and Alexander legally separated, and in 1905, Varvara left Russia to take up residence in Paris. In the ensuing years, their two mansions with all the

Kelkh Chanticleer egg (1904)

furnishings were sold to pay off mounting debts. But, as the Easter eggs were not included in the inventory of objects and decorations, they were not sold with their houses. According to Alexander Kelkh at the time of his arrest and trial by the Communists in 1930, Varvara left Russia with a collection of *objets d'art*, which probably included all her Easter eggs (although other documents of that period claim that she was residing with her husband in his house at 13, Glinka Street).

The Kelkhs marriage was formally annulled in 1915, according to the Russian Orthodox tradition of revoking a marriage after a separation of 10 years. The Bazanov companies went into liquidation, and the Promyshlennosty Company was sold in 1910 to Lena Gold Fields, a British firm.

In view of the anti-German sentiments which were rampant in Russia during the First World War, Alexander Kelkh adopted the Russian Orthodox faith and changed his name from Alexander Ferdinandovich to Alexander Fedorovich. Alexander, now unemployed, married for the second time. After the Revolution, he and his family were forced to move from city to city looking for work, returning to

St Petersburg (renamed Petrograd and then Leningrad), where he supported himself and his family as a street vendor selling cigarettes.

According to Alexander's statement when he was already a prisoner in 1930,[61] he and Varvara had corresponded in the 1920s. She had sent him money and had tried to convince him to join her in Paris with his new family. Alexander declined, not wanting to become a financial burden. He knew that she was no longer involved in business and could barely support herself on her dwindling capital.

The records show that in 1930 Alexander Kelkh was arrested and tried by the Communists in Leningrad.[62] He was convicted and sentenced to hard labour in a Siberian gulag where he perished along with millions of other Russians.

After the Revolution, six of the seven Kelkh eggs appeared in around 1920 and were offered for sale by the jeweller, Morgan, in the Rue de la Paix in Paris. They were acquired by Mr Zolotnitzky who sold them through his shop, A La Vieille Russie, to an American collector. It was not until 1979 that they were revealed to have been made for the Kelkh family by reference to the contemporary notes made in 1922 by Leon Grinberg of A La Vieille Russie in Paris. Varvara Kelkh's whereabouts in Paris become difficult to trace soon after her correspondence with Alexander ended in 1928.

Tradition has it that a total of seven Easter eggs were made over a period of seven years for Varvara Kelkh. Although the authors searched the archives in Russia for conclusive evidence, no documentation was found. The House of Fabergé's missing ledgers most probably contain the relative information required to establish fully which of these Easter eggs were actually purchased by the Kelkh family. The seven eggs, pictured on pages 72–76, comprise:

> 1898: the first Easter egg – the Hen egg. Sold in Cairo by Sotheby's London, 10 March 1954, lot 165, the Palace Collections of Egypt, ex-collection of King Farouk. Now in the FORBES Magazine collection.
>
> 1899: the second Easter egg – the Twelve Panel egg. Now in the Collection of Her Majesty Queen Elizabeth II.
>
> 1900: the third Easter egg – the Pine Cone egg. Sold by Christie's, Geneva, 10 May 1989 for SFr 5,280,000. Now in the collection of Mrs Joan B. Kroc, San Diego, California.
>
> 1901: the fourth Easter egg – the Apple Blossom egg. Sold at Sotheby's, Geneva, 19 November 1996 for SFr 1,433,500. Now in a private collection.
>
> 1902: the fifth Easter egg – the Rocaille egg. Now in a private collection.
>
> 1903: the sixth Easter egg – the Bonbonnière egg. Went to auction at Christie's New York, 30 October 1990, but did not make the reserve price, and was later sold privately to an American collector.
>
> 1904: the seventh Easter egg – the Chanticleer egg. Now in the FORBES Magazine collection.

10

Undocumented Easter Eggs

One only has to peruse the many inventory lists of Imperial property confiscated by the Provisional Government to realize that Easter eggs were traditional gifts given to family members as tokens of love and esteem. But not all of the Easter eggs listed in the Imperial inventories were made by the House of Fabergé and not all of the Fabergé eggs that made their way to the West are Imperial. The Mintslov diaries and archives in Russia indicate that Maria Fedorovna enjoyed patronizing various European jewellers and goldsmiths. At the 1891 French Exhibition in Moscow, the Parisian jeweller, Bourdier, presented the Empress with a large blue enamelled Easter egg.[63] It is thus certain that the Empress' collection contained Easter eggs made by other jewellers in addition to those made by the House of Fabergé.

Because of the lack of documentary proof, it has so far been relatively easy to attach the title Imperial to Easter eggs created by the House of Fabergé and by jewellers working during the same period. However, the newly discovered archival documentation has made it possible to clarify the subject.

THE RESURRECTION EGG
FORBES Magazine Collection

In the Moscow Armoury inventory of 1922 there is a reference to a 'crystal egg, containing figures on a gold stand with eight diamonds, roses and pearls'[64] which was kept with the objects confiscated by the Bolsheviks. This is the closest description the authors have found corresponding to the Resurrection egg in the FORBES Magazine Collection. However, some information published here for the first time, concerning an auction in 1934, seems to eliminate it from the list of Imperial Easter eggs.

On 15 March 1934, a large group of Fabergé *objets de luxe* was auctioned at Christie's in London. The auction was clearly a major event in the saleroom calendar and elicited great interest from the Fabergé family and past employees, as well as the press. Among those present at the sale was H.C. Bainbridge, manager of the House of Fabergé's London branch before its closure in 1917.

The information garnered from the documents cited below, which include a catalogue from the Christie's auction,[65] gives a new perspective on this egg. Prior to the auction, Bainbridge wrote to Eugène Fabergé:

Resurrection egg

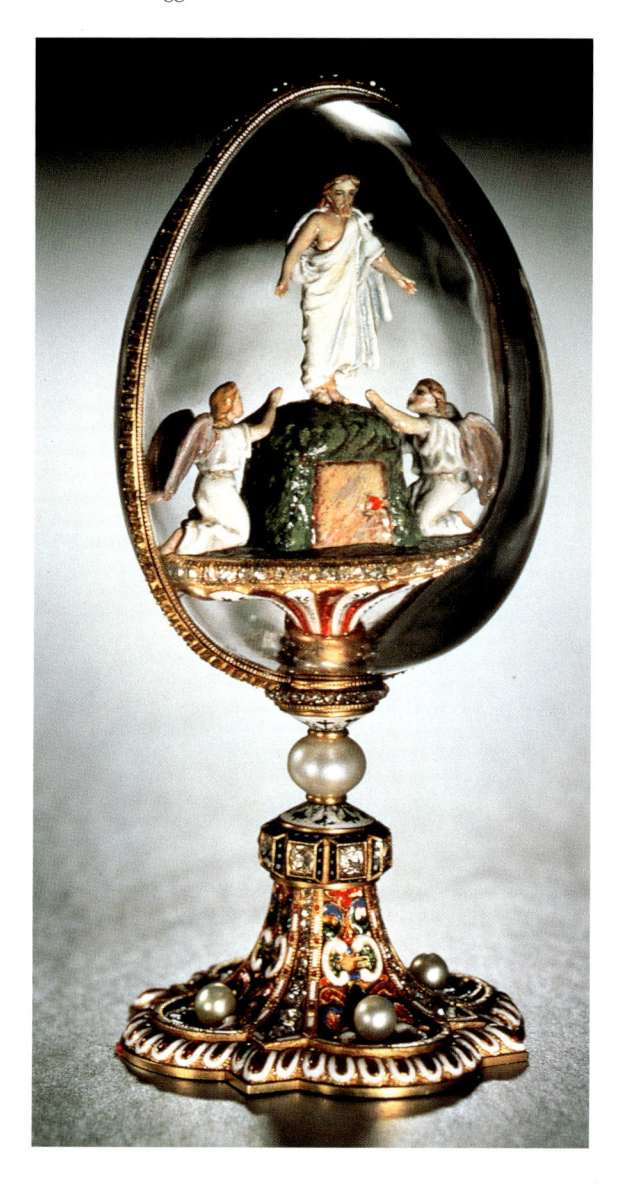

11 March, 1934

Dear Eugène,

I will attend the sale at Christie's and find out what you ask. As a matter of fact it is only a collection of small things, with nothing much of value, except perhaps the egg in white enamel with the yolk,[66] *which has historic interest more than anything else.*

And again:

13 March, 1934

Dear Eugène,

... As I told you there are none of the Imperial Easter eggs on sale except the original one like a hen's egg...[67]

Notes and drawings were sketched in the margins of the catalogue. Sale prices along with some of the names of the purchasers were also recorded. These drawings include a sketch of 'Lot 86, A Reliquary' which corresponds to the Resurrection egg now in the FORBES Magazine collection. Next to the drawing there was the notation, 'crystal egg with 3 figures in enamel, about size of duck egg and in all 6 inches high w/stand', 'Mr R.S. Taylor, £110.'

In addition to the Resurrection egg, Mr Taylor also purchased 'Lot 55, A Gold Easter Egg', which had been auctioned minutes earlier. He paid just £85 for this treasure, now known as the Hen egg (FORBES magazine collection), the first Imperial Easter egg made by Carl Fabergé for Tsar Alexander III. The Resurrection egg has the hallmark of Mikhail Perkhin, who died in August 1903, and we have shown that all of the Imperial Easter eggs for the years up to and including 1903 have been identified by invoices.

BLUE STRIPED ENAMEL EASTER EGG
Private Collection

In 1951 the Blue Striped Enamel Easter egg was shown for the first time in a loan exhibition at the Hammer Galleries in New York. Armand Hammer did not, at that time, describe the egg as having Imperial provenance, but gave the following description:

170. Easter Egg: trois-couleur gold, blue enamel: Imperial crown finial, sapphires, diamonds: contains aquamarine bunny, ruby eyes. 4¼ x 2 (Perchin).

When the egg next appeared, Imperial attributes were assigned to it and it was said to have been made between 1885 and 1891.[68] Almost 30 years later, in the 1986-87 Munich exhibition catalogue, the egg was accompanied by the following description:

Enamelled gold Imperial Easter egg. Provenance: According to tradition presented by Tsar Alexander III to his wife between 1885 and 1890. Alternatively, presented to the Tsarevich between 1890 and 1894.[69]

After a painstaking study of all the archival material, the authors did not find any documented evidence of this egg.

THE SPRING FLOWERS EGG
FORBES Magazine Collection

In the mid-1960s, the Spring Flowers egg appeared in the estate of shipping magnate, Lansdell K. Christie, and in 1964 was acquired by the FORBES Magazine Collection.

In 1993, the Spring Flowers egg was discussed by Marina Lopato who wrote:

In this author's opinion, the privately owned Ribbed Blue Enamel egg and the Forbes Spring Flowers egg dated 1890 (or before 1899) should not be included amongst the Imperial eggs since they bear inventory numbers. None of the other Imperial easter eggs was given an inventory number by the firm for obvious reasons.[70]

Spring Flowers egg

It does appear that the Imperial Easter eggs were never given inventory numbers by the House of Fabergé as each egg was commissioned for the Tsar and there was no need to attach numbers to the eggs, and yet the Spring Flowers egg is scratched with the inventory number 44374.[71]

After a careful and thorough search of the invoices presented by Carl Fabergé to the Tsars for the Imperial Easter eggs, as well as other relevant material in the archives, we were unable to identify the Spring Flowers egg in any of the documents.

NICHOLAS II EQUESTRIAN EGG
Private Collection

The Nicholas II Equestrian egg was sold on 27 April 1977 at Christie's, Geneva. Several years later the egg reappeared at Christie's New York, but its authenticity was questioned by specialists who had previously recognized it as an Imperial Easter egg made by Carl Fabergé. The egg was then withdrawn from the sale.

THE 1917 TWILIGHT EGG
Private Collection

This egg first appeared on 10 November 1976 at an auction at Christie's, Geneva. According to Christie's research, the provenance was Imperial, the egg was intended to be given by Tsar Nicholas II to either the Empress Alexandra Fedorovna or the dowager Empress in 1917. In 1977 the egg was included as Imperial in a major Fabergé exhibition at the Victoria and Albert Museum in London.

Thorough research into all the relevant documentation, which has only recently been possible, and the identification of the two 1917 eggs, as discussed in Chapter 7, eliminates the Twilight egg from the list of Imperial Easter eggs.

The following three eggs have been included in this chapter as they are among the most exquisite of all the non-Imperial Fabergé eggs commissioned by the nobility and wealthy industrialists.

Twilight egg

DUCHESS OF MARLBOROUGH EGG

This Easter egg was made by the House of Fabergé for the Duchess of Marlborough (née Consuelo Vanderbilt) when the Duke and Duchess visited Russia in 1902. It is now in the FORBES Magazine Collection.

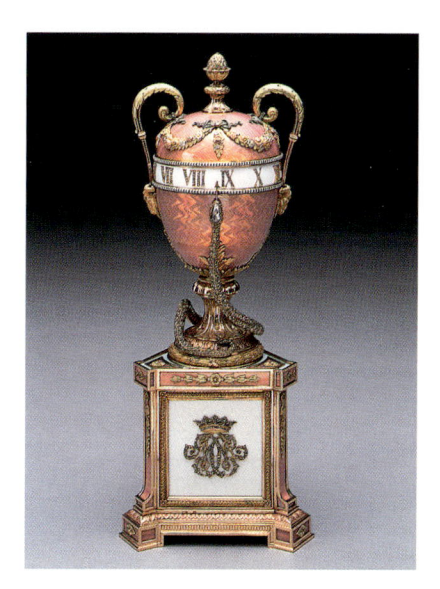

NOBEL ICE EGG

This Easter egg, which had not been seen for 55 years, was sold at Sotheby's, Geneva, on 19 November 1996, for SFr 421,500. The egg was originally commissioned by Dr Emmanuel Nobel, a wealthy oil baron and one of Fabergé's most important clients. The delicate 'frosted snowflake' motif of this Easter egg was conceived by the talented designer, Alma Theresia Pihl, who was also responsible for the designs of the enchanting Winter (43) and Mosaic (46) Easter eggs.

Nobel Ice egg

Duchess of Marlborough egg

YUSUPOV EGG

The immense wealth of the old aristocratic Yusupov family was said to be greater than that of the Romanovs. In 1907, Prince Felix Yusupov commissioned this delightful pink enamel clock Easter egg from the House of Fabergé, to present to his wife, Princess Zenaïda, on the occasion of their 25th wedding anniversary. It is now in the Edouard and Maurice Sandoz Foundation, Switzerland.

Yusupov egg

11

The Kremlin Collection

by Tatiana Muntian

During the night of 16 to 17 September 1917, a 40-wagon train arrived in Moscow, carrying 'especially valuable items of property of the former palace administration', evacuated from Petrograd by the Provisional Government because of the prevailing military situation. Eighty-four crates containing treasures from the Anichkov Palace, including most of the Imperial Easter eggs and other items manufactured by the House of Fabergé for the Imperial family, were delivered for storage to the Armoury, where they were received by the Armoury curators.[72] The act of acceptance is dated 19/20 September 1917, thus marking a new stage in the life of Fabergé works of art belonging to the last of the Romanovs – a life full of drama, with many events still left unexplained.

Until 1922, the Imperial Easter eggs remained packed in crates and trunks and stored on the Armoury premises. It is difficult to determine the exact number of Easter eggs thus stored, because of the extreme brevity of their descriptions in the inventories of the Emperor's property. Some of the Easter gifts are easily recognizable, such as 'Nephrite egg with gold ornaments, two diamonds and rose-cut diamonds, containing a model of the Alexander Palace' (34), 'Silver egg containing a gold model of a railway train' (22), 'Crystal egg with one emerald and rose-cut diamonds, containing a folding frame' (14), or 'Gold egg with diamonds and rose-cut diamonds, containing a gold carriage with a pear-shaped diamond' (16). However, quite a few of the descriptions are so vague that they do not allow positive identification – for instance, 'Gold egg with diamonds and roses', 'One gold egg with enamel containing a flask', or 'Gold toilet-case egg with diamonds, rubies, sapphires and emeralds' (5). Some of the eggs listed in the inventory ('Gold pendant egg', 'Stone egg in gold setting', or 'Silver egg with red enamel') are probably not part of the corpus of Imperial Easter eggs. However, it can be assumed that over 40 such eggs were among the collection.

The staff of the Armoury Museum kept a careful watch on these and all the other treasures consigned to it, 'keeping all the containers intact and undamaged during the height of the revolution'.[73] They remained undisturbed for more than four years, until January 1922, when the Commission of the Plenipotentiary for the Listing and Conservation of Valuables began to operate at the Armoury. Representatives of the State Depository of Valuables, Workers' and Peasants' Inspection Units and the Museum and Armoury Department began to sort out the colossal riches of the various Court institutions. Museum employees recorded that they had worked 'at an unusually fast rate, sorting several hundred articles a day, irrevocably determining their future and significance in a few moments and for a long time bearing the oppressive burden of the extremely exacting requirements of the Gokhran [State depository of valuables]'.[74] Carl Fabergé's son Agathon, a gemologist and a specialist in precious stones and diamonds, was released from prison to help evaluate the hoarded treasures, and was re-imprisoned after he had performed this task.

Between 17 February and 24 March 1922, the Imperial Easter eggs and other valuables temporarily stored in the Museum were transferred by the Glavmuseum, represented by the Director of the Armoury, Mikhail Sergeievich Sergeiev, to the Plenipotentiary of the Council of People's Commissars and the expert of the State Depository of Valuables, Ivan Gavrilovich Chinariov. They were entrusted with selling treasures abroad to bolster the economy of the fledgling Soviet Republic.

Sixteen eggs were received from the Foreign Currency Fund of the People's Commissariat for Finance under an Act dated 17 June 1927, as follows:

(1) the Memory of Azov egg (7) of 1891
(2) the Caucasus egg (9) of 1893
(3) the Revolving Miniatures egg (14) of 1896
(4) the Pelican egg (17) of 1898
(5) the Pansy egg (19) of 1899
(6) the Trans-Siberian Railway egg (22) of 1900
(7) the Peter the Great egg (28) of 1903
(8) the Moscow Kremlin egg (30) of 1906
(9) the Alexander Palace egg (34) of 1908
(10) the Standard egg (36) of 1909
(11) the Alexander III Equestrian egg (37) of 1910
(12) the Tsarevich egg (42) of 1912
(13) the Romanov Tercentenary egg (44) of 1913
(14) the Mosaic egg (46) of 1914
(15) the Red Cross egg (48) of 1915
(16) the Steel Military egg (50) of 1916

However, they were not sold immediately, and later in the year were returned to the Armoury, where they were joined by eight others received from the Central Depository of the Moscow Jewellers' Community as follows:

(17) the Danish Palaces egg (6) of 1890
(18) the Renaissance egg (10) of 1894 (noted as being 'empty')
(19) the Bouquet of Lilies Clock egg (20) of 1899
(20) the Basket of Wild Flowers egg (24) of 1901
(21) the Clover egg (26) of 1902
(22) the Napoleonic egg (41) of 1912
(23) the Grisaille egg (45) of 1914
(24) the Red Cross egg (47) of 1915

In 1930 the expert valuation commission of Antikvariat, an office engaged in the purchase and sale of antiques, selected 12 Easter eggs from the Armoury, six of them by M. Perkhin and five by G. Wigström (nos. 2-5, 7, 12, 15, 17, 18, 22-24 of the lists above). Museum officials tried to delay the transfer of those and other exhibits to Antikvariat, but a document marked 'urgent and secret' arrived from Narkompros (the government agency in charge of cultural policy), containing the stern warning that responsibility for retaining museum treasures intended for sale on foreign markets, and thus for hampering the financial plan of the USSR, was to be fully assumed by the Director of the Museum. The document further stated that it was inadmissible to delay 'the implementation of decisions that had already been made'.[75] On the basis of this document and a special instruction from the Council of People's Commissars, the Director of the Armoury, S.I. Monakhtin, and the Scientific Deputy Director, V.K. Klein, handed over the Easter eggs 'suitable for export' on 21 June 1930.

Three years later, in 1933, Antikvariat took away five more eggs from the Armoury collection. The Museum officials did all they could to prevent the sale of these masterpieces on foreign markets: Director Monakhtin wrote to the Science Department of the People's Commissariat for Education of the USSR that the removal of those articles from the Museum would have the effect of destroying it as a historical and artistic complex and that 'this will make it impossible to set up a Marxist-Leninist exhibition', but the Commandant of the Kremlin, comrade Peterson, ordered all the items selected by Antikvariat to be handed over. However, the Museum did manage with great difficulty to keep the Clover egg (26) and the Memory of Azov egg (7).

The eggs that were sold were dispersed throughout the world; some changed owners several times, and some disappeared without trace. Only ten Imperial Easter eggs were left in Russia and the rest of this chapter is devoted to a discussion of them.

The earliest egg in the Kremlin collection, made in 1891 (no. 7), cost the Emperor Alexander III 4500 roubles. It was presented to the Empress Maria Fedorovna and dedicated to a journey to the Far East undertaken by the Imperial couple's two sons, Nicholas and George. The maritime part of the journey took place aboard a cruiser of the Imperial fleet, *Memory of Azov*, named in honour of an earlier Russian warship *Azov*, the first vessel in Russian history to be entitled to fly the flag of the Cross of St George. Yet the miniature gold and platinum model of the ship, the surprise, bears the inscription *Azov*. Why is this? The suggestion once made, that the small surface of the ship's side could not accommodate its full name, does not seem convincing: there were no such limitations for the masters of the House of Fabergé, who manufactured the finest, most fragile miniature models – the gold Siberian train, for instance, features many minute inscriptions on its carriages. It can only be surmised that the inscription *Azov* was intended to evoke the glorious history of the old ship and its series of resounding victories.

The miniature gold ship, on an aquamarine plate with gold mounting, is fitted with a loop by which it can be drawn from the heliotrope egg-container in a gold-chased setting with diamonds. Its design carries on the maritime theme: the dark green heliotrope gives the impression of the sea depths, and the shells with their stylized, convoluted whorls and colours – symbols of the sea – are reminders of the Tsarevich's journey round the world from 1890 to 1891. It was unsuccessful for George and particularly so for Nicholas, who was struck on the head with a sword in the Japanese city of Otsu. For those who are aware of this unfortunate event, the blood-red drops on the heliotrope suddenly acquire a special, ominous meaning.

There is another interesting aspect of the design of this article: in some publications, alongside the name of the great Perkhin, in whose workshop the egg was made and whose personal stamp it bears, we find the name of Yurii Nikolaï, without any reference to archival or documentary sources. The jewellers who worked for Fabergé are well known – not only the workmasters, but also the apprentices, chasers, enamellers, engravers, stoneworkers and sculptor-modellers – but nowhere do we find the name of Nikolaï, which inevitably leads to the question why his name has been coupled with that of a leading master of the firm. An Armoury inventory card of 1959 indicates that the starting-point for attributing the surprise to Nikolaï was an oral account by an anonymous visitor to the Armoury. This visitor announced after touring the Museum that he was the nephew of Yurii Adamovich Nikolaï, who had been born in Finland into a woodcutter's family, and worked for Fabergé. According to the visitor, Nikolaï had executed the model of the yacht *Standard* which had been the surprise in one of the eggs in 1909. Thereafter, other surprises, such as the model of the cruiser *Memory of Azov* and even the clockwork Siberian Train, were also attributed to Yurii Nikolaï, the uncle of the unknown tourist. He mentioned 1875 as the year of his uncle's birth, so he would only have been 16 in 1891, when the Memory of Azov egg was made. The tourist's tale, recorded on a card yellowed with age, was subsequently embroidered with various details. It was concluded that Yurii Nikolaï came from a simple, working-class family, had not enough money to set up his own workshop and therefore did not use a personal stamp.

The House of Fabergé certainly had connections with a Nikolaï family. When Carl Fabergé's son, Eugène Gottlieb, was baptized in 1874, the godparents were the master cabinet-maker Gottlieb Jakobs, Carl Fabergé's father-in-law, and Mrs Wilhelmina Nikolaï, née Fabergé. Two years later, in 1876, when Agathon Fedor Fabergé was baptized, his godfather was the merchant Fedor Nikolaï.[76] However, Yurii Nikolaï remains a shadowy and possibly fictitious character.

The Memory of Azov egg is thematically linked with the Trans-Siberian Railway egg (22). In Vladivostok, after a long journey aboard the cruiser, the Tsarevich Nikolai Alexandrovich 'was pleased to lay the foundations for work on the construction of the Siberian railway', and by the year 1900 the work was practically completed. This is the event commemorated by the egg. In the invoice submitted by Carl Fabergé to the Cabinet of the Imperial Court and paid in January 1901, it is stated that the egg was prepared for April 1900 and was valued at 7000 roubles. This massive, heavy article is the only Imperial Easter egg that Fabergé made in the neo-Russian style. It is decorated with opaque polychrome enamel in a stylized scroll pattern, combined with the fashionable transparent enamel on a *guilloché* background. The egg is crowned with a moulded, three-sided double-headed eagle and is supported by silver-gilt marching gryphons holding shields and swords in their claws (a feature of the Romanov coat-of-arms), fastened on to a massive onyx base with a silver mounting. The egg is girdled by a silver band engraved with a map of the Russian Empire and the railway between St Petersburg and Vladivostok, the uncompleted sections being marked with a dotted line.

The egg contains a gold and platinum clockwork model of the Siberian train, together with a tiny gold key for winding the fine, complicated mechanism that sets the model in motion. The miniature express train consists of a locomotive with diamond headlights, a mail van and three passenger carriages with rock-crystal windows bearing inscriptions – 'Ladies', 'Smokers' and 'Non-smokers' – and indications of the class of compartment and the number of seats. The last section of the train is the church-carriage, modelled on the carriage built in 1896 and blessed in the presence of the Emperor and Empress in the name of St Olga, the patron saint of Nicholas II's eldest daughter.

The Memory of Azov and Trans-Siberian Railway eggs are typical examples of presents created by the firm to commemorate important events in the life of the Empire and of the Imperial family, but other eggs were more intimate in conception and can be seen as tokens of Nicholas II's love for his wife. The diamond-studded gold hour-hand of the Bouquet of Lilies Clock egg of 1899 (20) looks like an arrow shot from Cupid's bow, and the general concept of this Easter present, modelled on an antique French clock of the late 18th century, makes use of the symbolic language of flowers. Thus, the egg is wreathed in magnificent agate lilies, with matt, creamy petals and sparkling gold and diamond pistils and stamens, which seem to be growing out of a garland of multi-coloured gold roses. The combination of roses, symbols of love, and lilies signifying purity and innocence, together with torches whose flames turn into foliate patterns, suggests the beneficent flame of family love and the eternal flowering of inextinguishable passion. In the invoice submitted to the Cabinet, this work is referred to as 'Easter egg, clock', followed by its description: 'L. [i.e. Louis] XVI, yellow enamel with roses [the reference here is to the rose-faceted diamonds with which the egg is liberally sprinkled], bouquet of white chalcedony lilies and small pendant egg with roses'.[77] This last detail is now missing: the little pendant was probably attached to the gold clock key.

Although Fabergé often derived inspiration from the art of the past, he also used up-to-date styles. The most poetic and intimate eggs in the collection were carried out in the art nouveau style. An example is the Clover egg (no. 26) of 1902, one of the last to be executed under the direction of M. Perkhin. The fine open-work gold background of the egg, in the form a three-leaf clover, is filled in with transparent emerald-green enamel and the leaves are partly sprinkled with tiny diamonds. The egg contains gold wire claws that held the now missing surprise. Archival sources show that these contents were 'a large four-leaf clover with 23 diamonds and rose-cut diamonds and 4 miniatures'.[78] At the time the egg was made, the Imperial couple had four children and the four leaves may well have held portraits of them. The theme of the gift thus becomes clear: according to popular belief, to find a four-leaf clover is very rare and lucky, and in this case the surprise symbolized the union of two lovers and the fulfilment of the Emperor's boyhood dream to marry Alexandra.

The floral or plant-like forms typical of art nouveau made it particularly suitable for an intimate family theme. Examples of this are the Lilies of the Valley egg (no. 18), decorated with miniature portraits of Nicholas II and his two daughters, presented to his wife, and the Pansy egg (19), made for the Dowager Empress, containing a heart bearing portraits of members of the Imperial family.

Archival documents not only shed light on missing surprises and other details, but also help to specify the names of the eggs and to establish their dates, which had been regarded as incontrovertible. The Moscow Kremlin egg (30) used to be referred to as the 'Music-box Model of the Kremlin', although it is neither the one nor the other. Fabergé described it himself: 'The Moscow Kremlin egg of different coloured gold and enamel, white egg representing the Cathedral of the Dormition (the Uspenski Cathedral), with music, on a white onyx pediment' and valued it at 11800 roubles.[79] According to the document, the egg was delivered to the Emperor in 1906, although the year 1904 is twice stamped on the article itself. This discrepancy is probably explained by the historical events of the period (see Chapter 6). The egg celebrates the visit paid by the Emperor and Empress to Moscow, for Easter 1903, and was probably intended to be presented at the Easter of the following year. However, the beginning of 1904 saw the outbreak of the Russo-Japanese War, which proved disatrous for Russia. Franz Birbaum noted in his memoirs that in times of armed conflict the firm either did not make any Easter eggs or made cheaper and simpler ones. The reasons for this were the call-up of master craftsmen for military service (as during the First World War, when the firm was almost forced to close) and also urgent orders for articles such as military decorations and badges for war invalids and members of their families.

It is possible that the Emperor himself did not confirm his annual Easter order in those hard times, and there may also have been some trivial, non-political reason for the delay – for instance, the musical mechanism might not have been ready, although the egg itself had been completed.

Another factor came into play in mid-1904, with the long-awaited birth of the heir to the throne, the Tsarevich Alexei Nikolaievich, which of course had to be reflected in the Easter presents for 1905. Birbaum notes in his memoirs that the egg of that year was in the form of a cradle, with garlands of flowers and an oval portrait of the Tsarevich inside. That may be why the Moscow Kremlin egg was again put off for a year. Another possible reason for the postponement was that, early in 1905, Nicholas II's 'favourite uncle' and brother-in-law, the 'friend of Emperors', Grand Duke Sergei Alexandrovich, was assassinated in the Kremlin by a socialist-revolutionary terrorist. This was the first and only instance of the murder of a member of the ruling dynasty in the ancient citadel of the Moscow Tsars, and the Moscow Kremlin egg would of course have been a reminder of that fact. The egg was delivered a year after the murder, when the impact of the event had become less acute.

The pediment of the egg contains a musical mechanism, wound by a gold key and playing two Cherubim chants – triumphal Easter hymns. In 1903, when the Tsar and Empress had spent Holy Week and Easter Week in Moscow, Nicholas II had very much admired the Cherubim chant sung during the liturgy at the Uspenski Cathedral in the Kremlin. Apparently the Emperor had turned to the master of the Synodal Choir, Orlov, praised the singing and asked, 'Whose Cherubim chant did the choir sing during the liturgy?' 'Kastelskii's', replied Orlov. Carl Fabergé had either heard this story or had received special instructions on the subject from the Court.

The Moscow Kremlin egg is a very free variation on the theme of the Kremlin architecture. The decoration of the egg, made of translucent white enamel and crowned with a polished gold cupola, was inspired by the architecture of the Cathedral of the Dormition, and its festive, lighted interior may be seen through one of the windows. The red-gold pedestal consists of two reproductions each of the Spasskaia and Vodovsvodnaia towers, connected by quaint, fantastic lattices. The three storeys are connected by 35-step ladders, which are particularly, and perhaps deliberately, accentuated. It is possible that this virtuoso work embodies through the language of symbols (church, ladder) the idea of aspiration towards God, of spiritual renewal, the idea of a Temple of the Universe in which the worlds of God and man unite.

The temple is a most ancient symbol of the Old Testament and Christian traditions, and its appearance in a magnificent Easter present is appropriate. It is also possible that in this case the temple signifies the central symbol of freemasonry. This theory is speculative, but the egg could be interpreted as an illustration of the freemasons' basic ideas about the constitution of a spiritual temple within oneself under the guidance of a Master, the ascent up the ladder of degrees of enlightenment, the stages of advancement towards the truth. In the early 20th century freemasonry had spread among the widest variety of social groups. Contemporaries have noted that there were no professions, institutions or societies in which there were no freemasons. Even the title pages of the textbooks used by students of the Baron von Steiglitz Central School of Technical Drawing in St Petersburg (from which many of the artist-designers working for Fabergé had graduated) were stamped with the central masonic sign – a circle containing a square forming a six-pointed star. Freemasonry had penetrated into the highest social circles, including the Imperial family.

As the years went by, Fabergé made the symbolism of the Easter presents more and more complicated. One of the most interesting works in this respect is the Alexander Palace egg of 1908 (34), with a miniature copy of the Alexander Palace at Tsarskoie Selo, liberally decorated with 'incrusted gold, 54 rubies, 1,805 roses in a pattern, 2 diamonds and 5 miniatures of the Imperial children'. This is one of the most expensive eggs in the Kremlin collection – the Emperor paid Fabergé 12,300 roubles for it.

The egg is made of nephrite, decorated with gold-encrusted thyrsi, entwined with two branches symbolizing the male and female principles and wreathed in pine cones with diamond nuts – symbols of labour and endeavour, the results of which are proliferation and plenty. Five watercolour portraits of the children of Nicholas II and

Alexandra Fedorovna are placed between the thyrsi. As in the heart of the Pansy egg given by the Emperor to his wife in the year of their tenth wedding anniversary, the beloved children's faces are framed in tiny diamonds.

At the top and bottom ends of the egg, large, flat, triangular diamonds are placed in combination with three smaller ones to form six-pointed stars, in this case probably signifying the Star of Bethlehem which heralded the birth of the infant Christ. From ancient times, the six-pointed star has symbolized happiness, prosperity and sometimes royal children. Incidentally, the little heart which is the surprise in the Pansy egg, depicting the children and grandchildren of the Empress Maria Fedorovna, is surmounted by a six-pointed star. The terrible fate that befell the children of the last Russian Tsar ten years after the creation of this egg reminds us of another symbolic meaning of the six-pointed star, which is sometimes held to signify departed royal children 'numbered among the saints'.[80]

But let us go back to the time of the creation of the Easter gift on the theme of the Imperial family, with portraits of the little heir to the throne and the lovely young Grand Duchesses. It is probably not by chance that nephrite of a particularly bright shade of green was chosen for this egg: Carl Fabergé himself was very fond of green, which he called the colour of hope, and moreover green has always symbolized youth, flowering, the triumph of life, joy, spring and growth. The surprise in the egg is a model of a palace, surrounded by lawns, shrubberies and flower-beds of different coloured gold. The Imperial family seldom left the confines of this palace, and the last of the Romanovs were thus aptly called 'the prisoners of Tsarskoie Selo'. It may also not be by chance that the miniature Imperial palace, placed on its little gold table, seems to be fenced off from the rest of the world by the ideal, closed shape of a circle.

The following year, 1909, an Easter egg was made at H. Wigström's workshop featuring a model of the Imperial yacht *Standard* (36) as the surprise. The Imperial family spent quite a lot of time aboard this vessel, built in Copenhagen in 1896, which Nicholas II used to call 'my dear yacht'. The Imperial naval standard, with a black double-headed eagle on a gold background, flies from the fine mast of the miniature gold ship plying through crystal waves. The appearance and fittings of the yacht are reproduced faithfully to the last detail, down to a revolving steering wheel and platinum lifeboats.

For the egg itself, Carl Fabergé chose the antique Renaissance style, the noble and exquisite forms of which are evoked by the architectonic, richly carved base and the prevalence of horizontal lines. The combination of rock crystal, lapis lazuli and a very fine enamelled gold setting forms a magnificent whole. The lapis lazuli pediment, of an exceptionally beautiful dark blue colour, is in the form of two intertwined dolphins which, together with the double-headed eagles at each end of the egg, symbolize Imperial power. The egg with the 'floating yacht' is mounted on their tails, and the intention may have been to convey the idea of the protective power of dolphins as saviours of the drowning and rulers of the kingdom of the seas. In fact the magnificent Imperial yacht later met with a sad fate: it foundered on a coastal reef, and the royal lifeboat carrying the heir to the throne was fired on and nearly sunk by the coastguards. By a miracle, Tsarevich Alexei escaped.

The revolving globe which was the surprise in the egg for 1913 (44), celebrating the tercentenary of the Romanov dynasty, symbolizes power over the whole world. The globe is made of burnished steel, the deep blue of which represents the seas, while the continents are fashioned in different colours of gold. In fact, these are two northern hemispheres attached to one another, on which the territory of the Russian Empire is represented twice – first with the boundaries of 1613 and secondly with those of the reign of the last Romanov. The ornamentation of the egg makes liberal use of the symbols of power. Its surface, covered with opalescent enamel along the *guilloché* background, is decorated with applied chased heraldic eagles, Imperial wreaths and crowns. The egg is mounted on a hollow silver-gilt three-sided figure of a heraldic eagle, fastened to a circular purpurine base imitating the Imperial coat of arms. The secret of making purpurine – heavy, poured, gold-flecked glass invented by old Venetian masters – was rediscovered after a long period of trial and error by Petukhov, a worker at the technological laboratory of the Imperial Glassworks, who also worked for the House of Fabergé. The egg is covered by a veritable gallery of 18 miniature portraits of ruling members of the Romanov dynasty painted by the artist V. Zuiev. The portraits are arranged in three rows, in chronological order from which Fabergé departed in only one case – the Emperor Peter I is presented, not in 'his own' row, but to the right of Nicholas II, almost in the centre. This may have been the special wish of the client, who wanted to show that his reign, like that of Peter I, marked a series of great reforms and victories, or perhaps the decision was made by Carl Fabergé himself.

The last Easter present (50) was executed during the First World War and was dedicated to the decoration of the Emperor Nicholas II with the Order of St George, IVth Class. The cross and the ribbon of the Order are affixed at the top of the surprise, which is an easel in the form of the monogram of the Empress Alexandra Fedorovna, bearing a miniature on ivory representing Nicholas II and Tsarevich Alexei at the battle front. This egg, mounted on a stand consisting of four artillery shells, is distinguished from other Easter gifts by its severe and restrained purity of form. Emphasis is laid on the smooth, perfectly polished steel surface. The applied gold decorations are formal and simple. The egg bears the Empress' monogram, the Moscow coat of arms and a heraldic double-headed eagle with arrows and a laurel wreath in its claws – symbols of war and ultimate victory. In spite of the minimal representational elements used, this egg is one of the works which most comprehensively conveys the spirit and mood of its time. The atmosphere of those difficult years is wonderfully reflected in the miniature portraits executed by the artist V. Zuiev in subdued shades of grey. A gloomy day, a lowering sky, a bare, leafless tree in the foreground – all this creates a joyless backdrop for the central characters, the Tsar and the heir to the throne, in their grey greatcoats, studying a map with some military commanders. The artists and jewellers had evidently been assigned the task of showing the day-to-day aspects of war and representing the Tsar at the centre of military operations.

Current Location of Imperial Easter Eggs

KREMLIN ARMOURY MUSEUM, MOSCOW

7. Memory of Azov egg
20. Bouquet of Lilies Clock egg
22. Trans-Siberian Railway egg
26. Clover egg
30. Moscow Kremlin egg
34. Alexander Palace egg
36. Standard egg
37. Alexander III Equestrian egg
44. Romanov Tercentenary egg
50. Steel Military egg

FORBES MAGAZINE COLLECTION, NEW YORK

1. Hen egg
10. Renaissance egg
12. Rosebud egg
16. Coronation egg
18. Lilies of the Valley egg
21. Cockerel egg
39. Bay Tree egg
40. Fifteenth Anniversary egg
49. Order of St George egg

VIRGINIA MUSEUM OF ARTS, RICHMOND
(BEQUEST OF LILLIAN THOMAS PRATT)

14. Revolving Miniatures egg
17. Pelican egg
28. Peter the Great egg
42. Tsarevich egg
47. Red Cross egg with Imperial Portraits

THE MATILDA GEDDINGS GRAY FOUNDATION,
NEW ORLEANS MUSEUM OF ART

6. Danish Palaces egg
9. Caucasus egg
41. Napoleonic egg

THE ROYAL COLLECTION, HER MAJESTY QUEEN
ELIZABETH II

24. Basket of Wild Flowers egg
38. Colonnade egg
46. Mosaic egg

THE EDOUARD AND MAURICE SANDOZ FOUNDATION,
SWITZERLAND

29. Swan egg
33. Peacock egg

THE MARJORIE MERRIWEATHER POST COLLECTION
AT THE HILLWOOD MUSEUM, WASHINGTON, DC

11. Twelve Monograms egg
45. Grisaille egg

THE WALTERS ART GALLERY, BALTIMORE

23. Gatchina Palace egg
32. Rose Trellis egg

THE INDIA EARLY MINSHALL COLLECTION,
CLEVELAND MUSEUM OF ART

48. Red Cross egg with Triptych

PRINCE RAINIER III OF MONACO COLLECTION

3. Blue Serpent Clock egg

PRIVATE COLLECTIONS (USA)

8. Diamond Trellis egg
19. Pansy egg
31. Cradle with Garlands egg
43. Winter egg

MISSING EASTER EGGS

2. Hen egg with sapphire pendant
4. Cherub egg with chariot
5. Nécessaire egg
13. Alexander III egg
15. Mauve Enamel egg
25. Empire Nephrite egg
27. Danish Jubilee egg
35. Alexander III Commemorative egg

Total of 50 Imperial Easter eggs:
8 missing, 42 in museums and private collections

Kremlin Armoury Museum, Moscow	10
FORBES Magazine Collection, New York	9
Pratt Collection, Virginia Museum of Arts	5
Matilda Geddings Gray Foundation, New Orleans	3
Her Majesty Queen Elizabeth II	3
Edouard and Maurice Sandoz Foundation, Switzerland	2
Marjorie Merriweather Post Collection, Washington	2
Walters Art Gallery, Baltimore	2
India Early Minshall Collection, Cleveland	1
His Serene Highness Prince Rainier III of Monaco	1
Private Collections, USA	4

*Catalogue Raisonné
of the Fabergé
Imperial
Easter
Eggs*

I

1885

The Hen Egg

Presented by
Tsar Alexander III to his
wife, the Empress Maria
Fedorovna, Easter 1885
(24 March)

*(The FORBES Magazine
Collection, New York)*

Tsar Alexander III succeeded to the throne after the assassination of his father Alexander II on 1 March 1881. He commissioned this gift to be given to Empress Maria Fedorovna to celebrate the 20th anniversary of their betrothal in 1865.

DESCRIPTION

Surprises:	Golden hen.
	Diamond replica of the Imperial Crown (missing).
	Miniature ruby Easter egg (missing).
Height:	Shell: 2½ inches (6.4 cm); Yolk: 1⁹⁄₁₆ inches (4 cm);
	Hen: 1⅜ inches (3.5 cm).
Marks:	Unmarked.

Shell: Gold, matt white enamel; Yolk: Gold; Hen: Varicoloured gold, rubies.

The Imperial Hen Egg is enamelled in opaque white, and polished to give the effect of an eggshell. The shell conceals a removable surprise of a matt yellow, gold yolk. Inside the yolk sits a plump golden hen, its feathers realistically depicted in varicoloured gold. The hen originally contained an exquisite diamond replica of the Imperial Crown with a tiny ruby pendant suspended from it. Both of these surprises have been separated from the egg, and their present whereabouts are unknown. A letter from the Emperor to his brother, Grand Duke Vladimir Alexandrovich, shows that the surprise within the Hen egg, which was originally destined to be a ring, was changed.

1 February 1885
This could be very nice indeed. I would suggest replacing the last present by a small pendant egg of some precious stone. Please speak to Fabergé about this, I would be very grateful to you... Sasha. [81]

DOCUMENTS

The following description appears in the account books of N. Petrov, Assistant Manager of His Imperial Majesty's Cabinet:

> *White enamel Easter egg, with crown, decorated*
> *with rubies, diamonds and rose-cut diamonds*
> *(including 2 ruby pendant eggs – 2700 roubles)* [82]   *4151 r.*

The account books also contain the following reference:

> *9 April (1885):*
> *To the jeweller Fabergé for a gold egg with precious*
> *stones. 4151 roub. 75 kop.*
> *11 April. Appropriation No. 337.* [83]

On 8 February 1889, N. Petrov compiled a list of the first four Imperial Easter eggs, from 1885 to 1888, which confirms that the eggs were presented to the Empress Maria Fedorovna. Alexander III purchased no jewellery items from Fabergé in 1885 and 1887 other than Easter eggs, and the amounts given in the account books correspond exactly to the figures appearing in Petrov's list, which follows:

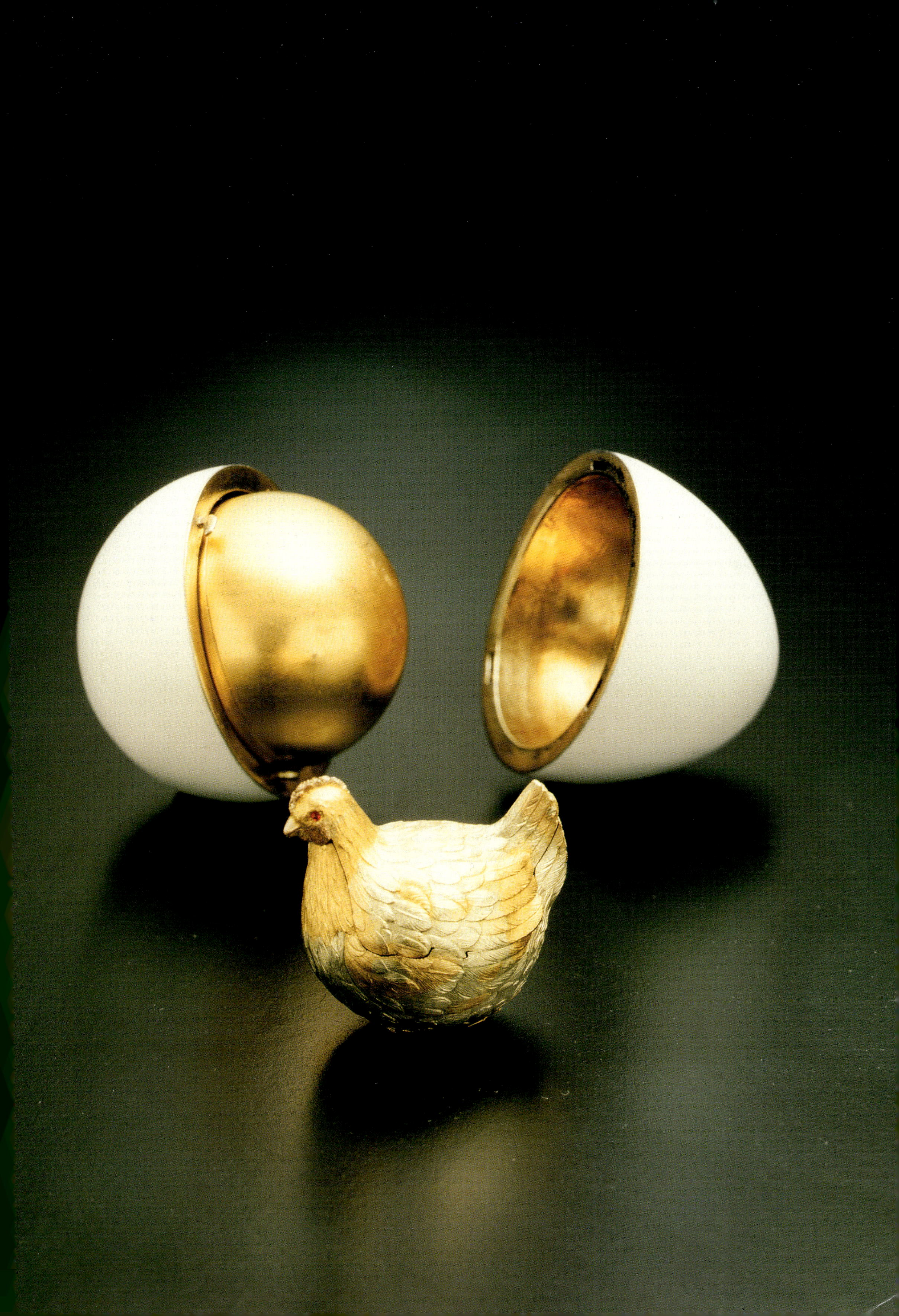

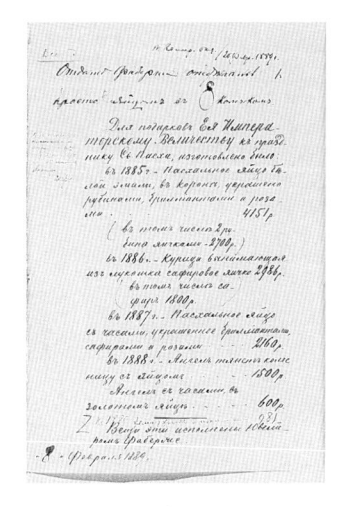

20 February 1889
Give to Fabergé to execute a simple pendant egg with a small ring.

For presentation to Her Imperial Majesty on the occasion of the Holy Feast of Easter, the following articles have been prepared:
In 1885 – white enamel Easter egg, with crown,
decorated with rubies, diamonds and rose-cut diamonds   4151 r.
(including 2 ruby pendant eggs – 2700 roubles)
In 1886 – hen picking a sapphire egg out of a basket   2986 r.
(including a sapphire – 1800 roubles)
In 1887 – Easter egg with clock, decorated with sapphires
and rose-cut diamonds   2160 r.
In 1888 – Cherub drawing a chariot containing an egg   1500 r.
Cherub with clock in gold egg   600 r.
{added in pencil} In 1889 pearl pendant egg 981 –
These articles have been executed by the jeweller Fabergé
8 February 1889

[Note pencilled in the margin: *Under the small ring there is a plate with rose-cut diamonds round it. I shall ask for an explanation tomorrow*]. [84]

History

1885–1917 Kept at the Anichkov Palace.

1917 Confiscated by Kerensky's provisional government, along with other treasures, and taken from the Anichkov Palace to the Moscow Kremlin Armoury.

Silver egg, painted white, containing a gilt egg and hen. [85]

1934 15 March, sold at Christie's, London for £85.
On 13 March, two days before the sale, H.C. Bainbridge wrote to Eugène Fabergé regarding several Fabergé objects which were coming up for auction at Christie's, London.

Dear Eugène,
I enclose two catalogues – {added in ink} *I can get more if you want them – which I got from Christie's today. As I told you there are none of the Imperial Easter eggs on sale except the original one like a hen's egg. It is a quite small collection of umbrella tops, small bell pushers, etc.* [86]

Subsequently owned by Lady Grantchester, wife of the first Baron Grantchester, and by A La Vieille Russie, Inc., New York.

1978 Acquired by FORBES, Inc.

2

Hen Egg with Sapphire Pendant

1886

Presented by
Tsar Alexander III to his
wife, the Empress Maria
Fedorovna, Easter 1886
(13 April)

(Whereabouts unknown)

It is probable that this Easter egg was designed to celebrate the 20th anniversary of the marriage of Tsar Alexander III and Maria Fedorovna.

DOCUMENTS

The following description appears in the account books of N. Petrov, Assistant Manager to the Cabinet:

> *Hen picking a sapphire egg out of a basket*   2986 r.
> *(including sapphire – 1800 roubles)* [87]

The documents on the execution of this present contain no mention of any large egg in which the hen might have been concealed, but it is known that 35 roubles were paid for two cases, which seems to indicate that the hen and the basket with the egg were placed in two separate containers.

N. Petrov confirms in his report that this Imperial Easter egg was made by the House of Fabergé for the Empress Maria Fedorovna.[88]

The documents in the Cabinet's dossier for the commission of the second Easter egg (see pages 96–97) include a series of questions submitted by Fabergé to the Court Minister. The answers were noted in pencil in the margin by N. Petrov, who was recording the quotes of the Court Minister.

For the manufacture of a hen picking an egg out of a wicker basket, it is necessary to know:
Q. What is the time limit for the execution of the article?
A. It would be preferable to have it finished by Easter, but not if this is detrimental to the quality.

Q. Should the hen itself be fashioned of silver only, or should it be sprinkled with rose-cut diamonds?
A. It must be made of gold without rose-cut diamonds.

Q. Should the pendant egg be removable or should it be firmly attached to the beak?
A. It must be loose.
15 February 1886

Petrov's file on the execution of this egg began on 15 February 1886 and ended on 24 April 1886.

HISTORY

1886–1917 Kept at the Anichkov Palace.

1917 Confiscated by Kerensky's provisional government, along with other treasures, and taken from the Anichkov Palace to the Moscow Kremlin Armoury.

1922 One of the items on the list of confiscated treasures transferred from the Anichkov Palace to the Sovnarkom:

1 silver hen, speckled with rose-cut diamonds, on gold stand. [89]

After the 1922 inventory, the egg disappeared.

Inv: 463/1860 File: 22
Category: 1   Box: 5853

No. 22

FILE
HIS IMPERIAL MAJESTY'S CABINET
1ST SECTION
OFFICE

Regarding the execution by the jeweller Fabergé of a hen made of gold and rose-cut diamonds picking a sapphire pendant egg out of a basket, and for payment of 2986 roubles 25 kopeks for the said article.

Begun, 15 February 1886   Ended, 24 April 1886

For the manufacture of a hen picking an egg out of a wicker basket, it is necessary to know:

1. What is the time limit for the execution of the article?
[annotation in pencil in the margin] *It would be preferable to have it finished by Easter, but not if this is detrimental to the quality.*

2. Should the hen itself be fashioned of silver only or should it be sprinkled with rose-cut diamonds?

3. Should the pendant egg be removable, or should it be firmly attached to the beak?

15 February 1886

[annotation in pencil in the margin] *Yes, it must be – 17 Feb. 1886 –*

N. Petrov

By order of the Minister, the 'hen picking a pendant egg out of a basket' has been ordered on the understanding that the said hen will be made of metal without rose-cut diamonds.

Meanwhile, the jeweller Fabergé who is carrying out this order has declared that the chicken must be fashioned with rose-cut diamonds, since otherwise it will be ugly and will look as though it is made of bronze

[annotation in pencil in the margin] *Reported to the Minister. Agreed to use rose-cut diamonds in the article.*
N. Petrov

N. 1665/247   21 April 1886
977   20 April 1886

The hen brought by the jeweller Fabergé is being sent today by courier. If inspection of this article does not elicit any comment from your Excellency, kindly return the invoice for payment.

N. Petrov
Saturday, 5 April 1886

3
Blue Serpent Clock Egg

1887

Presented by
Tsar Alexander III to his
wife, the Empress Maria
Fedorovna, Easter 1887
(5 April)

*(Prince Rainier III of
Monaco collection)*

Documents

The following description appears in the account books of N. Petrov, Assistant Manager to the Cabinet:

> *Easter egg with clock, decorated with diamonds,*   2160 r.
> *sapphires and rose-cut diamonds.* [90]

N. Petrov confirms in his report, 8 February 1889, that this egg was made by Fabergé for the Empress Maria Fedorovna.[91]

The account books also contain the following reference:

> *18 May (1887)*
> *To the jeweller Fabergé for an egg with clock.*
> *2160 roubles*
> *20 May. Appropriation No. 814.* [92]

History

1887–1917 Kept at the Anichkov Palace.

1917 Confiscated by Kerensky's provisional government, along with other treasures, and taken from the Anichkov Palace to the Moscow Kremlin Armoury.

1922 One of the items on the list of treasures confiscated, which were transferred from the Anichkov Palace to the Sovnarkom.

Gold egg with clock with diamond pushpiece on gold pedestal with 3 sapphires and rose-cut diamonds. [93]

Among the Easter eggs belonging to the Empress Maria Fedorovna, displayed in a vitrine at the 1902 von Dervis exhibition is an egg matching the design of the Blue Serpent Clock egg in the collection of His Serene Highness Prince Rainier III of Monaco (see pages 54-55). This is probably the Clock egg referred to in Fabergé's invoice (see page 94) and, although the design and descriptions appear to match in every detail, the sapphires referred to are missing.

The egg pictured in this enlargement of a section of the Empress Maria Fedorovna's vitrine matches exactly the shape of the Blue Serpent Clock egg opposite.

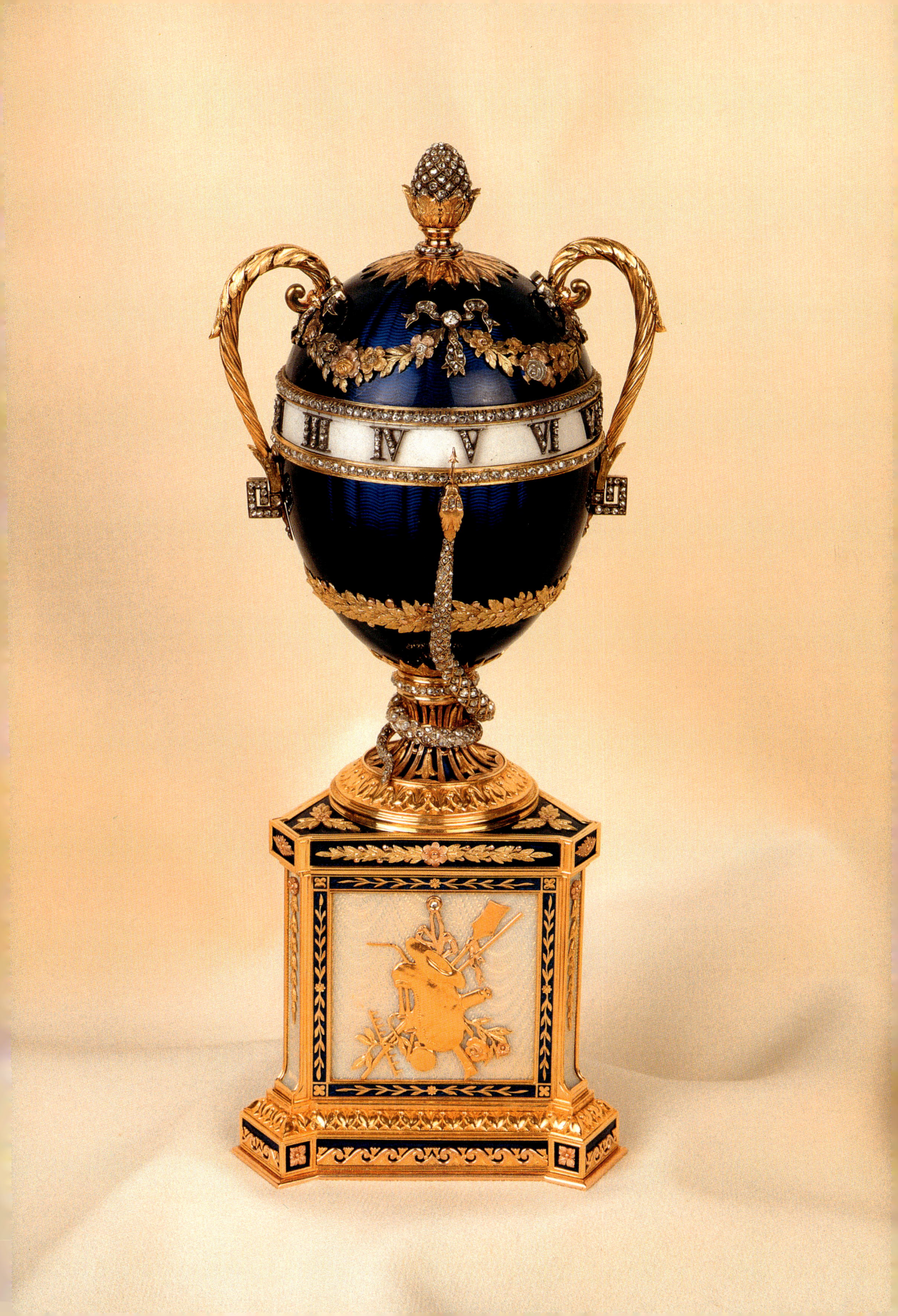

4
Cherub Egg with Chariot

1888

Presented by
Tsar Alexander III to his
wife, the Empress Maria
Fedorovna, Easter 1888
(24 April)

(Whereabouts unknown)

Documents

The following description appears in the account books of N. Petrov, Assistant Manager to the Cabinet:

Cherub pulling a chariot containing an egg	1500 s.r.
Cherub with clock in gold egg. [94]	600
	2100 s.r.

[s.r. = silver roubles]

N. Petrov confirms in his report, 8 February 1889, that this egg was made by Fabergé for the Empress Maria Fedorovna. [95]

History

1888–1917 Kept at the Gatchina Palace, but the following item on the list of Easter eggs at the Gatchina Palace in 1891-1892 shows that the Emperor and Empress travelled with some of their most beautiful gifts including this egg.

28 March 1891
Her Imperial Majesty arranged the following items in the main study:
'One cherub pulling a two-wheeled chariot containing an egg.' Taken on 16 May by the valet Ivoshkin when Their Majesties travelled to Moscow. Issued by Mikhailov. Their Majesties returned it on 18 March 1892. [96]

1917 Confiscated by Kerensky's provisional government, along with other treasures, and taken from the Anichkov Palace to the Moscow Kremlin Armoury.

Gold egg, decorated with small diamonds and a sapphire, and pediment consisting of a two-wheeled chariot with cherub. [97]

1922 One of the items on the list of treasures confiscated, and transferred from the Anichkov Palace to the Sovnarkom.

1 gold egg-shaped flask with 1 sapphire and diamonds, on stand in the form of a chariot. [98]

1934 It is quite possible that the 1888 Easter egg was among the objects sold by Armand Hammer in 1934 at Lord and Taylor, New York, as the following description implies:

No. 4524 – Miniature Amour [cherub] *holding wheelbarrow with Easter egg. Made by Fabergé.* [99]

The egg has since disappeared and its whereabouts are unknown.

5
Nécessaire Egg

1889

Presented by
Tsar Alexander III to his
wife, the Empress Maria
Fedorovna, Easter 1889
(9 April)

(Whereabouts unknown)

INVOICE

Nécessaire egg, Louis XV style 1900 r.
St Petersburg, 4 May 1889 [100]

This is the lowest amount paid to Fabergé for an Easter egg.

HISTORY

1889-1917 Kept at the Gatchina Palace, but the following item on the list of Easter eggs at the Gatchina Palace in 1891-1892 shows that the Emperor and Empress travelled with some of their most beautiful gifts including this egg.

28 March 1891
Her Imperial Majesty arranged the following items in the main study:
One item in the form of an egg, decorated with stones, containing ladies'
toilet articles, 13 pieces
Taken on 16 May by the valet Ivoshkin, when Their Majesties travelled to Moscow.
Issued by Mikhailov. [101]

1917 Confiscated by Kerensky's provisional government along with other treasures, and taken from the Anichkov Palace to the Moscow Kremlin Armoury.

Gold nécessaire egg, decorated with multicoloured precious stones. [102]

1922 One of the items on the list of treasures confiscated and transferred from the Anichkov Palace to the Sovnarkom.

1 gold nécessaire egg, with diamonds, rubies, emeralds and 1 sapphire. [103]

1949 The first Fabergé exhibition in Europe was held at Wartski, London in November, 1949. An intriguing entry was discovered in the exhibition catalogue [104] which probably refers to the missing Imperial Louis XV Nécessaire Easter egg given by Tsar Alexander III to the Empress Maria Fedorovna in 1889. Unfortunately, Wartski were unable to provide additional information that might help in tracing this egg.

6
1890
Danish Palaces Egg

Presented by
Tsar Alexander III to his
wife, the Empress Maria
Fedorovna, Easter 1890
(1 April)

*(New Orleans Museum of Art:
Matilda Geddings Gray
Foundation Collection)*

This egg was a nostalgic reminder to the Empress of her Danish heritage. She derived great pleasure from the enjoyable times spent at her royal residences and sailing on the Imperial yachts.

Description

Workmaster: Mikhail Perkhin.
Miniaturist: Konstantin Yakovlevich Kryzhitski.
Surprise: Ten-panel screen with miniatures.
Height: Egg: 4 inches x 2 inches (10.1 cm x 6.7 cm).
Marks: FABERGÉ, M.P. (in Cyrillic), assay mark of the city of St Petersburg, 56.

Egg: Green, rose and varicoloured gold, *guilloché* enamel, star sapphire, cabochon emerald, rose-cut diamonds, crimson velvet lining.

Screen: Green, rose and varicoloured gold, watercolour on mother-of-pearl.

A splendid Louis XVI style egg in translucent opalescent pink *guilloché* enamel ground over equilateral crosses. The twelve panels are divided by borders of laurel leaves, rose-cut diamonds, and cabochon emerald bosses at the intersections. A star sapphire finial is surrounded by rose-cut diamonds and chased gold laurel leaves. The egg opens to reveal its surprise, a folding ten-panel screen, snugly fitted into a crimson velvet pocket. Each panel displays an Imperial Russian yacht or royal palace known to the Empress. The panels, painted by the court miniaturist, Konstantin Yakovlevich Kryzhitski, signed and dated 1889, rest on Greek meander feet surmounted by a chased varicoloured gold wreath flanked by branches of laurel leaves. In the highly detailed views, Kryzhitski captured the shimmering luminous quality of the Danish late afternoon skies on thin panels of lustrous mother-of-pearl.

The following is a list of the miniatures concealed within the egg:

Imperial yacht *Polar Star*; Amalienborg Palace, Copenhagen; Villa Hvidøre, Copenhagen; Fredensborg Palace, summer residence; Bernsdorff Palace, Copenhagen; Kronborg Castle, Elsinore; Cottage Palace, in Alexandria Park in Peterhof; Cottage Palace, in Alexandria Park in Peterhof – south main entrance; Gatchina Palace; Imperial yacht *Tsarevna*.

The yachts conveyed the Empress from Russia to visit her family in Denmark every year. The Cottage Palace in the Alexandria Park in Peterhof was given by Alexander II to his son, the Tsarevich Alexander.

The two miniatures of the Cottage Palace, in the Alexandria Park in Peterhof, have been incorrectly referred to by all previous authors as the 'Gatchina dacha'.[105]

The seaside estate of Hvidøre near Copenhagen was to be the final home of the Empress after her escape from Russia during the Revolution. It was there that she died in 1928.

Invoice

30 March: Gold egg with pink enamel,   4260 s.r.
Louis XVI style
St Petersburg, 9 May 1890[106]   [s.r. = silver roubles]

History

1890–1917 Kept at the Gatchina Palace, but the following item from the list of Easter eggs at the Gatchina Palace in 1891–1892 shows that the Emperor and Empress took it with them when they travelled.

Egg consisting of 10 pieces (small folding screen). His Majesty took it to Petersburg on 31 December 1891. His Majesty returned it on 28 March 1892. [107]

1917 Confiscated by Kerensky's provisional government, along with other treasures, and taken from the Anichkov Palace to the Moscow Kremlin Armoury.

Gold egg, covered with pink enamel, with diamonds and emeralds, containing a small mother-of-pearl screen with landscapes in gold frames. [108]

1922 One of the items on the list of treasures confiscated, and transferred from the Anichkov Palace to the Sovnarkom.

1 gold screen-egg with rose-cut diamonds and pearl on gold stand. [109]

1930 Officially sold by Antikvariat for 1500 roubles. [110]
Later owned by Hammer Galleries, New York; Mr and Mrs Nicholas H. Ludwig.

1930s Acquired by Mrs Matilda Geddings Gray.

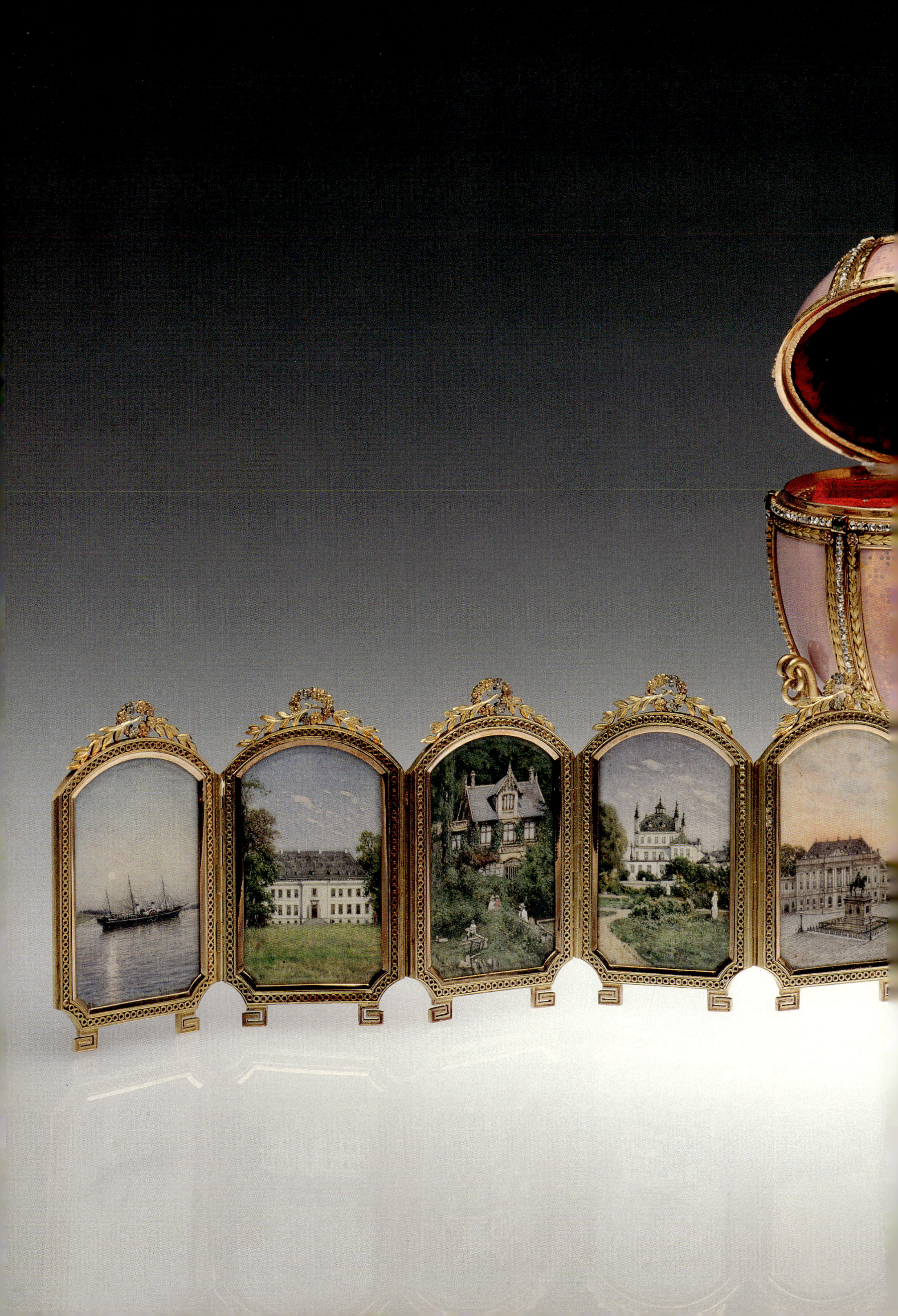

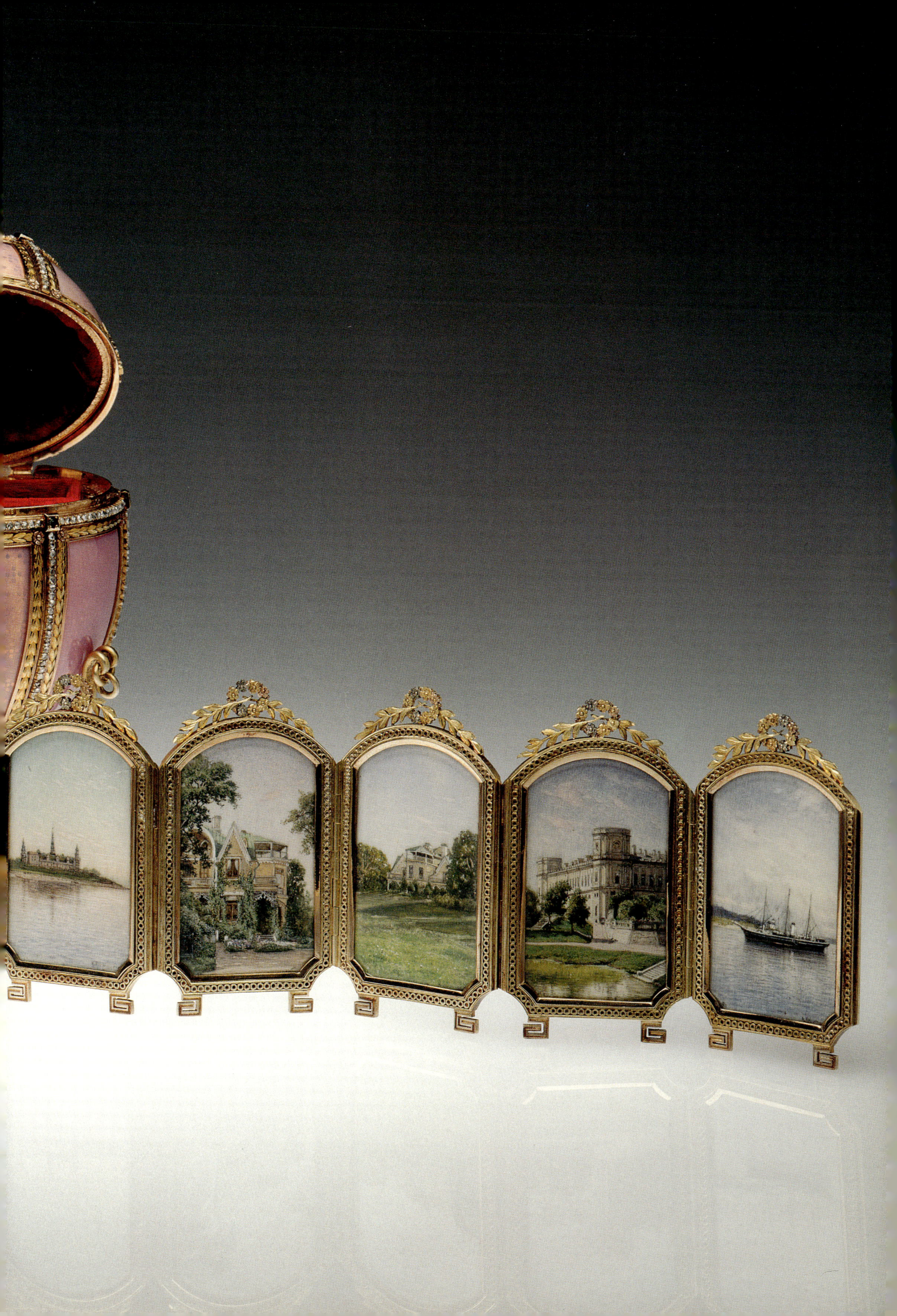

7

1891

Memory of Azov Egg

Presented by
Tsar Alexander III to his
wife, the Empress Maria
Fedorovna, Easter 1891
(21 April)

(Moscow Kremlin Armoury Museum)

The cruiser *Memory of Azov* was named in honour of the Russian battleship *Azov*, which took part in the Battle of Navarino in 1827 and was the first ship in the Russian navy to be awarded the flag of St George. In 1890-1891, Tsar Alexander III arranged for his son and heir, Nicholas, to sail to the East on the *Memory of Azov*, accompanied by his brother George. They visited India, China and Japan and their journey lasted over nine months.

This Easter egg was designed to commemorate that journey. It was presented to the Empress while her two sons were still travelling. The surprise is a miniature model of the *Memory of Azov*, made of gold and platinum and set on an aquamarine.

While in Japan, Nicholas was attacked by a disturbed Japanese policeman who tried to behead him with a sword. After he recovered from his head wound, he continued with the tour's prearranged itinerary and sailed to the naval port of Vladivostok, where he laid the foundation stone of the eastern terminus of the Trans-Siberian Railway. The 1900 Trans-Siberian Railway egg (22) commemorates the construction of that railway line.

DESCRIPTION

Workmaster: Mikhail Perkhin.
Surprise: Gold model of the cruiser *Memory of Azov*.
Height: Egg: 3⅝ inches x 2¾ inches (9.3 cm x 7.0 cm);
Cruiser: 2¾ inches x 1½ inches (7.0 cm x 4.0 cm).
Marks: Stamped FABERGÉ, M.P. (in Cyrillic), assay mark of the city of St Petersburg, 72.

Gold, platinum, silver, diamond, rose-cut diamonds, ruby, jasper, aquamarine, velvet.

This Louis XV style polished jasper egg is appliqued with yellow gold rococo scrolls, set with brilliant-cut diamonds and chased gold flowers. When the ruby and diamond clasp is pressed, the fluted gold bezel of the egg opens to reveal an exquisitely detailed tiny gold and platinum replica of the cruiser *Memory of Azov*, its portholes made of rose-cut diamonds. The egg is lined in green velvet. The name *Azov* is engraved on the stern of the ship, which appears to be slicing through the aquamarine waters.

Although the egg was made in Perkhin's workshop, the surprise, according to Eugène Fabergé, was by August Holmström:

Paris, June 5th, 1934
... by the old Holmström, who especially put all his art to make the tiny ship as natural as possible, so that the guns were movable and all the rigging exactly copied after nature... Even the chains of the anchors were movable. [111]

INVOICE

Jasper egg with diamonds, Louis XV style, and model of the 'Memory of Azov'   4500 r.
St Petersburg, 24 May 1891 [112]

106

107

HISTORY

1891–1917 Kept at the Gatchina and Anichkov Palaces. This is one of the eggs on the inventory list of Easter eggs at the Gatchina Palace in 1891-1892 that the Emperor and Empress sometimes travelled with.

27 November 1891
Deposited the following items in the main study:
One item in the form of a dark colour egg, decorated with stones and
containing a model of a ship.
Taken to Petersburg on 31 December 1891.
[signed] Valet Dinne
His Majesty returned it on 28 March 1892. [113]

1917 Confiscated by Kerensky's provisional government, along with other treasures, and taken from the Anichkov Palace to the Moscow Kremlin Armoury.

Jasper egg, in gold mounting, decorated with diamonds, containing a gold model of a vessel. [114]

1922 One of the items on the list of treasures which were transferred from the Anichkov Palace to the Sovnarkom.

Jasper egg in gold setting with diamonds, containing gold model of a ship. [115]

The Memory of Azov egg was never sold to the West and remained in Russia.

Early Fabergé photograph of the Memory of Azov egg with its surprise.

8

1892

Diamond Trellis Egg

Presented by
Tsar Alexander III to his
wife, the Empress Maria
Fedorovna, Easter 1892
(5 April)

(Private Collection)

DESCRIPTION

Workmaster: August Holmström.
Surprise: Miniature ivory elephant (now missing).
Height: 4¼ inches (10.8 cm).
Marks: Stamped FABERGÉ, A.H. (in Cyrillic), assay mark of the city of St Petersburg.

The pale green jadeite egg is contained within a softly swirling rose-cut diamond trellis which originates from a larger rose-cut diamond at the egg's apex. The miniature clockwork elephant surprise has been separated from the egg, and its whereabouts are unknown.

INVOICE

Jadeite egg with rose-cut diamonds, elephant and 3 cupids
St Petersburg, 6 May 1892 [116]   4750 r.

HISTORY

1892–1917 Kept at the Anichkov Palace. Described in the list of Easter eggs at the Gatchina Palace in 1891–1892:

One egg of pale-green stone, opening into two halves, set in gold, decorated with small rose-cut diamonds. [117]

A silver group on a round pale-green stone slab represents three little boys holding an egg of pale-green stone, opening into two parts, decorated outside by a trellis of small rose-cut diamonds. The egg is lined with white satin with a space for the figure of an elephant and a key for winding it. [118]

Ivory figure of an elephant, clockwork, with a small gold tower, partly enamelled and decorated with rose-cut diamonds, on its back; the sides of the figure bearing gold decorations in the form of two crosses, each with five white precious stones. The elephant's forehead is decorated with the same kind of stone. The tusks, trunk and harness are decorated with small rose-cut diamonds, and a black mahout is seated on its head. [119]

1917 Confiscated by Kerensky's provisional government, along with other treasures, and taken from the Anichkov Palace to the Moscow Kremlin Armoury.

Nephrite egg in gold mounting with diamond trellis; nephrite pediment with three silver cupids. [120]

1922 One of the items on the list of treasures that were transferred from the Anichkov Palace to the Sovnarkom.

Ivory model of an elephant in gold setting with rose-cut diamonds and diamonds [perhaps the surprise for the Diamond Trellis egg]. [121]

1 nephrite egg in gold setting with lattice of 2 diamonds and and rose-cut diamonds, on stand with 3 silver figures. [122]

1960 The egg was in the estate of the late T.B. Kitson and was sold on 5 December 1960 at Sotheby's, London, for £2,400 to the antique dealer, Drager.

Diamond Trellis egg displayed in the Empress Maria Fedorovna's vitrine at the 1902 von Dervis exhibition (see pages 54-55).

The catalogue illustration shows the Easter egg supported by three silver cupids on a silver and stone base, together with its original case. However, even though the catalogue states that the base with the cupids, which has since disappeared, bears English import marks for 1908, the authors believe that this was the original base made for the Diamond Trellis egg. The cherubs represented the three little sons of the Tsar and Empress: Grand Dukes Nicholas (later Tsar Nicholas II), George and Michael.

Unfortunately, permission was not given to reproduce a coloured photograph of the Diamond Trellis egg.

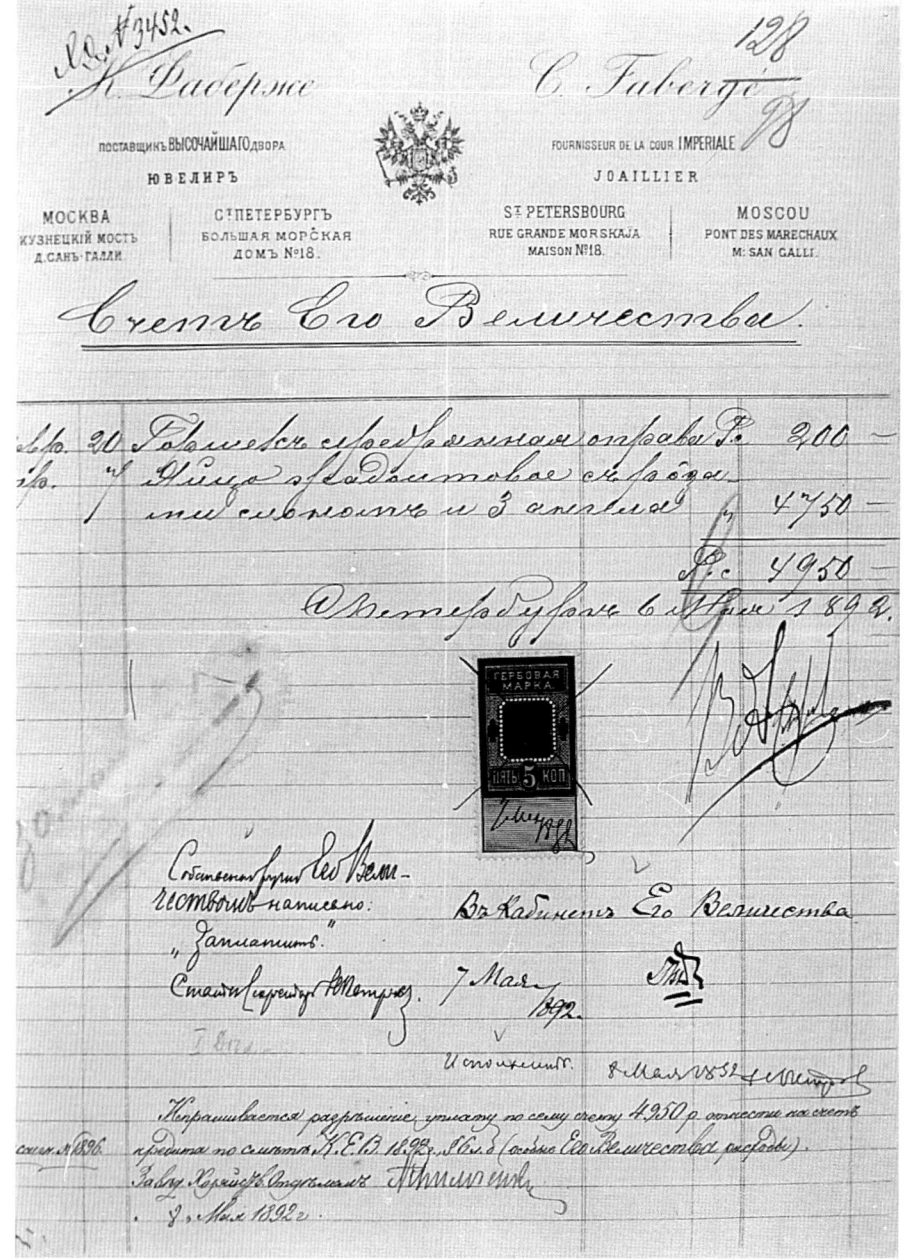

OPPOSITE: *Diamond Trellis Easter egg shown with its original stand. After the Easter egg was sold in 1960, the base with the three cherubs, as well as the original box, was separated and lost.*

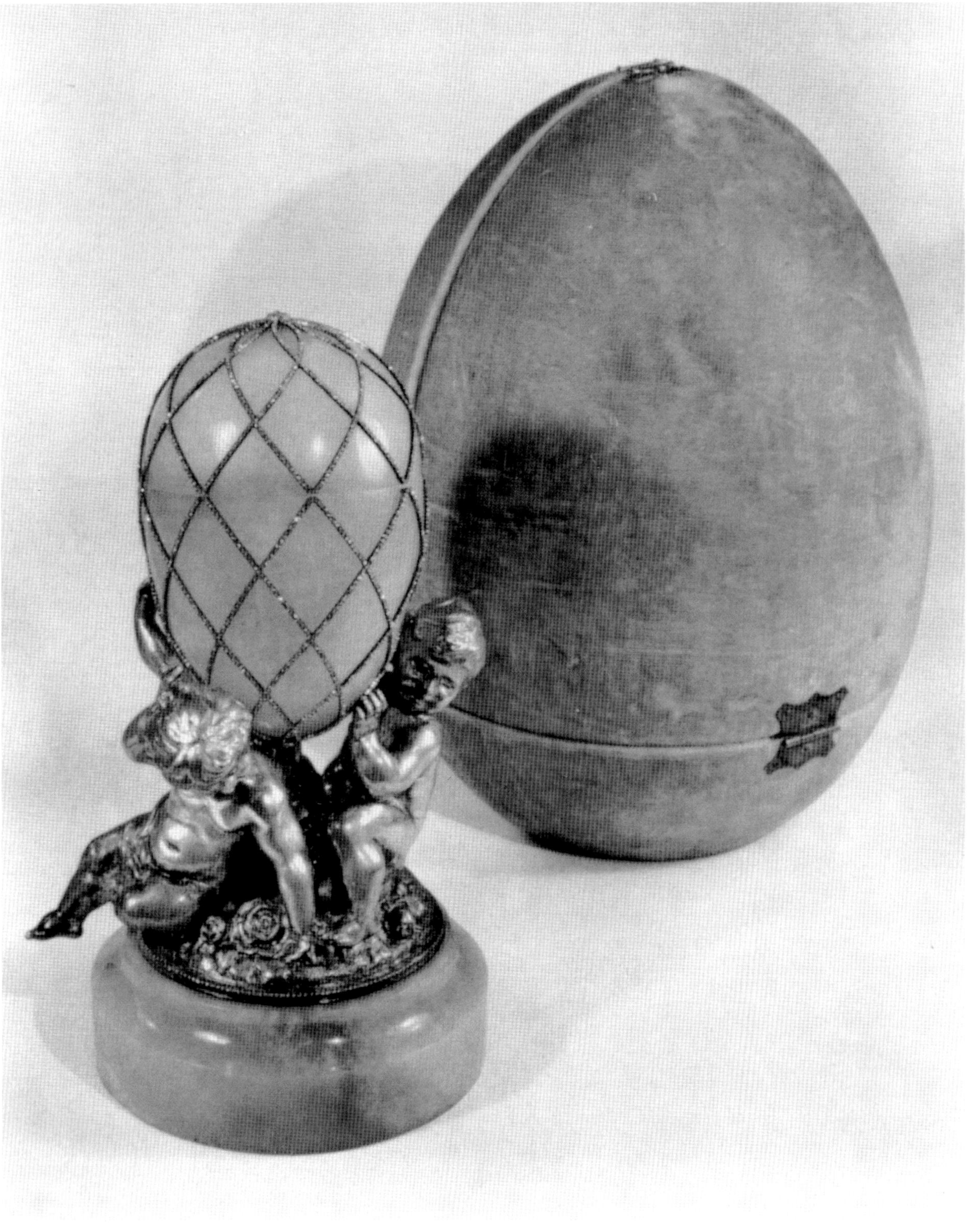

9
1893
Caucasus Egg

Presented by
Tsar Alexander III to his
wife, the Empress Maria
Fedorovna, Easter 1893
(28 March)

*(New Orleans Museum of Art:
Matilda Geddings Gray
Foundation Collection)*

Description

Workmaster: Mikhail Perkhin.
Miniaturist: Konstantin Yakovlevich Kryzhitski.
Surprise: Ivory miniatures of the Imperial hunting lodge at Abastuman.
Height: 3⅝ inches x 2⅞ inches (9.2 cm x 7.2 cm).
Marks: FABERGÉ, M.P. (in Cyrillic), assay mark of the city of St Petersburg, 72.

Varicoloured gold, silver, platinum, *guilloché* enamel, rose-cut diamonds, portrait diamond, pearls, crystal, ivory, watercolour.

A masterpiece of the 18th-century-inspired enamelling techniques at which Fabergé excelled. The crimson *guilloché* enamel shell is draped with four-colour gold floral swags held by diamond-tied bows. The four oval hinged covers reveal views of the Imperial hunting lodge at Abastuman, an elaborate Russian *dacha* (country villa). These highly detailed miniatures were completed and signed by Kryzhitski in 1891, when Abastuman became the principal residence of Grand Duke Georgii Alexandrovich (1871–1899) following his collapse from tuberculosis in 1891 while on a world tour with his brother, the Tsarevich Nicholas Alexandrovich. The oval doors are surrounded by seed pearls which are flanked by fluted columns. Each door bears a diamond-set numeral, forming the date 1893, within a diamond wreath. A miniature of the Grand Duke in naval uniform can be seen through the large portrait diamond set at the apex of the egg.

Invoice

> *Red enamel egg, Louis XVI style, with portrait,*   5200 r.
> *diamonds and four miniatures*
> *St Petersburg, 22 May 1893* [123]

Tsars Alexander III and Nicholas II purchased Easter eggs from the House of Fabergé annually for 32 years. An indication that this yearly ritual was not automatic can be found in a note sent in 1893 by the Minister of the Imperial Court, Count I.I. Vorontsov-Dashkov, to Alexander III.

> *Fabergé has submitted his egg as usual. Are we authorized to accept it?*

The letter bears a note from the Emperor reading:

> *Of course.* [124]

This would indicate that an authorization was required every time for such substantial expenditure.

History

1893–1917 Kept at the Anichkov Palace.

1917 Confiscated by Kerensky's provisional government, along with other treasures, and taken from the Anichkov Palace to the Moscow Kremlin Armoury.

Gold egg, covered with red enamel and diamond decorations in medallions with pearls and diamonds. [125]

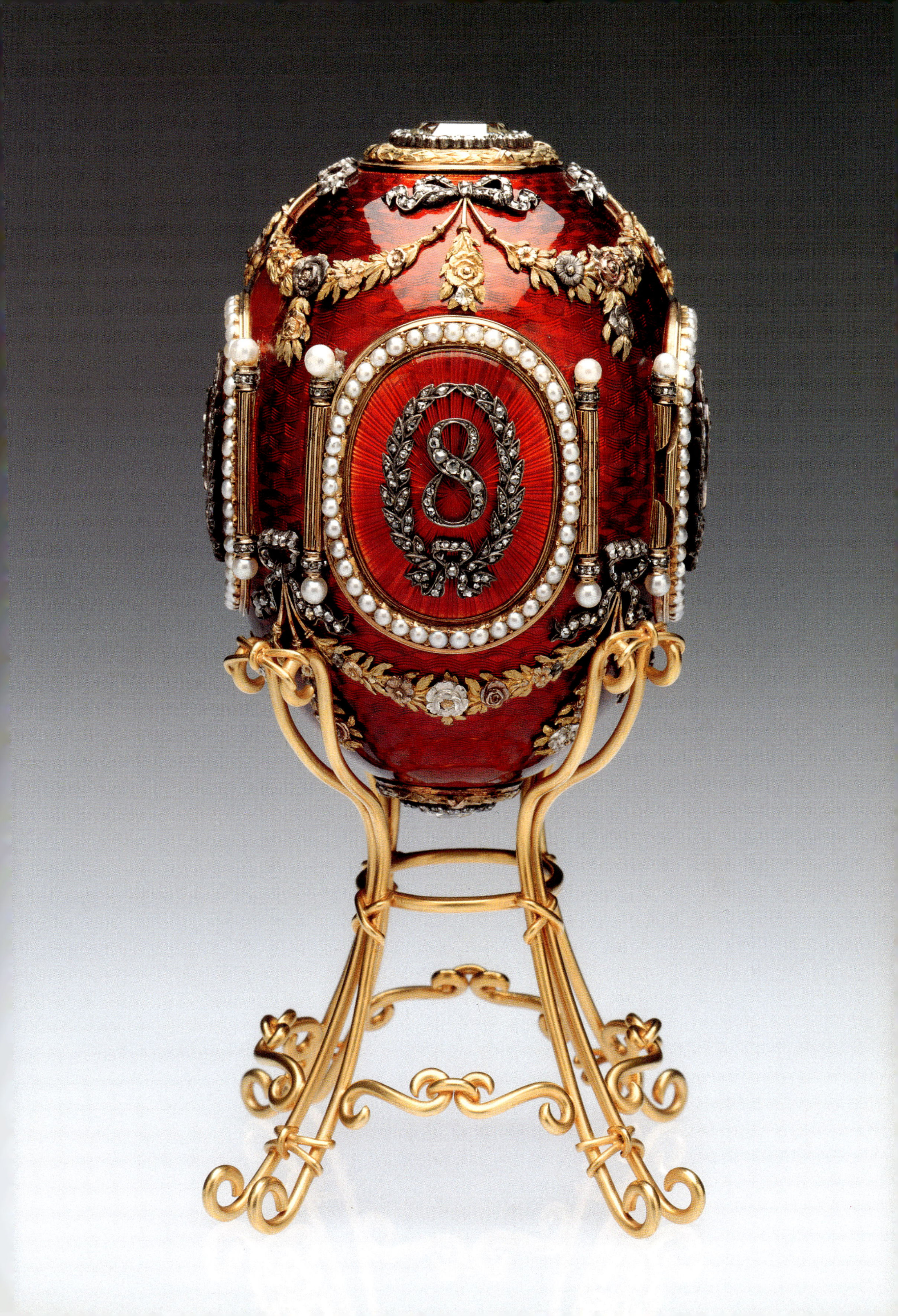

1922 One of the items on the list of treasures confiscated and transferred from the Anichkov Palace to the Sovnarkom.

1 gold egg with 2 diamonds and rose-cut diamonds, covered with portraits and landscapes. [126]

1930 Officially sold by Antikvariat for 5000 roubles. [127]

1930s Purchased by the Coca Cola heiress, Mrs Matilda Geddings Gray from Hammer Galleries Inc., New York.

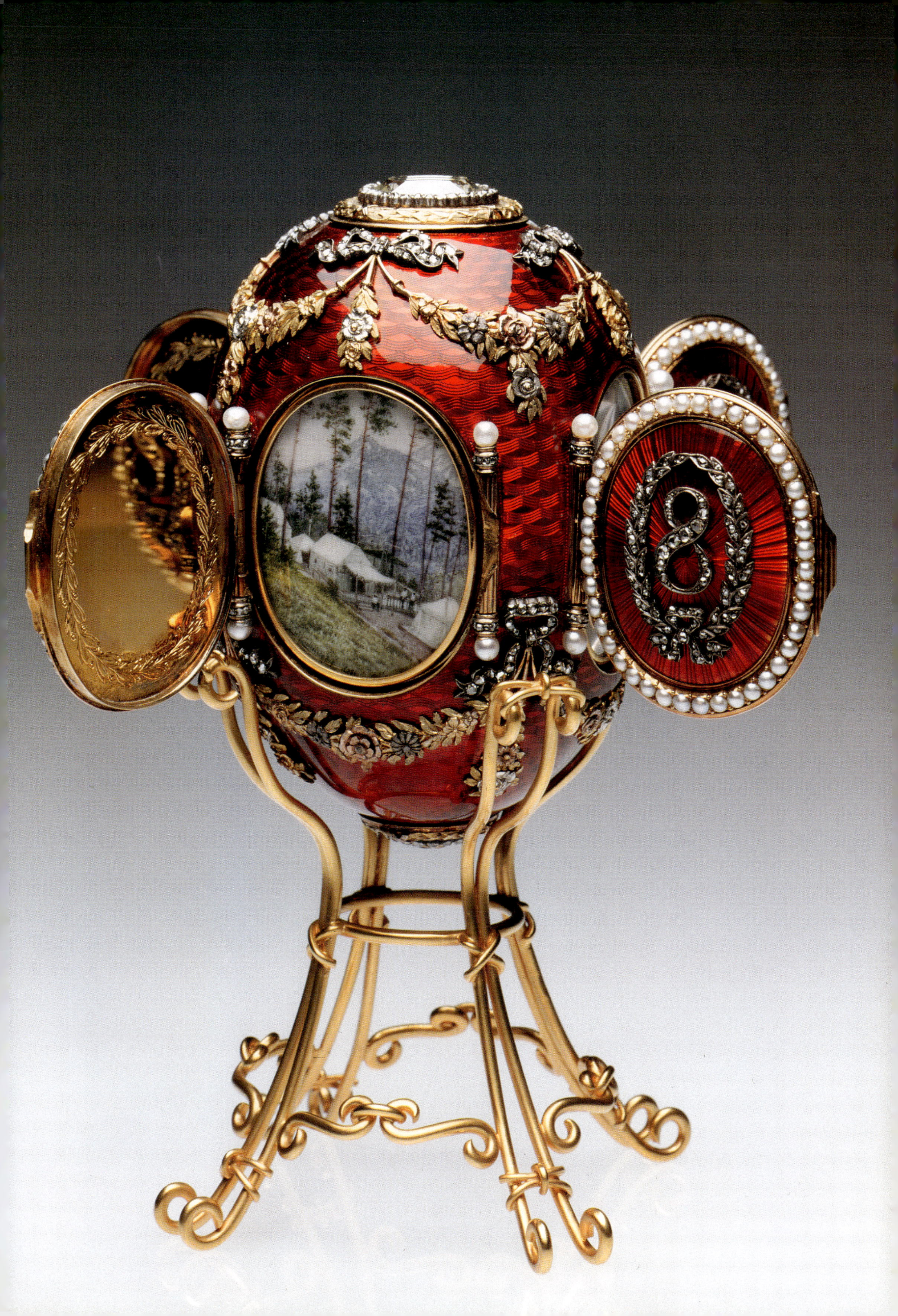

10

1894

Renaissance Egg

Presented by
Tsar Alexander III to his
wife, the Empress Maria
Fedorovna, Easter 1894
(17 April)

*(The FORBES Magazine
Collection, New York)*

This was the last Easter egg given by Tsar Alexander III to the Empress as he died eight months after its presentation. The design of the egg is modelled after an 18th-century casket by Le Roy, now in the Grüne Gewölbe, Dresden.

DESCRIPTION

Workmaster: Mikhail Perkhin.
Height: 5¼ inches (13.3 cm).
Marks: FABERGÉ, M.P. (in Cyrillic), assay mark of St Petersburg, 56.

White agate, gold, green, red, blue, black and white enamel, diamonds, rubies.

The egg rests horizontally on a richly enamelled base; mounted at both ends are chased gold lions' heads gripping rings in their mouths. Diamond and ruby flowers adorn the intersections of the white enamel trellises. The year 1894 is set in diamonds at the top of the egg, centering a diamond and an oval strawberry enamel medallion. The whereabouts and even the nature of its surprise are unknown.

INVOICE

18th century casket by Le Roy that was the inspiration for the Renaissance egg.

*Agate egg, gold mounting, enamelled in the
Renaissance style, with diamonds, rose-cut diamonds,
pearls and rubies*   4750 r.
St Petersburg, 6 May 1894 [128]

History

1894–1917 Kept at the Anichkov Palace.

1930 Officially sold by Antikvariat for 1500 roubles.[129] Later owned by Hammer Galleries Inc., New York, Mr and Mrs Henry Talbot de Vere Clifton, England; Mr and Mrs Jack Linsky, New York and A La Vieille Russie, Inc., New York.

1966 Purchased by FORBES, Inc.

11

1895

Twelve Monograms Egg

Presented by
Tsar Nicholas II to his
mother, the Dowager
Empress Maria Fedorovna,
Easter 1895 (2 April)

*(Hillwood Museum,
Washington DC)*

In October 1894 Alexander III died. Carl Fabergé was faced with a difficult problem. Barely six months remained until the following Easter. The new Tsar, Nicholas II, decided to continue the tradition of giving an Easter egg to his wife, Alexandra Fedorovna, as well as one to his mother, the Dowager Empress Maria Fedorovna. It is probable that Fabergé had to change the subject of the egg to reflect the Dowager Empress's sorrow, and she was presented with this elegant, subdued Easter egg.

DESCRIPTION

Workmaster: Mikhail Perkhin.
Height: 3⅛ inches (7.9 cm).
Marks: Stamped FABERGÉ, M.P. (in Cyrillic), assay mark of the city of St Petersburg, 56.

The upper and lower halves of the Twelve Monograms egg are each divided into six panels. Between each panel are rose-cut diamonds, and diamonds around the rim where the egg opens. The panels are engraved with elaborate patterns in red gold against the deep royal blue enamel. The diamond-set crowned ciphers of the Empress and Alexander III encircle the upper and lower halves of the egg. The inside of the egg is covered with velvet lining for the surprise, which is now missing.

INVOICE

31 March entry:

> *Blue enamel egg, Louis XVI style,*   4500 r.
> *St Petersburg, 9 May 1895* [130]

The Emperor, after receiving the invoice, wrote on it:

> *The underlined items to be shared between
> the Empress AΘ [Alexandra Fedorovna] and myself,
> cost 4500 roubles, ½ share, 2250 roubles.* [131]

HISTORY

1895–1917 Kept at the Anichkov Palace.

1902 Among the Fabergé objects shown at the charity exhibition sponsored by the Empress Alexandra Fedorovna at the von Dervis mansion in St Petersburg (see page 55).

1949 Mrs Marjorie Merriweather Post, whose husband, Mr Joseph E. Davies, was the American Ambassador to Moscow, purchased this Easter egg in Italy in 1949 from Mrs G.V. Berchielli. It is thought she may have been a friend of Mrs Frances Rosso, the American wife of the Italian Ambassador in Moscow, when the Davieses were in Moscow. Mrs Rosso and Mrs Post remained friends until the death of Mrs Rosso in 1969. [132]

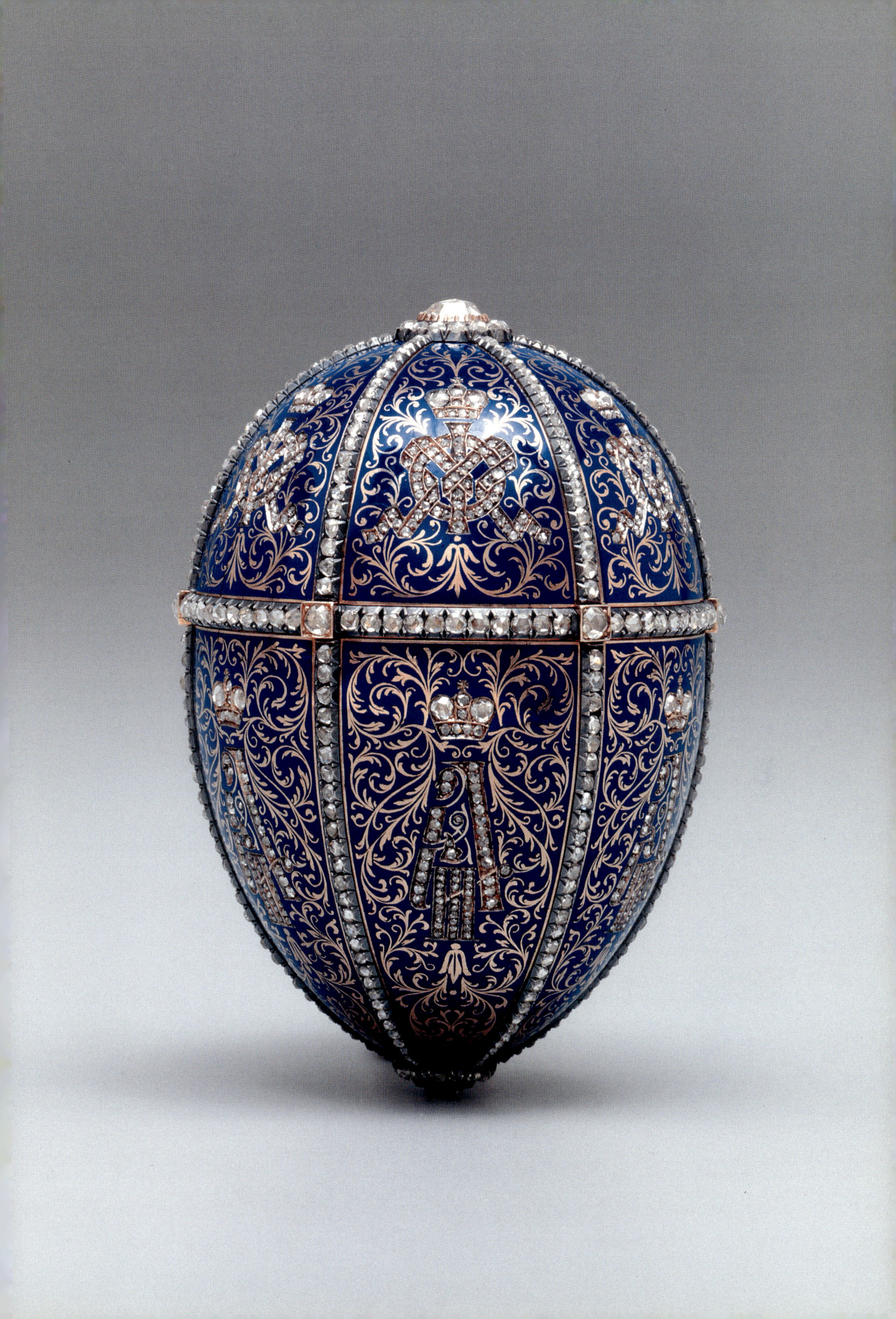

1895

Rosebud Egg

Presented by
Tsar Nicholas II to his
wife, the Empress
Alexandra Fedorovna,
Easter 1895 (2 April)

*(The FORBES Magazine
Collection, New York)*

Alexander III died on 20 October 1894. Tsar Nicholas II came to the throne and an Easter egg had to be made urgently for the new Empress, Alexandra Fedorovna, whom he had married on 14 November, just a few weeks after the death of his father. In Germany, Alexandra Fedorovna's native country, yellow was regarded as the noblest and worthiest colour for a rose (the golden rose), and Fabergé therefore considered this to be an appropriate surprise within this egg for her.

DESCRIPTION

Workmaster: Mikhail Perkhin.
Surprises: Yellow enamel rosebud concealing a miniature diamond replica of the Imperial crown (now missing).
Height: Egg: 2⅝ inches (6.8 cm); Rosebud: 1³⁄₁₆ inches (3 cm).
Marks: FABERGÉ, M.P. (in Cyrillic), assay mark of the city of St Petersburg, 56.

Egg: Varicoloured gold, translucent red and opaque white enamel, diamonds, velvet lining.

Surprise: Gold, opaque green and yellow enamel.

The striking translucent strawberry red enamel egg is divided by rows of diamonds between bands of opaque white enamel. Green-gold laurel swags and wreaths, diamond set Cupid's arrows and ribbons embellish the egg. A hinged yellow and green enamelled rosebud is concealed inside the egg. This flower when opened revealed its own surprise, a miniature diamond replica of the Imperial crown. The diamond crown's present whereabouts are unknown. A table diamond is mounted at the egg's apex through which can be seen a portrait of Nicholas II, and the year 1895 is set beneath a rose diamond at the base.

INVOICE

31 March entry:

Red enamel egg with crown   3250 r.
St Petersburg, 9 May 1895 [133]

HISTORY

1895–1917 Kept in the study of Her Imperial Highness Alexandra Fedorovna at the Winter Palace. It was displayed on the second shelf from the top in the corner showcase between the door leading into the bedroom and the window.

On 10 April 1909, N. Dementiev, Inspector of Premises of the Imperial Winter Palace, described this Easter egg when he inventoried articles in the Imperial family's private apartments.[134]

Egg, Louis XVI style, covered with red enamel, decorated with green gold wreaths and garlands, and bows and arrows of rose-cut diamonds. The egg is entwined with four bands of rose-cut diamonds. The top is encircled by a strip of rose-cut diamonds and a band of white enamel, containing a flat diamond covering a portrait of the Emperor Nicholas II. The lower part of the egg is similarly encircled by a strip of rose-cut diamonds and a band of white enamel containing a flat diamond, covering

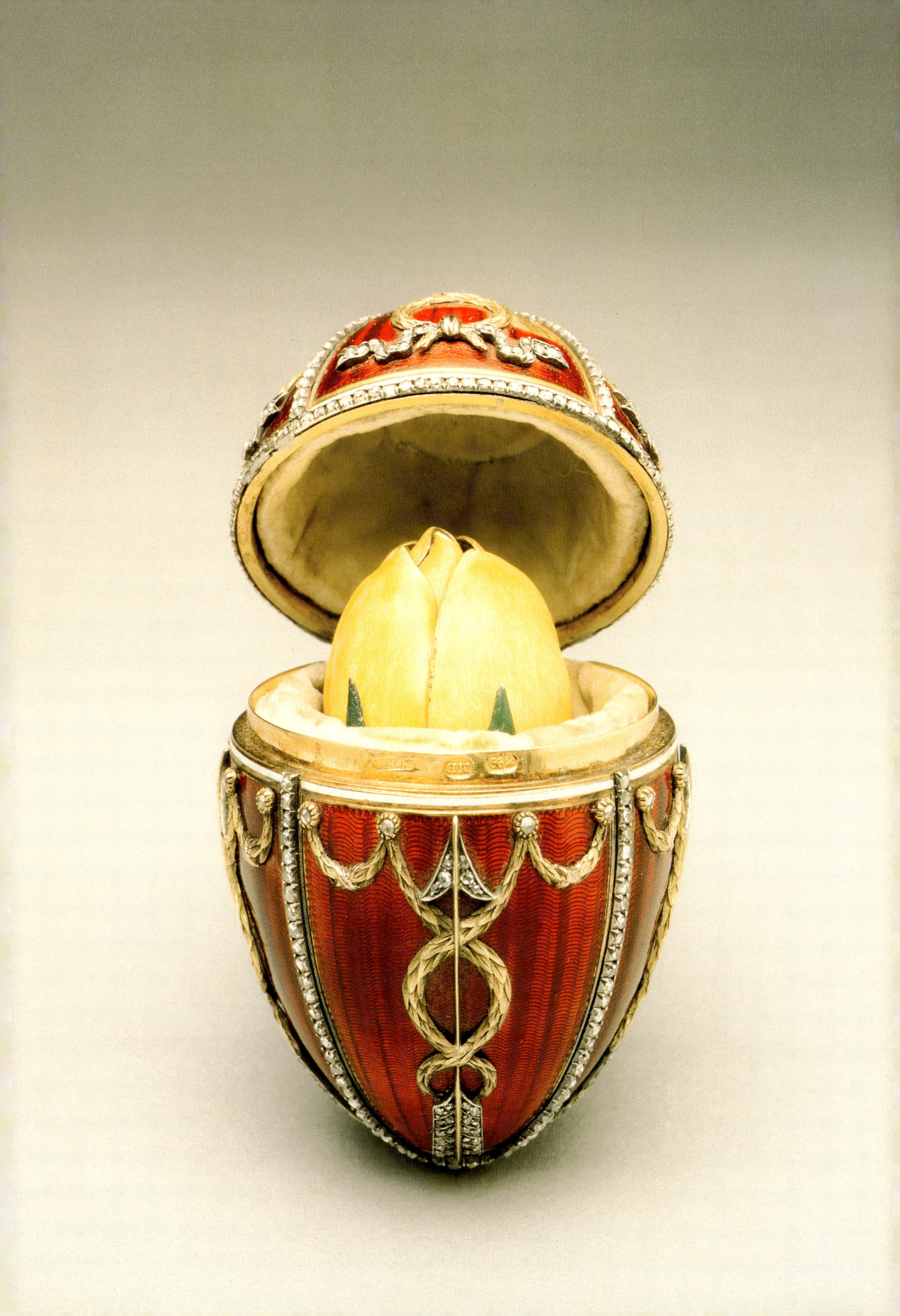

the date 1895. The egg contains a rosebud of yellow enamel with a green enamel stem. The flower opens into two halves, containing an Imperial crown entirely made of rose-cut diamonds, with two cabochon rubies. [135]

1917 Confiscated by Kerensky's provisional government, along with other treasures, and taken from the Anichkov Palace to the Moscow Kremlin Armoury.

1922 One of the items on the list of treasures confiscated and transferred from the Anichkov Palace to the Sovnarkom.

1 gold egg with diamonds and rose-cut diamonds, containing a flower and a crown of rose-cut diamonds. [136]

Later owned by Wartski, London; Charles Parsons, England; Mr and Mrs Henry Talbot de Vere Clifton, England; Fine Art Society, London.

1985 Acquired by FORBES, Inc.

13

1896

Alexander III Egg

Presented by
Tsar Nicholas II to his
mother, the Dowager
Empress Maria Fedorovna,
Easter 1896 (24 March)

(Whereabouts unknown)

Once again, Fabergé chose blue for this Easter egg. It featured six portraits of the late Emperor Alexander III. According to a tradition established by Fabergé, many of the hand-painted miniatures in the Easter eggs celebrated important achievements and events in the lives of Their Imperial Majesties. As this year was the 30th anniversary of the marriage of Maria Fedorovna and Alexander Alexandrovich, the miniatures probably highlighted the accomplishments of the Imperial family during this period.

INVOICE

3 April entry:

> *Blue enamel egg, 6 portraits of H.I.M.*
> *Emperor Alexander III, with 10 sapphires*
> *and rose-cut diamonds and mounting*   3575 r.
> *St Petersburg, 12 April 1896*[137]

HISTORY

1896–1917 Kept at the Anichkov Palace.

It is known that the Dowager Empress' palaces were pillaged and looted during the Revolution and it is probable that this was when the Alexander III egg disappeared.

123

1896

14

Revolving Miniatures Egg

Presented by
Tsar Nicholas II to
his wife, the Empress
Alexandra Fedorovna,
Easter 1896 (24 March)

*(Virginia Museum of Fine Arts,
Richmond, bequest of Lillian
Thomas Pratt)*

DESCRIPTION

Workmaster: Mikhail Perkhin.
Miniaturist: Johannes Zehngraf (signed on all but two miniatures).
Surprise: Revolving miniatures with views of Imperial palaces.
Height: 9 ³/₄ inches (24.7 cm).
Marks: M.P. (in Cyrillic), assay mark of the city of St Petersburg.

Rock crystal, gold, green enamel, diamonds, cabochon emerald.

This rock crystal egg contains 12 gold-framed miniatures showing views of palaces in Germany, Great Britain and Russia, connected with the life of the Empress. They revolve around a fluted gold column that terminates in an elaborate setting with a large cabochon Siberian emerald finial. The circular rock crystal plinth is decorated with bands of rose-cut diamonds and brightly coloured *champlevé* enamel monograms of the Empress, as Princess Alix of Hesse and the Rhine prior to her marriage, and as the Russian Empress, Alexandra Fedorovna.

INVOICE

3 April entry:

> *Rock crystal egg with rock crystal pedestal, 12 miniatures,
> with emerald, rose-cut diamonds and mounting*   6750 r.
> *St Petersburg, 12 April 1896* [138]

HISTORY

1896–1917 Kept in the study of Her Imperial Majesty Alexandra Fedorovna at the Winter Palace. It was displayed on the first shelf from the top in the corner showcase between the door leading into the bedroom and the window.

On 10 April 1909, N. Dementiev, Inspector of Premises of the Imperial Winter Palace, described this Easter egg when he inventoried articles in the Imperial family's private apartments. [139]

Transparent rock crystal egg banded with green enamel containing rose-cut diamonds. The upper edge of the band is connected by a rosette of rose-cut diamonds...The egg stands on a gold neck, the upper part of which represents the letter A in red and blue, with a crown of rose-cut diamonds underneath. The lower part of the neck consists of repetitions of the initials AΘ...In the middle of the crystal egg is an engraved gold column to which six tiny frames are attached...The frames contain different miniature landscapes on both sides and revolve around the column, which is set in motion by the emerald at the top of the egg. [140]

1917 Confiscated by Kerensky's provisional government, along with other treasures, and taken from the Anichkov Palace to the Moscow Kremlin Armoury.

1922 One of the items on the list of treasures confiscated and transferred from the Anichkov Palace to the Sovnarkom.

1 crystal egg with 1 emerald, containing gold folding frame. [141]

1930 Officially sold by Antikvariat for 8000 roubles. [142]

1940s Purchased by Lillian Thomas Pratt from Hammer Galleries, New York.

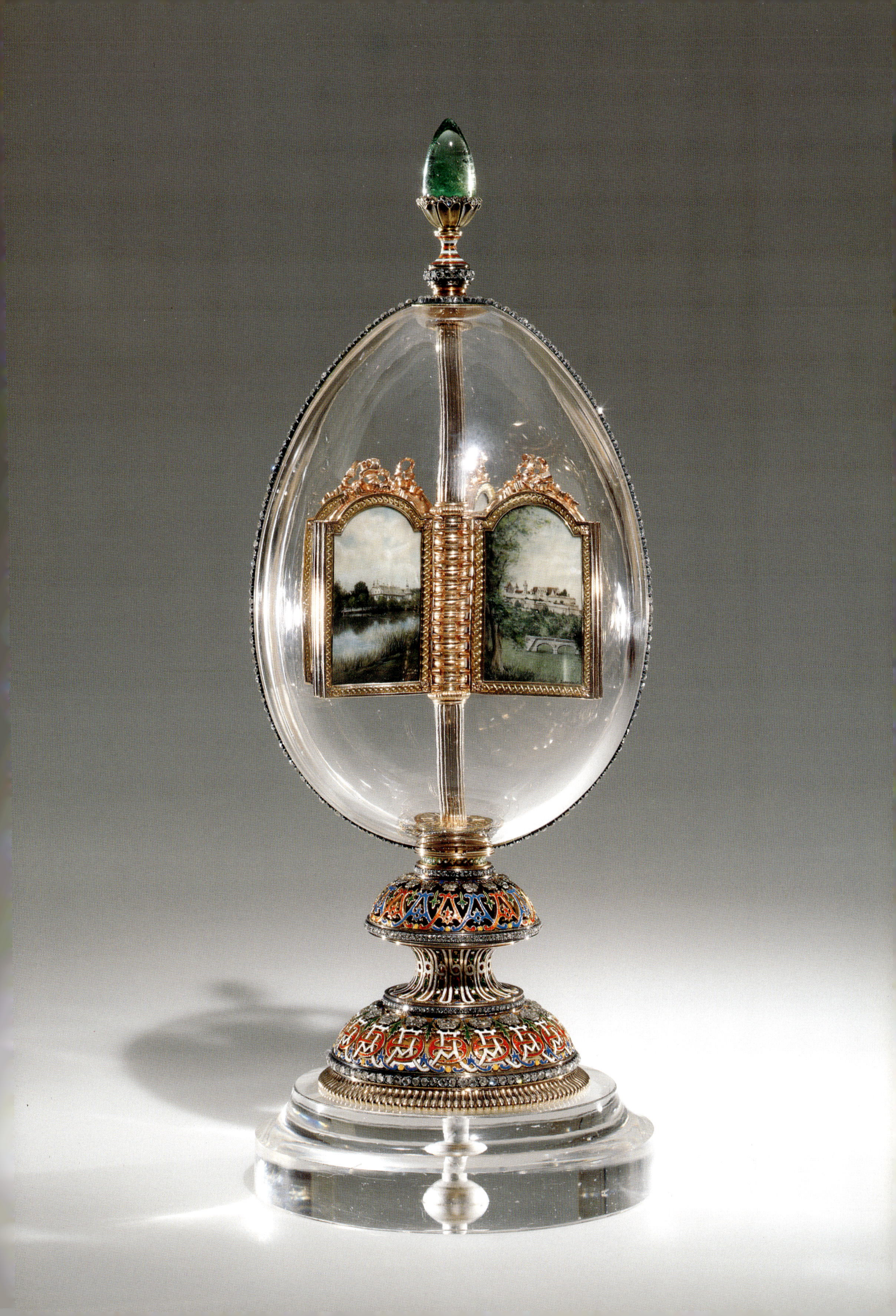

15

1897

Mauve Enamel Egg

Presented by
Tsar Nicholas II to his
mother, the Dowager
Empress Maria Fedorovna,
Easter 1897 (13 April)

(Whereabouts of egg unknown; surprise now identified as the Heart Surprise Frame in the FORBES Magazine Collection, New York)

The authors believe that the surprise of the missing Mauve Enamel Easter egg is the Heart Surprise Frame in the FORBES Magazine Collection. It contains three miniatures representing Tsar Nicholas II, Empress Alexandra Fedorovna, and Grand Duchess Olga, their first-born daughter.

DESCRIPTION OF SURPRISE

Height: 3¼ inches (8.2 cm) closed.
Marks: K. FABERGÉ (in Cyrillic).

Gold, translucent strawberry and shamrock green *guilloché* enamel, opaque white enamel, diamonds, pearls.

The splendid translucent strawberry *guilloché* heart frame surprise opens out into the shape of a three-leaf clover portraying oval miniatures of Tsar Nicholas II, Empress Alexandra Fedorovna, and their daughter, Grand Duchess Olga, and is bordered by rose-cut diamonds on shamrock green *guilloché* enamel background. The heart, which displays the year 1897, is set with rose-cut diamonds and is supported on a stand of white opaque enamel, laurel leaves, a strawberry enamel base, and bands of rose-cut diamonds. A spring mechanism in the shaft is triggered by pushing the central pearl in the base which causes the trefoil of miniatures to snap shut, leaving only the heart displayed.

INVOICE

18 April entry:

> *Mauve enamel egg, with 3 miniatures*   3250 r.
> *St Petersburg, 17 May 1897* [143]

HISTORY

1897–1917 Kept at the Anichkov Palace.

1978 Sold at Christie's, Geneva, 26 April. The description in the catalogue identifies the miniature of the child as the Tsar's second-born daughter, Grand Duchess Tatiana, but this is not possible, as she was born 29 May 1897, and was just over one month old when the egg was presented to the Dowager Empress. The miniature is not of a new-born baby, but of an older child, her sister Olga, born 3 November 1895. The following year the Empress Alexandra Fedorovna was presented with the superb Lilies of the Valley egg (18) which contained as its surprise miniatures of the Emperor Nicholas II and daughters, Olga and Tatiana. The miniature portrays Tatiana, even one year later, as a very young baby.

1978 Acquired by Forbes Inc. Previously in the collection of Lydia, Lady Deterding, Paris.

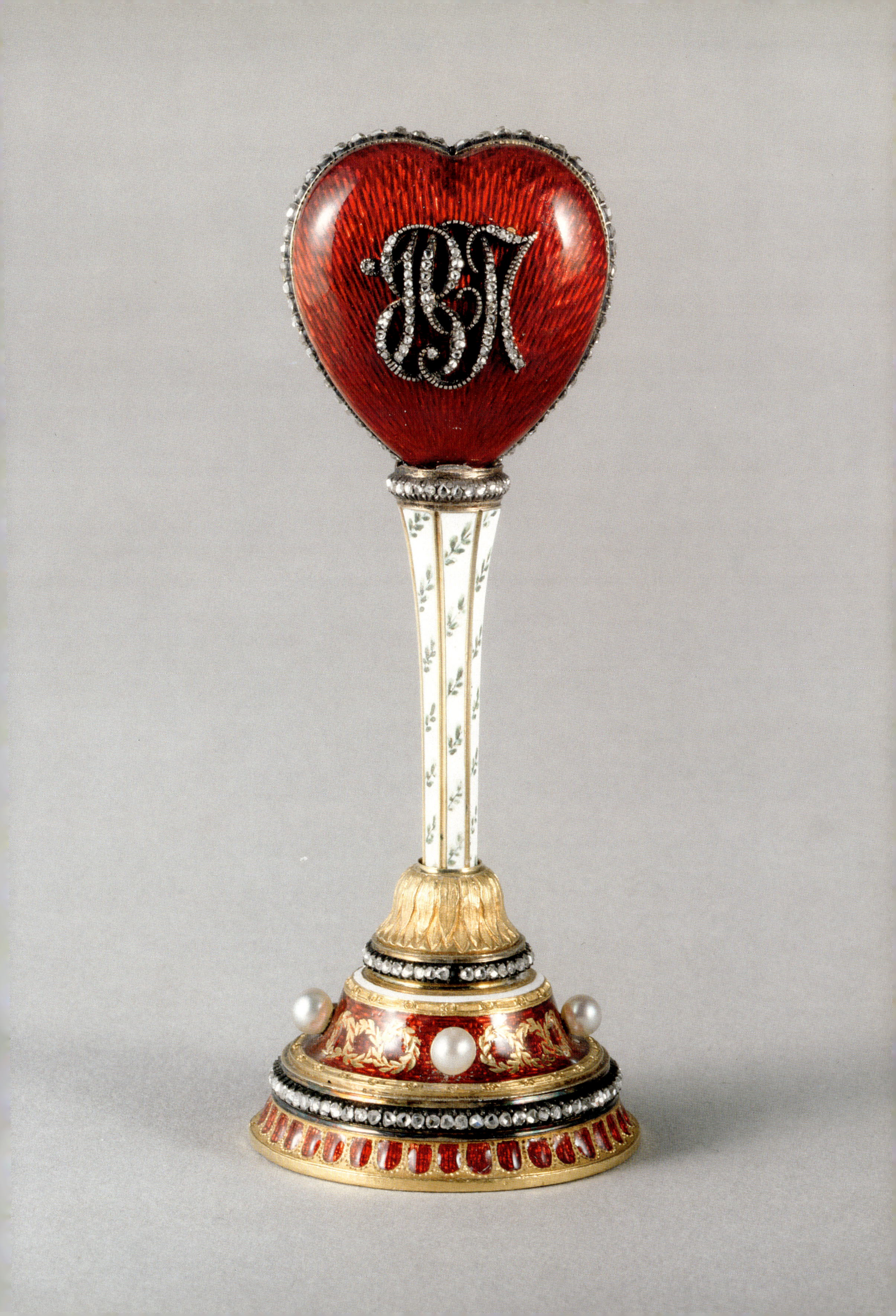

Кабинетъ Е. В. уплатилъ
24 Мая 1899

К. Фаберже C. Fabergé

ПОСТАВЩИКЪ ВЫСОЧАЙШАГО ДВОРА — FOURNISSEUR DE LA COUR IMPÉRIALE

ЮВЕЛИРЪ — JOAILLIER

МОСКВА	С. ПЕТЕРБУРГЪ	St PETERSBOURG	MOSCOU
КУЗНЕЦКІЙ МОСТЪ ДОМЪ № 4.	БОЛЬШАЯ МОРСКАЯ ДОМЪ № 16	RUE GRANDE MORSKAJA MAISON № 16	PONT DES MARÉCHAUX MAISON № 4.

Его Императорскому Величеству

Апрѣля 18	яйцо желтой эмали и карета	Р.	5500.—
	яичко изумрудовое съ бриллiантами		1000.—
	станокъ зеркальнаго стекла съ жадеитомъ		150.—
	яйцо mauve эмали съ 3-мя мiнiатюрами		3250.—
Мая 8	брошка XXX: 1 бриллiантъ		6000.—
	1 изумрудъ пандалокъ		3200.—
	мал. бриллiанты и работа		2300.—
		Р.	21.400.—

С. Петербургъ, 17 Мая 1899

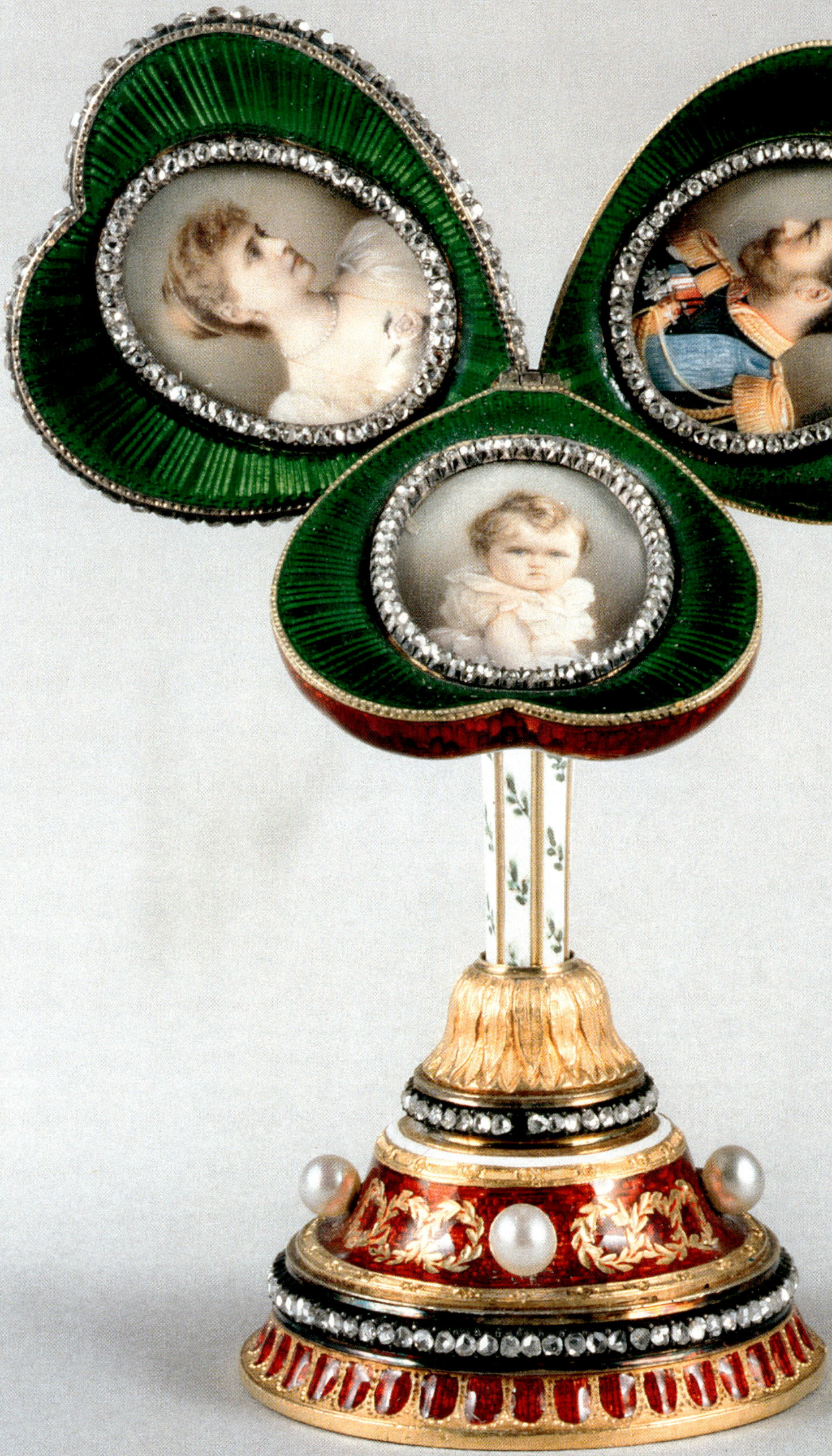

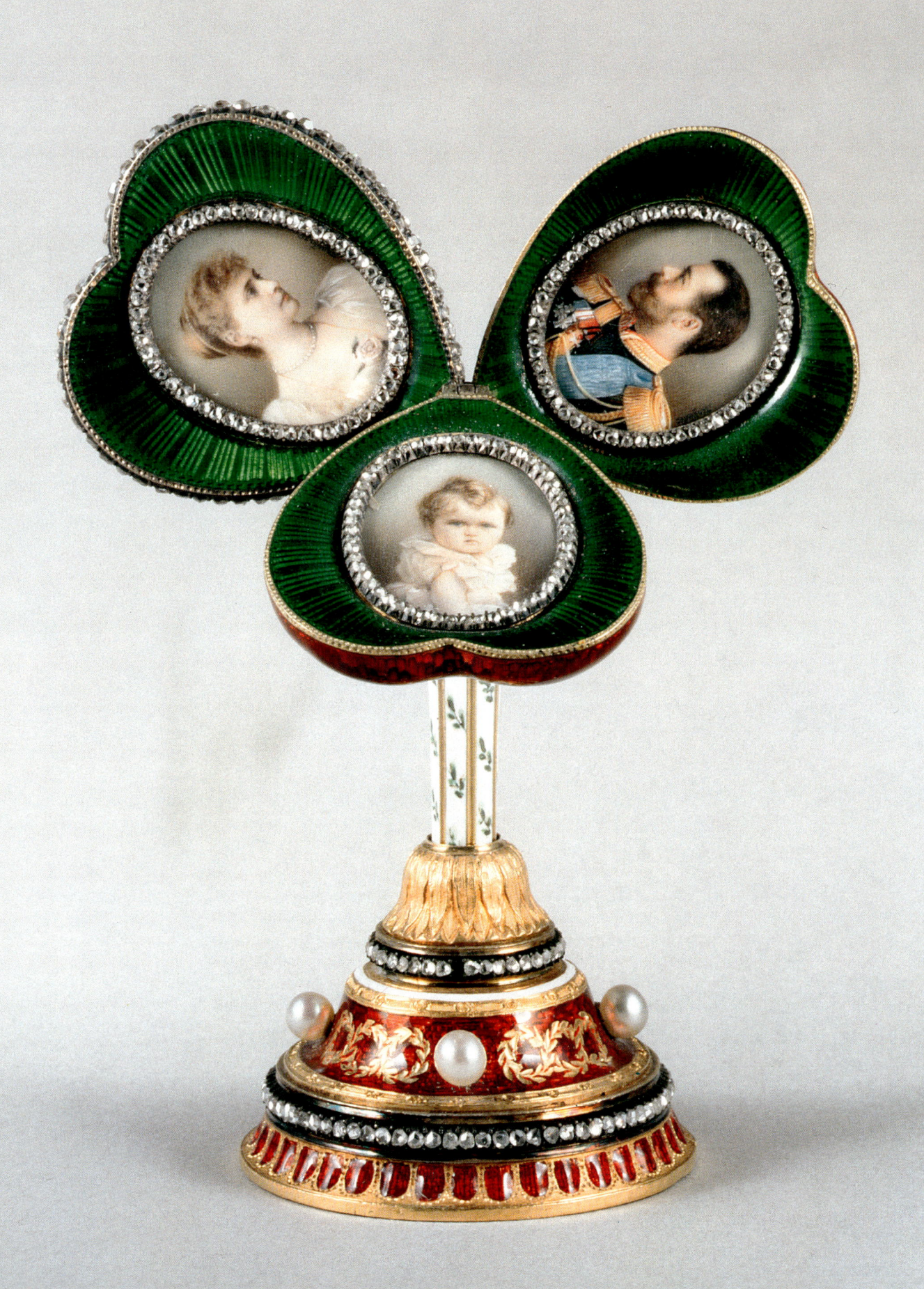

16

1897

Coronation Egg

Presented by
Tsar Nicholas II to
his wife, the Empress
Alexandra Fedorovna,
Easter 1897 (13 April)

(*The FORBES Magazine
Collection, New York*)

On 9 May 1896, Nicholas and Alexandra were crowned in the Uspenski (Dormition) Cathedral in Moscow. Nicholas recorded the ceremonial procession from the Kremlin to the Cathedral in his diary: 'I was riding on Norma, Mama was sitting in the first gold carriage and Alix in the second, alone also.' During the ceremony Nicholas took the large Imperial crown from the Metropolitan and placed it on his own head. Alexandra sank to her knees in obeisance before him. Nicholas removed the crown and gently touched her head with it. She rose and they kissed each other, then proceeded to their golden thrones where Nicholas was proclaimed Emperor and Autocrat of all the Russias. A million citizens descended upon Moscow to catch a glimpse of their new Emperor and Empress. All European royalty were invited to attend this sumptuous event, commemorated in this appropriately lavish egg.

DESCRIPTION

Workmaster: Mikhail Perkhin.
Surprise: Coach.
Length: 5 inches (12.7 cm).
Marks: M.P. (in Cyrillic), Wigström etched into the inner surface of the shell, assay mark of the city of St Petersburg, 56.

Varicoloured gold, translucent lime yellow enamel, opaque black and blue enamel, diamonds, velvet lining.

COACH

Workmaster: George Stein.
Length: 3¹¹⁄₁₆ inches (9.3 cm).

Gold, platinum, translucent strawberry red enamel, diamonds, rubies, rock crystal.

This magnificent red gold and lime yellow translucent enamel egg is encased in a gold laurel leaf trellis design. Black enamelled double-headed eagles of the Romanov family crest, each set with a rose-cut diamond, are mounted at each intersection. The colours of the egg are an allusion to the gold ermine-trimmed robes worn by Their Imperial Majesties to their coronation. Concealed inside this elaborate shell is a gold replica of the Imperial Coronation coach that the Empress rode in to the ceremony. George Stein laboured for 15 months, 16 hours a day, to complete this surprise in time for Easter 1897.[144] A tiny emerald pendant egg once hung inside the coach. The monogram of Empress Alexandra Fedorovna is emblazoned in rose-cut diamonds and set beneath a portrait diamond at the apex of the egg. The date 1897 appears beneath a smaller portrait diamond at the bottom of the egg. The Coronation egg is visible in a photograph taken at the 1902 exhibition of Imperial treasures at the von Dervis mansion. On the shelf above the Coronation egg is an elaborate glass case that houses the coach (see page 55).

INVOICE

18 April entry:

Yellow enamel egg and carriage	5500 r.
Emerald pendant egg with diamonds	1000 r.
Bevelled glass case with jadeite stand	150 r.
St Petersburg, 17 May 1897 [145]	

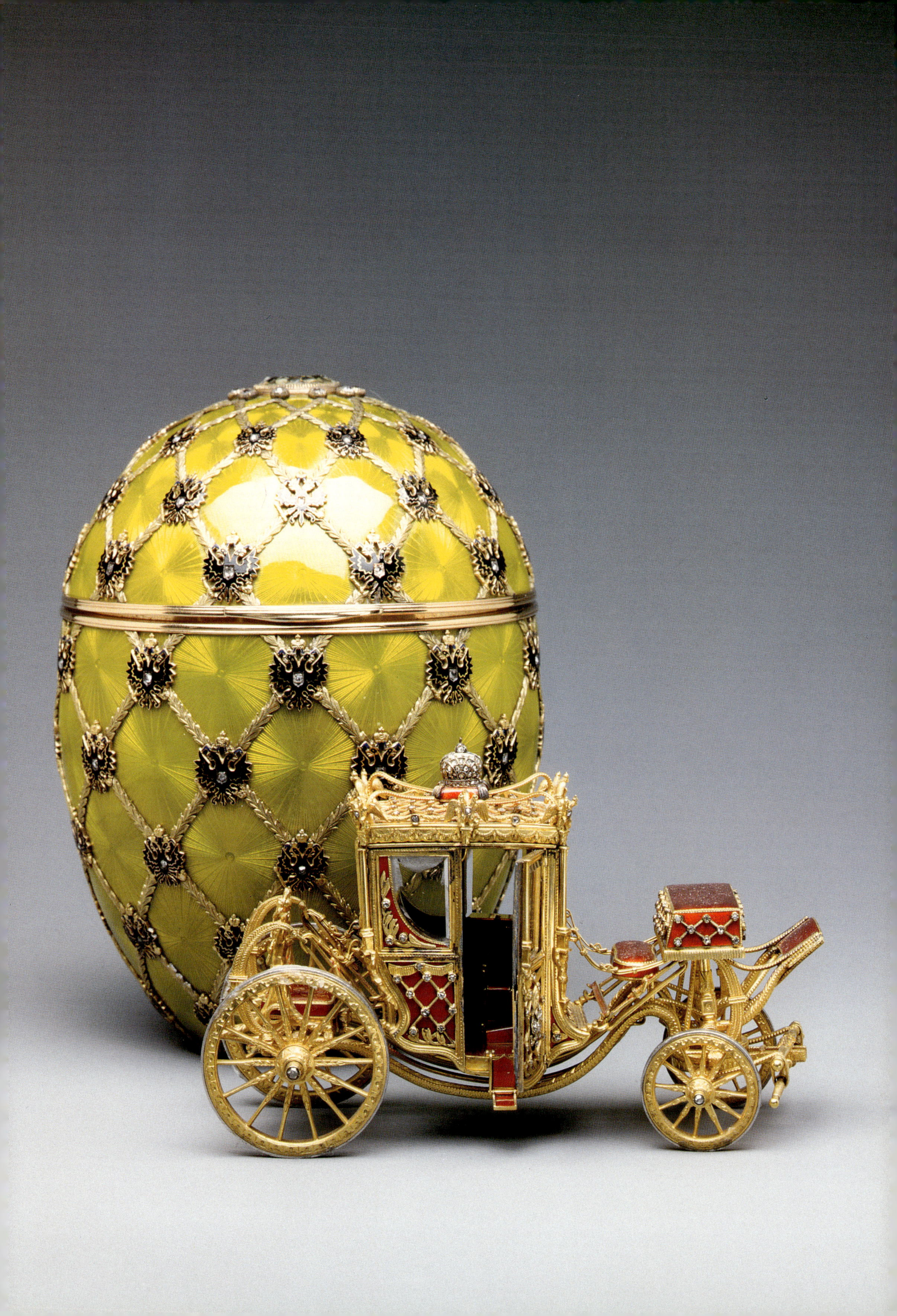

HISTORY

1897–1917 Kept in the study of Her Imperial Majesty Alexandra Fedorovna at the Winter Palace. It was displayed on the second shelf from the top in the corner showcase between the door leading into the bedroom and the window.

On 10 April 1909, N. Dementiev, Inspector of Premises of the Imperial Winter Palace, described this Easter egg when he inventoried articles in the Imperial family's private apartments.[146]

Egg covered with yellow enamel and a lattice-work of green gold strips, with a black enamel eagle and a single rose-cut diamond at each intersection. The base of the egg is encircled with a smooth gold band. The upper part of the egg contains a small, round gold frame surrounded by 10 diamonds and surmounted by the initials AΘ, the letter A made of rose-cut diamonds and Θ of rubies, under a crown made of rose-cut diamonds and one ruby. The lower part of the egg holds a chased rosette of green gold, with a circle of rose-cut diamonds surmounting a flat diamond covering the date 1897. The egg is lined with white velvet which serves as a nest for the model State carriage described in this inventory under no.190. The egg rests on a silver-gilt wire stand.[147]

SURPRISE IN THE EGG

Small gold model of a State carriage, decorated with red enamel, with eagles made of rose-cut diamonds on the doors and surmounted by an Imperial crown of rose-cut diamonds. The carriage contains a yellow diamond pendant egg (briolette). It is placed on a rectangular jadeite pediment with a silver-gilt rim and is contained in a rectangular glass case with silver-gilt edging. Silver-gilt Imperial crowns are placed at each of the four corners of the case.[148]

The invoice from the House of Fabergé lists the pendant egg as an emerald, whereas the inventory taken at the Winter Palace in 1909 says the carriage contains a yellow diamond pendant egg (briolette). It is unfortunate that the pendant egg is missing from the surprise, but the authors believe that while the invoice from the House of Fabergé accurately describes the original pendant in the surprise, it is quite possible that the pendant egg was replaced at some time.

1917 Confiscated by Kerensky's provisional government, along with other treasures, and taken to the Moscow Kremlin Armoury.

1922 One of the items on the list of treasures transferred from the Anichkov Palace to the Sovnarkom.

1 gold egg with diamonds and rose-cut diamonds, containing a gold carriage with a pear-shaped diamond.[149]

1979 Acquired by Mr Forbes, August 1979, from Wartski (together with the 1898 Lilies of the Valley egg (18)) for $2.16 million.[150]

17

1898

Pelican Egg

Presented by
Tsar Nicholas II to his
mother, the Dowager
Empress Maria Fedorovna,
Easter 1898 (5 April)

*(Virginia Museum of Fine Arts,
Richmond, bequest of Lillian
Thomas Pratt)*

The Pelican Egg was presented to the Dowager Empress in celebration of the 100th anniversary of the founding of the charitable institutions by the Empress Maria Fedorovna, wife of Paul I, of which the Dowager Empress was also Patroness. The dates 1797 and 1897 are engraved on the shell of the Easter egg and an inscription on the rose gold exterior reads: 'Visit our vineyards, O Lord, and we shall live in Thee'.

Description

Workmaster: Mikhail Perkhin.
Miniaturist: Johannes Zehngraf.
Surprise: Miniatures of buildings in St Petersburg that housed educational institutions for women of privilege.
Height: Egg: 4 inches, (10.2 cm); Egg with stand: 5¼ inches (13.3 cm).
Marks: FABERGÉ, M.P. (in Cyrillic), assay mark of the city of St Petersburg, 56, stand marked 'Fabergé'.

Gold, diamonds, enamel, pearls, ivory, watercolours.

The Empire-style Pelican Easter egg is a visual allegory celebrating charity and good works. The egg is surmounted by an opalescent white enamel pelican, the ancient symbol of self-sacrifice, her outstretched diamond-studded wings protect her little nestlings, which in this case represent the daughters of the aristocracy. As the nestlings clamour for food, she plucks at her own breast to feed them. Near the top of the shell an engraving of the pelican family repeats the sculptural motif.

Most of Fabergé's Easter eggs contain separate surprises that are moved within the shell or can be taken out completely, but the entire Pelican egg itself is the surprise. The egg unfolds to become a screen of gold oval frames, each surrounded with seed pearls. The frames hold eight miniatures by Johannes Zehngraf depicting buildings in St Petersburg that housed educational institutions for women of means. The egg rests on an Empire-style varicoloured gold stand decorated with crowned eagles.

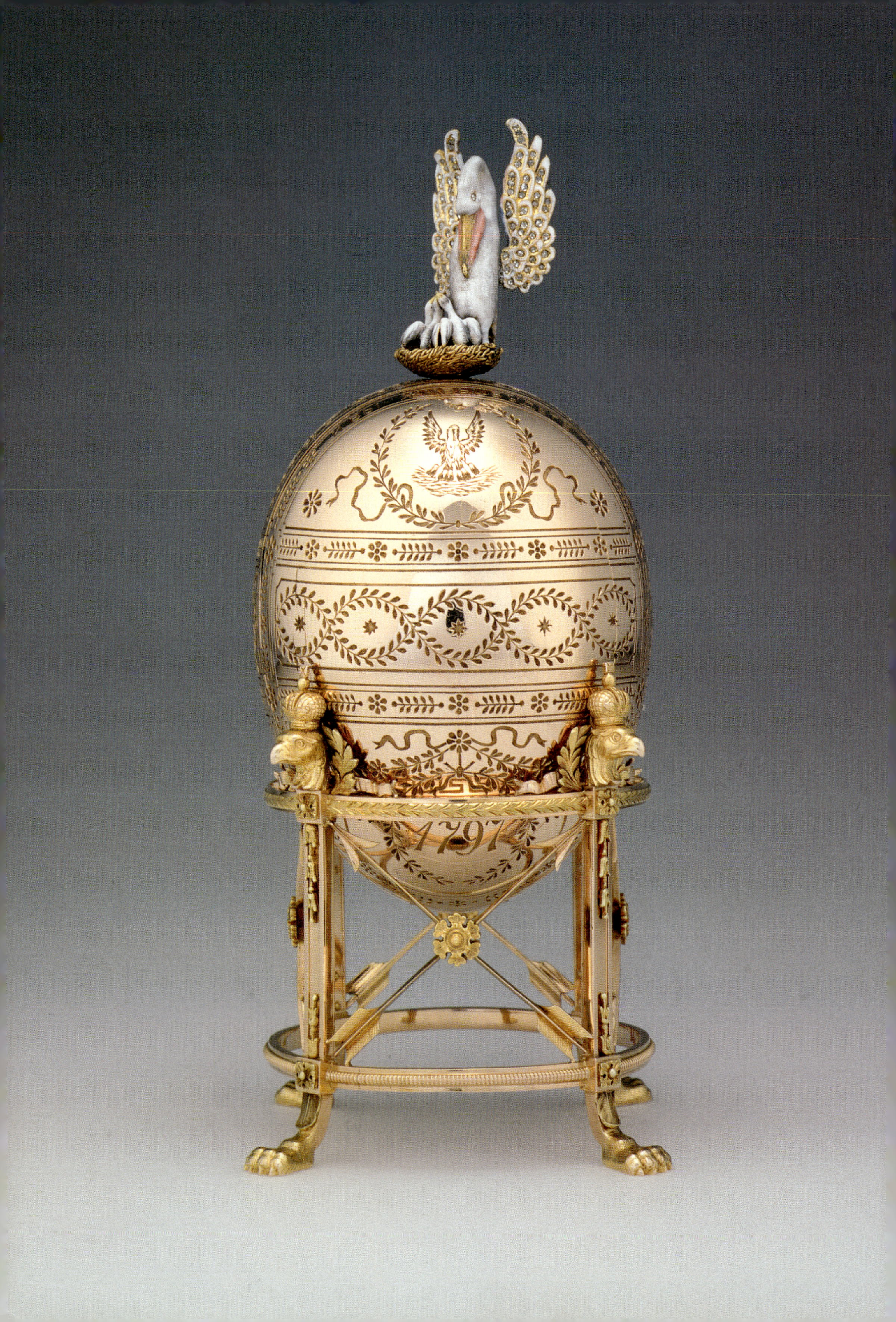
1797

INVOICE

10 April entry:

> *Gold egg, Empire style, 9 miniatures*   3600 r.
> *St Petersburg, 7 May 1898*[151]

For many years, the Pelican egg was ascribed to 1897, but the invoice found shows that this egg was in fact presented to Maria Fedorovna for Easter 1898. Although the egg separates into eight miniatures, the invoice refers to nine of them. Perhaps Fabergé considered the Pelican (the symbol of maternal love) to be the ninth miniature, as it was enamelled and painted in the fashion of many of the other miniatures.

HISTORY

1898–1917   Kept at the Anichkov Palace.

1902   Included in the charity exhibition sponsored by Empress Alexandra Fedorovna at the von Dervis mansion in St Petersburg (see page 55).
A newspaper article refers to this egg as being:

... surmounted by a diamond pelican, the Empress Maria's personal emblem, and contains small screens with miniature images of all the institutions of which Her Majesty is a patron.[152]

1917   Confiscated by Kerensky's provisional government, along with other treasures, and taken from the Anichkov Palace to the Moscow Kremlin Armoury.

Gold folding screen egg with medallions, decorated with pearls and surmounted by an enamelled swan [should read pelican], *four-legged gold pediment.*[153]

1930   Officially sold by Antikvariat for 1000 roubles.[154]

1930s   Acquired by Lillian Thomas Pratt from Hammer Galleries, New York.

18

Lilies of the Valley Egg

1898

Presented by
Tsar Nicholas II to his
wife, the Empress
Alexandra Fedorovna,
Easter 1898 (5 April)

*(The FORBES Magazine
Collection, New York)*

Both Fabergé and the Empress Maria Fedorovna loved flowers. This exquisite art nouveau style Easter egg was an ever-present reminder to her of the resplendent perfumed gardens on the Imperial palaces' grounds. The Dowager Empress described her grandchildren's delight in decorating the palace rooms with bouquets of flowers from the palace grounds:

25 May 1906
For the past four weeks we are having wonderful summer weather. Everything is green like in the month of June, and all the flowers are blooming at the same time and the lilacs are all over... Our rooms are fragrant with the smell of lilacs and birch-trees. It is delicious. My grandchildren spend the whole day in the garden and bring me back bouquets of lilies of the valley, which are plentiful. [155]

DESCRIPTION

Workmaster: Mikhail Perkhin.
Miniaturist: Johannes Zehngraf.
Surprise: Miniatures of Tsar Nicholas II in military uniform and his two daughters, the Grand Duchesses Olga and Tatiana.
Height: 7⅞ inches (20 cm).
Marks: M.P. (in Cyrillic), assay mark of the city of St Petersburg, 56.

Gold, translucent pink and green enamel, diamonds, rubies, pearls, rock crystal.

The green gold stalks, and pearl and rose-cut diamond lilies of the valley scale the sides of the rose-coloured *guilloché* enamel egg, their leaves realistically enamelled translucent green on gold. The egg is supported upon four green gold cabriole legs with tiny diamonds embedded in the leaves. The surprise, three miniature portraits of Tsar Nicholas II and Grand Duchesses Olga and Tatiana, rises out of the egg when a pearl button is turned. The diamond-set oval miniatures, by Zehngraf, are surmounted by a rose-cut diamond and cabochon ruby miniature replica of the Imperial crown. The reverse side of the miniatures is engraved with the date the Easter egg was presented, 5 IV 1898.

INVOICE

10 April entry:

> *Pink enamel egg with three portraits, leaves of green enamel*
> *and lilies of the valley of pearls and rose-cut diamonds*   6700 r.
> *St Petersburg, 7 May 1898* [156]

HISTORY

1898–1917 Kept in the study of Her Imperial Majesty Alexandra Fedorovna at the Winter Palace. It was displayed on the first shelf from the top in the corner showcase between the door leading into the bedroom and the window.

On 10 April 1909, N. Dementiev, Inspector of Premises of the Imperial Winter Palace, described this Easter egg when he inventoried articles in the Imperial family's private apartments. [157]

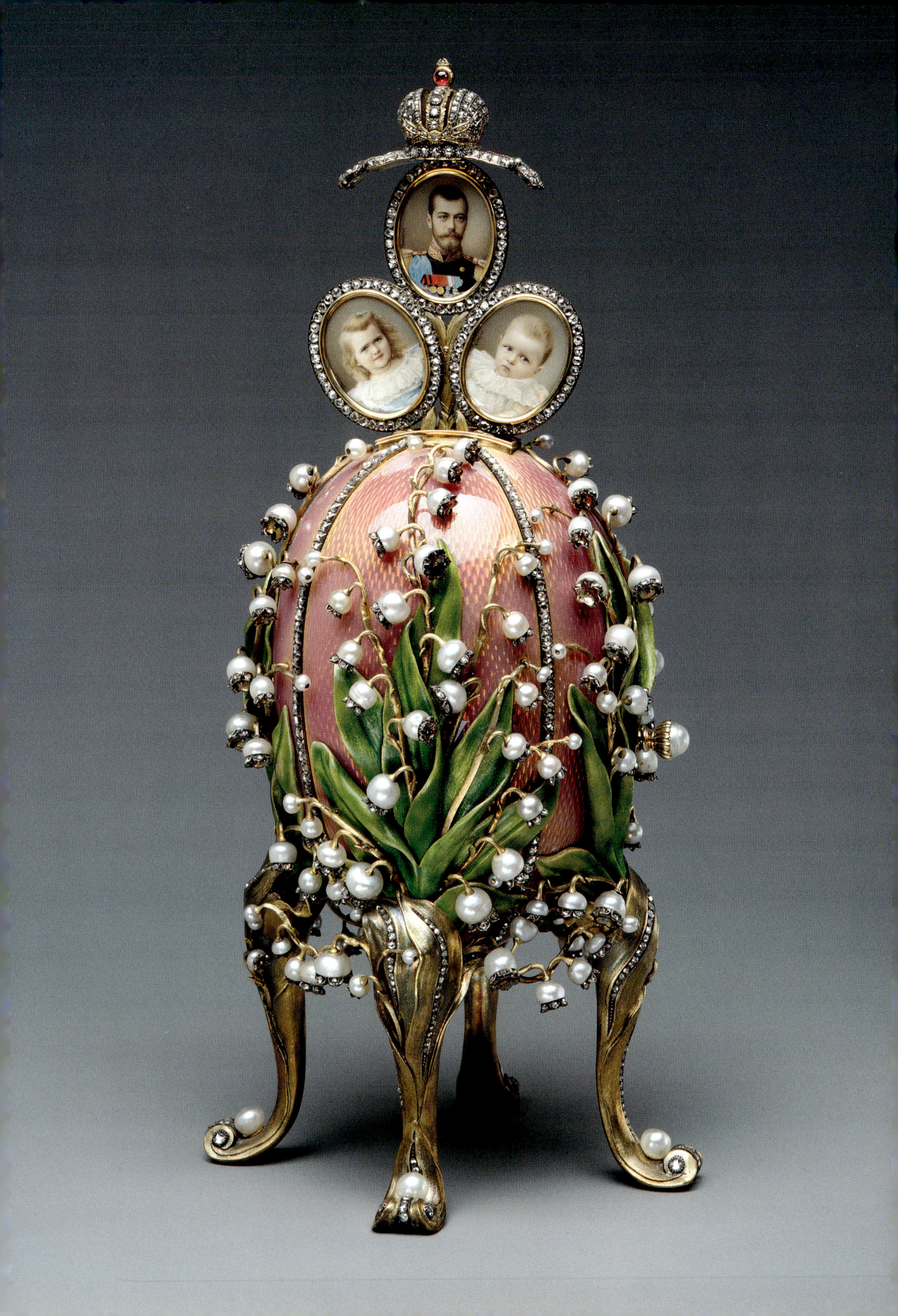

Egg covered with pink enamel, on a four-legged gold stand, the legs representing leaves of lilies of the valley, which are decorated with rose-cut diamonds: a pearl is placed at the tip of each leg. Green enamel lily of the valley leaves cover the body of the egg, and the whole is decorated with lilies of the valley made of pearls and rose-cut diamonds. The egg is surmounted by an Imperial crown made entirely of rose-cut diamonds and containing two cabochon rubies. At the side of the egg there is a button with a single pearl which, when pressed, causes the crown to rise and disclose three miniature medallions framed in rose-cut diamonds. The frames contain portraits of the Emperor Nicholas II and the Imperial children (Olga and Tatiana). The reverse side of the medallions is engraved with the figures 5-IV-98. [158]

1902 Included in the charity exhibition sponsored by Empress Alexandra Fedorovna at the von Dervis mansion in St Petersburg (see page 55). A newspaper article notes that:

The Empress Alexandra Fedorovna's collection contains an egg containing a miniature bouquet of lilies of the valley, surrounded by moss: the flowers are made of pearls, the leaves of nephrite, and the moss of finest gold strands. [159]

At the exhibition, the Lilies of the Valley Easter egg was placed near the Lilies of the Valley Basket (now in the New Orleans Museum of Art: Matilda Geddings Gray Foundation Collection) and it is that basket that is lined with the moss of 'finest gold strands' referred to by the journalist. The egg is not surrounded by moss, so the journalist has confused these two similarly designed objects.

1917 Not accounted for in any of the inventories of Imperial treasures confiscated by Kerensky's provisional government.

1979 Acquired by Forbes Inc. from Wartski (together with the 1897 Coronation egg (16)) for $2.16 million (see page 132).

19

1899

Pansy Egg

Presented by
Tsar Nicholas II to his
mother, the Dowager
Empress Maria Fedorovna,
Easter 1899 (18 April)

(Private Collection, USA)

DESCRIPTION

Workmaster: Mikhail Perkhin.
Surprise: Heart-shaped frame on a gold easel with eleven miniatures.
Height: Egg: 5¾ inches (14.6 cm).
Marks: Assay mark of St Petersburg regional assay department, 88.

Nephrite, silver-gilt, diamonds, white, red, green and violet enamel.

The polished and carved nephrite art nouveau style Easter egg is decorated with violet enamelled pansies, their lower petals encrusted with rose-cut diamonds. A silver-gilt base of spiralling and twisting leaves and twigs supports the egg which opens to reveal a magnificent varicoloured gold easel upon which sits an exquisite diamond-set translucent white *guilloché* enamel heart with eleven tiny miniatures. The heart-shaped frame is bordered with rose-cut diamonds and surmounted with a diamond-set Imperial crown. At the pinnacle of the easel is a diamond-set Star of Bethlehem surrounded by a gold wreath and the year 1899.

Each strawberry-red enamel cover is monogrammed with the initials of a member of the Imperial family, whose miniature portrait is revealed when opened. Reading from left to right and top to bottom, the portraits depict: Tsarevich Georgii Alexandrovich, younger brother of Tsar Nicholas II; Grand Duke Alexander Mikhailovich, husband of Grand Duchess Xenia Alexandrovna, the Tsar's sister; Tsar Nicholas II; Princess Irina Alexandrovna, subsequently Princess Yusupov, daughter of Grand Duke Alexander Mikhailovich and Grand Duchess Xenia Alexandrovna; Grand Duchess Olga Nikolaievna, the first child of the Emperor and the Empress; Grand Duchess Tatiana Nikolaievna, their second child; Grand Duke Mikhail Alexandrovich, youngest brother of the Tsar; the Empress; Prince Andrei Alexandrovich, brother of Princess Irina; and Grand Duchesses Olga Alexandrovna and Xenia Alexandrovna, sisters of the Tsar.

INVOICE

> *Easter egg, with pansies, containing a heart with
> the monogram 'M' and a crown of rose-cut diamonds,
> 11 miniatures, diamonds and rose-cut diamonds.*   5600 r.
> *St Petersburg, 17 July 1899* [160]

HISTORY

1899–1917 Kept at the Anichkov Palace.

1900 Exhibited at the *Exposition Universelle*, the Paris World Fair.

1902 Included in the charity exhibition sponsored by the Empress Alexandra Fedorovna at the von Dervis mansion in St Petersburg (see pages 54-55). The egg is described as follows in a newspaper article:

> *... the exhibits belonging to the Empress Maria Fedorovna include a group of family portraits (miniatures) of the Emperor, the Empress Alexandra Fedorovna and the August son, daughter and grandchildren of Her Majesty the Empress Maria Fedorovna. The miniatures are arranged in a precious heart-shaped frame, placed on an easel. Each portrait, no bigger than a silver five-kopek piece is surmounted by a ruby.* [161]

Another newspaper covering the exhibition also mentions the Pansy Easter egg:

In the showcase with articles belonging to Her Majesty the Empress Maria Fedorovna, one's special attention is attracted to a heart-shaped silver portrait frame, decorated with precious stones. This frame, not more than 5 cm high, contains a multitude of miniature portraits of members of the Imperial Family, each no bigger than a split-pea, but so exquisitely painted that it is in no way inferior to a full-size detailed portrait. The impression is that these miniatures were painted by some Lilliputian artist. [162]

1917 Confiscated by Kerensky's provisional government, along with other treasures, and taken from the Anichkov Palace to the Moscow Kremlin Armoury.

Jasper egg, with gold mounting, decorated with diamonds; containing a small heart-shaped gold screen under a crown, decorated with diamond monograms in red enamel medallions. [163]

1930 Officially sold by Antikvariat for 7,500 roubles. [164]

1947 Purchased by Matilda Geddings Gray and given to her niece on the occasion of her first wedding anniversary in 1947.

141

Bouquet of Lilies Clock Egg

1899

Presented by Tsar Nicholas II to his wife, the Empress Alexandra Fedorovna, Easter 1899 (18 April)

(Moscow Kremlin Armoury Museum)

Description

Workmaster: Mikhail Perkhin.
Surprise: Ruby and rose-cut diamond pendant egg (now missing).
Height: 10⅝ inches (27 cm).
Marks: FABERGÉ, M.P. (in Cyrillic), assay mark of St Petersburg regional assay department, 56 and Y.L. (initials of St Petersburg Standard Board regional manager and inspector, Yakov Lyapunov).

Gold, platinum, rose-cut diamonds, chalcedony, *guilloché* enamel.

The elegance and grandeur of this Louis XVI style yellow-gold *guilloché* enamel clock makes it one of Fabergé's most distinctive Easter eggs. The shape of the clock egg, which sits on an enamelled gold scrolled rectangular base bearing the date '1899' in diamonds, forms a vase crowned with a delicate bouquet of lilies carved from chalcedony. The pistils of the flowers are set with three small diamonds, with the leaves and stems carved in green gold. The body of the enamelled egg is mounted on both sides with varicoloured gold scrolls, and divides into twelve panels outlined by diamond-set strips. The white opaque enamel ribbon-dial is inlaid with twelve diamond-set Roman numerals which revolves round the perimeter of the egg. A drawn diamond-studded bow and arrow indicates the time. The miniature ruby and rose-cut diamond pendant surprise that originally hung from the egg has since disappeared. The clock mechanism was wound with a fluted gold key.

Invoice

1 Easter egg, Louis XVI clock, yellow enamel with rose-cut diamonds, bouquet of lilies of white chalcedony and ruby pendant egg with rose-cut diamonds   6750 r.
St Petersburg, 17 July 1899 [165]

History

1899–1917 Kept in the study of Her Imperial Majesty Alexandra Fedorovna at the Winter Palace. It was displayed on the second shelf from the top in the corner showcase between the door leading into the bedroom and the window.

On 10 April 1909, N. Dementiev, Inspector of Premises of the Imperial Winter Palace, described this Easter egg when he inventoried articles in the Imperial family's private apartments. [166]

The Clock egg consists of a vase of flowers in Louis XVI style. The egg is covered with orange enamel with 12 vertical strips of rose-cut diamonds. The clock face is a horizontal band of white enamel between two strips of rose-cut diamonds, and the figures are made of rose-cut diamonds. The top of the egg bears a rosette of laurel leaves made of green gold; above this rosette is a collar of smooth red gold, surmounted by a wreath of red and yellow gold and platinum roses with green gold leaves. Above this wreath is a bouquet with green gold stems and leaves and flowers of light-coloured agate with hearts of gold and roses. The egg is supported on both sides by ornamental handles of green and red gold studded with roses... The lower part of the egg is placed on a green gold rosette resting on an orange enamel neck decorated with one band of roses and six vertical rose strips... The clock-egg is mounted on a rectangular pedestal made of gold and covered with orange enamel, with decorations of red and

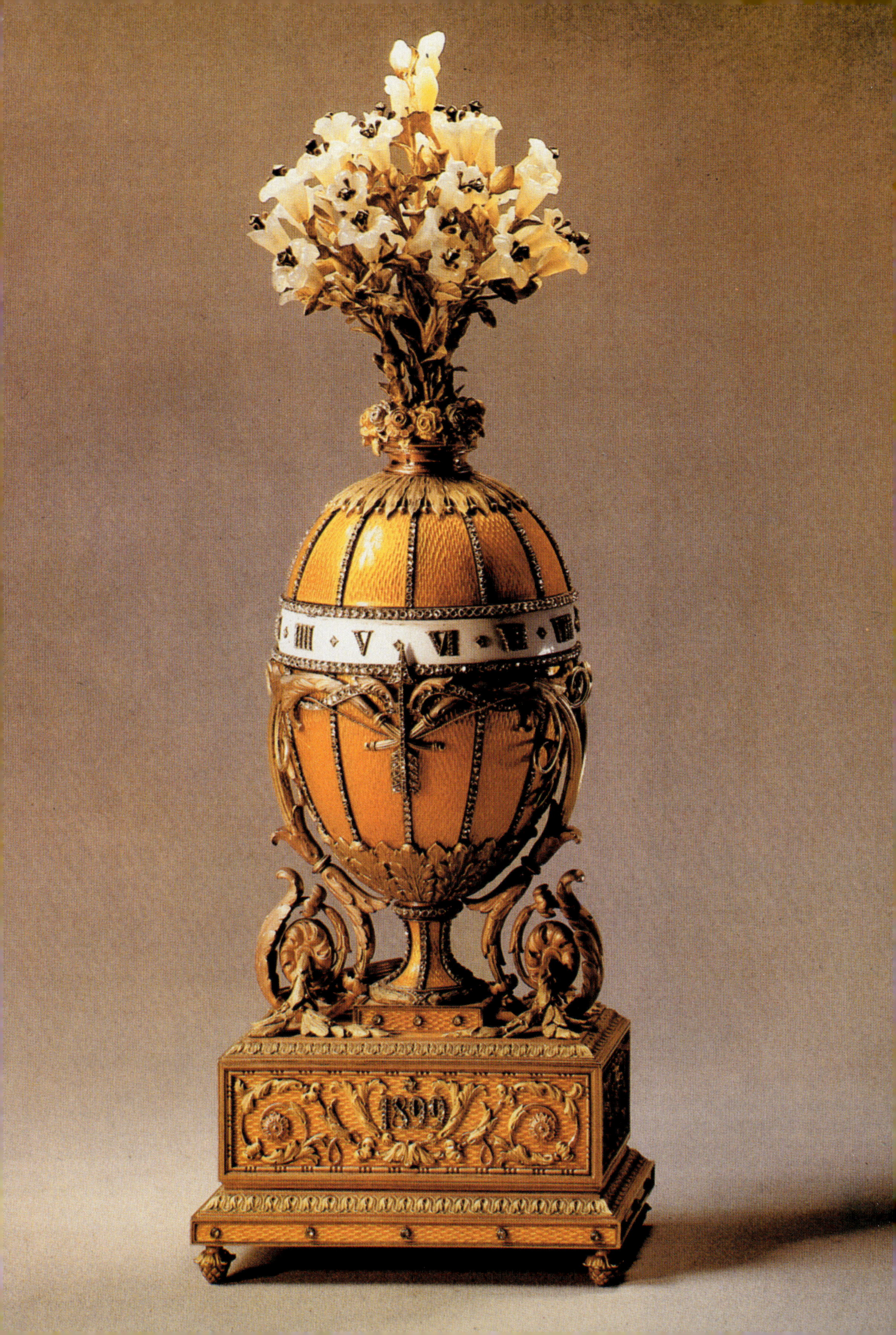
1899

green gold. The base pediment of enamel is studded with 16 rose-cut diamonds. One side of the pedestal bears the date 1899 picked out in rose-cut diamonds and surmounted by a star consisting of one rose-cut diamond. The pedestal rests on four short legs of green and red gold. [167]

1917 Confiscated by Kerensky's provisional government, along with other treasures, and taken from the Anichkov Palace to the Moscow Kremlin.

1922 One of the items on the list of treasures transferred from the Anichkov Palace to the Sovnarkom, may be the Bouquet of Lilies Clock egg:

1 gold clock in the form of a vase with rose-cut diamonds [168]

Antikvariat did not sell the Bouquet of Lilies Clock egg and it remained in Russia.

Early Fabergé photograph of the Bouquet of Lilies Clock egg pictured with the original ruby pendant egg surprise (now missing).

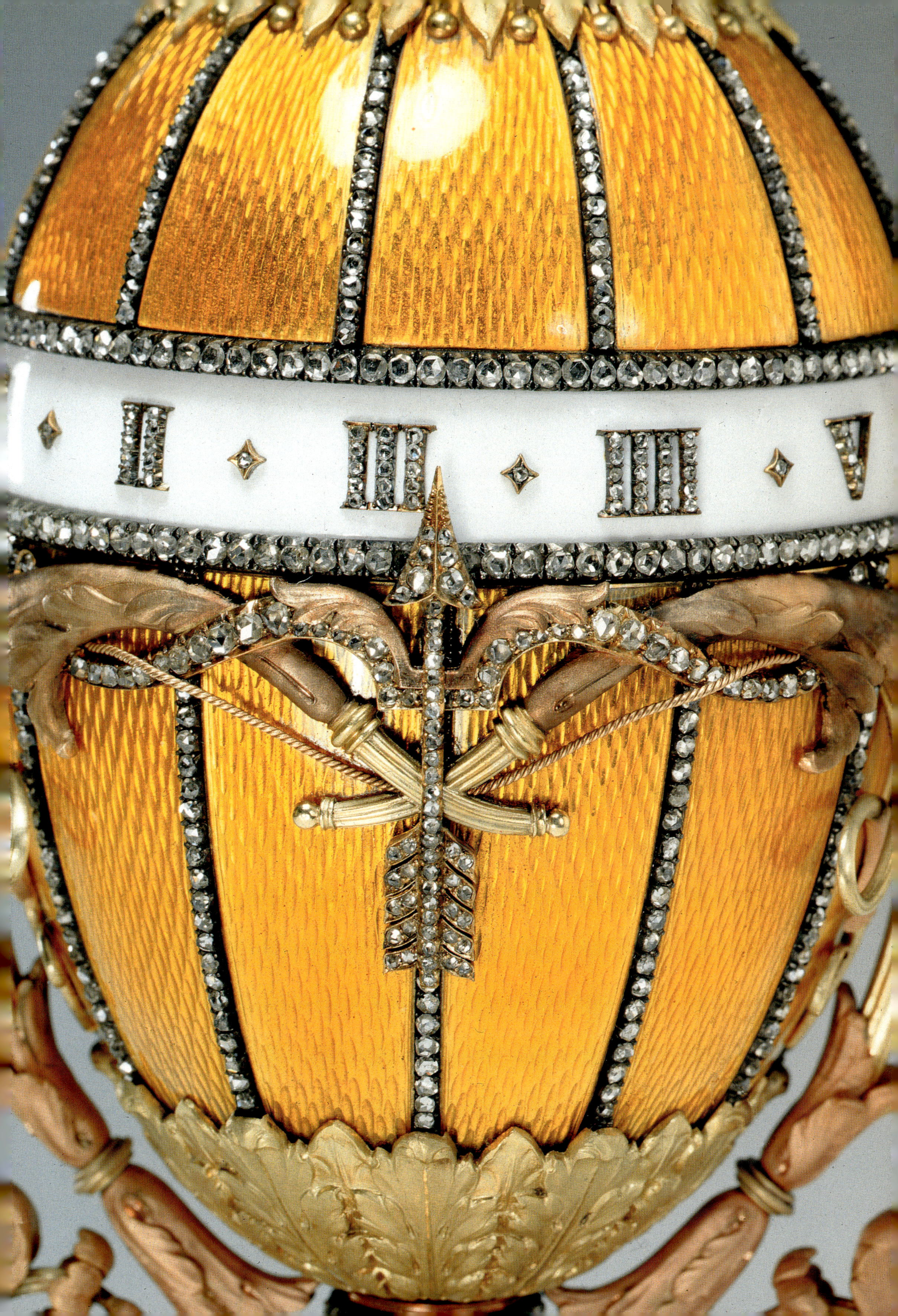

1900

21

Cockerel Egg

Presented by
Tsar Nicholas II to his
mother, the Dowager
Empress Maria Fedorovna,
Easter 1900 (9 April)

*(The FORBES Magazine
Collection, New York)*

The famous ormolu automaton Peacock Clock in the Winter Palace, made by James Cox (d. 1788), was the inspiration for both the Cockerel egg, formerly referred to as the Cuckoo egg, and the 1908 Peacock egg (33). For over 20 years, Carl Fabergé gave his time and expertise, voluntarily and without recompense, to the Hermitage, repairing, restoring, and classifying its treasures. Fabergé, together with a mechanic, were known to have examined and repaired the mechanism of the automaton Peacock Clock, and familiarity with the large-scale mechanical work of art led to the design, in miniature, of the 1900 Imperial Cockerel Easter egg.

DESCRIPTION

Workmaster: Mikhail Perkhin.
Surprise: Cockerel emerges crowing and flapping its wings when a button is pressed.
Height: 8 inches – open (20.3 cm).
Marks: FABERGÉ, M.P. (in Cyrillic), assay mark of St Petersburg regional assay department, 56.

Varicoloured gold, translucent violet and green enamel, opalescent white and oyster enamel, opaque lilac enamel, diamonds, rubies, pearls, feathers.

The elaborately designed Cockerel egg table clock is enamelled in translucent violet over a *guilloché* wavy patterned ground. The clock face, which is surrounded by pearls and white enamel, features rose-cut diamond numerals and red-gold clock hands. When the button is pressed, a gold grille at the top of the egg opens up, and the surprise, a naturally plumed and feathered cockerel, rises out of the egg, perched on a gold platform, crowing while its beak opens and shuts and its wings flap. The bird descends into the egg once the crowing has ceased and the grille closes shut. The date 1900 is inscribed beneath a portrait diamond on top of the grille. The base is beautifully worked in gold with swags and trellis designs; three large rose-cut diamonds and three gold and white enamelled *torchères* help support the egg.

INVOICE

*Easter egg of violet enamel, with cockerel and clock,
with one lozenge diamond, 188 rose-cut diamonds,
2 rubies*   6500 r.
St Petersburg, 13 January 1901[169]

Fabergé usually sent his bill for an egg to the Cabinet or the Ministry of the Court almost immediately after delivery, at any rate within one or two months at the most. However, Fabergé's bill for this particular egg (and The Trans-Siberian Railway egg (22) made in the same year) was not received by the Imperial Cabinet until January 1901 – an unprecedented delay of eight months. This was probably due to the fact that Fabergé was away from St Petersburg for an extended period of time. He participated as a member of the expert commission of the 1900 World Exhibition in Paris which ran from April to November. It was on this occasion that Fabergé was awarded the presitigious French order of the Legion of Honour.

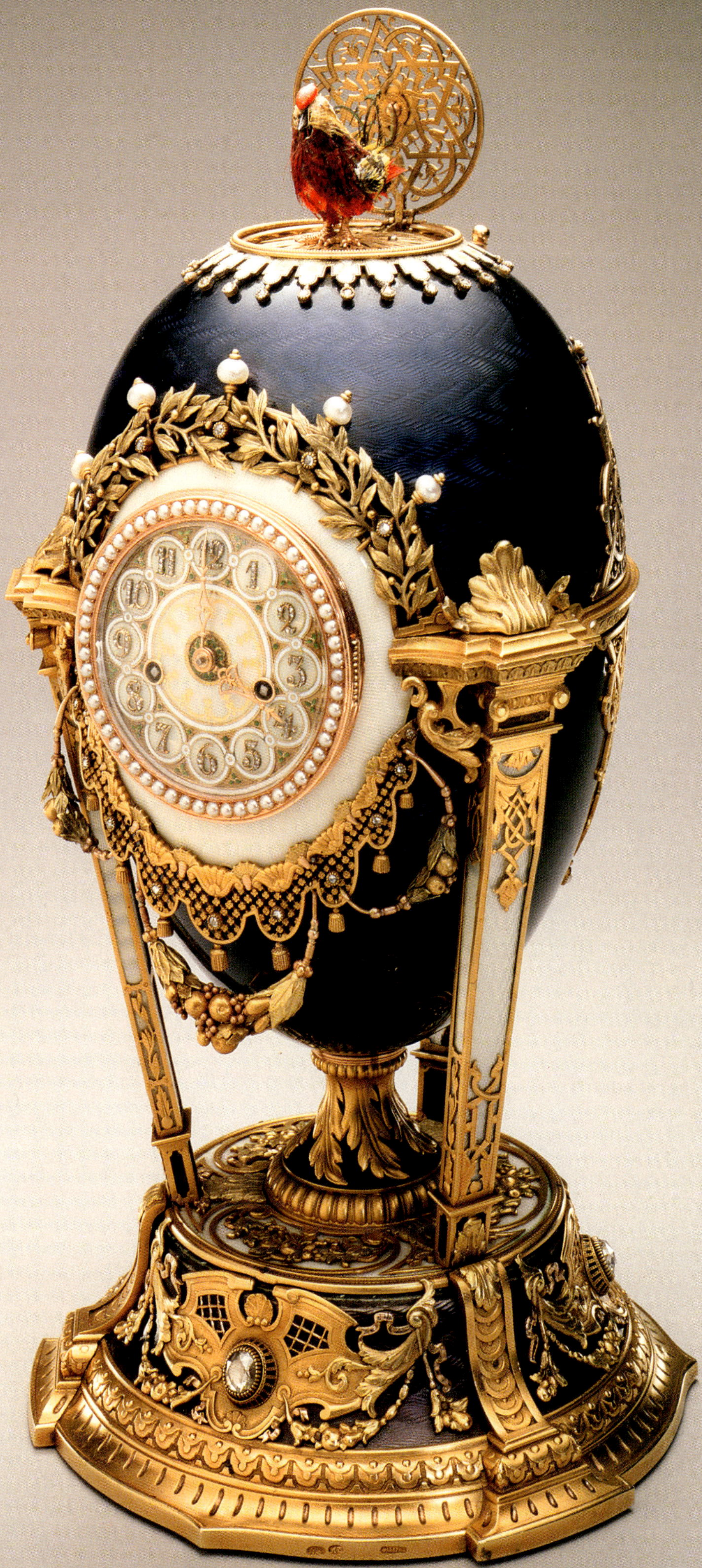

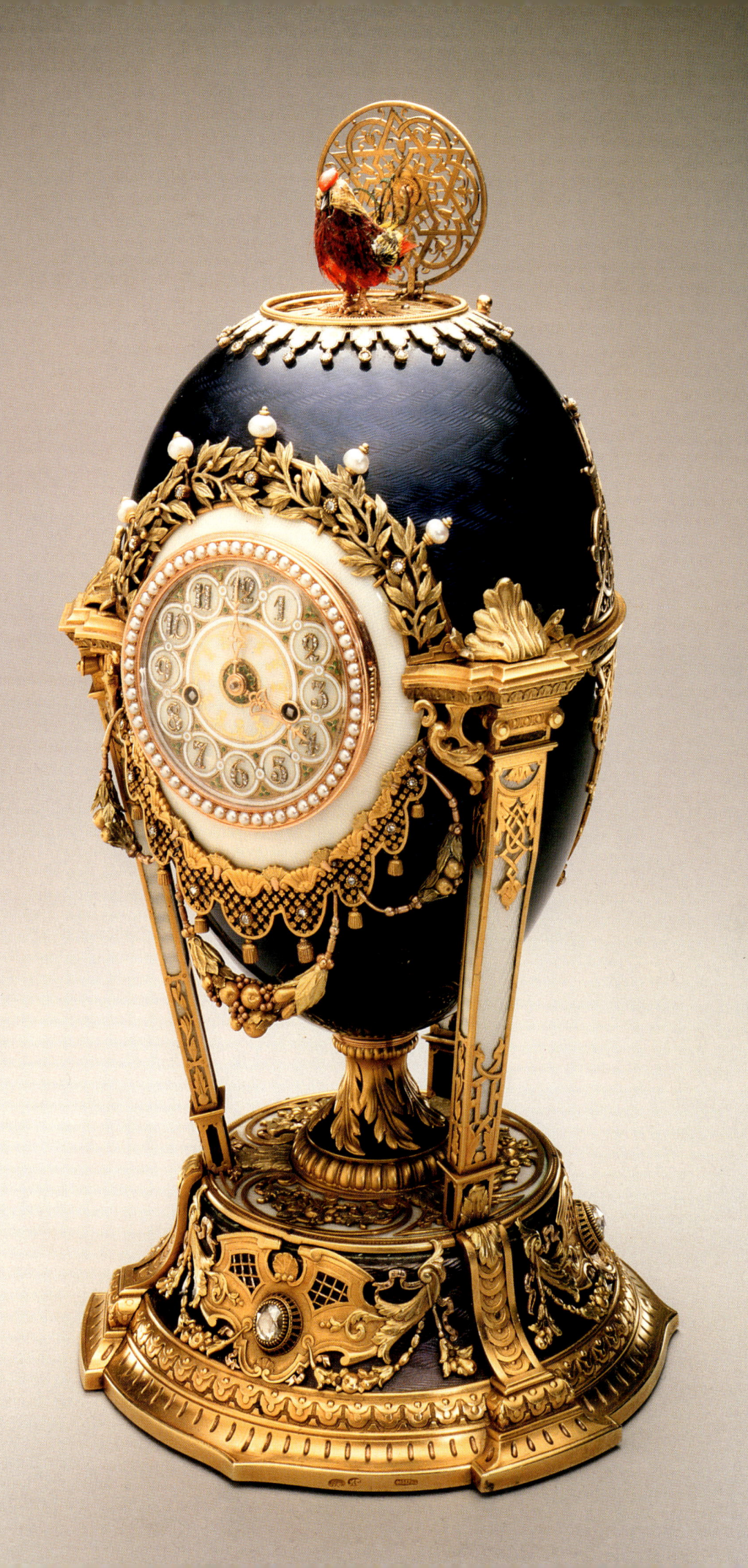

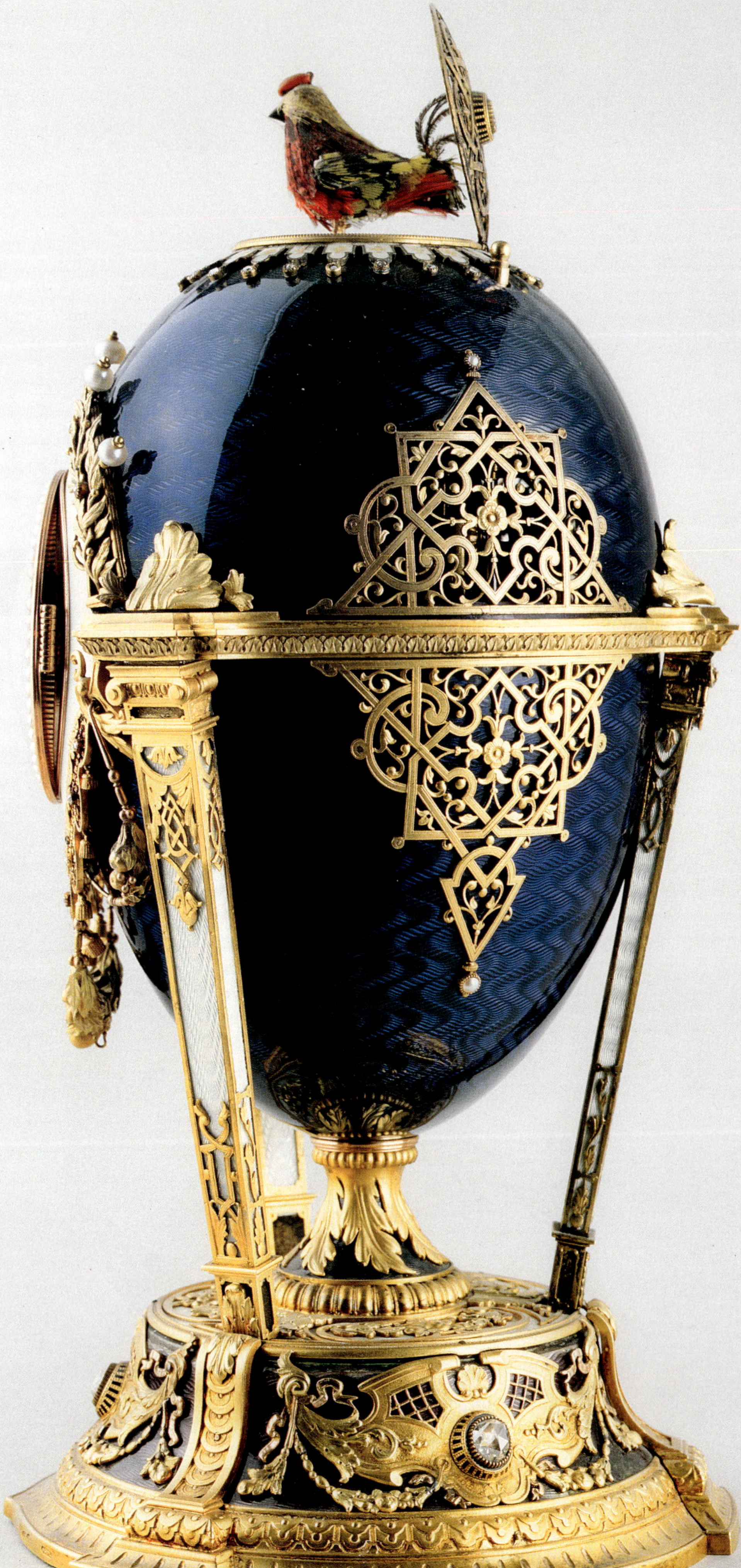

HISTORY

1900–1917 Kept at the Anichkov Palace.

1917 Confiscated by Kerensky's provisional government, along with other treasures, and taken from the Anichkov Palace to the Moscow Kremlin Armoury.

Clock in the form of an egg of violet enamel, on tripod, decorated with pearls and diamonds. [170]

1973 Sold as the Cuckoo Egg at Christie's, Geneva, 20 November, for SFr 620,000.

1979 Sold at Christie's, New York, for $354,287 to Mr and Mrs Bernard C. Solomon, Beverly Hills, California.

11 June 1985 Sold as the Cuckoo Egg at Sotheby's, New York for $1.76 million to Mr Forbes ($1,905,200). [171]

Early Fabergé photograph of Cockerel egg

22

1900

Trans-Siberian Railway Egg

Presented by
Tsar Nicholas II to his
wife, the Empress
Alexandra Fedorovna,
Easter 1900 (9 April)

*(Moscow Kremlin Armoury
Museum)*

In 1891, while Nicholas II was still the heir to the throne, his father, Alexander III, arranged for him to sail on the Imperial cruiser *Memory of Azov* to the Far East, where he visited India, China, and Japan. On his return to Russia, he called in at the naval port of Vladivostok, where he laid the foundation stone at the eastern terminus of the Trans-Siberian Railway, which linked European and Asian parts of Russia, in particular the cities of St Petersburg and Moscow with the naval port of Vladivostok.

In 1900 the railway line was almost complete and the Trans-Siberian Easter egg commemorated this great feat of engineering. The silver egg was decorated with the route of the Trans-Siberian Railway, the sections of line that had not yet been completed being indicated by dotted lines.

DESCRIPTION

Workmaster: Mikhail Perkhin.
Surprise: Miniature working model of a train.
Dimensions: Height of egg: 10¼ inches (26 cm); Height of coach: 1⅛ inches (2.6 cm); Length of train: 15¾ inches (39.8 cm).
Marks: FABERGÉ, M.P. (in Cyrillic), assay mark of St Petersburg regional assay department, 56 and Y.L. (initials of St Petersburg Standard Board regional assay manager and inspector, Yakov Lyapunov).

Gold, platinum, silver, rose-cut diamonds, ruby, onyx, rock crystal, wood, *guilloché* enamel, velvet.

The egg is divided into three parts. The central silver section is engraved with the map of Russia and the route of the Trans-Siberian Railway. It bears the inscription 'The route of the Grand Siberian Railway in the year 1900'. The top and lower portions of the egg are decorated in translucent green enamel over gold, applied with blue and orange enamel mounts. A three-sided gold-plated silver heraldic eagle, bearing the Imperial crown, rises from the lid. The egg is supported by three Romanov griffins cast in gold-plated silver, each brandishing a sword and shield and mounted on a white onyx triangular-form stepped base.

An exquisitely detailed working model of the train is inserted into the egg, section by section. Its platinum locomotive, with ruby lantern and rosette headlights, pulls five gold coaches, their windows made of rock-crystal. The coaches are engraved with inscriptions identifying their various functions. The first coach reads: 'Siberia through train'; the second, third and fourth coaches: 'Ladies', 'Smokers' and 'Non-smokers'. Additional information and designations are also engraved on the coaches. They are: on the second: '2nd class, 24 seats'; and on the third and fourth: '1st class, 18 seats'. The fifth, and last coach, is designated 'Chapel'. The train, when wound with a tiny gold key, ran for several metres.

INVOICE

*Easter egg of green enamel, with Siberian
train, ruby, pearls and rose-cut diamonds*   7000 r.
St Petersburg, 13 January 1901 [172]

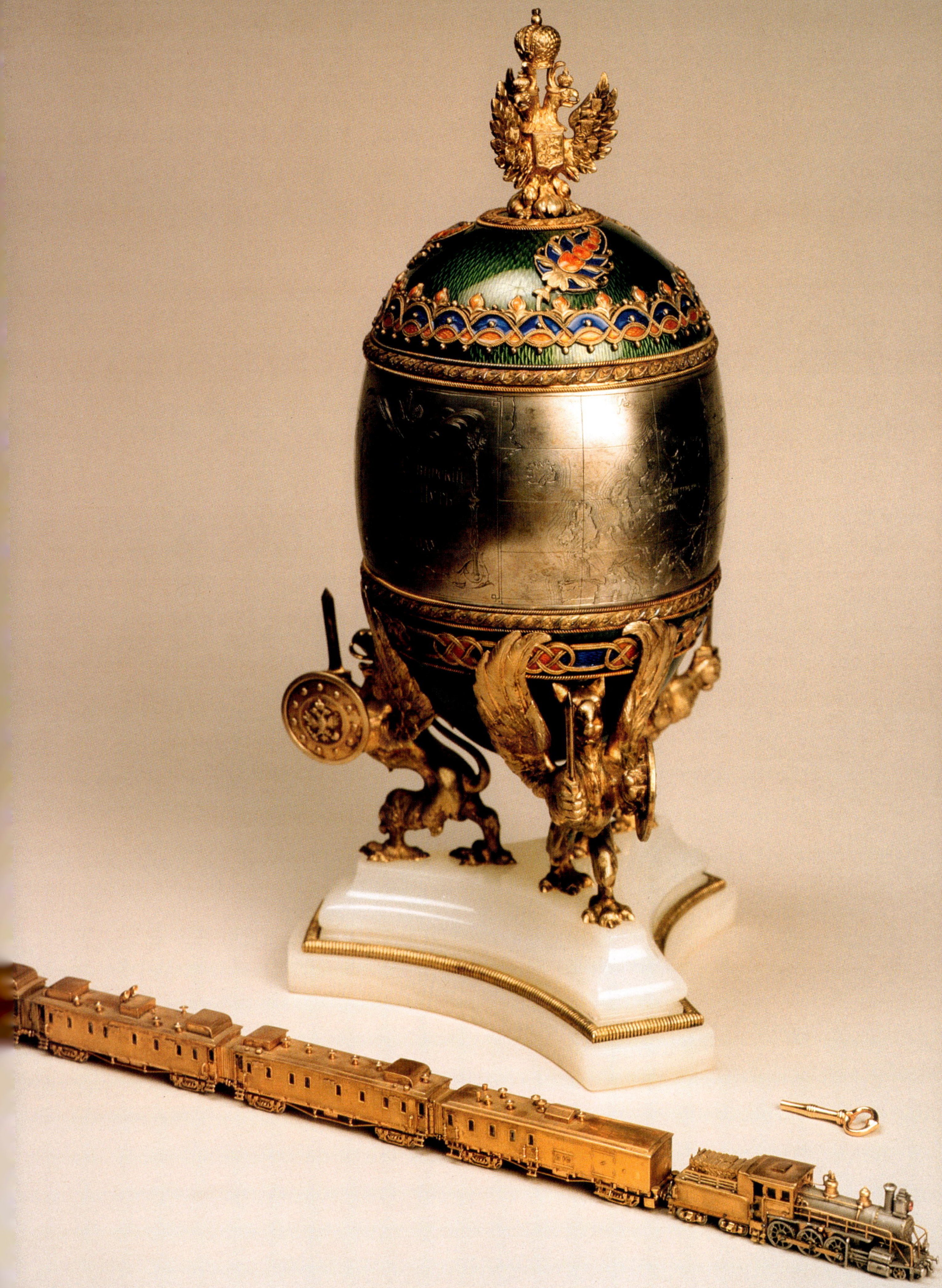

History

1900–1917 Kept in the study of Her Imperial Majesty Alexandra Fedorovna at the Winter Palace. It was displayed on the first shelf from the top in the corner showcase between the door leading into the bedroom and the window.

On 10 April 1909, N. Dementiev, Inspector of Premises of the Imperial Winter Palace, described this Easter egg when he inventoried articles in the Imperial family's private apartments.[173]

Silver egg on a triangular white onyx pedestal, the rim of the pedestal of ribbed silver gilt. The pedestal bears three gilded griffins supporting an egg on their wings. The central part of the egg is made of silvered metal engraved with a map of Siberia, in the middle of which appears an engraved coat of arms surmounted by a crown and bearing the inscription 'The Great Siberian Railway, 1900'. The lower part of the egg and its lid are covered with green enamel and blue and orange enamel decorations. The lower rims of the lid and of the middle part of the egg are bordered with green and red gold. The lid is surmounted by a silver-gilt figure of a three-sided eagle under a crown. Inside the egg is a velvet case containing models of five carriages and a locomotive. The carriages and the tender are made of gold, and the locomotive of platinum. The overhead light of the locomotive is represented by a ruby and the model is accompanied by a gold key. [174]

1902 Included in the charity exhibition sponsored by the Empress Alexandra Fedorovna at the von Dervis mansion in St Petersburg (see page 55). The Trans-Siberian Railway egg is described in a newspaper article as follows:

Another interesting article is the gold miniature of the Trans-Siberian railway – Direct line to Siberia – which has been taken out of its special egg and is shown separately. The train consists of several carriages attached to one another, each no more ⅔ of an inch long, the last being a model of the church-carriage used on the Siberian railway. The workmanship of this exquisite little object is so fine that it gives an accurate idea of the composition of the Siberian express train, down to the carriages labelled 'Smokers' and 'Non-smokers'. [175]

Another newspaper article covering the exhibition states:

... the Empress Alexandra Fedorovna's collection includes... an egg containing a whole miniature train of the Great Siberian Railway... [176]

1917 Confiscated by Kerensky's provisional government, along with other treasures, and taken from the Anichkov Palace to the Moscow Kremlin Armoury.

1922 One of the items on the list of treasures transferred from the Anichkov Palace to the Sovnarkom.

1 silver egg with gold model of a railway train. [177]

The Trans-Siberian Railway egg was not sold by Antikvariat to the West and remained in Russia.

С.-ПЕТЕРБУРГЪ
МОСКВА
УФА
ОМСКЪ
САМАРА

23
Gatchina Palace Egg

1901

Presented by
Tsar Nicholas II to his
mother, the Dowager
Empress Maria Fedorovna,
Easter 1901 (1 April)

(The Walters Art Gallery, Baltimore)

The Gatchina Palace was the Dowager Empress. favourite winter residence. This egg reminded her of it whenever the Court removed to another palace.

Description

Workmaster: Mikhail Perkhin.
Surprise: Replica of the Gatchina Palace.
Height: 5 inches (12.7 cm).

Gold, varicoloured gold, green, red, yellow and white enamel and pearls.

Regarded as one of Fabergé's best compositions, this superb, delicate egg, is enamelled opalescent white, the shell engraved on a gold moiré *guilloché* ground. It is divided vertically into six panels by strips of tiny seed pearls and horizontally at its hinged centre. The sections are decorated with pink ribbon-tied swags and roses from which hang classical motifs and symbols of the arts and sciences, endeavours actively encouraged by the Dowager Empress. When the egg is opened, a wonderfully rendered model of the Gatchina Palace near St Petersburg, is revealed. It is modelled in four-coloured gold; the minutely detailed exterior includes diminutive trees, bridges and a cannon. Under the model of the palace, a velvet-lined space originally concealed some precious jewel, now lost.

Invoice

*Easter egg, white enamel, 1 large rose-cut diamond,
1 lozenge diamond and pearls, with Gatchina Palace*   5000 r.
St Petersburg, 16 April 1901 [178]

History

1901–1917 Kept at the Anichkov Palace.

1902 Included in the charity exhibition sponsored by the Empress Alexandra Fedorovna at the von Dervis mansion in St Petersburg (see pages 54-55). The Gatchina Palace Easter egg was mentioned in a newspaper article as follows:

... a third [Easter egg] of gold, containing a picture of Her Majesty's winter residence, the Gatchina Palace. [179]

Another newspaper covering the exhibition writes:

Most of these exhibits are precious Easter eggs made by the jeweller Fabergé: one of them contains a superbly fashioned gold model of the Gatchina Palace no more than an inch high. [180]

1930 Bought by Henry C. Walters (1848–1931) of Baltimore, together with the Rose Trellis egg (32) from the antiques dealer Alexander Polovtsov, a Russian emigré in Paris. Polovtsov, a former superintendant at the Gatchina Palace, left Russia in 1921, and shortly afterwards was in business in Paris selling Russian treasures. Mr Walters, a railroad baron and an avid art collector, bequeathed his collection to the Walters Art Gallery, Baltimore, which was founded by his father.

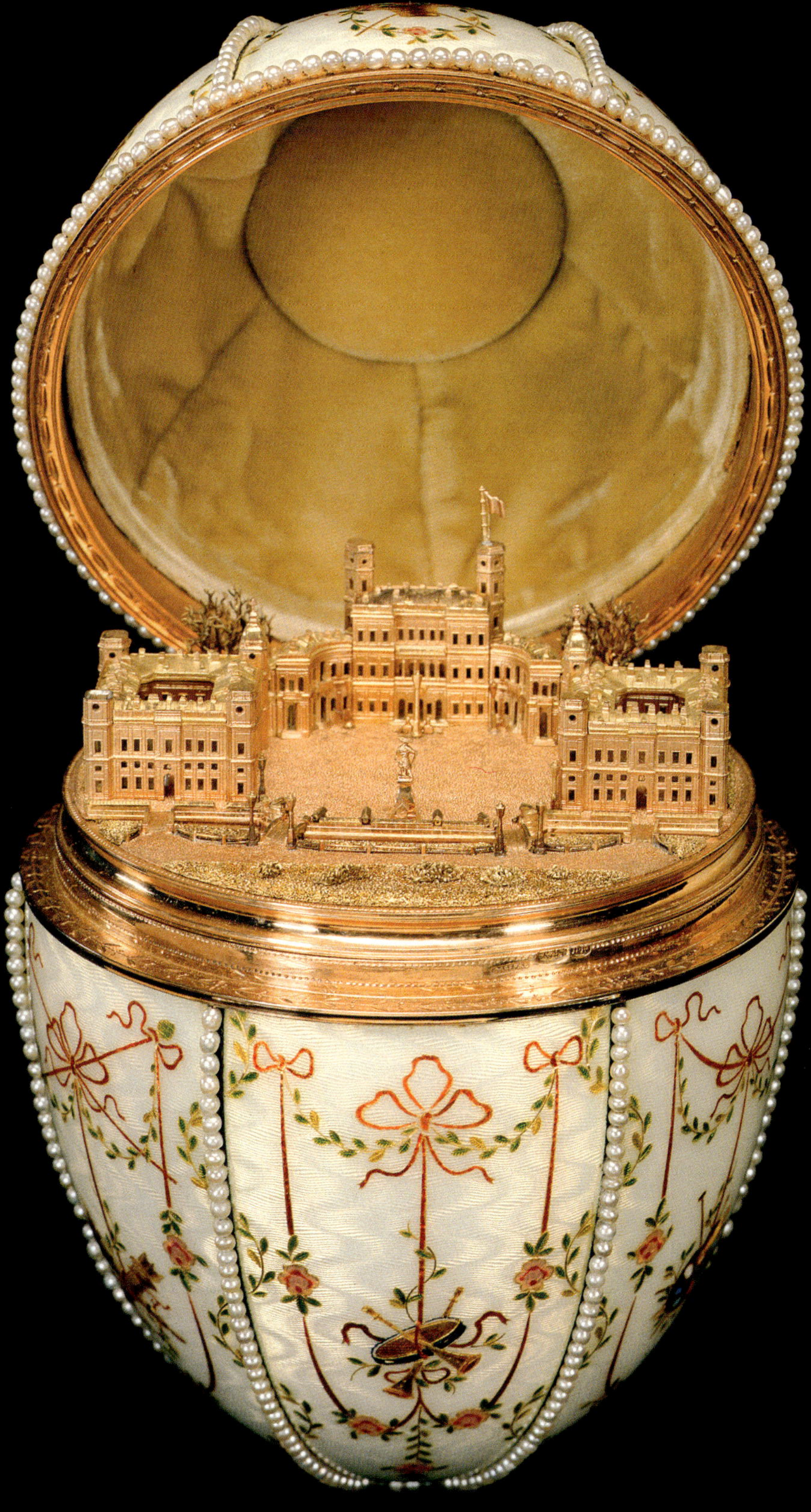

24

Basket of Wild Flowers Egg

1901

Presented by
Tsar Nicholas II to his
wife, the Empress
Alexandra Fedorovna,
Easter 1901 (1 April)

*(Collection of Her Majesty
Queen Elizabeth II)*

Description

Height: 9 inches (23 cm).
Marks: Apparently unmarked.

Silver, parcel-gilt, oyster *guilloché* and blue enamel, rose-cut diamonds.

This delightful Easter egg is designed as a vase containing a profusion of wild flowers, which are enamelled on gold in a variety of colours; the leaves and moss are of gold. The oyster *guilloché* and blue enamel egg is embellished with a delicate trellis design applied with rose-cut diamonds. The basket handle is mounted with numerous rose-cut diamonds. The neck of the vase bears the date 1901 in rose-cut diamonds set in silver.

In a photograph taken at the 1902 von Dervis mansion exhibition, the entire body of the egg, including the base, is enamelled white. Between then and 1949, when H.C. Bainbridge illustrated it in his book, the colour of the enamel on the pedestal had changed from white to blue. The egg's base had most probably been re-enamelled due to the damaged it sustained after the Revolution. In 1933, the damage was recorded: 'The enamel on the leaves and in two places on the basket is damaged'.[181]

Invoice

*Easter egg, white enamel. Basket with bouquet of wild flowers,
with 4176 rose-cut diamonds and 10 pearls*   6850 r.
St Petersburg, 16 April 1901[182]

Until the recent discovery of this invoice by the authors, the egg's Imperial provenance was doubted. Even Henry Charles Bainbridge, the manager of the firm's London branch, was misinformed. This is not as strange as it may sound, as Bainbridge was far removed from the St Petersburg shop. It is well known that the Imperial Easter eggs were made under a cloud of secrecy, and known only to those who were directly involved in their production. Bainbridge writes:

This is not an Imperial Easter Egg, and for whom it was made is not known.[183]

History

1901–1917 Kept in the study of Her Imperial Majesty Alexandra Fedorovna at the Winter Palace. It was displayed on the second shelf from the top in the corner showcase between the door leading into the bedroom and the window.

On 10 April 1909, N. Dementiev, Inspector of Premises of the Imperial Winter Palace, described this Easter egg when he inventoried articles in the Imperial family's private apartments.[184]

Vase in the form of a basket-egg, entirely covered with white enamel. The body, stem and pediment are decorated with a design representing an interlacing lattice made entirely of rose-cut diamonds. The vase has a horseshoe-shaped handle decorated with bows, the whole made of rose-cut diamonds. The vase is filled with moss of green gold, in which there is a bouquet of wild flowers made of different-coloured enamel. The vase bears the date 1901 picked out in rose-cut diamonds.[185]

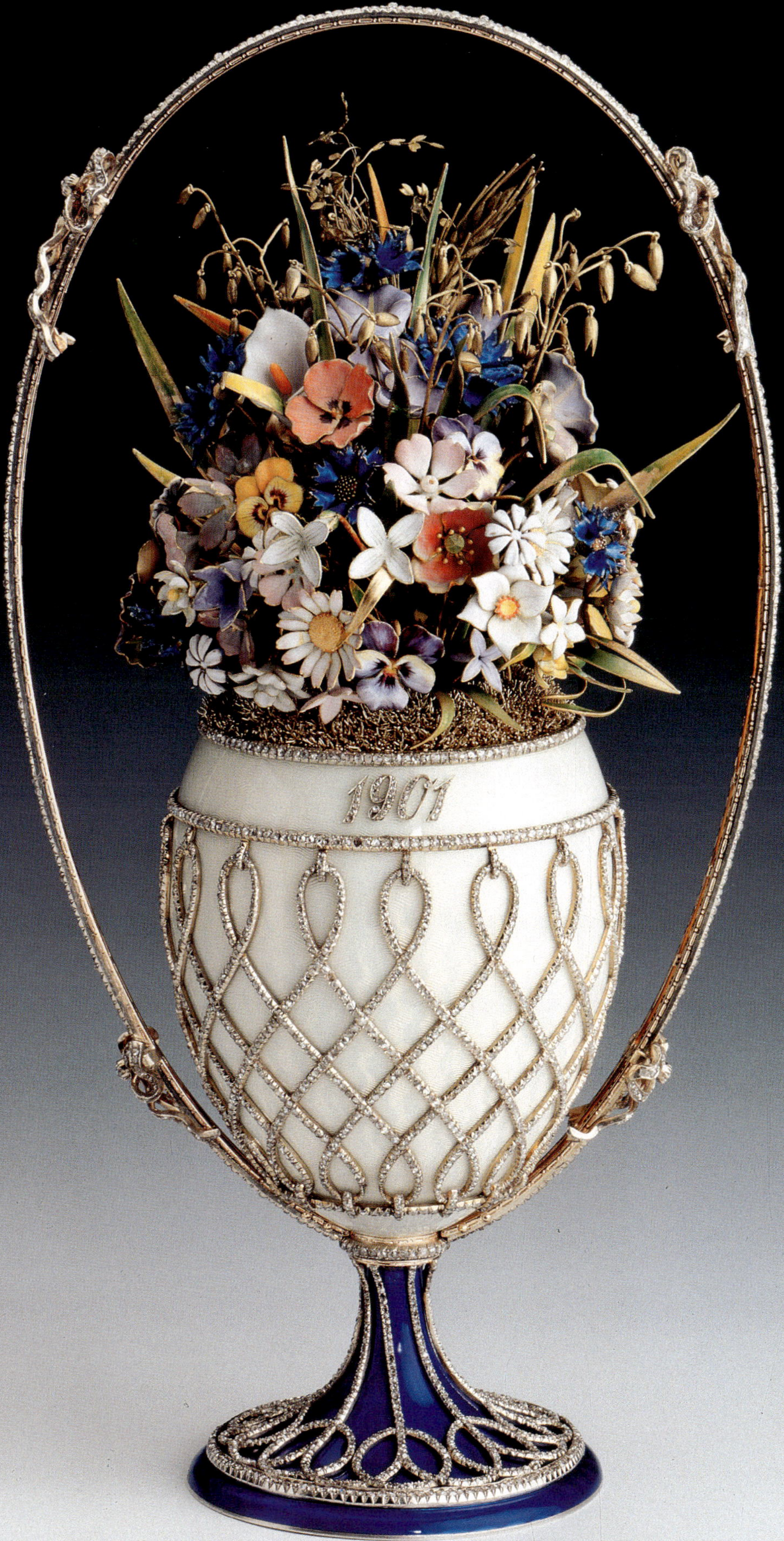
1901

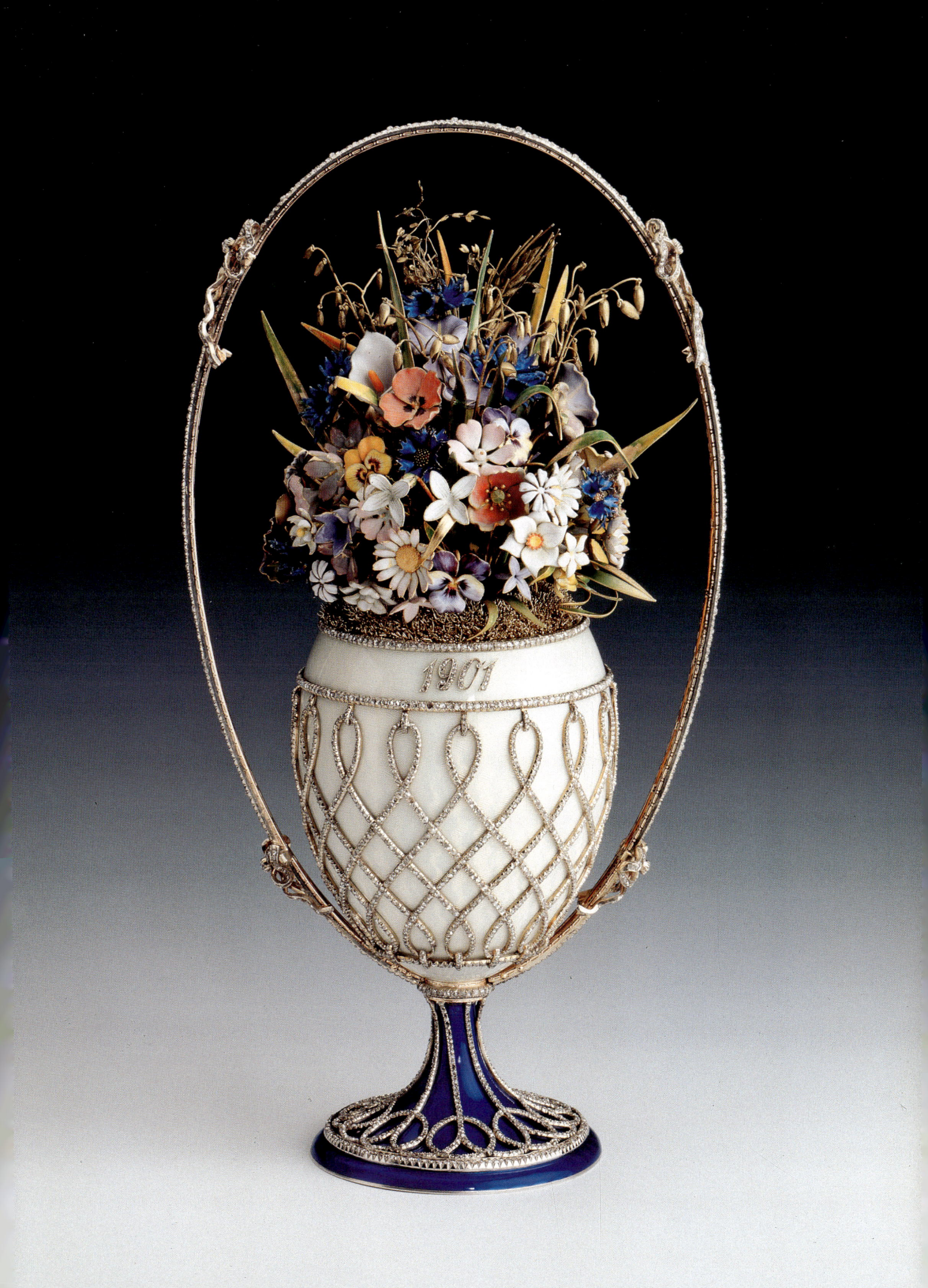

1902 Included in the charity exhibition sponsored by Alexandra Fedorovna at the Von Dervis mansion in St Petersburg (see page 55).

1917 Confiscated by Kerensky's provisional government, along with other treasures, and taken from the Anichkov Palace to the Moscow Kremlin Armoury.

1922 One of the items on the list of treasures confiscated and transferred from the Anichkov Palace to the Sovnarkom.

1 gold and enamel egg with rose-cut diamonds, in the form of a vase with flowers. [186]

1933 Officially sold by Antikvariat for 2,000 roubles. [187]

This Imperial Easter egg appears in Queen Mary's list of bibelots acquired in 1933, but as there is no invoice or record of payment for the egg in the Royal Archives it may be presumed to have been given as a present to the Queen. [188]

Contemporary photograph of the Basket of Wild Flowers egg displayed at the 1902 von Dervis exhibition (see page 55). Note that the enamel pedestal and vase are both white.

25

1902

Empire Nephrite Egg

Presented by
Tsar Nicholas II to his
mother, the Dowager
Empress Maria Fedorovna,
Easter 1902 (14 April)

(Whereabouts unknown)

Karl Woerffel, a stone carver and one of the founders of the gem-carving company, Russkiye Samotsvety, held the concession in Russia for Siberian nephrite. This beautiful semi-precious stone was favoured by the Tsars for their gifts, and they tightly controlled the amount of nephrite mined thus increasing its value. In the 50-year period preceding the Revolution a total of only 50 tons had been utilized throughout Russia. Carl Fabergé was given special permission to keep four tons of the finest nephrite in the courtyard of the House of Fabergé in St Petersburg, thereby making it readily available to his workmasters and designers. Whenever an item was designed to be made of nephrite, one of the stone carvers would walk out to the courtyard and cut off a piece. In 1924, the remaining nephrite in Fabergé's courtyard was confiscated and delivered to Russkiye Samotsvety, where it was subsequently broken up and used to make many small nephrite objects. [189]

INVOICE

Nephrite and gold EMPIRE *egg, with 2 diamonds and miniature*   6000 r.
St Petersburg, 10 May 1902 [190]

HISTORY

1902–1917 Kept at the Anichkov Palace.

1917 Confiscated by Kerensky's provisional government, along with other treasures, and taken from the Anichkov Palace to the Moscow Kremlin Armoury.

Nephrite egg on gold stand, with medallion portrait of the Emperor Alexander III. [191]

1922 One of the items on the list of treasures confiscated and transferred from the Anichkov Palace to the Sovnarkom may be this egg.

1 nephrite egg with rose-cut diamonds. [192]

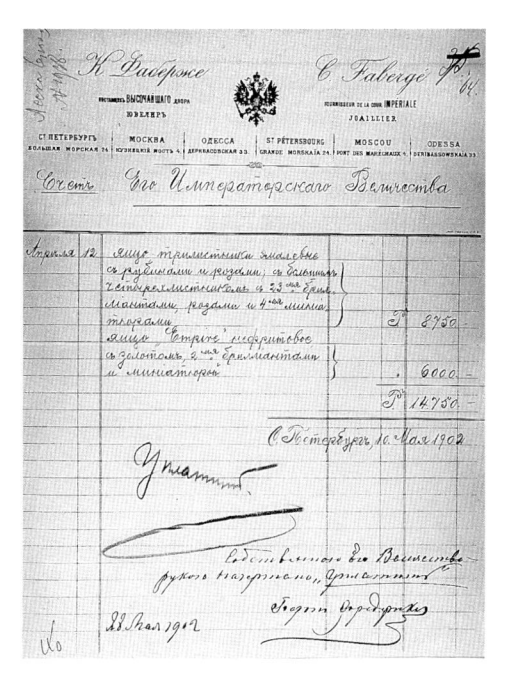

26

1902

Clover Egg

Presented by
Tsar Nicholas II to his
wife, the Empress
Alexandra Fedorovna,
Easter 1902 (14 April)

*(Moscow Kremlin Armoury
Museum)*

DESCRIPTION

Workmaster: Mikhail Perkhin.
Height: 3⅜ inches (8.5 cm).
Surprise: Four-leaf clover with four miniatures (now missing).

Gold, green enamel, diamonds, rubies.

The entire shell of this extraordinary egg is covered in *plique-a-jour* green enamel and diamond-studded three-leaf clovers. *Calibré*-cut ruby ribbons are threaded between the clover leaves, and a gold tripod, also embellished with clover leaves, supports the egg. A large cabochon ruby surrounded by diamonds is set at the point of the egg. Presumably the miniatures were of the four daughters of the Emperor and Empress.

INVOICE

12 April entry:

> *Enamel clover egg with rubies and rose-cut diamonds,*
> *with large four-leaf clover, 23 diamonds, rose-cut diamonds*
> *and 4 miniatures.* 8750 r.
> *St Petersburg, 10 May 1902* [193]

HISTORY

1902–1917 Kept in the study of Her Imperial Majesty Alexandra Fedorovna at the Winter Palace. It was displayed on the first shelf from the top in the corner showcase between the door leading into the bedroom and the window.

On 10 April 1909, N. Dementiev, Inspector of Premises of the Imperial Winter Palace, described this Easter egg when he inventoried articles in the Imperial family's private apartments. [194]

> *One gold egg covered with a transparent green enamel trefoil and trefoils of rose-cut diamonds. In some places the trefoils are intertwined with ribbons made of tiny rubies. At the top of the egg is an engraved ruby surrounded with rose-cut diamonds. The egg opens, and on the upper edge of its lower part runs a gold openwork rim along which the initials Aθ and five crowns are repeated and the date 1902 appears once. The egg is mounted on a gold stand representing clumps of clover.* [195]

1917 Confiscated by Kerensky's provisional government, along with other treasures, and taken from the Anichkov Palace to the Moscow Kremlin Armoury.

1922 One of the items on the list of treasures and transferred from the Anichkov Palace to the Sovnarkom.

> *Gold egg with green transparent enamel, approx. 1,178 rose-cut diamonds, approx. 232 rubies. 1 large ruby, gold and platinum.* [196]

The Clover egg was never sold by Antikvariat to the West and remained in Russia.

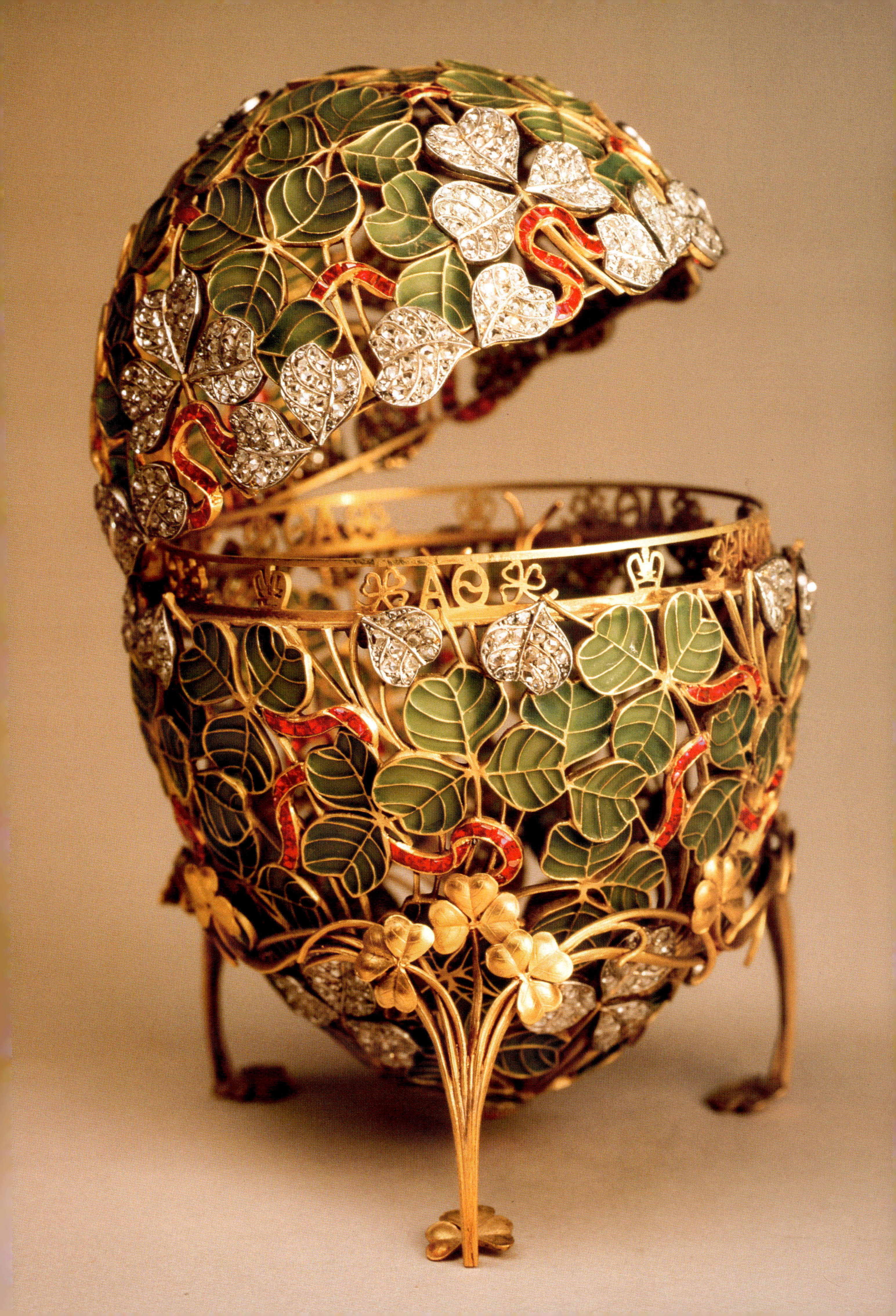

27

1903

Danish Jubilee Egg

Presented by
Tsar Nicholas II to his
mother, the Dowager
Empress Maria Fedorovna,
Easter 1903 (6 April)

(Whereabouts unknown)

The most important family event for Maria Fedorovna in 1902 was her visit to Copenhagen for the 50th anniversary of the accession of her father, King Christian IX, to the throne of Denmark. This golden jubilee was commemorated in this egg.

DESCRIPTION

Although the egg has long been missing, its appearance is known through photographs. One of the photographs from the Tatiana Fabergé archives shows an egg with a miniature portrait of King Christian. A detailed description of the egg was given by H.C. Bainbridge in the June 1934 issue of *The Connoisseur*.[197] He writes:

Miniatures of the late King of Denmark and his Queen are framed as the surprise feature in the Imperial egg... The outer surface is in light blue and white enamel with ornaments in gold and precious stones. On the top are the armorial bearings of the Danish Royal Family, and it is supported by Danish heraldic lions.[198]

INVOICE

Gold egg, Louis XIV style, with two miniatures   7535 r.
St Petersburg, 29 April 1903[199]

HISTORY

1903–1917 Kept at the Anichkov Palace.

Nicholas II wrote the following letter to his mother, the Dowager Empress Maria Fedorovna, while she was in Copenhagen:

3 April, 1903
I am sending you a Fabergé Easter present. I hope it will arrive safely. There are no secrets in it – the egg simply opens from the top.[200]

After the Empress received the egg she brought it back with her to Russia and kept it at the Anichkov Palace. Nothing is known of its fate after the Revolution.

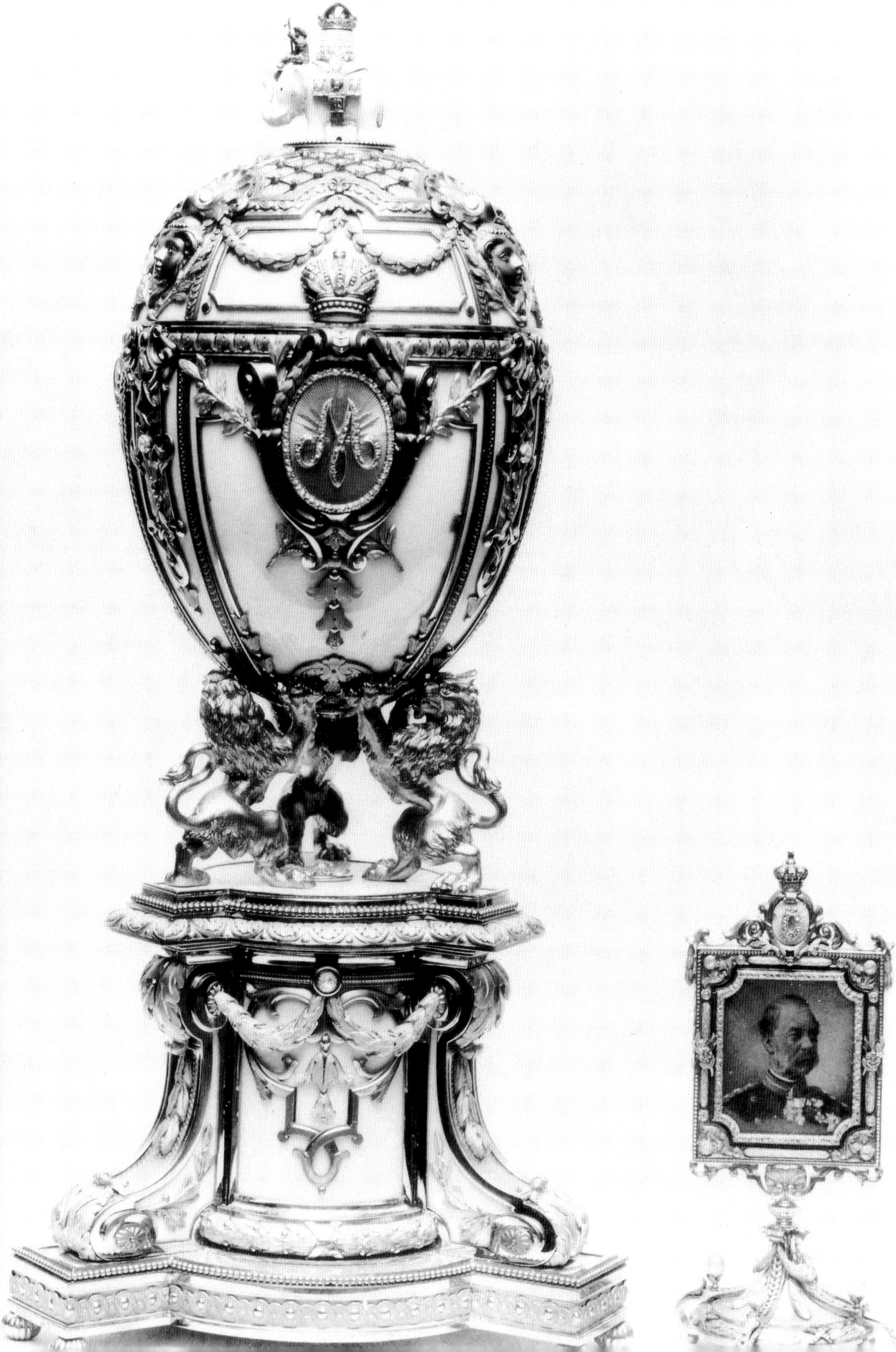

28

1903

Peter the Great Egg

Presented by
Tsar Nicholas II to his
wife, the Empress
Alexandra Fedorovna,
Easter 1903 (6 April)

*(Virginia Museum of Fine Arts,
Richmond, bequest of Lillian
Thomas Pratt)*

DESCRIPTION

Workmaster: Mikhail Perkhin.
Surprise: Miniature bronze equestrian statue of Peter the Great, supposedly modelled by Georgii Malyshev.
Height: Egg: 4⅜ inches (11.1 cm); Statue: 1%₁₆ inches (3.9 cm).
Marks: Egg: M.P. (in Cyrillic), 1903, engraved K.FABERGÉ, M.P. (in Cyrillic), 1903, St Petersburg assay mark
Statue: K.FABERGÉ (in Cyrillic).

Varicoloured gold, platinum, diamonds, rubies, enamel, bronze, sapphire, watercolour, ivory, rock crystal.

This lavish rococo-revival style egg celebrates the 200th anniversary of the founding of St Petersburg by Peter the Great in 1703. Stylistically, the inspiration was a French *nécessaire* with a clock, now in the Hermitage. The egg's extravagant design and four miniatures, each covered with rock crystal and mounted in a gold cartouche, attest to Russia's political and economic achievements by paying tribute to both Peter the Great and Tsar Nicholas II. Their portraits appear on both sides of the egg. The variance in their lifestyles is captured in the pictures of their dwellings: from Peter the Great's humble log cabin, said to have been built with his own hands, to the glorious thousand-room Winter Palace, where Nicholas II hosted lavish court balls. The symbolic dates of 1703 and 1903, studded in diamonds, are mounted above these miniatures. An enamelled wreath, centred with Tsar Nicholas II's own monogram in diamonds, circles the top half of the shell. The shell of the egg is richly embellished with laurel leaves and roses, Russian symbols of triumph and pride, and bulrushes, representing the marshy land upon which Peter the Great built his city.

When the lid of the Easter egg is raised, a gilt bronze replica of Falconet's massive equestrian statue of Peter the Great on horseback stands upon a large sapphire rock. This famous monument, commissioned by Catherine the Great, was unveiled in 1782; it still stands on the banks of the Neva River.

INVOICE

Gold egg with monument to Emperor Peter I   9760 r.
St Petersburg, 29 April 1903 [201]

HISTORY

1903–1917 Kept in the study of Her Imperial Majesty Alexandra Fedorovna at the Winter Palace. It was displayed on the second shelf from the top in the corner showcase between the door leading into the bedroom and the window.

On 10 April 1909, N. Dementiev, Inspector of Premises of the Imperial Winter Palace, described this Easter egg when he inventoried articles in the Imperial family's private apartments. [202]

Gold egg, chased in Louis XV style, the design decorated in places with rose-cut diamonds and rubies. On the top of the lid are the initials NII-A under a crown, made of rose-cut diamonds and surrounded by a wreath of green and red enamel intertwined with a white enamel ribbon. Four water-colour medallions are set in the body of the egg, representing

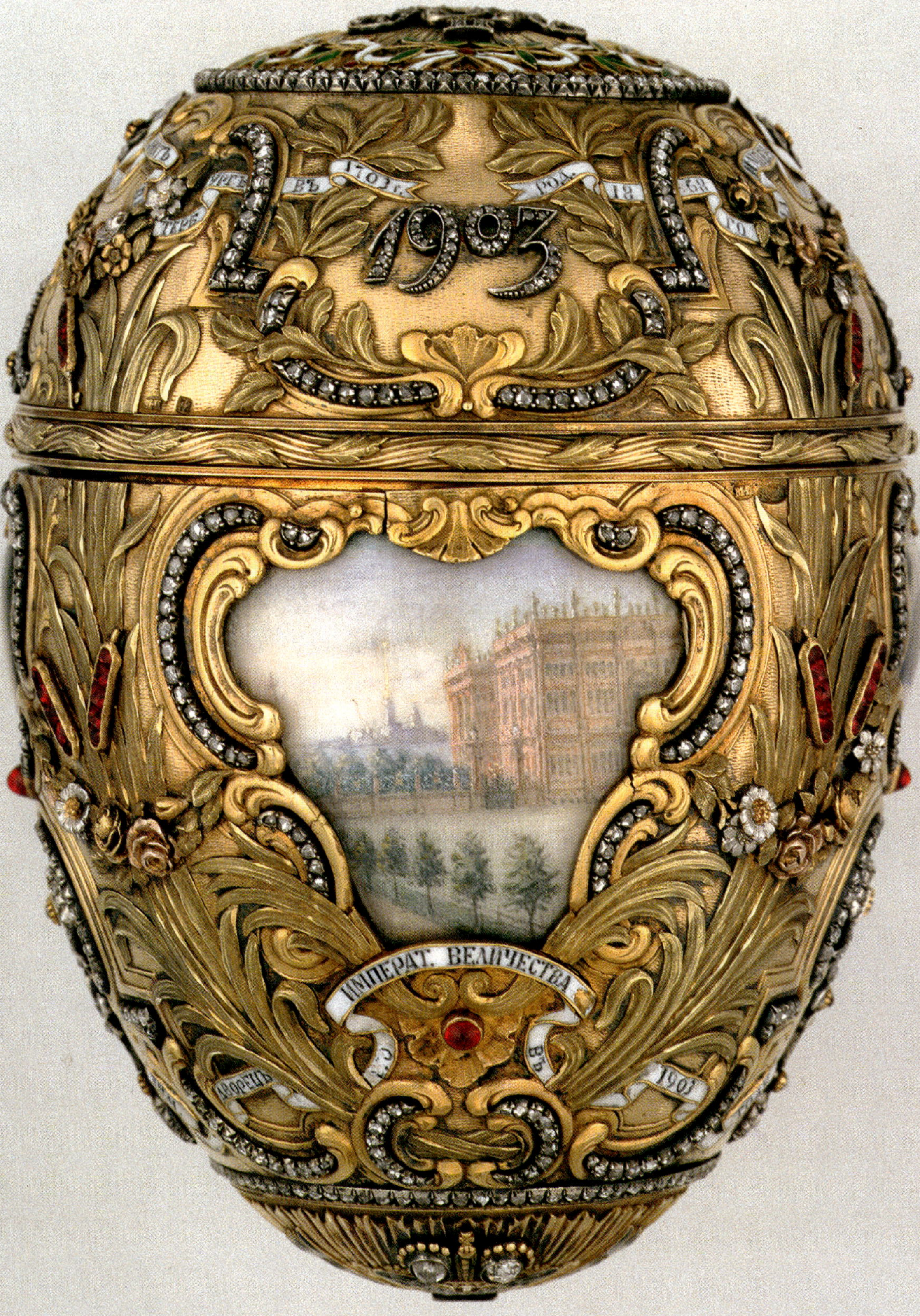
1903
ИМПЕРАТ. ВЕЛИЧЕСТВА
ВЪ
1901

Early photograph of the Peter the Great Monument. Unveiled in 1782, it still stands on the banks of the river Neva.

Their Imperial Majesties Nicholas II and Peter the Great, the Winter Palace and Peter the Great's little house. At the bottom of the egg is a black enamel eagle, with a flat diamond in the middle and 2 rose-cut diamonds in the crown. The egg bears the inscriptions 'The Emperor Nicholas II, born in 1868, came to the Throne in 1894' and 'The Emperor Peter the Great, born in 1672, founded Saint Petersburg in 1703'. Two dates made of rose-cut diamonds are inserted between these inscriptions, 1703 on one side and 1903 on the other. The lower part of the egg also bears the inscriptions 'The first little house of Emperor Peter the Great in 1703' and 'The Winter Palace of His Imperial Majesty in 1903'. The inside of the lid is lined with yellow enamel and contains a gold plate on which a model of the monument to the Emperor Peter the Great is mounted. The platform supporting the monument, the railing, columns, posts and chains are all made of gold; the rock is of black stone, and the figures of the Emperor and his steed are also made of chased gold. The inscription engraved on the rock reads: 'To Peter the First from Catherine the Second, 1782 – Petro Primo Catherina Secunda MDCCLXXXII.' The egg rests on a stand made of red silver-gilt wire. [203]

1917 Confiscated by Kerensky's provisional government, along with other treasures, and taken from the Anichkov Palace to the Moscow Kremlin Armoury.

1922 One of the items on the list of treasures transferred from the Anichkov Palace to the Sovnarkom.

1 gold egg with rose-cut diamonds, containing a model of the Peter I monument. [204]

1933 Officially sold by Antikvariat for 4,000 roubles. [205]

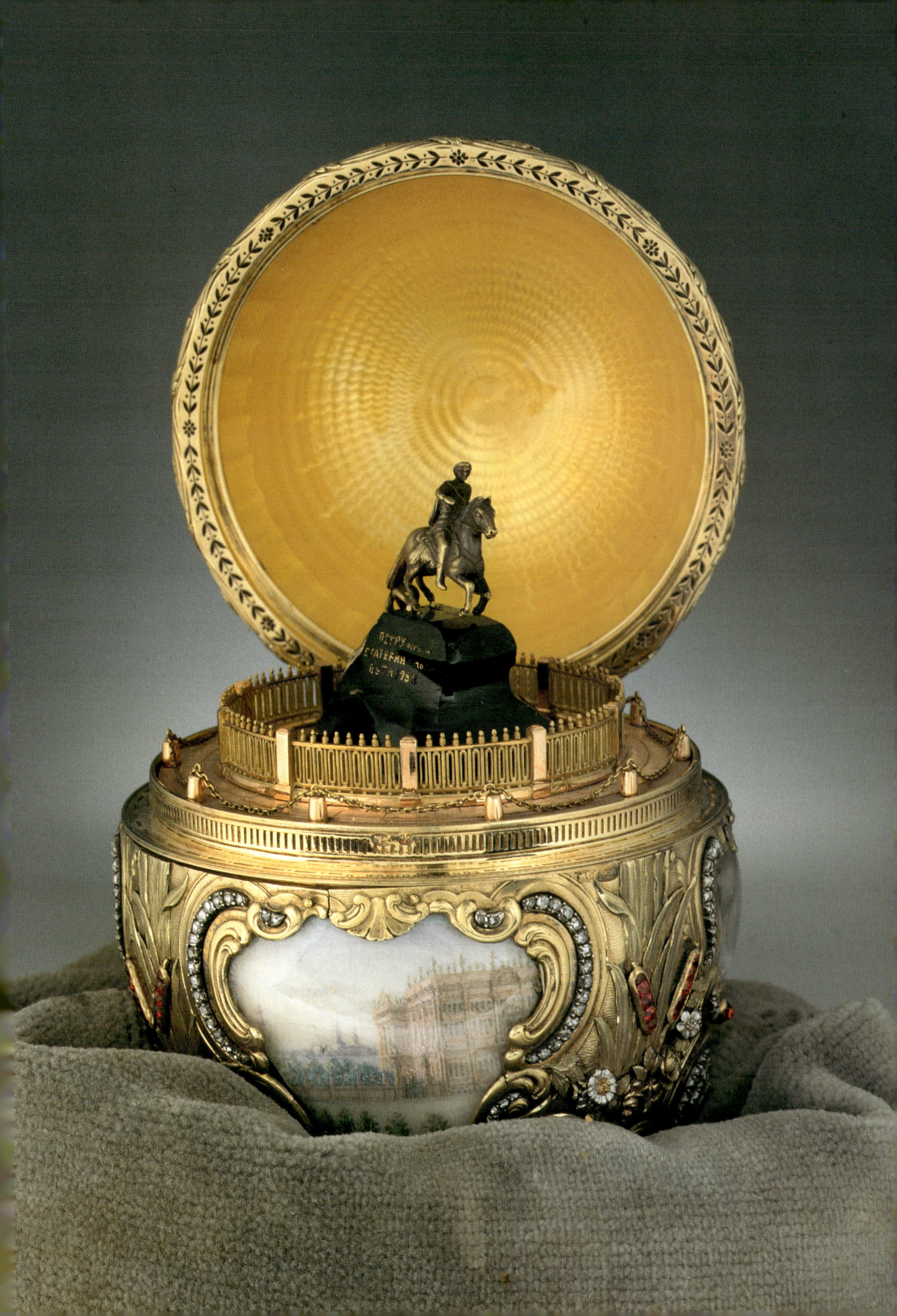

29

1906

Swan Egg

Presented by
Tsar Nicholas II to his
mother, the Dowager
Empress Maria Fedorovna,
Easter 1906 (16 April)

*(The Edouard and Maurice
Sandoz Foundation,
Switzerland)*

The swan is a symbol of family life and of the permanence of marriage ties, since swans are devoted to one another and always live in pairs. This bird was therefore appropriate as a theme for an egg presented to Maria Fedorovna in the year of the 40th anniversary of her wedding.

The design of the miniature mechanical silver swan appears to have been inspired by a life-size silver automaton, made by John Cox, which was exhibited at the Paris World Exhibition in 1867 and is now in the Bowes Museum, Barnard Castle, County Durham. Fabergé drew upon another Cox automaton, on display in the Winter Palace, for the mechanical 1900 Cockerel (21) and 1908 Peacock (33) eggs.

Description

Workmaster: Unknown
Surprise: Miniature mechanical swan 2³⁄₁₆ inches (5.5 cm)
Height: 3⅞ inches (9.9 cm).
Marks: FABERGÉ, assay mark of St Petersburg, 56 and Y.L. (initials of St Petersburg regional assay manager and inspector, Yakov Lyapunov).

Varicoloured gold, mauve enamel, rose-cut diamonds, platinum, aquamarine.

Fabergé must have chosen this feminine design to please the Empress, and it was a well known fact that mauve was one of her favourite colours. The matt opaque mauve enamel shell is decorated with a trellis design of rose-cut diamond-set bows. A large portrait diamond is mounted at the apex of the egg, over the date 1906. The egg opens to reveal the exquisite surprise of a silver-plated gold mechanical swan sitting on a miniature aquamarine lake encased within a basket of four-coloured gold water lilies. When wound by the mechanism found under one of the wings, the swan spreads both wings, displaying all its feathers, and appears to glide gracefully upon the surface of the aquamarine while moving its webbed feet and stretching its elegant neck.

Invoice

1 April entry:

> *Egg, Louis XVI style, opaque mauve enamel, with bows of rose-cut diamonds and 2 diamonds, containing a mechanical gold silver-plated swan on an aquamarine pediment.* 7200 r.
> *St Petersburg, 7 June 1906* [206]

The invoice reveals for the first time that the swan is made of gold plated with silver, rather than of silver, as previously thought.

History

1906–1917 Kept at the Anichkov Palace.

1917 Confiscated by Kerensky's provisional government, along with other treasures, and taken from the Anichkov Palace to the Moscow Kremlin Armoury.

Gold egg, covered with mauve enamel and decorated with diamonds, containing a small stone stand with a silver swan. [207]

1922 One of the items on the list of treasures confiscated and transferred from the Anichkov Palace to the Sovnarkom.

1 gold egg with 2 diamonds and rose-cut diamonds, containing a silver swan on a stone stand, gold handle broken off. [208]

1954 Sold by Sotheby's, Cairo on 10 March, from the palace collection of King Farouk, for £6,400 ($19,000).

30

1906

Moscow Kremlin Egg

Presented by
Tsar Nicholas II to his
wife, the Empress
Alexandra Fedorovna,
Easter 1906 (16 April)

(Moscow Kremlin Armoury Museum)

This egg was probably made to commemorate the Easter 1903 visit by the Emperor and Empress to the ancient capital of Moscow, which was regarded by all Russian society, and Muscovites in particular, as a significant event. It was the first time that Nicholas II and Alexandra Fedorovna had visited Moscow since their coronation festivities in 1896, when a catastrophe had occurred and thousands of people had accidentally perished at an outdoor feast.

Nicholas II's first cousin, Marie, Grand Duchess of Russia, recalled this tragic event:

Magnificent preparation had been made for the fêtes attending the ascension of the young Emperor and Empress. All was blighted, however, by a frightful accident at the Khodinsky Meadows where a distribution of gifts to the people was to take place. The crowd was far larger than had been expected and order could not be maintained by a carelessly organized police force. The crowd stormed the booths from which the gifts were to be distributed. Thousands of them were killed and maimed in the crush of the panic and stampede that followed.

In the court circles the disaster was little mentioned... but seemed under a cloud of sadness and premonition. All, perhaps without saying, regarded this catastrophe as a bad omen at the very beginning of the new reign. [209]

Although the egg had been produced at an earlier date, the outbreak of the Russo-Japanese war in 1904 delayed its presentation until 1906.

Description

Height: Egg and stand: 14³⁄₁₆ inches (36.1 cm);
Base: 7¼ inches x 7¼ inches (18.5 cm x 18.5 cm).
Marks: K. FABERGÉ (in Cyrillic), dated 1904 (in alphabetic numerals).

Gold, silver, onyx, glass, opaque and *guilloché* enamel, oil painting.

The decorative scheme of this Imperial Easter egg was inspired by the architecture of the Uspenski (Dormition) Cathedral in the Kremlin, in which the Tsars of Russia were crowned. The white opalescent enamel egg has a series of three-paned windows through which can be seen the interior of the cathedral, opulently decorated with carpets, tiny enamelled icons, and High Altar. A polished gold cupola sits atop the egg. Red gold turrets, towers, and staircases rise from the stylized Kremlin walls, their roofs covered in light-green translucent enamel. The two Spasskie Towers which bear the coat-of-arms of the Russian Empire and Moscow, are inset with chiming clocks, the dials each measuring approximately half-an-inch in diameter. A music box plays the melody of Tsar Nicholas II's favourite traditional hymn, *Izhe Kheruvimy*, triggered by a button at the back of the egg. At the bottom, the egg is dated '1904' in white enamel and it sits upon a white octagonal onyx base.

Invoice

1 April entry:

*Egg, 'Moscow Kremlin', of different coloured gold
and enamel, with a white enamel egg representing
the Uspenski Cathedral, with music, on a white
onyx pediment*   11800 r.
*St Petersburg, 7 June 1906
A. Fabergé {signed per pro C. Fabergé}* [210]

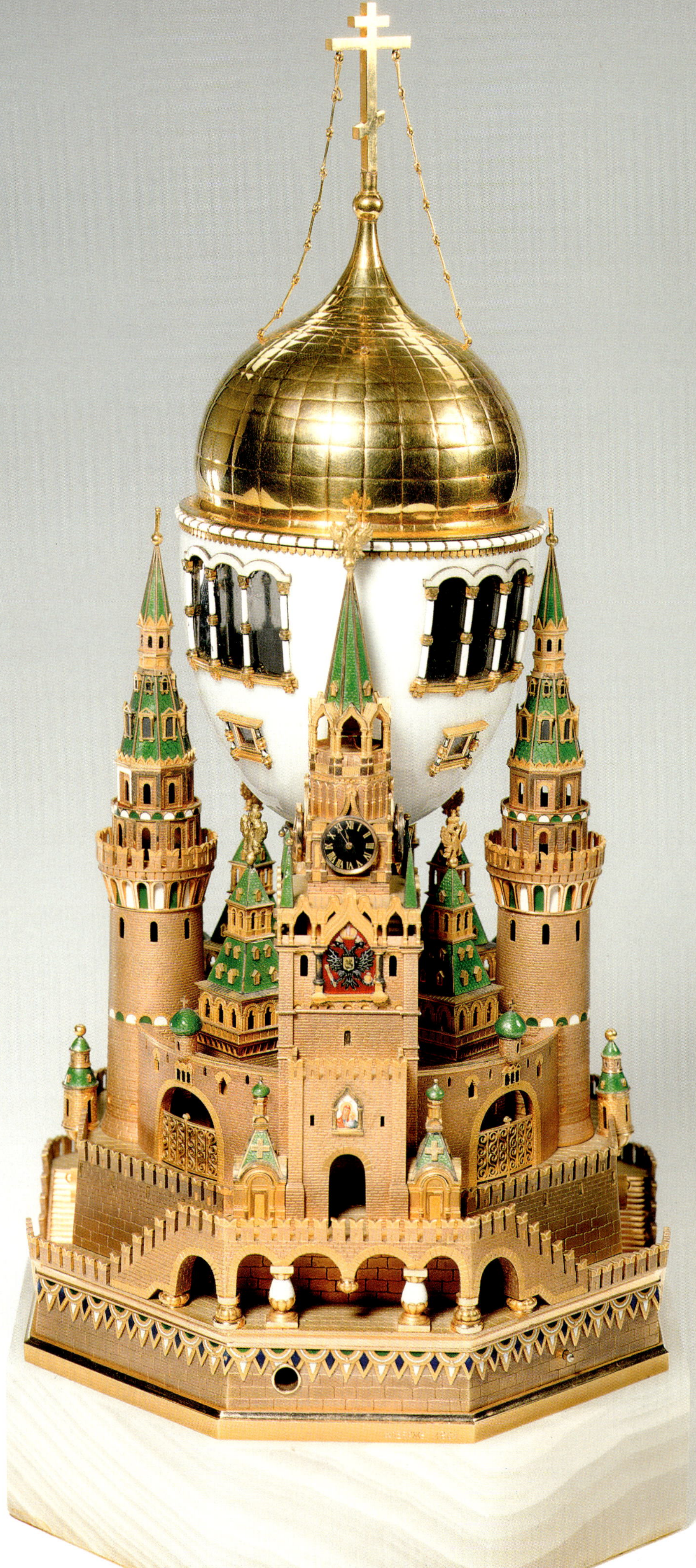

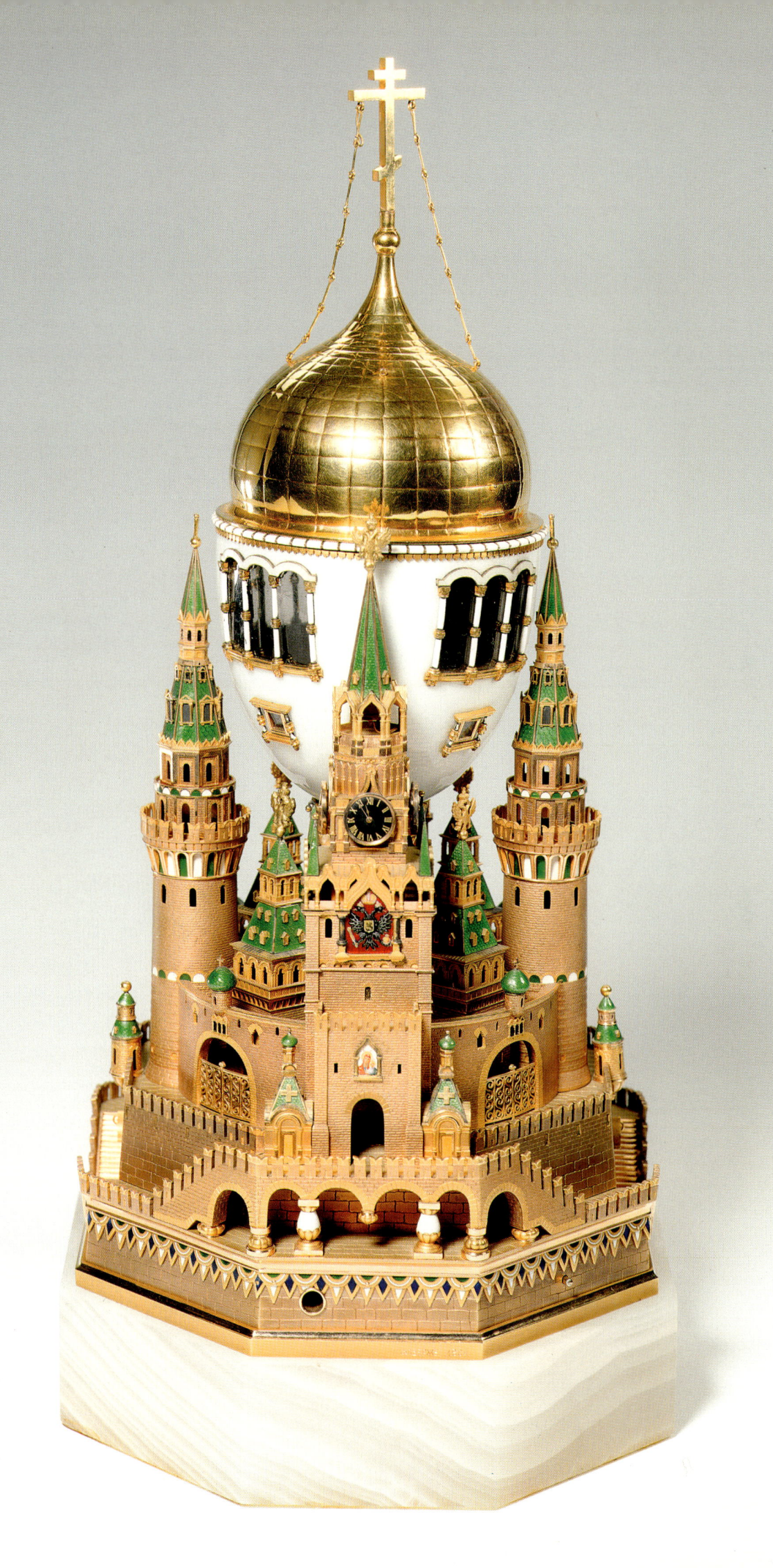

HISTORY

1906–1917 Kept in the Mauve Room of the Alexander Palace at Tsarskoie Selo.

1917 Confiscated by Kerensky's provisional government, along with other treasures and taken to the Moscow Kremlin Armoury.

1922 The inventory of treasures transferred to the Moscow Kremlin Armoury includes this entry:

1 egg in the form of the Kremlin, gold, with music. [211]

The Moscow Kremlin egg was never sold by Antikvariat to the West and remained in Russia.

Early Fabergé photograph of the Moscow Kremlin egg

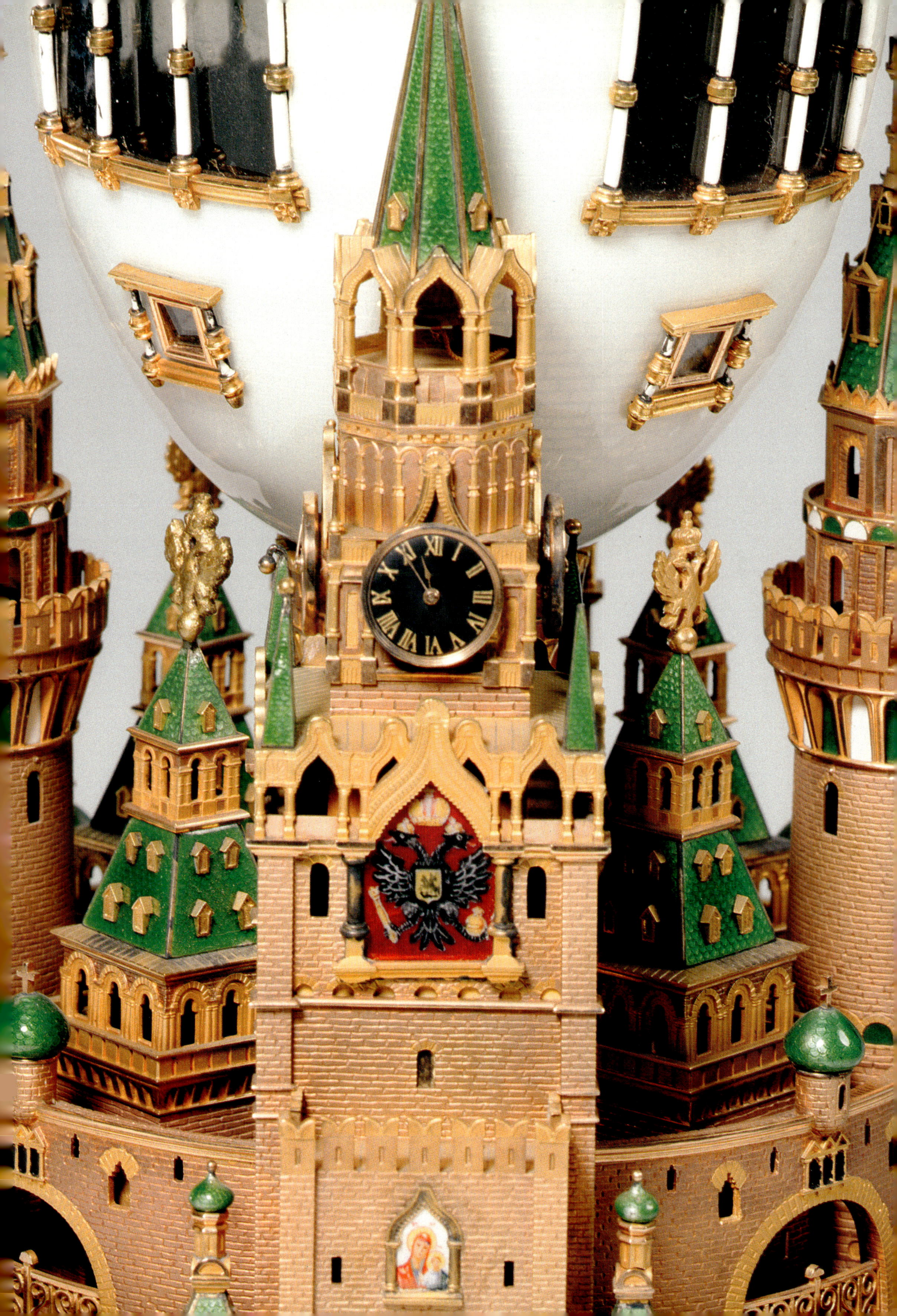

31

1907

Cradle with Garlands Egg

Presented by
Tsar Nicholas II to his
mother, the Dowager
Empress Maria Fedorovna,
Easter 1907 (22 April)

(Private Collection, USA)

For years, this delightful egg has been called the Love Trophy egg, but, as Franz Birbaum notes in his memoirs, it in fact celebrates the birth of Tsar Nicholas II and Empress Alexandra Fedorovna's long-awaited son and heir, the Tsarevich Alexei Nikolaievich:

The appearance and the contents were sometimes adapted to family events – for instance, when the heir to the throne was born, the Easter egg suggested a cradle decorated with garlands of flowers, and contained the first portrait of the heir in a medallion surrounded with diamonds. [212]

DESCRIPTION

Workmaster: Henrik Wigström.
Surprise: Miniature of the Imperial children on an easel (now missing).
Height: 5¾ inches (14.6 cm).
Marks: FABERGÉ (in Cyrillic), H.W., assay mark of St Petersburg regional assay department, 56.

Varicoloured gold, translucent sky blue and green enamel, opalescent oyster enamel, pink enamel, diamonds, rubies, pearls, white onyx.

This elegant pale blue *guilloché* enamel Easter egg, created in the Louis XVI style, is surmounted by a diamond-set gold basket with pink enamelled roses. A border of pink roses and green enamel vines is mounted above the hinged cover. The interior of the egg is lined in silk with a hollow of approximately 1 x 1¼ inches; this originally held the surprise which is now missing. The gold cradle is supported and encircled by four columns modelled as love trophies in the form of quivers of arrows and is mounted on an oval onyx base. A garland of pink roses and diamond-set flowers is hung between and around each of the columns.

INVOICE

21 April entry:

> *Blue and opalescent enamel egg, on white onyx stand, basket with enamel bouquet, garlands of various enamels, mountings of coloured golds with rose-cut diamonds, containing a white enamel easel with one ruby, pearls and rose-cut diamonds, one miniature of the Imperial children*   9700 r.
> *St Petersburg, 30 April 1907* [213]

HISTORY

1907-1917 Kept at the Anichkov Palace.

1992 Sold at Sotheby's, New York, 10 June, for $3.19 million.

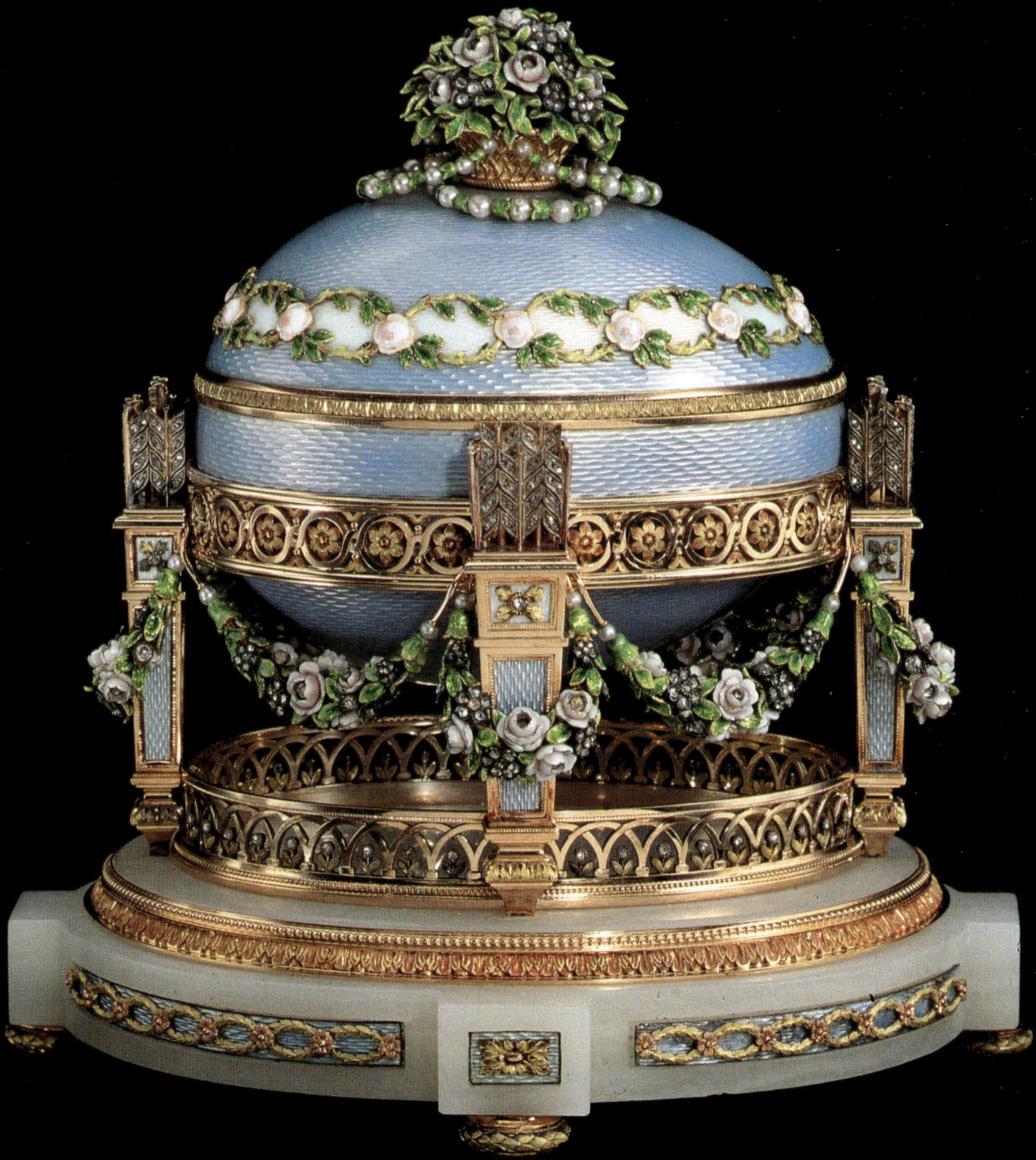

1907

32

Rose Trellis Egg

Presented by
Tsar Nicholas II to his
wife, the Empress
Alexandra Fedorovna,
Easter 1907 (22 April)

(The Walters Art Gallery, Baltimore)

Just as the Cradle with Garlands egg (31), celebrated the birth of the Tsarevich Alexei Nikolaievich, the son and heir of Nicholas and Alexandra, so did the Rose Trellis egg. Fabergé's sense of humour is brought out in an account of a conversation he had regarding a suitable design to commemorate the event:

When we were discussing the design for the next Easter egg in the year of the Tsarevich's birth, trying to adapt the subject to this event, someone observed the Heir to the Throne was appointed from birth to command all the army rifle regiments, and that fact might be used in the composition. 'Yes,' he [Fabergé] agreed, 'but then we'll have to represent his soiled swaddling clothes, since for the time being they are the only results of his rifle practice.' [214]

DESCRIPTION

Workmaster: Henrik Wigström.
Surprise: A diamond necklace with medallion and ivory miniature surrounded by diamonds of His Imperial Highness Grand Duke Tsarevich Alexei Nikolaievich (missing).
Height: 3 3/16 inch (7.7 cm).

Gold, yellow, green and pink enamel, diamonds.

The delicacy of the rose-cut diamond trellises overlaying the translucent green enamel shell is enhanced by the pink enamel roses centered within each lattice. These roses are set among gold vines and tiny emerald-green leaves. The swirls of the diamond trellises end at the egg's apex where a large diamond is mounted. The bottom point of the egg is also set with a large table diamond under which is the inscription 1907. The surprise, a diamond necklace with medallion and ivory miniature of the Grand Duke Tsarevich Alexei Nikolaievich, is now missing.

INVOICE

21 April entry:

Green enamel egg with branches of roses and enamel leaves, 1 diamond and rose-cut diamonds, containing a diamond necklace with medallion and miniature of His Imperial Highness the Grand Duke Tsarevich Alexei Nikolaievich. 8300 r.
St Petersburg, 30 April 1907 [215]

HISTORY

1907–1917 Kept in the study of Her Imperial Majesty Alexandra Fedorovna at the Winter Palace. It was displayed on the bottom shelf in the corner showcase between the door leading into the bedroom and the window.

On 10 April 1909, N. Dementiev, Inspector of Premises of the Imperial Winter Palace, described this Easter egg when he inventoried articles in the Imperial family's private apartments. [216]

Egg covered with pale green enamel. The body of the egg is covered with a trellis of rose-cut diamonds and pink enamel roses with green enamel leaves. At the top of the egg there is a rosette of small rose-cut diamonds with a large diamond in the centre. The bottom of the egg also contains a rosette of small diamonds, with a flat diamond in the middle, covering the inscription 1907. The egg rests on a stand of silver gilt wire.

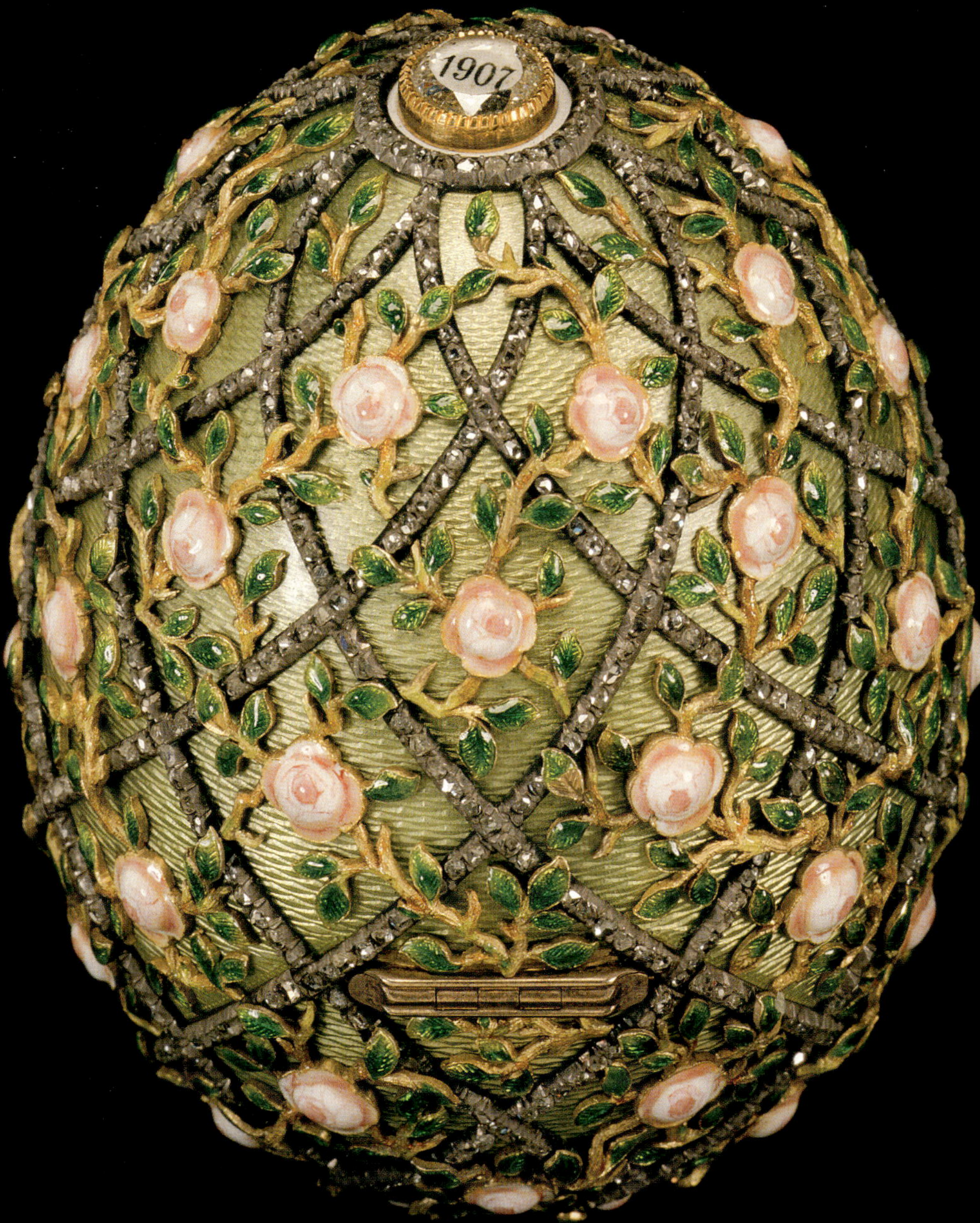
1907

A Fabergé album[217] of the Imperial Easter eggs presented to Alexandra Fedorovna between 1907 and 1916 gives much more detailed descriptions of these eggs, which makes it possible to distinguish between the eggs made for Maria Fedorovna and Alexandra Fedorovna during that period. Unfortunately, all the relevant photographs have disappeared.

Easter egg presented to Alexandra Fedorovna in 1907. Green enamel egg covered with a network of diamonds, intertwined with garlands of roses. Contains a portrait of the Heir on ivory, in the form of a medallion surrounded with diamonds, on a similar chain.

1917 Confiscated by Kerensky's provisional government, along with other treasures, and taken from the Anichkov Palace to the Moscow Kremlin Armoury.

1922 One of the items on the list of confiscated treasures transferred from the Anichkov Palace to the Sovnarkom.

1 gold egg with rose-cut diamonds and pearls, containing portrait. [218]

1930 Bought by Henry C. Walters of Baltimore from Alexander Polovtsov, a Russian emigré who owned an antiques business at 154, Boulevard Haussmann in Paris. Polovstov was formerly the superintendant at the Gatchina Palace who inventoried the Imperial family's property which had been confiscated by the provisional government. In 1921, he left Russia and set up a business in Paris selling Russian treasures. The following entry is from the diary of an English gentleman who was living in Russia at the time of the Revolution:

Sunday July 8, 1917

Alexander Polovtsov is making an inventory of everything in the palace of Gatchina... {he} is working for the Government, who are cataloguing the contents of all the Imperial Palaces. [219]

At the same time Walters bought the Gatchina Palace egg (23). On his death in 1931, Mr Walters left both eggs to the Walters Art Gallery, Baltimore.

1908

33
Peacock Egg

Presented by
Tsar Nicholas II to his
mother, the Dowager
Empress Maria Fedorovna,
Easter 1908 (13 April)

*(The Edouard and Maurice
Sandoz Foundation,
Switzerland)*

The famous ormolu automaton Peacock Clock in the Winter Palace, made by James Cox (d. 1788), was the inspiration for both the 1900 Cockerel egg (21) and the 1908 Peacock egg. For over 20 years, Carl Fabergé gave his time and expertise gratis to the Hermitage, repairing, restoring, and classifying its treasures. The archives show that Baron Fredericks, Minister of the Imperial Court, received a request, dated 25 June 1898, from A. Kunik, Chief Curator of the Hermitage, requesting permission for 'The Court Jeweller Fabergé... and a mechanic' to be admitted to the Hermitage 'to study the inner workings of the Peacock kept in the Hermitage Treasury' as a model for for a peacock ordered by His Imperial Majesty 'as a table decoration'.[220] The Fabergé country estate was near that of Prince Wyazemski where many peacocks were allowed to roam free and where the Prince also kept his private zoo. According to a story told by Tatiana Fabergé's father, one day, Carl's dog, unnerved by the cries of the Prince's peacocks managed to break free of his chain. He chased and killed one of the peacocks, then brought it home to his master to show off his prized catch.

DESCRIPTION

Workmaster: Henrik Wigström.
Surprise: Mechanical peacock.
Dimensions: Egg: 6 inches (15.25 cm); Length of peacock: 4¾ inches (12 cm).
Marks: FABERGÉ (in Cyrillic) and H.W., St Petersburg assay mark indistinct, 91.

Rock crystal, silver-gilt, precious stones, coloured enamel.

*Early Fabergé photograph
of the Peacock egg*

The surprise within is the focal point of this Louis XV style rock-crystal Easter egg. The mechanical enamelled peacock can be seen through the rock-crystal shell, roosting in the branches of a gold and enamel tree. When wound, the peacock struts around, with its head held high moving from side to side. Periodically, the peacock fans its beautifully enamelled tail. The Easter egg is mounted on an elaborate scrolled silver-gilt base bearing the Empress Maria Fedorovna's crowned monogram and the year 1908.

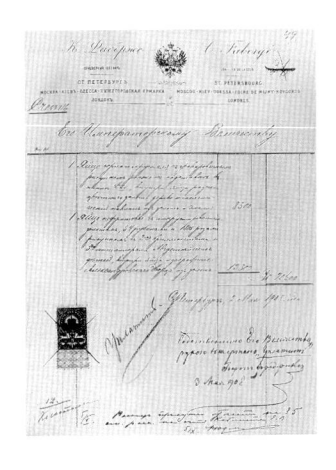

INVOICE

Rock crystal egg with rococo engraved design on a Louis XV style pediment, inside the egg a tree of various kinds of gold and a gold and enamel mechanical peacock   8300 r.
St Petersburg, 2 May 1908 [221]

HISTORY

1908–1917 Kept at the Anichkov Palace.

1917 Confiscated by Kerensky's provisional government, along with other treasures, and taken from the Anichkov Palace to the Moscow Kremlin Armoury.

Crystal egg, on pediment with bronze mounting, containing a peacock. [222]

1922 One of the items on the list of confiscated treasures transferred from the Anichkov Palace to the Sovnarkom.

1 crystal egg in silver setting, containing a peacock. [223]

The 18th-century automaton Peacock Clock in the Winter Palace that was the inspiration for the Peacock and the Cockerel (21) egg.

180

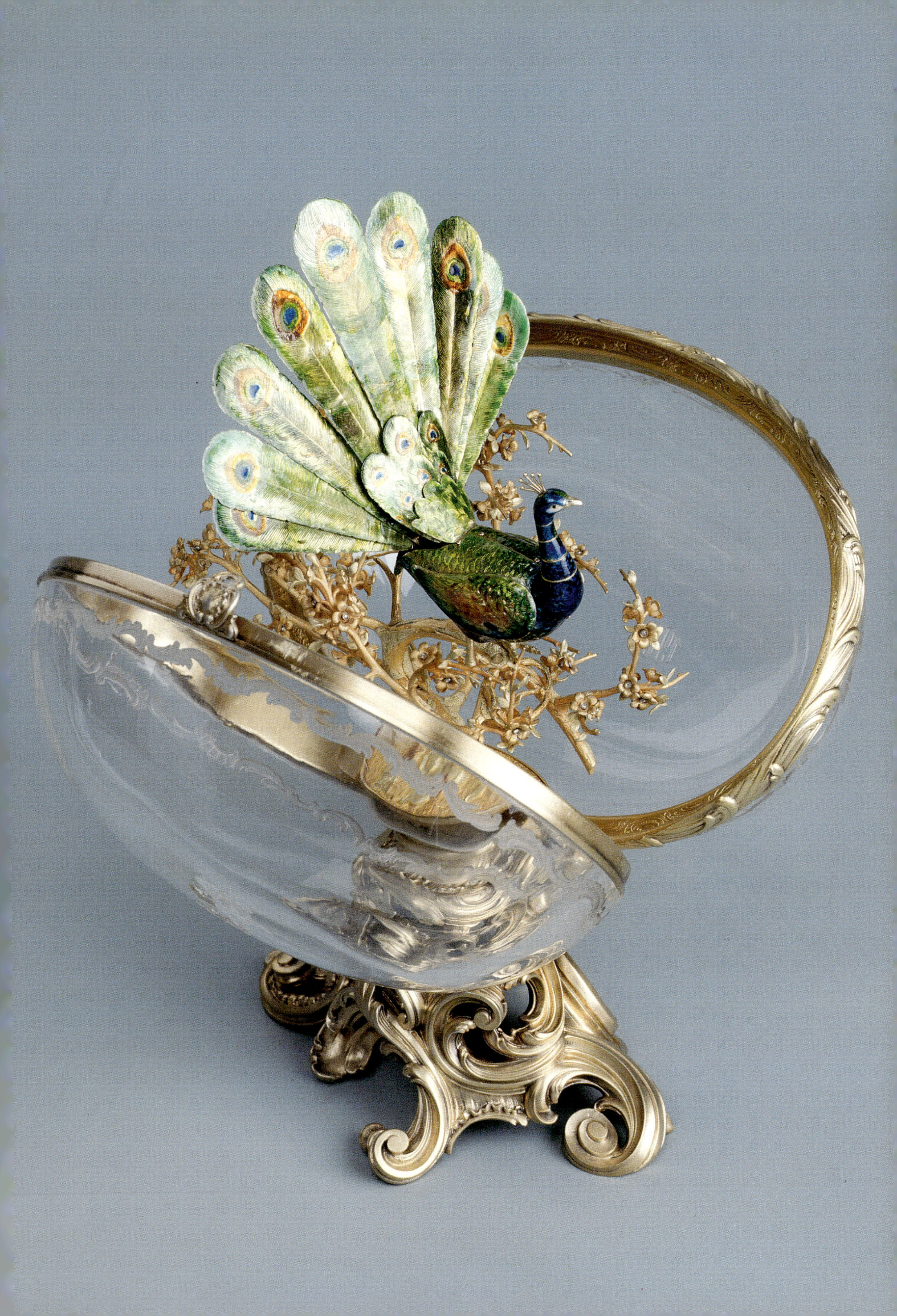

34
Alexander Palace Egg

1908

Presented by
Tsar Nicholas II to his
wife, the Empress
Alexandra Fedorovna,
Easter 1908 (13 April)

(Moscow Kremlin Armoury Museum)

DESCRIPTION

Workmaster: Henrik Wigström.
Surprise: Model of the Alexander Palace.
Height: Egg: 4 5/16 inches (11 cm);
Palace: 1 3/16 x 2 9/16 inches (3 cm x 6.5 cm).
Marks: Stamped FABERGÉ (in Cyrillic), H.W., assay mark of St Petersburg regional assay department, 72.

Gold, silver, diamonds, rose-cut diamonds, rubies, jade, rock crystal, glass, wood, velvet, bone and enamel.

This Siberian nephrite egg celebrates Tsar Nicholas II's five children. Their miniature watercolour portraits are framed in rose-cut diamonds, with their initials picked out in diamonds above their portraits. The dark green colour of the shell contrasts with the applied gold laurel leaves, diamond bows and flowers. The Empress Alexandra Fedorovna's monogram, AΘ, and the date 1908 are mounted beneath flat triangular diamonds at the apex of the egg. When opened, the egg reveals a tiny detailed model of the Alexander Palace, the Imperial family's favourite residence at Tsarskoie Selo. It is made of gold and silver, with windows of rock crystal; the roof is enamelled in light green. The palace is mounted on a gold table with an engraved inscription: TSARSKOIE SELO PALACE.

The stand for the egg was made in 1989 at the Moscow experimental jewellery factory by S. Bugrov from a sketch by T.D. Zharkova. The original stand has been lost.

INVOICE

Nephrite egg with gold incrustations, 54 rubies and 1805 rose-cut diamonds, design with 2 diamonds and 5 miniatures of the Imperial children, containing a representation of the Alexander Palace in gold   12300 r.
St Petersburg, 2 May 1908 [224]

HISTORY

1908–1917 Kept in the Mauve Room of the Alexander Palace at Tsarskoie Selo. The following is a description from a Fabergé album of the Imperial Easter eggs presented to Alexandra Fedorovna between 1907 and 1916. [225]

Easter egg presented to Alexandra Fedorovna in 1908, of nephrite inlaid with a pattern of diamond wreaths and garlands. The egg bears five medallions with portraits of Their Majesties' august children painted on ivory. The egg contains a miniature gold and enamel model of the Alexander Palace at Tsarskoie Selo.

1917 Confiscated by Kerensky's provisional government, along with other treasures, and taken from the Anichkov Palace to the Moscow Kremlin Armoury.

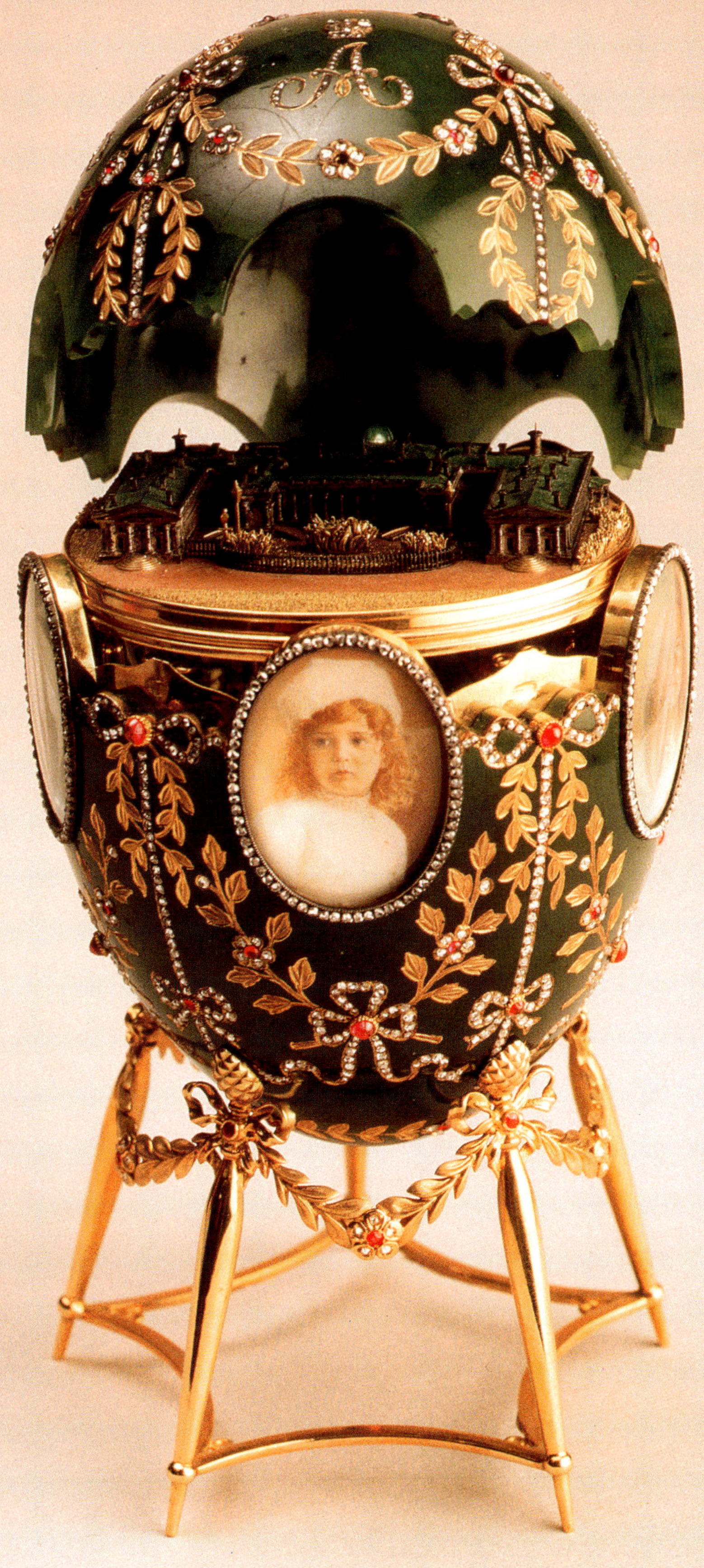

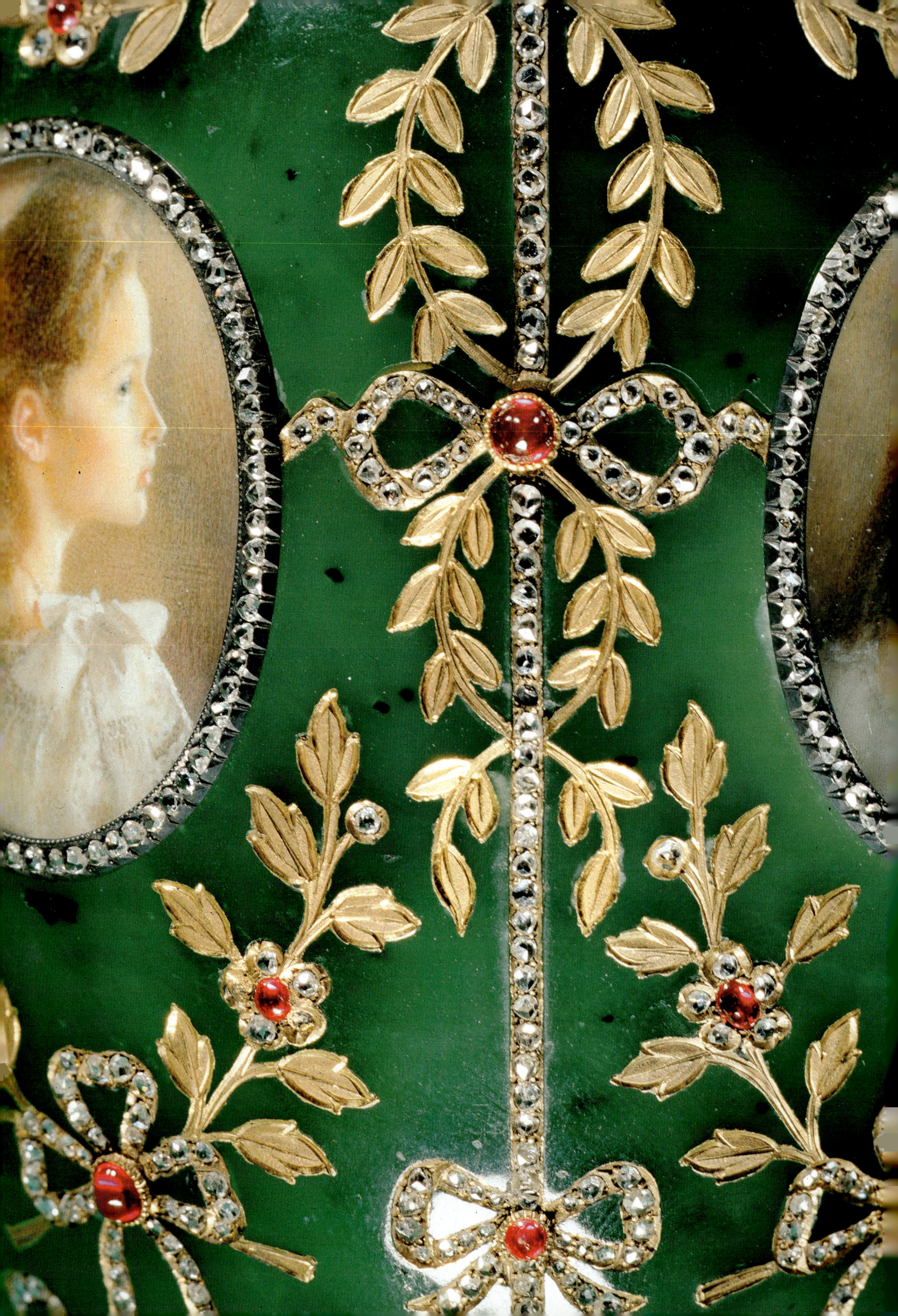

1922 One of the items on the list of confiscated treasures transferred from the Anichkov Palace to the Sovnarkom.

1 nephrite egg with gold ornamentation, 2 diamonds and rose-cut diamonds, containing a model of the Tsarskoselskii [Alexander] Palace. [226]

The Alexander Palace egg was never sold by Antikvariat to the West and remained in Russia.

1909

35
Alexander III Commemorative Egg

Presented by
Tsar Nicholas II to his
mother, the Dowager
Empress Maria Fedorovna,
Easter 1909 (29 March)

(Whereabouts unknown)

DESCRIPTION

The egg and its surprise disappeared after the Revolution, but a photograph exists. From this and the invoice, it appears that the body of the egg was in white opaque enamel with horizontal gold stripes and divided into five sections with vertical lines of rose-cut diamond laurel leaves. White enamel lozenge-shape diamond clusters are positioned around the middle of the egg, each mounted with diamond-set baskets, flowers and ribbons. Rose-cut diamond wreaths centered with diamond-set stars of Bethlehem are placed near the apex. Both ends of the egg are set with large diamonds. An inverted heart-shaped wire frame supported the egg, which originally concealed a miniature gold bust of Alexander III, on a lapis lazuli pediment. This Easter egg commemorated the 15th anniversary of his death.

In a 1934 article for *The Connoisseur* magazine H.C. Bainbridge wrote:

... Some of these Imperial gifts are of white opaque enamel, one such, decorated with brilliants set in platinum, enclosing a gold bust of Alexander III on a lapis-lazuli pedestal... [227]

INVOICE

Egg of opaque white enamel with gold stripes, decorated with 2 diamonds and 3467 rose-cut diamonds, inside a gold bust of Alexander III on a lapis lazuli pediment decorated with rose-cut diamonds   11200 r.
St Petersburg, 9 July 1909. C. Fabergé[228]

HISTORY

1909–1917   Kept at the Anichkov Palace.

Early Fabergé photograph of the Alexander III Commemorative egg.

1909

36

Standard Egg

Presented by
Tsar Nicholas II to his
wife, Empress Alexandra
Fedorovna, Easter 1909
(29 March).

*(Moscow Kremlin Armoury
Museum)*

This egg celebrates the third anniversary of the launching of the 128-metre-long Imperial yacht *Standard* which took place in February 1906. It was commissioned by Tsar Alexander III who had it built in Copenhagen. This floating palace brought the Imperial family much pleasure, transporting them on their annual journeys to the islands along the coast of Finland. The surprise within the Easter egg is an exquisitely produced miniature gold replica of the yacht.

DESCRIPTION

Workmaster: Henrik Wigström.
Surprise: Miniature replica of the Imperial yacht *Standard*.
Height: Egg: 6 inches (15.3 cm) – with base
Yacht: ¾ x 3 inches (2 cm x 7.5 cm).
Marks: K. FABERGÉ (engraved in italics), H.W., assay mark of St Petersburg regional assay department (indistinct), 72.

Gold, silver, diamonds, pearls, rock crystal, lapis lazuli and enamel.

This Renaissance style rock crystal egg consists of two parts hinged together. The gold setting with a carved inscription *Standard 1909* is decorated with diamonds, enamel and two lapis-lazuli figures of heraldic double-headed eagles. The stand – two intertwined lapis-lazuli dolphins – has a shaped rock crystal base. Inside the egg is a gold model of the *Standard* mounted on an undulating rock-crystal plate simulating water.

According to Eugène Fabergé in a letter he wrote to Bainbridge in Paris on 5 June 1934, the surprise was executed:

... by the old Holmström, who especially put all his art into making the tiny ship as natural as possible so that the guns were movable and all the rigging exactly copied... Even the chains of the anchors were movable. [229]

INVOICE

Rock crystal egg on rock crystal pediment, with two lapis lazuli dolphins, decorations of gold and enamel with 2 pearls, 4 diamonds and 1029 rose-cut diamonds, containing a model of the yacht 'Standard' in gold, platinum and enamel 12 400 r.
St Petersburg, 9 July 1909. C. Fabergé [230]

HISTORY

1909–1917 Kept in the study of Her Imperial Majesty Alexandra Fedorovna at the Winter Palace.

The following is a description from a Fabergé album of the Imperial Easter eggs presented to Alexandra Fedorovna between 1907 and 1916. [231]

Easter egg presented to Alexandra Fedorovna in 1909, of rock crystal in gold and enamel setting. At both ends of the egg, double-headed eagles of lapis lazuli with pearl pendants. The egg is placed horizontally on a lapis lazuli dolphin and is completed by a pedestal of rock crystal in a gold setting with white and green enamel. Contains a miniature model of the new Imperial yacht, 'Standard'.

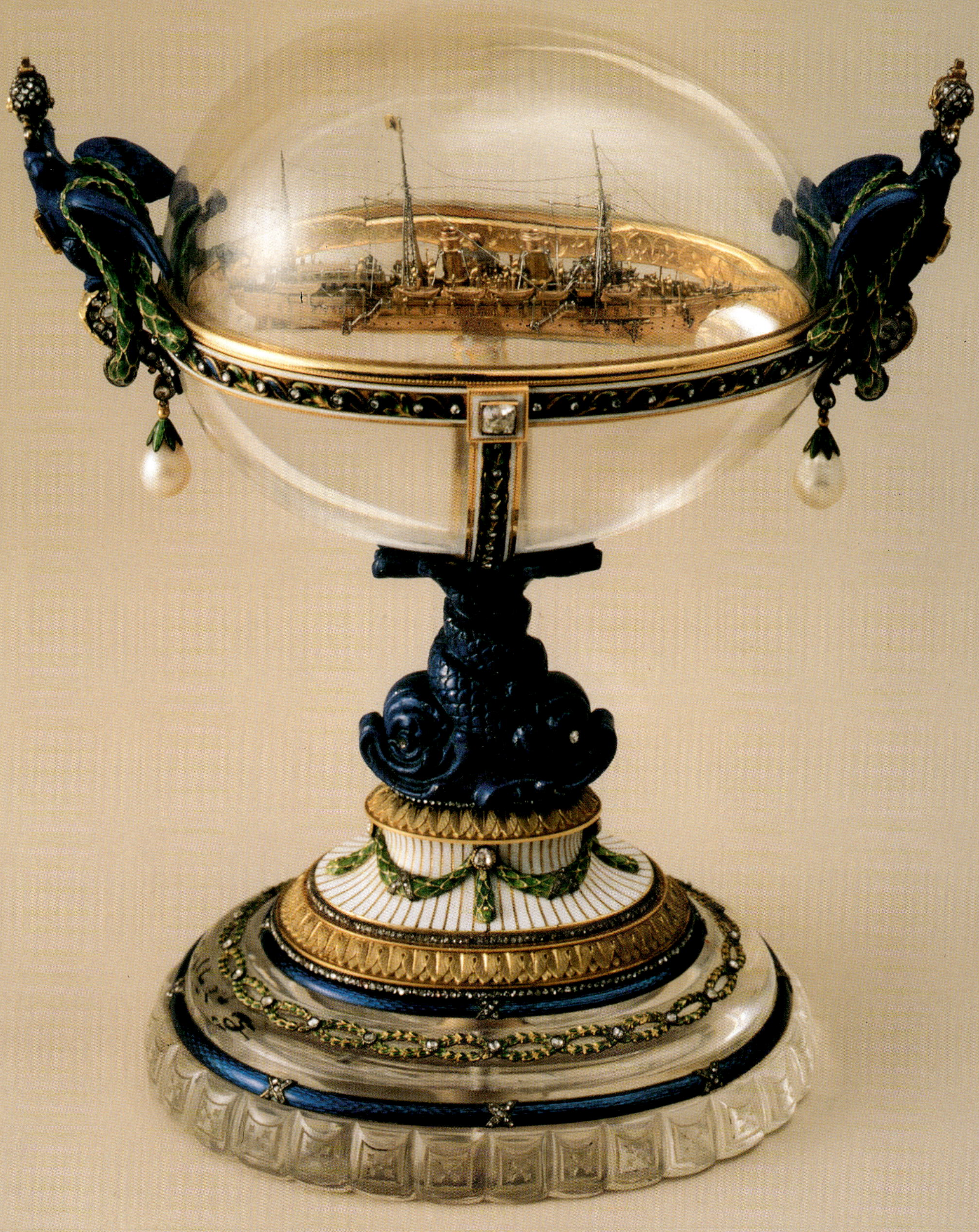

1917 Confiscated by Kerensky's provisional government, along with other treasures, and taken from the Anichkov Palace to the Moscow Kremlin Armoury.

1922 One of the items on the list of confiscated treasures transferred from the Anichkov Palace to the Sovnarkom.

1 crystal egg in gold setting, with 4 diamonds and rose-cut diamonds, containing a model of a ship. [232]

The Standard egg was never sold by Antikvariat to the West and has remained in Russia.

1910

37
Alexander III Equestrian Egg

Presented by
Tsar Nicholas II to his
mother, the Dowager
Empress Maria Fedorovna,
Easter 1910 (18 April)

(Moscow Kremlin Armoury Museum)

In 1909, a bronze monument of Tsar Alexander III, designed by the sculptor, Prince Paolo Troubetskoy, was unveiled in Znamensky Square in St Petersburg. To commemorate this important family event, Tsar Nicholas II gave his mother, the Dowager Empress Maria Fedorovna, this Easter egg, which contains a gold replica of the statue of her late husband. During the Revolution Troubetskoy's bronze statue was removed from its place of honour and has only recently been relocated in front of the Marble Palace.

DESCRIPTION

Surprise: Miniature replica of the Alexander III monument.
Height: Egg and base: 6⅛ inches (15.5 cm);
Monument: 1%₆ inches (5 cm x 4 cm).
Marks: FABERGÉ (engraved in italics).

Gold, platinum, rose-cut diamonds, rock crystal, lapis lazuli.

This is one of the most beautiful Easter eggs designed by Fabergé, entirely set in platinum and carved from a single, large piece of rock crystal. The upper part is decorated with an appliqué platinum lattice studded with small diamonds, a diamond tassled fringe and has platinum consoles on two sides, on which figures of heraldic double-headed eagles are mounted. The Renaissance style egg is mounted with a large diamond on the top. The stand is in the form of four platinum-winged half-length figures of cupids resting upon a shaped rock-crystal base. A gold model of the monument to Alexander III on a tall rectangular pedestal of lapis lazuli fits inside the egg.

Early photograph of Alexander III monument unveiled in 1909 in Znamensky Square, St Petersburg.

INVOICE

17 April entry:

> Large egg of engraved topaz in massive platinum
> mounting in the Renaissance style, on a similar pediment
> of the same topaz, 1318 rose-cut diamonds and 1 large diamond.
> Inside on a lapis lazuli pedestal a matt gold equestrian figure
> of Emperor Alexander III 14700 r.
> St Petersburg, 12 July 1910 [233]

[Note: Topaz is a Russian term for high quality rock crystal]

HISTORY

1910–1917 Kept at the Anichkov Palace.

1917 Confiscated by Kerensky's provisional government, along with other treasures, and taken from the Anichkov Palace to the Moscow Kremlin Armoury.

Crystal egg in silver mounting, decorated with diamonds, on pediment, containing a statue of Alexander III. [234]

1922 One of the items on the list of confiscated treasures transferred from the Anichkov Palace to the Sovnarkom.

1 crystal egg in silver setting with 7 diamonds and rose-cut diamonds, containing a gold model of the Alexander III monument. [235]

The Alexander III Equestrian egg was never sold by Antikvariat to the West and it remained in Russia.

The bronze monument of Tsar Alexander III on which the surprise was modelled now stands in front of the Marble Palace

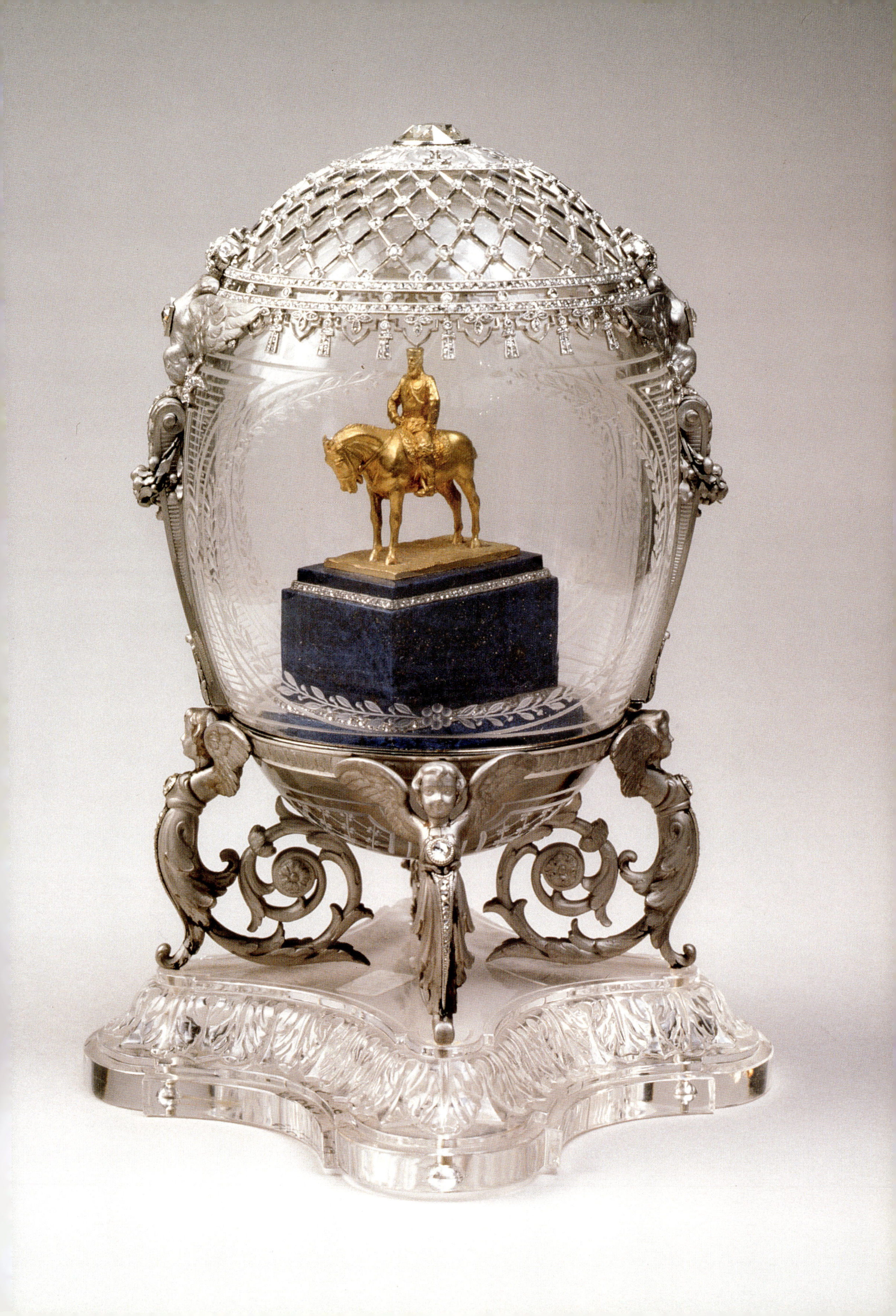

1910

38

Colonnade Egg

Presented by
Tsar Nicholas II to his
wife, the Empress
Alexandra Fedorovna,
Easter 1910 (18 April)

*(Collection of Her Majesty
Queen Elizabeth II)*

Fabergé modelled this romantic Easter egg on a Greek Temple of Love and endowed it with metaphorical symbolism. The cherubs around the base represent the Emperor and Empress four daughters (Olga, Tatiana, Maria, Anastasia) and the two doves inside the colonnade represent the enduring love which existed between the Imperial couple. Elevated above all is a cherub, depicting the young Tsarevich Alexei, demonstrating the significance the Imperial family placed upon the long-awaited birth of the heir to the throne.

Description

Workmaster: Henrik Wigström.
Height: 11 inches (28 cm).
Marks: FABERGÉ (in Cyrillic) and H.W., assay mark of St Petersburg regional assay department, 56.

Bowenite, varicoloured gold, pink and white *guilloché* enamel and rose-cut diamonds.

The rotary clock is in the form of a pink *guilloché* enamelled gold egg, surmounted by a silver-gilt cherub looking down and pointing to the clock's revolving chapter ring which is set with rose-cut diamond Arabic numerals and a diamond-studded arrowhead indicating the hour. The Temple of Love is completed by six pale-green bowenite columns wound with gold floral garlands terminating at Ionic capitals. The columns shelter two platinum doves nestling upon a matching pink *guilloché* enamel pedestal. Below the columns, seated on the round stepped bowenite base, are four silver-gilt cherubs holding elaborate varicoloured gold floral garlands.

Invoice

17 April entry:

> *Large clock egg in the form of a summer-house with a jadeite and enamel colonnade, Louis XVI style, with figures of cupids, quatre couleurs garlands and clock face of diamonds and enamel.* 11600 r.
> *St Petersburg, 12 July 1910* [236]

History

1910–1917 Kept in the study of Her Imperial Majesty Alexandra Fedorovna at the Winter Palace.

The following description is from a Fabergé album of the Imperial Easter eggs presented to Alexandra Fedorovna between 1907 and 1916. [237]

Easter egg presented to Alexandra Fedorovna in 1910. Clock-egg of pink enamel with rotating clock face, surmounted by a cupid pointing to the hour with a rod. The egg is placed on a colonnade of light green serpentine and the columns are entwined with garlands of roses of different colours of gold. In the centre there are two white platinum doves. The colonnade ends with a pedestal of serpentine, gold and pink enamel. At the corners of the pedestal, four cherubs (the Imperial children) hold garlands of roses.

1917 Confiscated by Kerensky's provisional government, along with other treasures, and taken from the Anichkov Palace to the Moscow Kremlin Armoury.

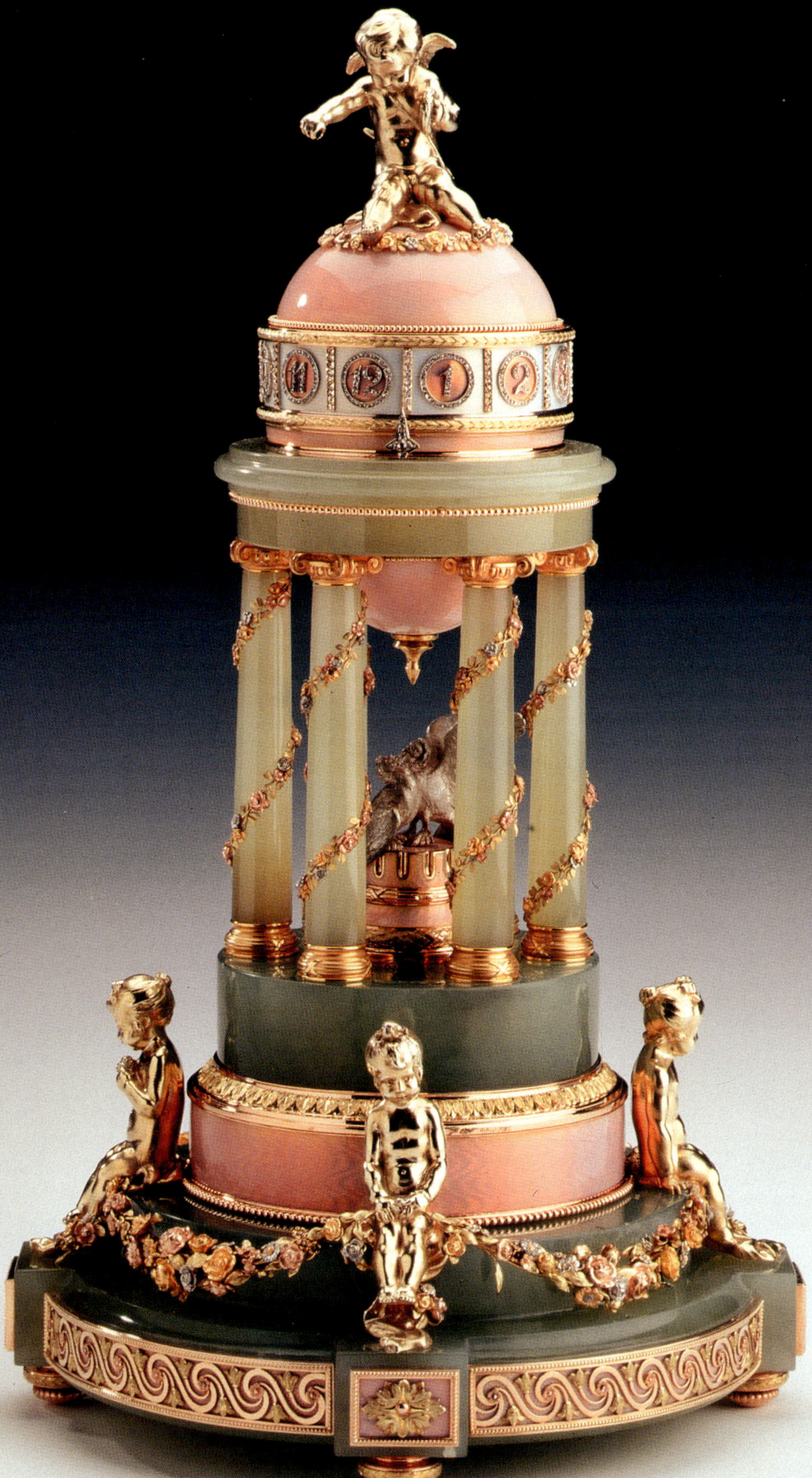

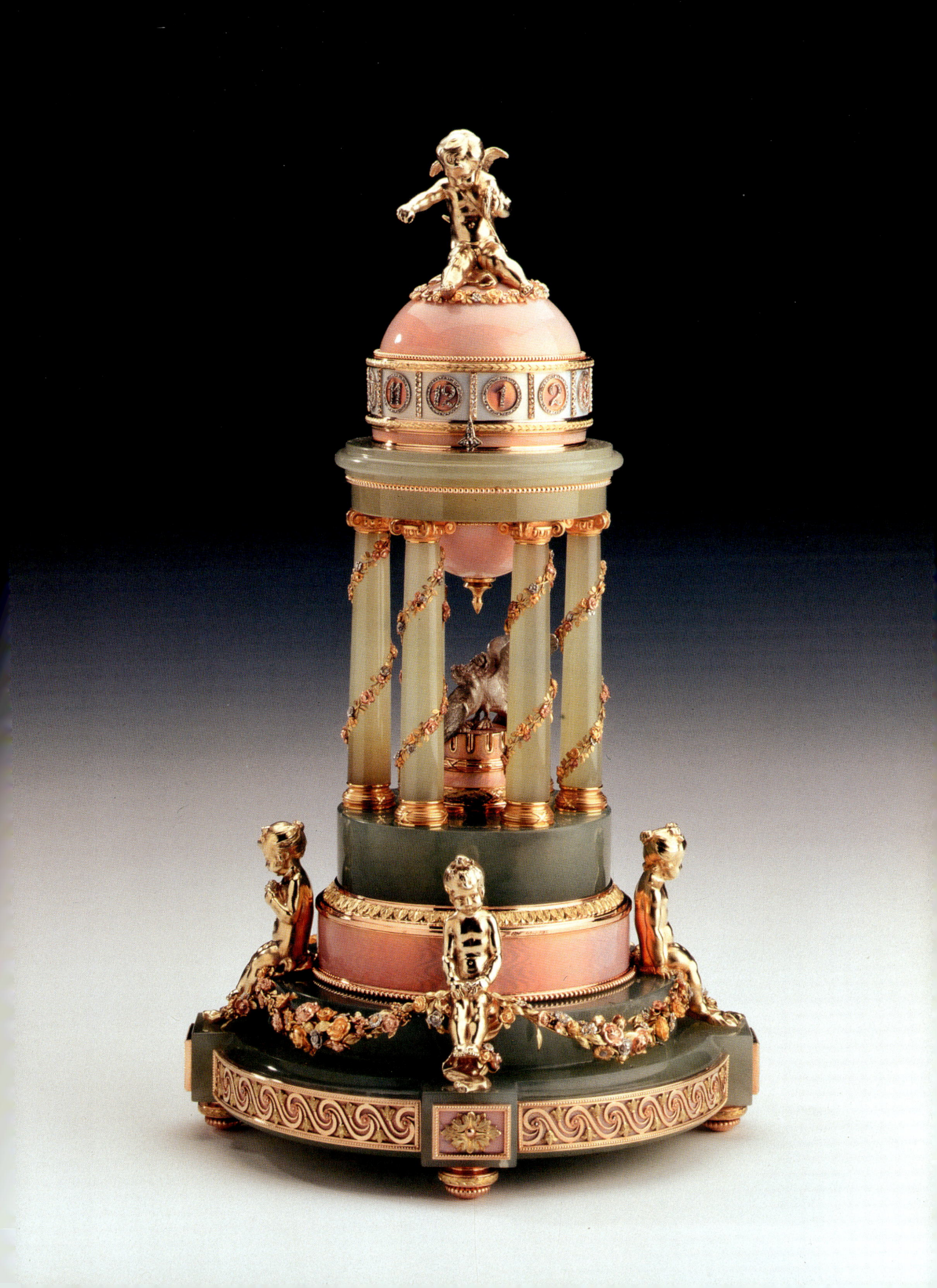

1922 One of the items on the list of confiscated treasures transferred from the Anichkov Palace to the Sovnarkom.

Desk clock in the form of a summer-house, in gold setting with roses. [238]

1933 This egg appears in Queen Mary's list of bibelots acquired in 1933, but as there is no invoice or record of payment for the egg in the Royal Archives it was probably presented as a gift to the Queen. [239]

Early Fabergé photograph of the Colonnade egg

Bay Tree Egg

1911

39

Presented by
Tsar Nicholas II to his
mother, the Dowager
Empress Maria Fedorovna,
Easter 1911 (10 April)

*(The FORBES Magazine
Collection, New York)*

DESCRIPTION

Height: 11 inches (28 cm).
Marks: FABERGÉ, dated 1911.

Gold, translucent green and opaque white enamel, nephrite, diamonds, citrines, amethysts, rubies, pearls, agate, feathers.

This egg, previously known as the Orange Tree egg, was inspired by French 18th-century musical orange trees. It is designed in the form of a bay tree with lush foliage of finely carved nephrite leaves. The modelled gold tree-trunk sits in a gold trellised agate box adorned with floral swags and mounted on a square solid nephrite base. The tree, which is laden with fruits carved from various gemstones, conceals a feathered songbird. The bird emerges singing from the top of the tree, when a button, which appears to be a fruit, is pressed and disappears again when the song is finished.

INVOICE

9 April entry:

> *1 Large egg in the form of a bay tree in gold, with
> 325 nephrite leaves, 110 opalescent white enamel
> flowerets, 25 diamonds, 20 rubies, 53 pearls,
> 219 rose-cut diamonds, 1 large rose-cut diamond.
> Inside the tree a mechanical songbird. In a
> rectangular tub of white Mexican onyx on a nephrite
> pediment, with 4 nephrite columns at the corners
> supporting green enamel garlands with pearls.*   12800 r.
> *St Petersburg, 13 June 1911* [240]

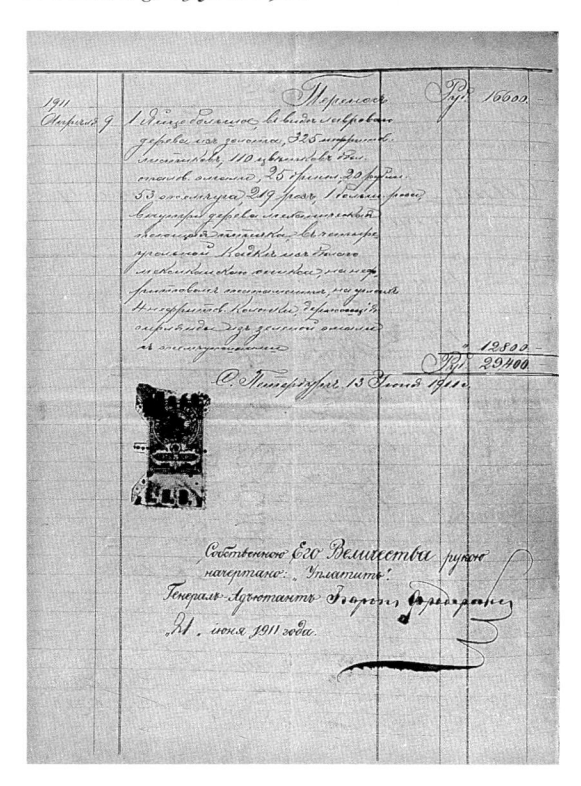

HISTORY

1911–1917 Kept at the Anichkov Palace.

1917 Confiscated by Kerensky's provisional government, along with other treasures, and taken from the Anichkov Palace to the Moscow Kremlin Armoury.

Nephrite bay tree on pediment, gold-mounted with multi-coloured precious stones and with song-bird. [241]

1922 One of the items on the list of confiscated treasures transferred from the Anichkov Palace to the Sovnarkom.

1 nephrite tree with songbird, gold ornamentation, rose-cut diamonds, diamonds, topazes, pearls and rubies. [242]

1947 Sold by Sotheby's, London, 10 July, for £1,650.

Previous owners include: Wartski, London; A.G. Hughes, England; Arthur E. Bradshaw; W. Magalow; Maurice Sandoz, Switzerland; A La Vieille Russie, New York, Mildred Kaplan, New York.

1966 Purchased by Forbes, Inc. for $35,000. [243]

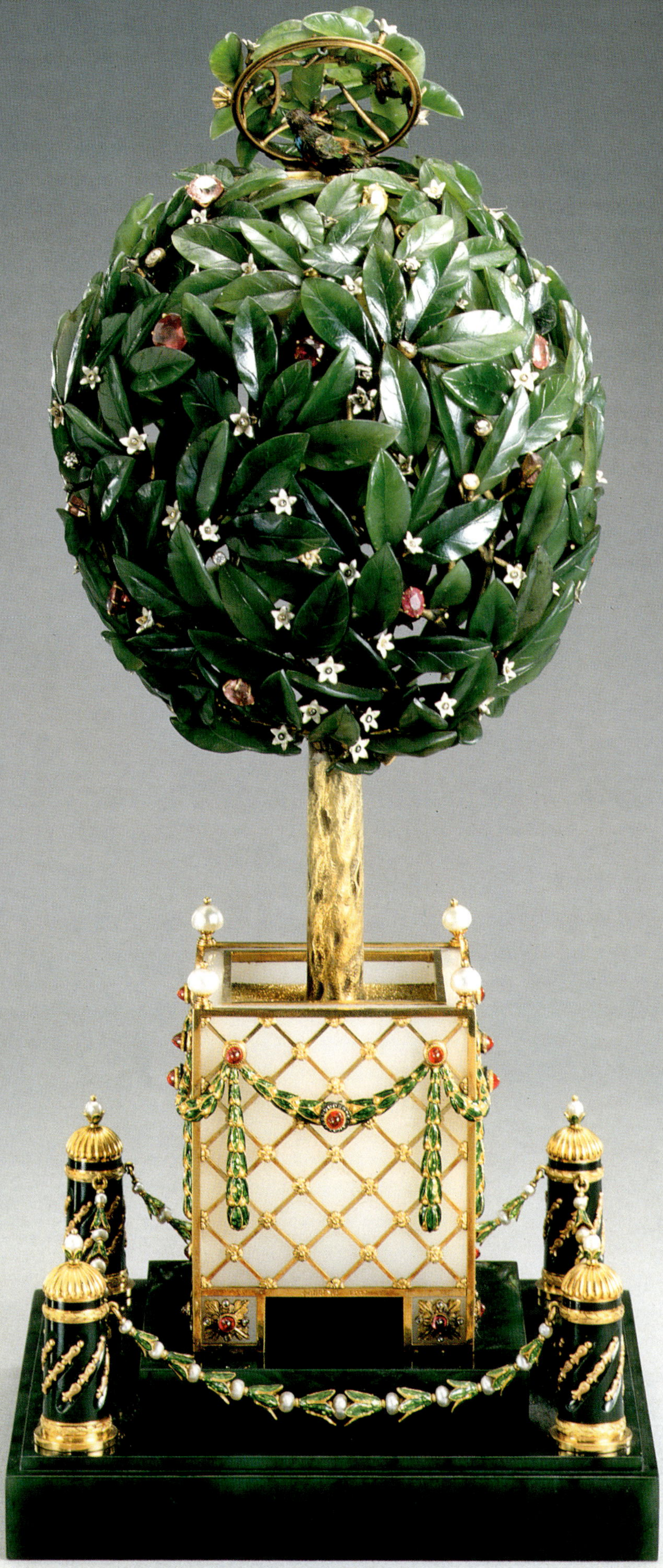

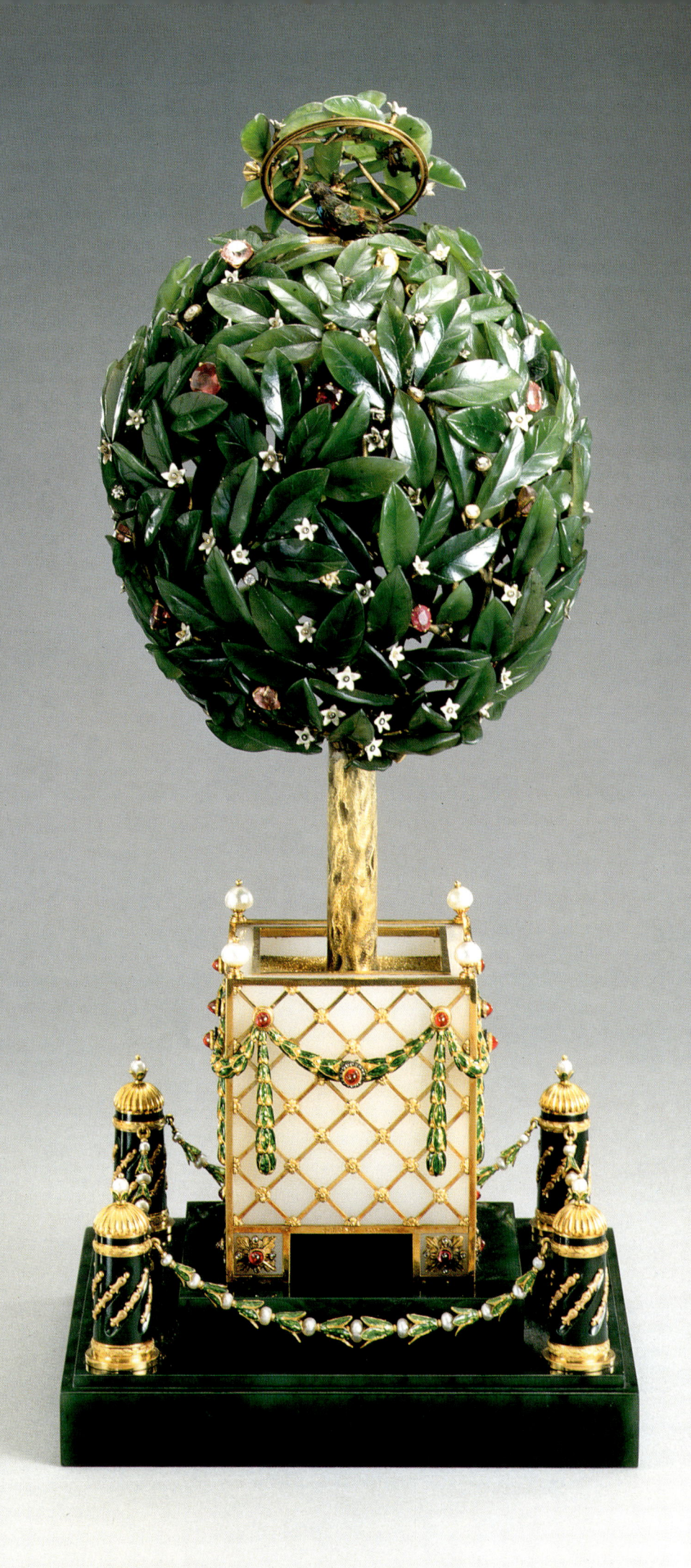

40

1911

Fifteenth Anniversary Egg

Presented by
Tsar Nicholas II to his
wife, the Empress
Alexandra Fedorovna,
Easter 1911 (10 April)

*(The FORBES Magazine
Collection, New York)*

DESCRIPTION

Height: 5⅛ inches (13 cm) without stand.

Gold, translucent green enamel, opaque white enamel, opalescent oyster enamel, diamonds, rock crystal.

The Fifteenth Anniversary Egg is the most personal of all the eggs created for Nicholas II and his wife, Alexandra Federovna, and one of the most exquisite Easter eggs produced by Fabergé. Made to commemorate the fifteenth anniversary of Tsar Nicholas II's accession to the throne, the egg is set with oval miniatures painted by Vassilii Zuiev of the Tsar, the Empress Alexandra and their four daughters. Additional rectangular miniatures depict the principal events of the reign up to 1911.

INVOICE

9 April entry:

*Large gold egg, Louis XVI style, opalescent white enamel
with green enamel garlands, 929 rose-cut diamonds,
1 diamond, 1 large rose-cut diamond.
16 miniatures by Zuiev:
Portraits:
His Majesty the Emperor
Her Majesty the Empress
His Highness the Heir-Tsarevich
The Grand Duchesses: Olga Nikolaievna, Tatiana
Nikolaievna, Maria Nikolaievna, Anastasia Nikolaievna
1. Procession in the Cathedral of the Dormition
2. The Holy Coronation of Their Majesties
3. The Emperor's Speech from the Throne
4. Transfer of the Relics of Saint Seraphim of Sarov
5. The Peace Palace at the Hague
6. The Emperor Alexander III Museum
7. The Emperor Alexander III Bridge in Paris
8. Unveiling of the monument to Peter I in Riga
9. The Poltava Celebrations (Swedish Grave)
Two vignettes, 1894 and 1911   16600 r.*

St Petersburg, 13 June 1911 [244]

HISTORY

1911–1917 Kept in the study of Her Imperial Majesty Alexandra Fedorovna at the Winter Palace.

The following is a description from a Fabergé album of the Imperial Easter eggs presented to Alexandra Fedorovna between 1907 and 1916. [245]

Easter egg presented to Alexandra Fedorovna in 1911. Made of opalescent enamel, divided into thyrsi by green enamel garlands. The thyrsi sections contain miniature paintings depicting the main events of the reign of Nicholas II, alternating with portraits of members of the Imperial family.

1966 Acquired by FORBES, Inc.

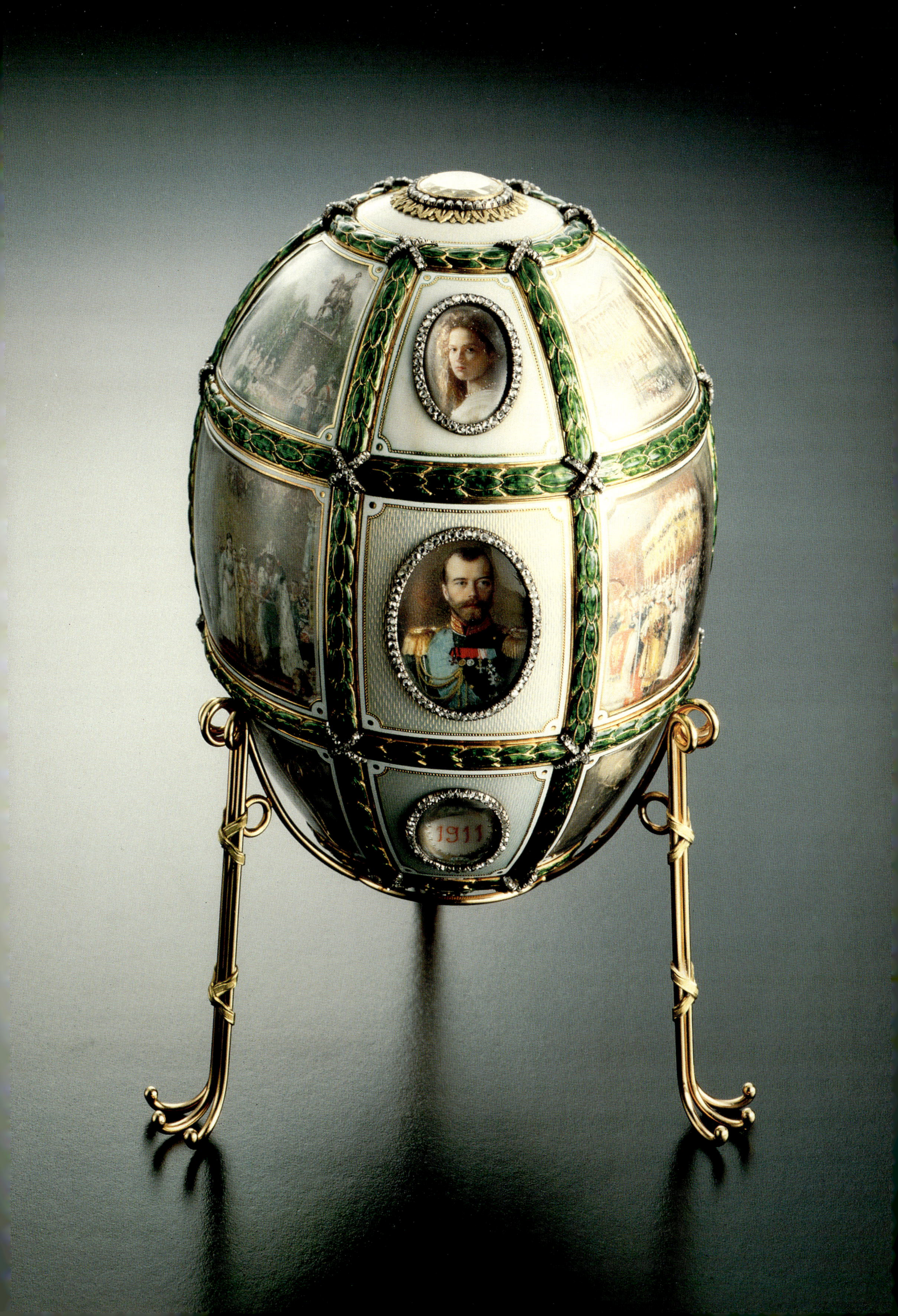
1911

1912

41
Napoleonic Egg

Presented by Tsar Nicholas II to his mother, the Dowager Empress Maria Fedorovna, Easter 1912 (25 March)

(New Orleans Museum of Art: Matilda Geddings Gray Foundation Collection)

This egg commemorates the centenary of the Russian victory over the armies of Napoleon which were defeated in 1812 following the battle of Borodino. The festivities for this centenary were used to enhance Russian patriotism.

DESCRIPTION

EGG:
Workmaster: Henrik Wigström.
Height: 4 inches (11.8 cm).
Marks: FABERGÉ, H.W., assay mark of St Petersburg.

SURPRISE: 6 miniatures signed and dated V. Zuiev 1912.

Gold, enamel, diamonds, platinum, ivory, velvet, silk.

Fabergé's green *guilloché* enamel Easter egg is decorated in the Empire style with double-headed eagles and trophies of war. Diamonds at the apex and base cover the cipher of the Dowager Empress and the date 1912.

As in the Danish Palaces Easter egg (6), the surprise is a folding screen.
On six panels Vasilii Zuiev has painted the regiments of which the Dowager Empress was honorary colonel.

Drawing of the Napoleonic Easter egg from Wigström's stock book

202

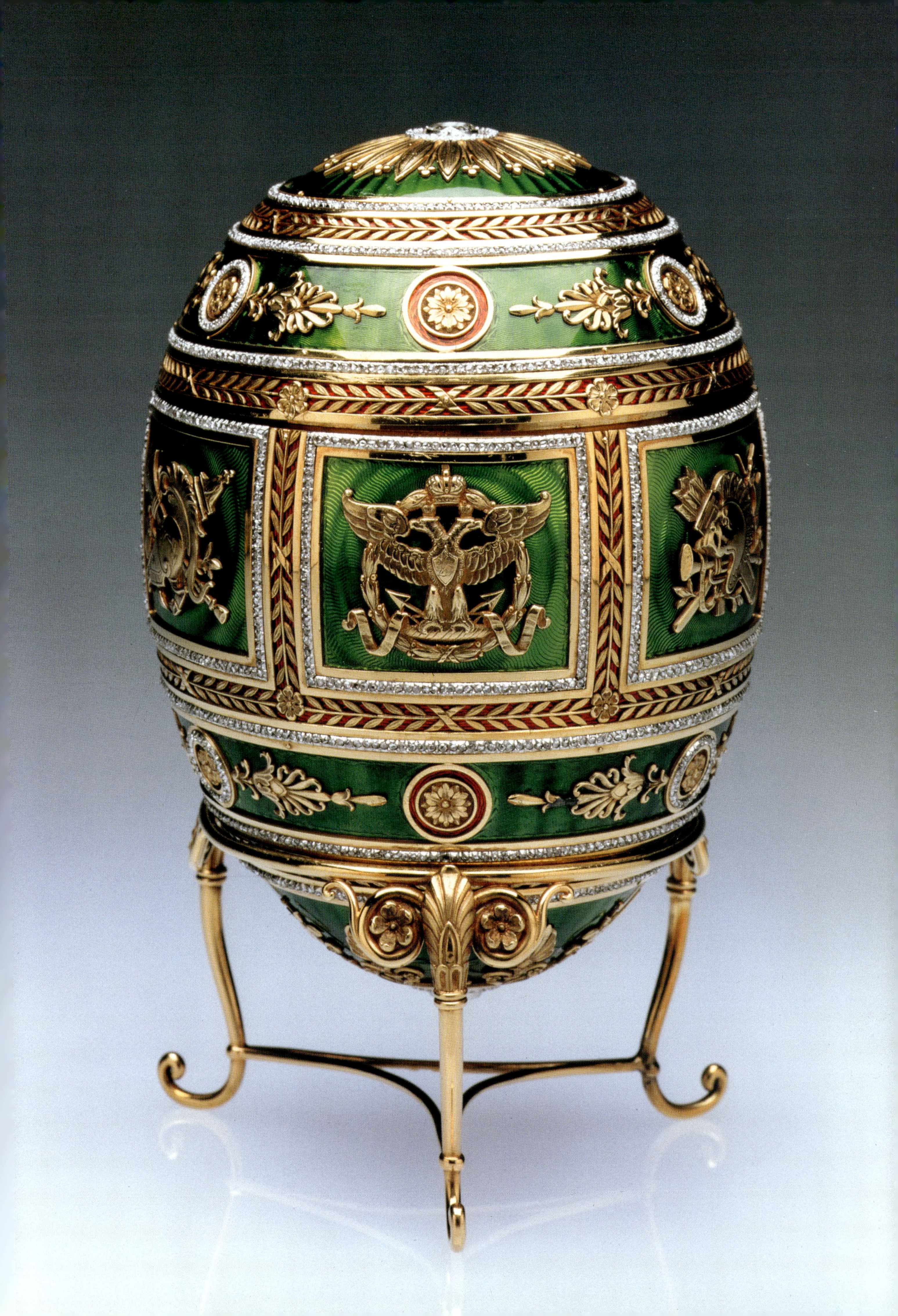

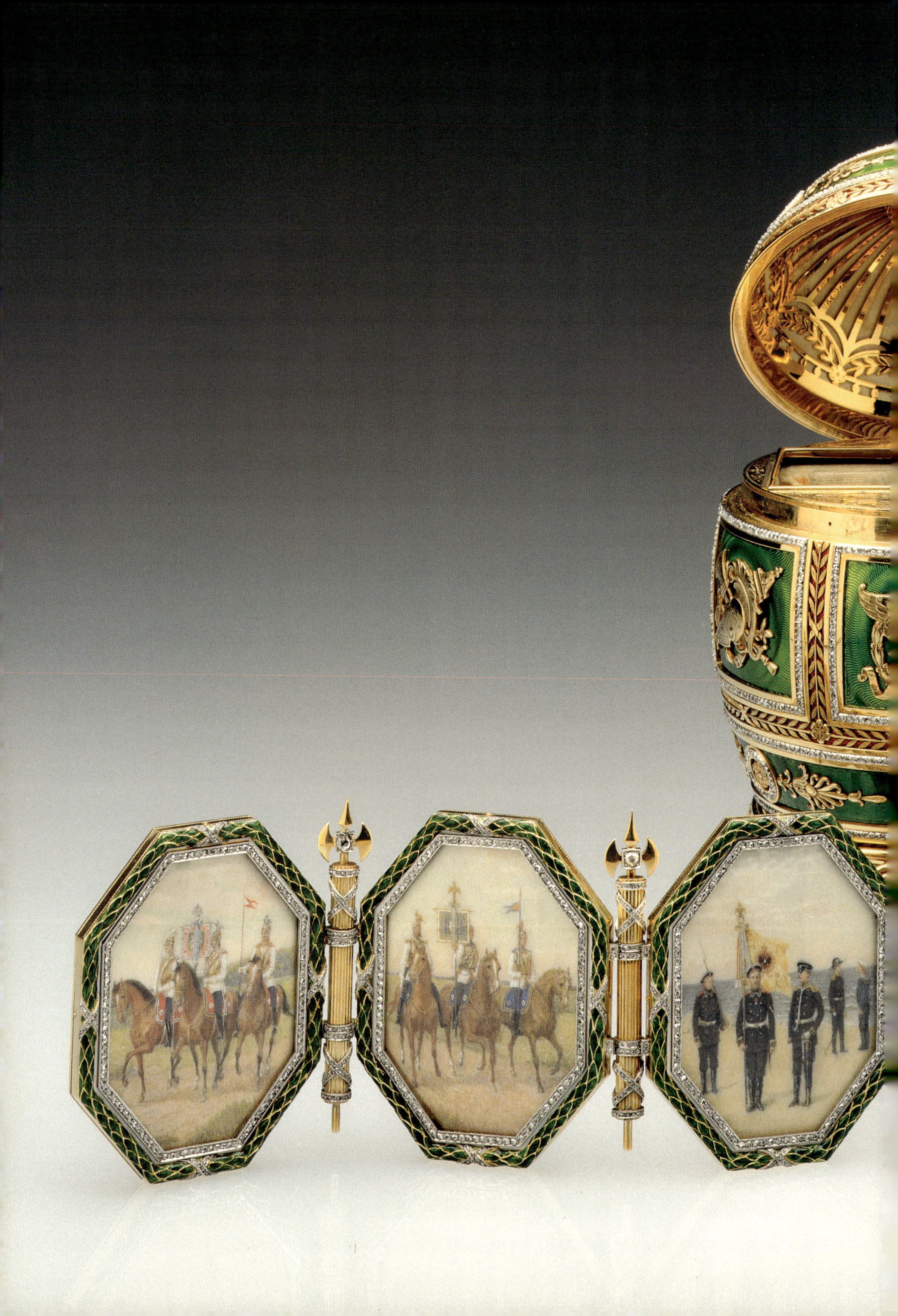

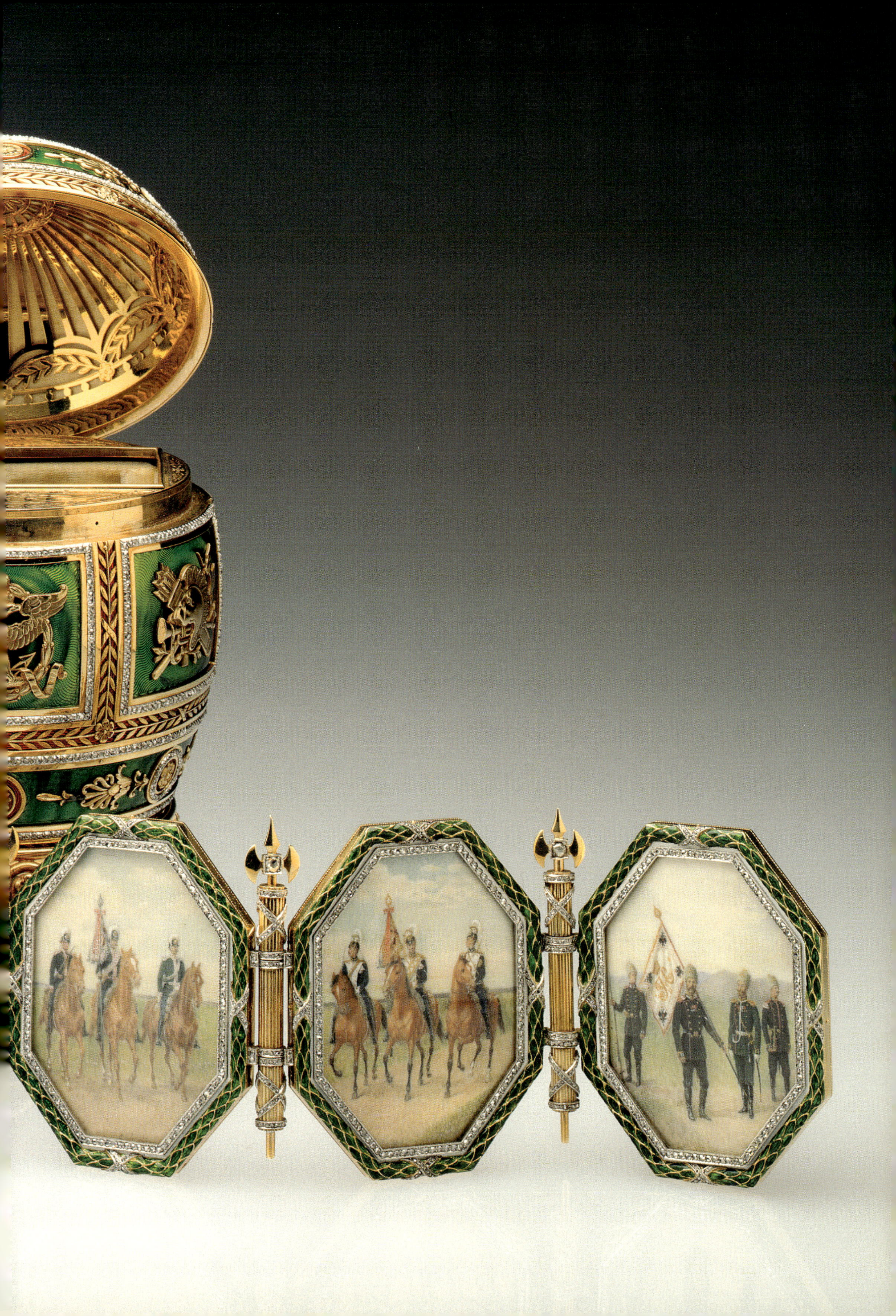

From left to right the regiments are Her Majesty's Regiment of the Chevaliers Guard, the Imperial Guard Cuirassiers, the Fleet of the Imperial Guard, the Second Pskov Dragoons, the Eleventh Chuguevskii Uhlans and the Eleventh East Siberian Rifles. The panels are framed in green enamelled laurel-leaf and diamond borders; the hinges are in the shape of axe-topped fasces. The reverse side of each miniature shows the crowned cipher of Maria Fedorovna on a green *guilloché* enamel disc in the centre of an opalescent white enamel panel.

INVOICE

Not found

No invoices have been found for the eggs presented in 1912, 1914, 1915 and 1916. This is because the documents of the Household Division of His Imperial Majesty's Cabinet for 1912–1917 were not deposited in the archives on the Fontanka, opposite the Anichkov Palace. After the October Revolution of 1917, the Cabinet documents were transferred to the Tsentarkhiv, and while they were being sorted between 1918 and 1939 a large part of them were unaccountably destroyed, leaving only some isolated documents, including the invoice for the eggs made in 1913. Yet the account books of His Imperial Majesty's Cabinet survived, as did the correspondence between Alexandra Fedorovna's Secretariat and the Cabinet concerning the submission of Fabergé's invoices for payment. They supply the following information regarding payment of Fabergé's invoices for the two Easter eggs produced in 1912 for Maria Fedorovna and Alexandra Fedorovna:

27 June 1912, invoice for the sum of 50897 r. 50 kop. [246]

HISTORY

1912–1917 Kept at the Anichkov Palace.

1917 Confiscated by Kerensky's provisional government, along with other treasures, and taken from the Anichkov Palace to the Moscow Kremlin Armoury.

1922 One of the items on the list of confiscated treasures transferred from the Anichkov Palace to Sovnarkom.

1 gold egg with rose-cut diamonds and large diamonds on gold stand, containing gold six-sided folding frame. [247]

1930 Officially sold by Antikvariat for 5,000 roubles. Later acquired by Matilda Geddings Gray from Hammer Galleries Inc., New York. [248]

1912

42

Tsarevich Egg

Presented by
Tsar Nicholas II to his
wife, the Empress
Alexandra Fedorovna,
Easter 1912 (25 March)

(Virginia Museum of Fine Arts, Richmond, bequest of Lillian Thomas Pratt)

The long-awaited birth in 1904 of the Heir-Tsarevich Alexei was a major cause for celebration. At last, a son was born to Nicholas and Alexandra. The Imperial couple's hopes and dreams were contingent upon Alexei surviving into adulthood. But, in 1911 he fell seriously ill (he had unfortunately inherited from his mother the haemophilia transmitted to descendants of Queen Victoria) and lingered for a time between life and death. A notice announcing his death was even prepared, but he survived, thanks, as the Empress believed, to the ministrations of Rasputin. His almost miraculous recovery made him an obvious subject for the following year's egg. The Imperial couple were extremely touched by the design. On 13 March 1912, Eugène Fabergé was sent to Livadia to present this Easter egg to the Tsar, while his father delivered the Napoleonic Easter egg to the Dowager Empress Maria Fedorovna. Eugène later recalled (in a letter written to H.C. Bainbridge on 5 June 1934):

... This lapis-lazuli egg made in 1912 – as the Tsar then dwelled at the Livadia Castle near Yalta on the south coast of the Crimea – I was ordered by father to carry personally to His Majesty. So, I made this voyage through all Russia... [249]

DESCRIPTION

Workmaster: Henrik Wigström.
Surprise: Diamond picture frame with miniature of Tsarevich Alexei.
Height: Egg: 4 15/16 inches (12.5 cm);
Frame: 3 3/4 inches (9.5 cm).
Marks: FABERGÉ (engraved), H.W.

Early Fabergé photograph of the Tsarevich egg

This regal rococo-style Easter egg carved from six pieces of finest lapis lazuli is encased in a profusion of gold decorative motifs. The inscriptions AΘ and 1912 are visible under the large table diamond set at the top and diamond solitaire at the bottom. Double-headed eagles, double-winged caryatids, floral scrolls, garlands and flower baskets embellish this opulent egg which conceals a diamond-studded double-headed eagle picture frame with a miniature portrait on ivory of the Tsarevich Alexei. The original gold stand, known from a vintage photograph, was separated from the egg during the Revolution and its whereabouts are unknown.

INVOICE

See Napoleonic egg (page 206).

HISTORY

1912–1917 Kept in the study of Her Imperial Majesty Alexandra Fedorovna at the Winter Palace.

The following is a description from a Fabergé album of the Imperial Easter eggs presented to Alexandra Fedorovna between 1907 and 1916. [250]

Easter egg presented to Alexandra Fedorovna in 1912. Made of lapis-lazuli in Louis XVI style, covered with open-work chased gold ornamentation. Contains a double-headed eagle of diamonds, on whose breast is a two-faceted portrait of Tsarevich Alexei (recto and verso).

1917 Confiscated by Kerensky's provisional government, along with other treasures, and taken to the Moscow Kremlin Armoury.

1930 Officially sold by Antikvariat for 8000 roubles. [251]

1933–1934 Purchased by Lillian Thomas Pratt from Armand Hammer's exhibition at Lord and Taylor, New York.

1913

43
Winter Egg

Presented by
Tsar Nicholas II to his
mother, the Dowager
Empress Maria Fedorovna,
Easter 1913 (14 April)

(Private collection, USA)

The Winter egg, designed by Alma Theresia Pihl, must have been inspired by the exceptionally harsh winter of 1911–12, which was the coldest Russia had experienced for over 25 years. Perhaps Alma observed the beautiful frost patterns on the window panes and used the designs in her project.

DESCRIPTION

Workmaster: Albert Holmström.
Designer: Alma Theresia Pihl.
Surprise: Basket full of wood anemones.
Overall height: 5⅝ inches (14.2 cm).
Egg height: 4 inches (10.2 cm).
Surprise height: 3¼ inches (8.2 cm).
Marks: (engraved on the surprise): FABERGÉ 1913

Platinum, gold, rock crystal, moonstone, rose-cut diamonds, white quartz, demantoid garnets, nephrite.

One of the finest Easter eggs produced by Fabergé. The frosted appearance of the egg which simulates ice crystals is attained by finely engraving the interior of the carved, thinly transparent body of the egg. The crystal exterior is similarly engraved and decorated all over with platinum and rose-cut diamond-set ice crystals. The egg sits upon a rock-crystal base formed as a block of melting ice dripping with rivulets of rose-cut diamonds. A glimpse of the surprise can be seen through the frosted egg, which opens at the diamond-set platinum rim to reveal an exquisite basket of wood anemones. Each flower in the platinum and rose-cut diamond double-handled trelliswork basket is carved from a single piece of white quartz with gold stems and stamens centred with demantoid garnets. The leaves of the flowers are delicately carved in nephrite, emerging from a bed of gold moss. The base of the basket is engraved FABERGÉ 1913. A cabochon moonstone mounted at the top of the egg is painted on the reverse with the date 1913.

INVOICE

13 April entry:

> *Large egg of white topaz* with frosting motifs of*
> *1508 rose-cut diamonds and inlaid in the*
> *topaz with borders set with 360 diamonds, on a*
> *topaz base shaped as a block of ice with rose-cut*
> *diamond icicles. Inside the egg is a small platinum basket*
> *decorated with 1378 rose-cut diamonds, in it white*
> *quartz snowdrops with nephrite leaves* 24600 r.
> *St Petersburg, 24 June 1913* [252]

*White topaz is the Russian term given to high quality rock crystal, and while the invoice states that the flowers are snowdrops, this may be poetic licence as the flowers bear a closer resemblance to wood anemones.

This is the highest amount paid by a Tsar for an Imperial Easter egg.

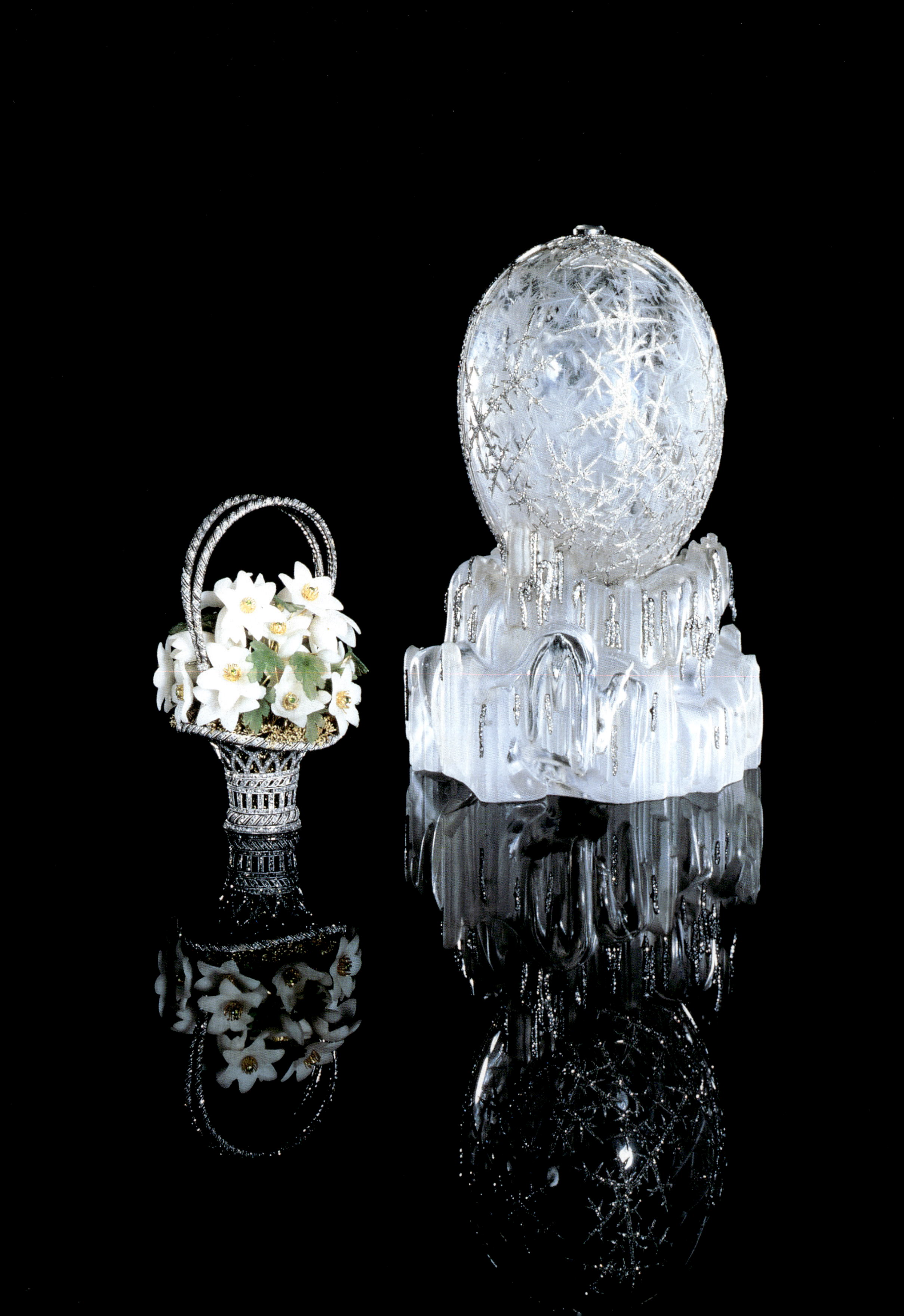

HISTORY

1913–1917 Kept at the Anichkov Palace.

1917 Confiscated by Kerensky's provisional government, along with other treasures, and taken from the Anichkov Palace to the Moscow Kremlin Armoury.

1922 One of the items on the list of confiscated treasures transferred from the Anichkov Palace to the Sovnarkom may be the egg in question.

1 crystal egg in silver setting with diamonds and rose-cut diamonds on stand. [253]

1934 Acquired by Lord Allington. Later owned by Sir Bernard Eckstein.

1949 Sold by Sotheby's, London, 8 February, for £1,700 ($4,760) to Mr Bryan Ledbrook.

1994 Sold by Christie's, Geneva, 16 November, for $5.6 million to a private collector.

211

44

1913

Romanov Tercentenary Egg

Presented by
Tsar Nicholas II to his
wife, the Empress
Alexandra Fedoronva,
Easter 1913 (14 April)

(Moscow Kremlin Armoury Museum)

The theme of this egg is the tercentenary of the House of Romanov, which had been founded by Mikhail Fedorovich Romanov in 1613. In 1912 the newspapers carried announcements of the impending bicentenary, in 1913, of the famous Gottorp Globe presented in 1713 to Peter I that held pride of place at the Kunstkamera in St Petersburg, and the idea seems to have inspired the designers of the egg.

Description

Workmaster: Henrik Wigström.
Height: 7½ inches (19 cm).
Marks: Stamped FABERGÉ (in Cyrillic) and H.W., assay mark of St Petersburg regional assay department.

Gold, silver, steel, diamonds, turquoise, crystal, purpurine, ivory.

This egg, with 18 miniature portraits of the Romanov Tsars, is supported by a shaft in the shape of a three-sided eagle. The golden egg is covered with white transparent enamel on a *guilloché* ground. The miniature portraits by Vassilii Zuiev, in 18 round diamond frames, depict rulers of the Romanov dynasty, from Mikhail Fedorovich to Nicholas II. The spaces between the portraits contain inlaid patterns of heraldic eagles, crowns, and Tsars' wreaths. A large diamond bearing the dates 1613 and 1913 is secured at the top of the egg, while a large triangular diamond fixed to the bottom end covers the monogram AΘ.

The inside of the egg is lined with opalescent enamel on a *guilloché* ground.
A rotating steel globe of dark blue enamel is secured inside the egg; it shows the territories of Russia in 1613 and 1913, represented in gold.

The base is constructed of purpurine, decorated with small enamel patterns, and secured on three supports cast in the shape of flattened pellets.

Invoice

13 April entry:

> *Large egg covered inside and out with white enamel.*
> *On the outside, 18 miniatures of members of the Romanov Dynasty*
> *by Zuiev, framed with 1115 rose-cut diamonds, under topazes.*
> *Between the miniatures, gold chased and engraved designs with*
> *Imperial crowns and fur caps. At each end of the egg, lozenge diamonds*
> *with* HER MAJESTY'S *cipher and the dates of the jubilee year.*
> *Inside, a blue steel globe with representation of two northern hemispheres.*
> *The continents are presented in relief, in different coloured golds.*
> *One hemisphere shows Russia in 1613 and the other Russia in 1913.*
> *The egg rests on a pediment consisting of a three-sided eagle*
> *standing on the Imperial coat of arms made of purpurine and enamel*
>
> 21300 r.

{copy from the original shield kept at the Armoury in Moscow}

St Petersburg, 24 June 1913 [254]

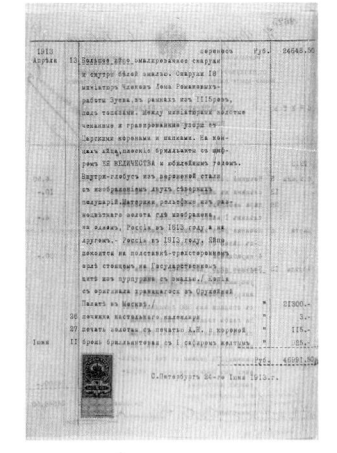

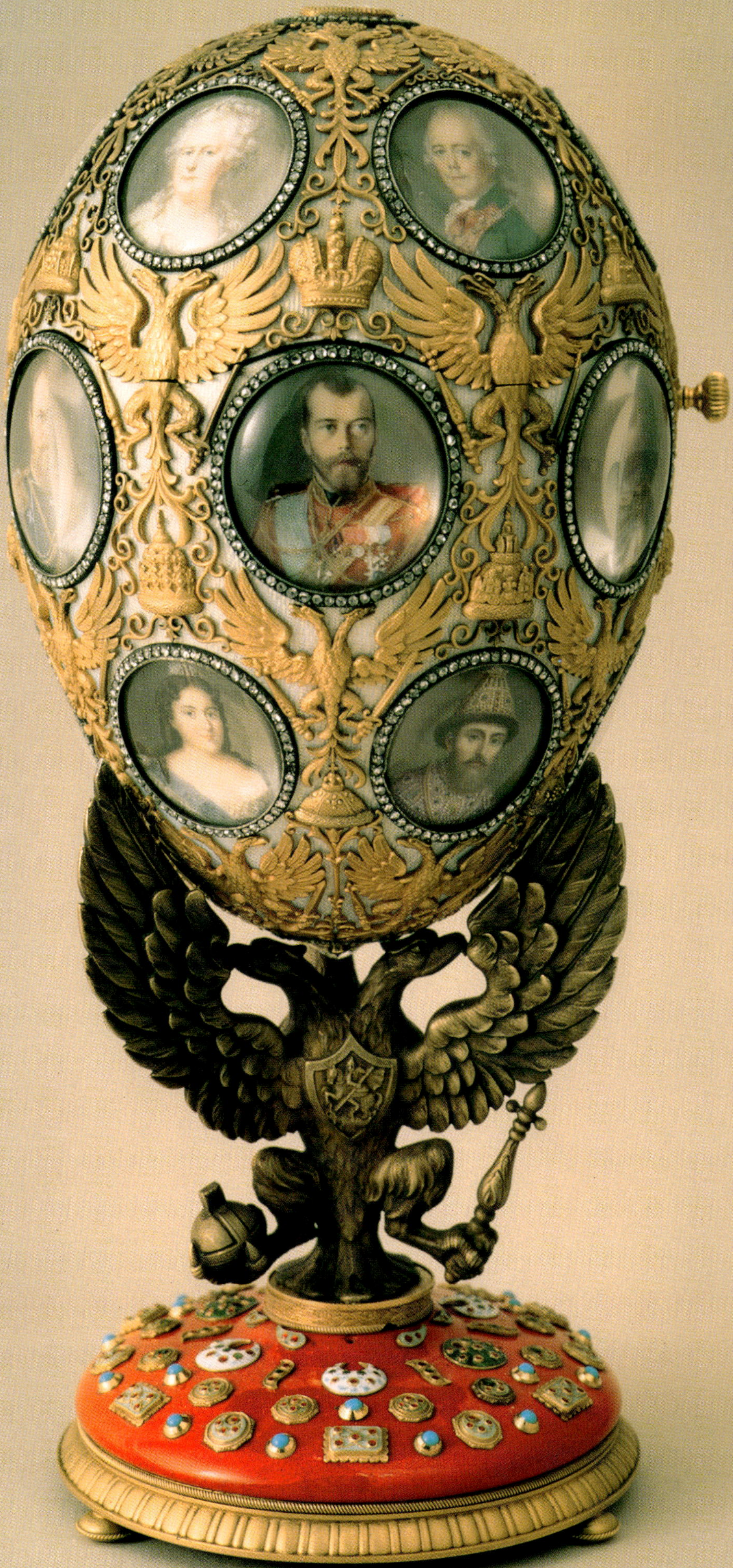

HISTORY

1913–1917 Kept in the study of Her Imperial Majesty Alexandra Fedorovna in the Winter Palace.

The following is a description from a Fabergé album of the Imperial Easter eggs presented to Alexandra Fedorovna between 1907 and 1916. [255]

Easter egg presented to Alexandra Fedorovna in 1913, commemorating the tercentenary of the rule of the House of Romanov. White enamel egg, covered with chased gold eagles and crowns, among them portraits of Tsars, Emperors and Empresses of the House of Romanov. The egg rests on a double-headed eagle on a pedestal representing the Imperial coat of arms. The egg contains a revolving globe, one half showing a relief map of Russia at the time of Mikhail Fedorovich (founder of the Romanov dynasty) and the other, a similar map of contemporary Russia (1913).

1917 Confiscated by Kerensky's provisional government, along with other treasures, and taken from the Anichkov Palace to the Moscow Kremlin Armoury.

1922 One of the items on the list of confiscated treasures transferred from the Anichkov Palace to the Sovnarkom.

1 gold egg with 2 diamonds and rose-cut diamonds, containing globe on stand with enamel (silver eagle). [256]

The Romanov Tercentenary egg was not sold by Antikvariat to the West and remained in Russia.

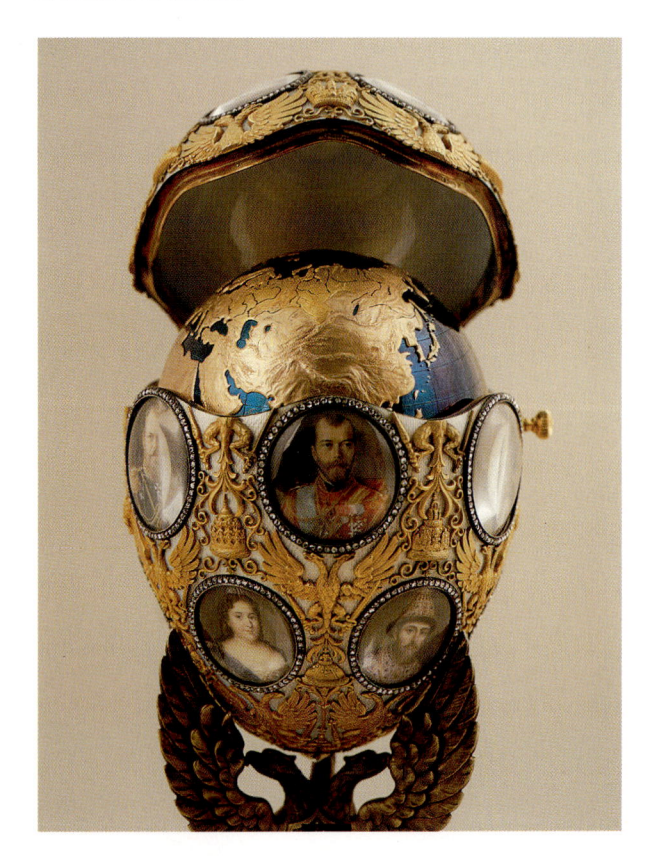

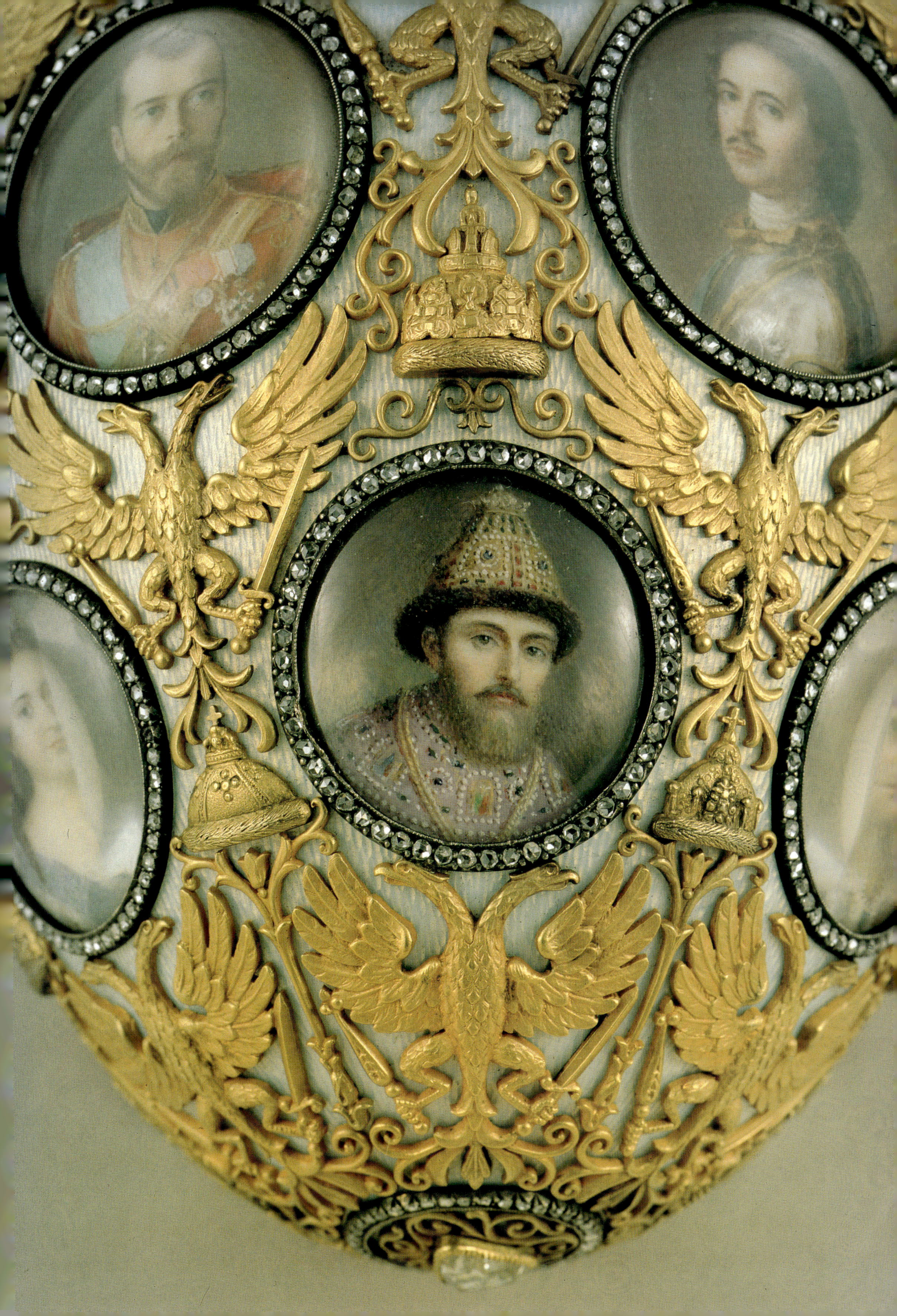

1914

45
Grisaille Egg

Presented by
Tsar Nicholas II to his
mother, the Dowager
Empress Maria Fedorovna,
Easter 1914 (6 April)

*(Hillwood Museum,
Washington DC)*

Fabergé's choice of design for the 1914 Easter egg may have been inspired by the Anichkov Palace where many of the ceilings are painted *en grisaille*. As this was the Empress's favourite palace the treatment of this Easter egg was no doubt particularly pleasing to her.

DESCRIPTION

Workmaster: Henrik Wigström.
Miniaturist: Vassilii Zuiev.
Height: 4¾ inches (12 cm).
Marks: Engraved FABERGÉ, H.W., assay mark of St Petersburg regional assay department.

Varicoloured gold, translucent pink and opaque white enamel, rose-cut diamonds, pearls.

This egg is in the Louis XVI style and was designed by Henrik Wigström. Vassilii Zuiev painted the two pink and white enamel panels with miniature allegorical scenes of the arts and sciences after François Boucher. Alternating with smaller enamelled ovals, featuring cherubs with attributes of the seasons, are musical instruments, tools of the arts and sciences, and trophies in four-colour gold mounted on cream *guilloché* enamel. Under a table diamond at the top are the initials of Maria Fedorovna, and the date 1914 is under a diamond at the bottom.

SURPRISE

Upon receiving the Easter egg from her son, Tsar Nicholas II, the Dowager Empress wrote to her sister Queen Alexandra. This important letter contains the only reference to the surprise inside the 1914 Easter egg, and also provides us with an excellent description:

8 April 1914

... He {Tsar Nicholas II} wrote me a most charming letter and presented me with a most beautiful Easter egg. Fabergé brought it to me himself. It is a true chef d'oeuvre in pink enamel and inside a porte chaise *carried by two negroes with Empress Catherine in it wearing a little crown on her head. You wind it up and then the negroes walk : it is an unbelievably beautiful and superbly fine piece of work. Fabergé is the greatest genius of our time. I also told him:* Vous êtes un génie incomparable... [257]

216

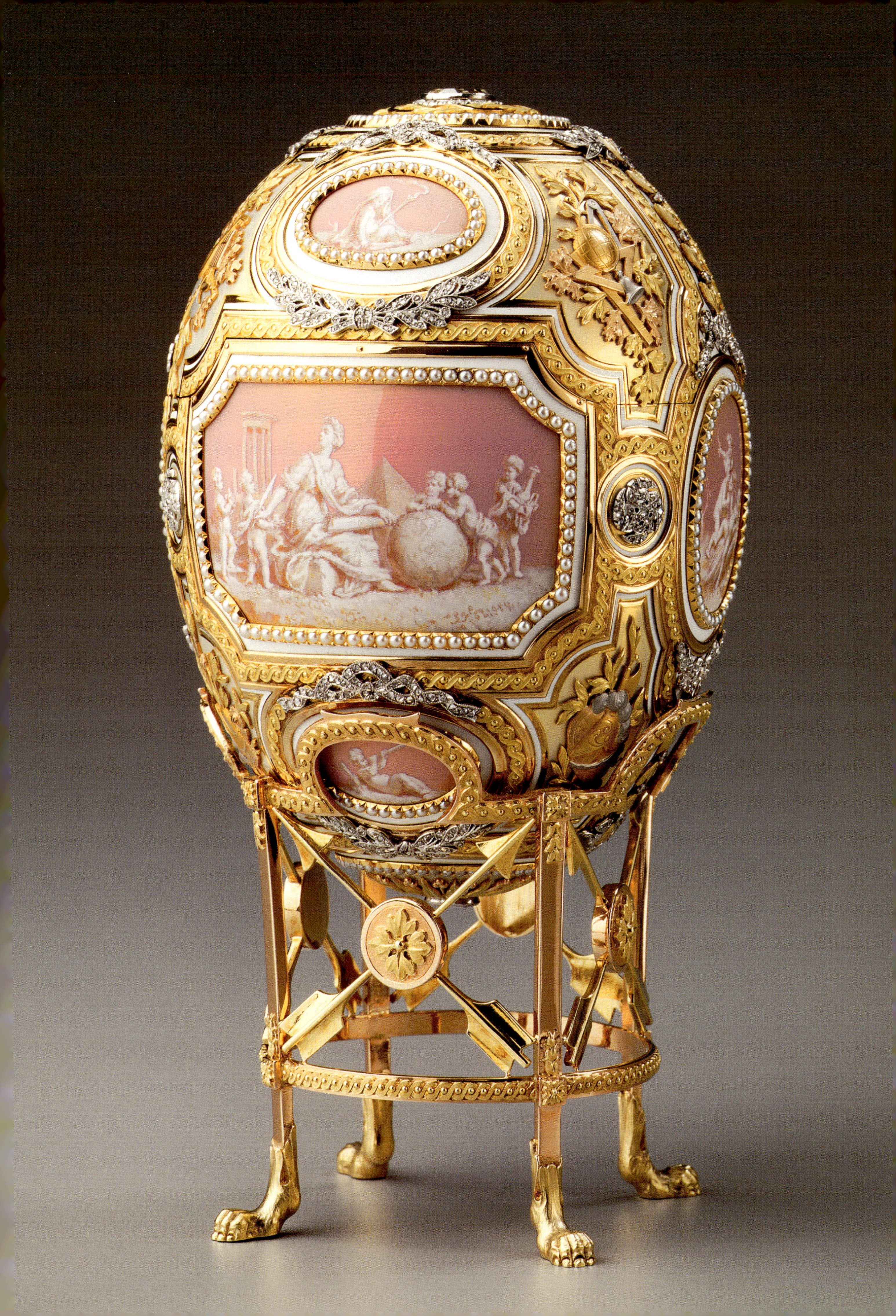

INVOICE

No invoice found (see page 206), but the account books of His Imperial Majesty's Cabinet and correspondence between Alexandra Fedorovna's Secretariat and the Cabinet supplies the following information regarding payment of Fabergé's invoices:

11 June 1914, invoice for the sum of 59,452 r. [258]

HISTORY

1914–1917 Kept at the Anichkov Palace.

1917 Confiscated by Kerensky's provisional government, along with other treasures, and taken from the Anichkov Palace to the Moscow Kremlin Armoury.
Gold egg with pink enamel medallions, decorated with pearls and and diamonds. [259]

1922 One of the items on the list of treasures confiscated which were transferred from the Anichkov Palace to the Sovnarkom.
1 gold and enamel sedan chair with 2 blackamoor bearers. [260]

1930 Officially sold by Antikvariat for 8000 roubles. [261]

1931 Presented as a gift to Marjorie Merriweather Post by her daughter, Eleanor Post.

1985, 13 November. An automated sedan chair matching the description in the Dowager Empress' letter in the late Charles Clore Collection was sold for SFr. 1,430,000 at Christie's, Geneva. Although the colours of this sedan chair are different from the Easter egg's subtle pink shades, it does fit the space prepared for the surprise inside the Easter egg and is similar in description to that of the sedan chair seized by the Bolsheviks from the Empress' palace. [262]

1914

46

Mosaic Egg

Presented by
Tsar Nicholas II to his
wife, the Empress
Alexandra Fedorovna,
Easter 1914 (6 April)

*(Collection of Her Majesty
Queen Elizabeth II)*

Alma Theresia Pihl, the designer of this egg, in keeping with the tradition of embroidering linens and other household items which she would bring to her marriage as part of the trousseau, was creating a *petit point* carpet. The central motif of her carpet was a medallion decorated with a bouquet of roses. A variation of this design appears on the Imperial Mosaic egg, and it was known within her family to have been the inspiration for this exquisite and delicate Easter egg.

DESCRIPTION

Workmaster: August Holmström.
Designer: Alma Theresia Pihl.
Height: 3⅝ inches (9.2 cm).
Marks: Engraved on the egg: C. FABERGÉ.
Surprise: Miniature of the five Imperial children.
Height: 3 1/16 inches (7.9 cm).
Marks: Engraved on the pedestal support: G. FABERGÉ 1914.

Yellow gold, platinum, diamonds, rubies, emeralds, topazes, sapphires, demantoid garnets, pearls.

The technical virtuosity displayed by Fabergé's craftsmen is overshadowed by the elegance and airiness of the design of this Easter egg. Each of the little precious stones were cut individually, taking into account the egg's curvature, and calibrated to fit perfectly into each space provided for them within the platinum lattice cage, which had actually been cut out and not welded. The following is a description of the results of their mastery:

Five gem-set medallions of floral bouquets are centred around the middle of the egg, each oval medallion surrounded by seed pearls and filets of white opaque enamel. A diamond is placed at the intersection of each medallion. Flanking the medallions are scrolls of smaller diamonds set between bands of pearls, and a large moonstone is mounted at the apex of the egg under which is the monogram of the Empress Alexandra Fedorovna and the date 1914. Concealed within the egg is a jewelled miniature frame with the profile heads of the five Imperial children painted *en camaieu-brun* on a pink enamel ground. Their names (Olga, Tatiana, Maria, Anatasia and Alexei) and the date 1914 are enamelled in sepia on the ivory enamelled border and a basket of flowers is painted in sepia against a pale green background. The border surrounding the medallion is highlighted with diamonds, green enamel and pearls and the pedestal is jewelled and enamelled.

This signature G. FABERGÉ is engraved on the surprise. Some authorities[263] have written that this is a distortion by the engraver of the letter C (for Carl), but we believe that there is no question of any mistake, and that Carl Fabergé marked on the Imperial Easter egg the 100th anniversary of the birth of his father – Gustav.

INVOICE
No invoice found (see page 206).

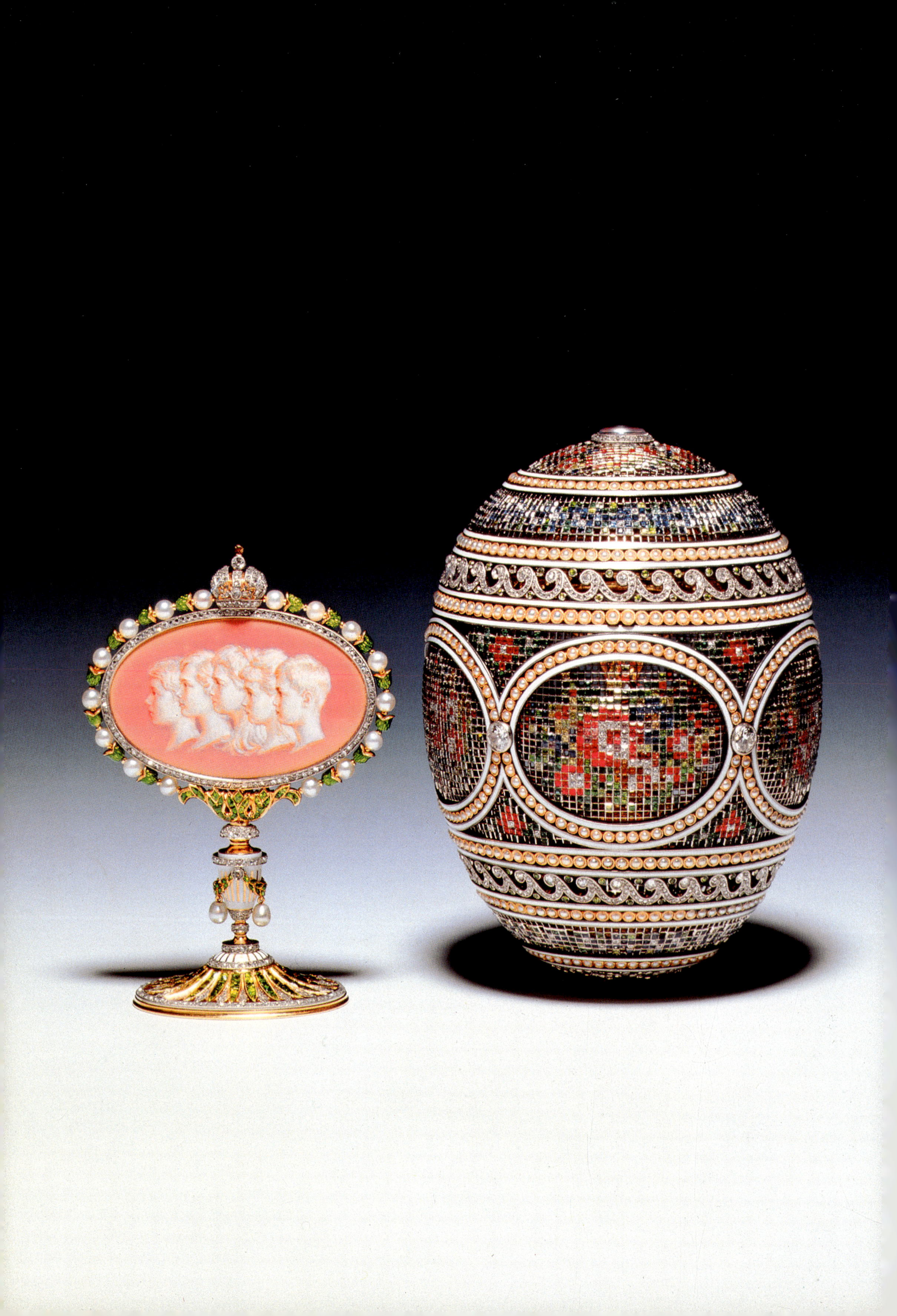

HISTORY

1914–1917 Kept in the study of Her Imperial Majesty Alexandra Fedorovna at the Winter Palace.

The following is a description from a Fabergé album of the Imperial Easter eggs presented to Alexandra Fedorovna between 1907 and 1916. [264]

Easter egg presented to Alexandra Fedorovna in 1914. Louis XVI style, open-work of different-coloured precious stones, pearls and white enamel. Contains a medallion with an Imperial crown on a gold and enamel pedestal. On one side of the medallion are portraits of their Majesties' five children, painted on ivory in cameo style, and on the other side, a basket of flowers and the children's names.

1917 Confiscated by Kerensky's provisional government, along with other treasures, and taken from the Anichkov Palace to the Moscow Kremlin Armoury.

1922 One of the items on the list of confiscated treasures transferred from the Anichkov Palace to the Sovnarkom.

1 gold egg as though embroidered on canvas, with diamonds, rose-cut diamonds and coloured gemstones, containing a portrait screen with rose-cut diamonds and pearls. [265]

1933 Officially sold by Antikvariat for 5000 roubles. [266]

1933 22 May – purchased by King George V from Cameo Corner, London. The invoice is addressed to His Majesty, the King, with the notation 'HALF COST: £250'. It is assumed that Queen Mary paid the other half of the cost of the egg, and she probably received the egg as a gift for her birthday on 26 May. [267]

47

Red Cross Egg with Imperial Portraits

1915

Presented by
Tsar Nicholas II to his
mother, the Dowager
Empress Maria Fedorovna,
Easter 1915 (22 March)

(Virginia Museum of Fine Arts, Richmond, bequest of Lillian Thomas Pratt)

During the First World War the Dowager Empress was very actively involved in Red Cross activities. Her daughters, Xenia and Olga, as well as other members of her family, acted as nurses in various hospitals. This involvement provides the theme for this egg.

DESCRIPTION

Workmaster: Henrik Wigström.
Height: 3½ inches (8.9 cm).
Surprise: Five-panel folding screen bearing miniatures of members of the Imperial family in Red Cross uniform.

Silver-gilt, opalescent white and red enamel, gold, mother-of-pearl.

The austerity measures instituted by the Tsar during the First World War are reflected in the design of this Easter egg. As Franz Birbaum notes in his memoirs:

During the war years the eggs were either not made at all or were manufactured very simply and at a low cost. [268]

The composition is simple, yet dignified. The body of the egg is covered with opalescent white *guilloché* enamel, and adorning the central band, written in stylized, gold, Church Slavonic lettering is the biblical legend 'Greater love hath no man than this, that a man lay down his life for his comrades', and two red enamelled crosses with the date 1914. The egg opens to reveal the five-panel folding screen surprise, bearing miniatures painted on mother-of-pearl. They are from left to right: Grand Duchess Olga Alexandrovna, Grand Duchess Olga Nikolaievna, Empress Alexandra Fedorovna, Grand Duchess Tatiana Nikolaievna, and Grand Duchess Maria Pavlovna the younger, when she was decorated with the St George's medal for her participation in Red Cross work. (Maria Pavlovna the younger was the cousin of Nicholas II and the sister of Dimitri Pavlovich, who participated in Rasputin's murder.)

INVOICE

No invoice found (see page 206), but the account books of His Imperial Majesty's Cabinet and correspondence between Alexandra Fedorovna's Secretariat and the Cabinet supplies the following information regarding payment of Fabergé's invoices:

10 July 1915, invoice for the sum of 3559 r. 50 kop. [269]

HISTORY

1915–1917 Kept at the Anichkov Palace.

1917 Confiscated by Kerensky's provisional government, along with other treasures, and taken from the Anichkov Palace to the Moscow Kremlin Armoury.

Gold egg, covered with white enamel and a red cross, on small stand, containing a small mother-of-pearl white enamel screen and with portraits of Imperial personages in a gold setting. [270]

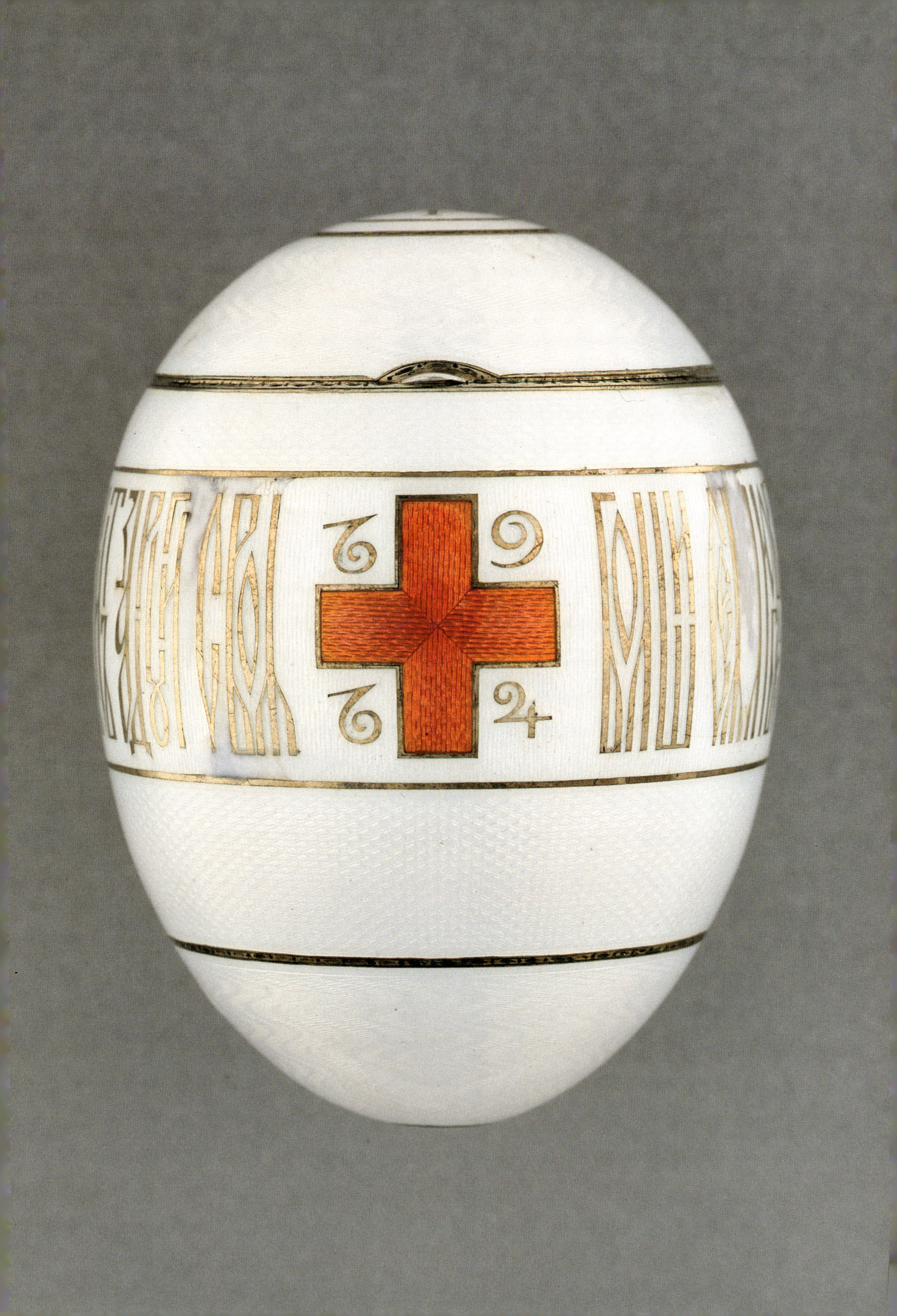

1922 One of the items on the list of confiscated treasures transferred from the Anichkov Palace to the Sovnarkom.

1 silver egg with enamel, on silver stand with screen inside. [271]

1930 Officially sold by Antikvariat for 500 roubles. [272]

1933 Purchased by Lillian Thomas Pratt from Armand Hammer's exhibition at Lord and Taylor, New York.

1915

48
Red Cross Egg with Triptych

Presented by
Tsar Nicholas II to his
wife, the Empress
Alexandra Fedorovna,
Easter 1915 (22 March)

(The Cleveland Museum of Art, The India Early Minshall Collection)

DESCRIPTION

Workmaster: Henrik Wigström.
Height: 3⅜ inches (8.5 cm)
Marks: FABERGÉ, H.W., 1915, assay mark of St Petersburg 1908-1917
Gold, silver, enamel, gold glass.

Wartime economy prevailed in the making of this egg and its comparatively austere decoration. A miniature of the *Resurrection* appears inside, flanked by St Olga and St Tatiana, patron saints of the two eldest Grand Duchesses. These miniatures previously thought to have been painted on ivory have recently been found to be executed in enamel on gold. On the exterior are portraits of the Grand Duchesses Olga and Tatiana wearing Red Cross uniforms.

INVOICE

No invoice found (see page 206).

HISTORY

1915–1917 Kept in the study of Her Imperial Majesty Alexandra Fedorovna at the Winter Palace.

The following is a description from a Fabergé album of the Imperial Easter eggs presented to Alexandra Fedorovna between 1907 and 1916. [273]

Easter egg presented to Alexandra Fedorovna in 1915 to commemorate the Imperial family's participation in the work of the Red Cross. White enamel egg with two red crosses, between them portraits of Olga Nicholaievna and Tatiana Nikolaievna wearing nurses head-dresses. Contains a triptych icon of the Resurrection in the 17th century style, flanked by smaller icons of Saint Olga and Saint Tatiana.

In her memoirs, Grand Duchess Maria wrote:

Upon the declaration of war the Empress, like the rest of us, felt the need of participating in the common cause. Her maternal instinct led her to choose as her war work the same which, for other reasons, I myself had chosen. She undertook the care of the wounded... and, having donned a nurse's uniform, she worked in a hospital at Tsarskoie Selo... [274]

1917 Confiscated by Kerensky's provisional government, along with other treasures, and taken from the Anichkov Palace to the Moscow Kremlin Armoury.

1922 One of the items on the list of confiscated treasures transferred from the Anichkov Palace to the Sovnarkom may be the egg in question.

1 gold egg with enamel and 2 crosses. [275]

1930 Officially sold by Antikvariat for 500 roubles. [276]

1943 Purchased by India Early Minshall from A La Vieille Russie, New York, for $4,400. [277]

1963 Presented by I.E. Minshall to the Cleveland Museum of Art.

49
Order of St George Egg

1916

Presented by
Tsar Nicholas II to his
mother, the Dowager
Empress Maria Fedorovna,
Easter 1916 (10 April)

*(The FORBES Magazine
Collection, New York)*

This egg commemorates the presentation to Tsar Nicholas II of the Order of St George (fourth class), which he received on 25 October 1915. The Order of St George, created by Catherine the Great in 1769, was given only for military bravery or specific military achievements. It was the most coveted military order in the Russian army. The cross made for Nicholas II was of cachalong, a stone found near Baikal Lake. [278]

DESCRIPTION

Height: 3 5/16 inches (8.4 cm) without the stand.

Silver, gold, translucent orange, opalescent white, opaque rose, pale green, white and black enamel, rock crystal.

The simple silver shell is a gesture to wartime austerity. Behind the medallion of the cross of the Order, a miniature of the Tsar is revealed when a small button below the badge is pressed. A miniature of the Tsarevich is similarly revealed from behind a St George Medal when a second button is pushed.

INVOICE

No invoice found (see page 206), but the account books of His Imperial Majesty's Cabinet and correspondence between Alexandra Fedorovna's Secretariat and the Cabinet supplies the following information regarding payment of Fabergé's invoices:

5 August 1916, invoice for the sum of 13,347 r. [279]

HISTORY

1916–1917 Kept at the Anichkov Palace.

1918 The Dowager Empress had the 1916 egg with her in Kiev, where she stayed in 1917 before moving on to the Romanov estates in the Crimea. The last in the series of eggs presented to the Empress, this was the only one taken by her to the West when she escaped from Russia, and it remained in her possession until her death. Her daughter, the Grand Duchess Xenia, inherited the egg and it remained in her collection until she died in 1960. Her son, Prince Vassilii Romanov, sold it through Sotheby's that year.

1961 Sold by Sotheby's, London, 27 November, for £11,000. Later owned by Fabergé, Inc. and A La Vieille Russie, New York.

1976 Purchased by FORBES, Inc.

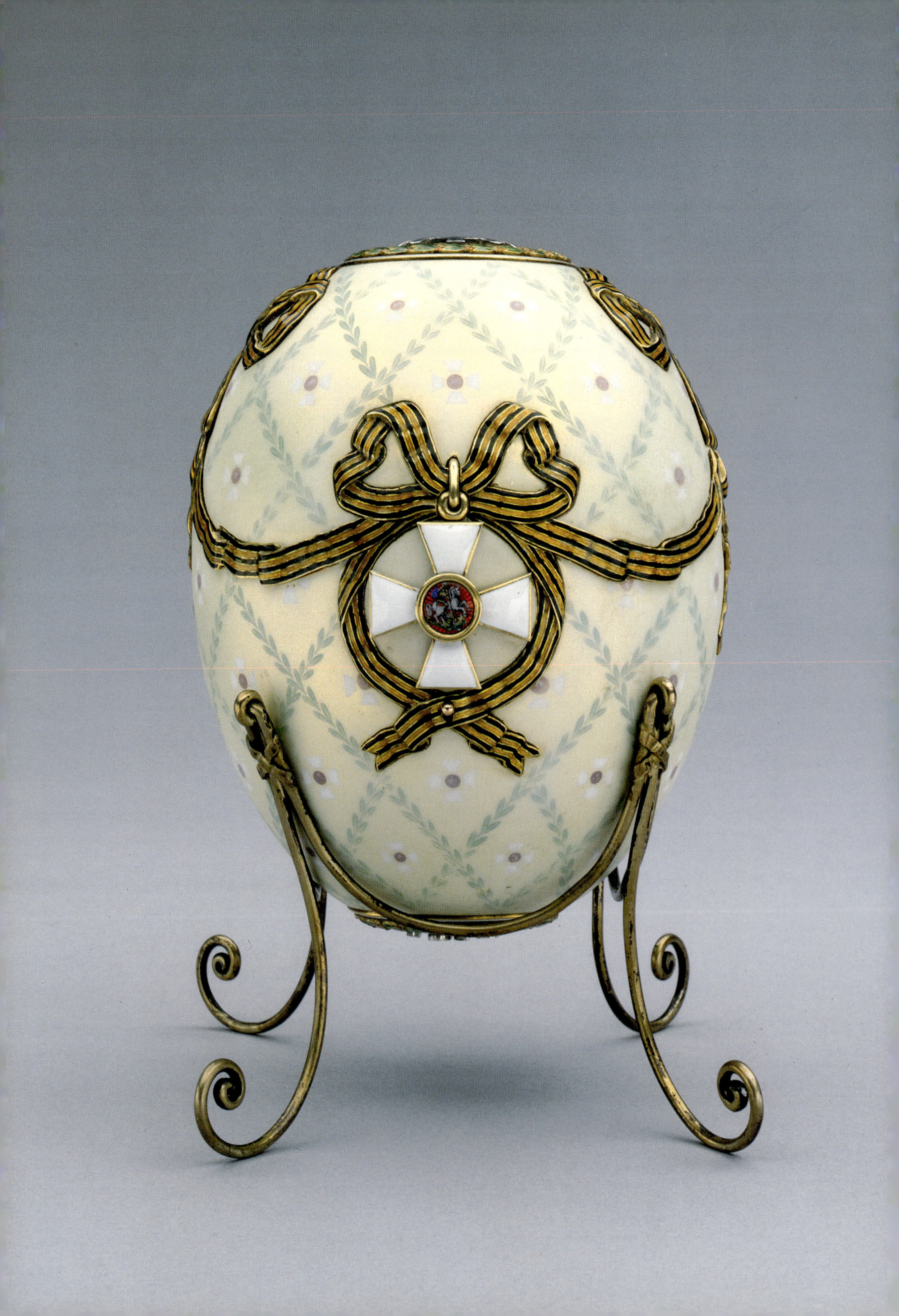

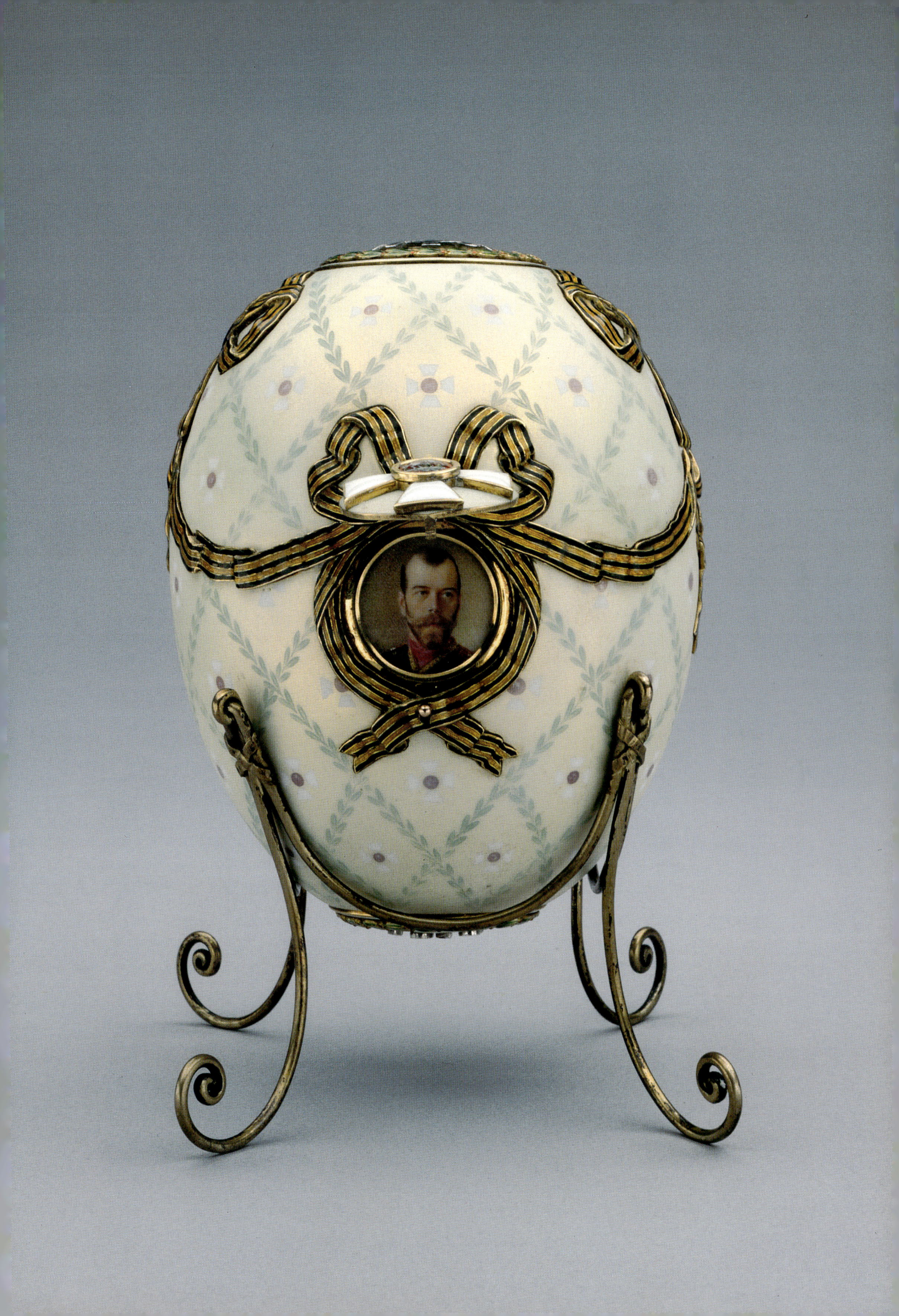

50

1916

Steel Military Egg

Presented by
Tsar Nicholas II to his
wife, the Empress
Alexandra Fedorovna,
Easter 1916 (10 April)

(Moscow Kremlin Armoury Museum)

The last of the Fabergé Imperial Easter eggs presented to the Empress, like the other made in the same year (49), commemorates the awarding of the Order of St George (fourth class) to Emperor Nicholas II. In August 1915, Nicholas became Supreme Commander of the Russian Armed Forces, replacing Grand Duke Nikolai Nikolaievich. The cross and ribbon of the Order are placed above the surprise, which is an easel with a miniature watercolour painting.

Description

Workmaster: Henrik Wigström.
Surprise: Miniature watercolour of Tsar Nicholas II and the Tsarevich at the front lines. First on left (with long moustache) is probably General Alexei Alexeievich Brussilov.
Height: Egg and stand: 6½ inches (16.7 cm).
Easel: 2%6 inches (6.5 cm).
Miniature: 1¹⁵⁄₁₆ x 2⅜ inches (5 x 5.5 cm).
Marks: FABERGÉ, H.W., assay mark of St Petersburg regional assay department, 72.

Gold, steel, nephrite.

The Steel egg is decorated with the gold Imperial Crown and appliques of the heraldic double-headed eagle with arrows and a laurel wreath in its claws – symbols of war and ultimate victory – and the Moscow coat of arms, the figure of St George, the date 1916 and the monogram of Empress Alexandra Fedorovna, AΘ. The stand is in the form of four artillery shells mounted on a nephrite pedestal. The watercolour miniature is set in a gold frame decorated with the Imperial crown and the ribbon and cross of the Order of St George. The miniature is fastened to an easel in the shape of Empress Alexandra Fedorovna's monogram.

Eugène Fabergé described the Steel egg in a letter written in English to H.C. Bainbridge on 27 June 1934.

Answering your last letter I got today, I beg to inform you that the Red Cross egg was not the last one we have made. There was another one, which, also for economy in connection of the war, my father decided to execute in blackened steel only with the Empress Alexandra Fedorovna's initials in gold and inside with an easel in steel too, bearing a miniature (square) representing the Tsar with the Tsarevich in conversation with the generals of the staff on the front; it was painted by Zuiev. Sorrily I can't remember the parallel egg for the Empress Maria Fedorovna. The above mentioned I have delivered personally in the Tsar's name and by His Majesty's special order sent by wire from the front, to Empress Alexandra, who has been surrounded by all her five children the eve before Easter, while my father went on the same purpose to Empress Maria. [280]

Eugène Fabergé also pointed out that this Easter egg had been designed by Gustav Shkilter (1874–1954), a Latvian who was one of the firm's artists and an instructor at the Baron von Steiglitz School of Technical Drawing.

Invoice

No invoice found (see the entry for the 1916 Order of St George Easter egg, 49, page 227)

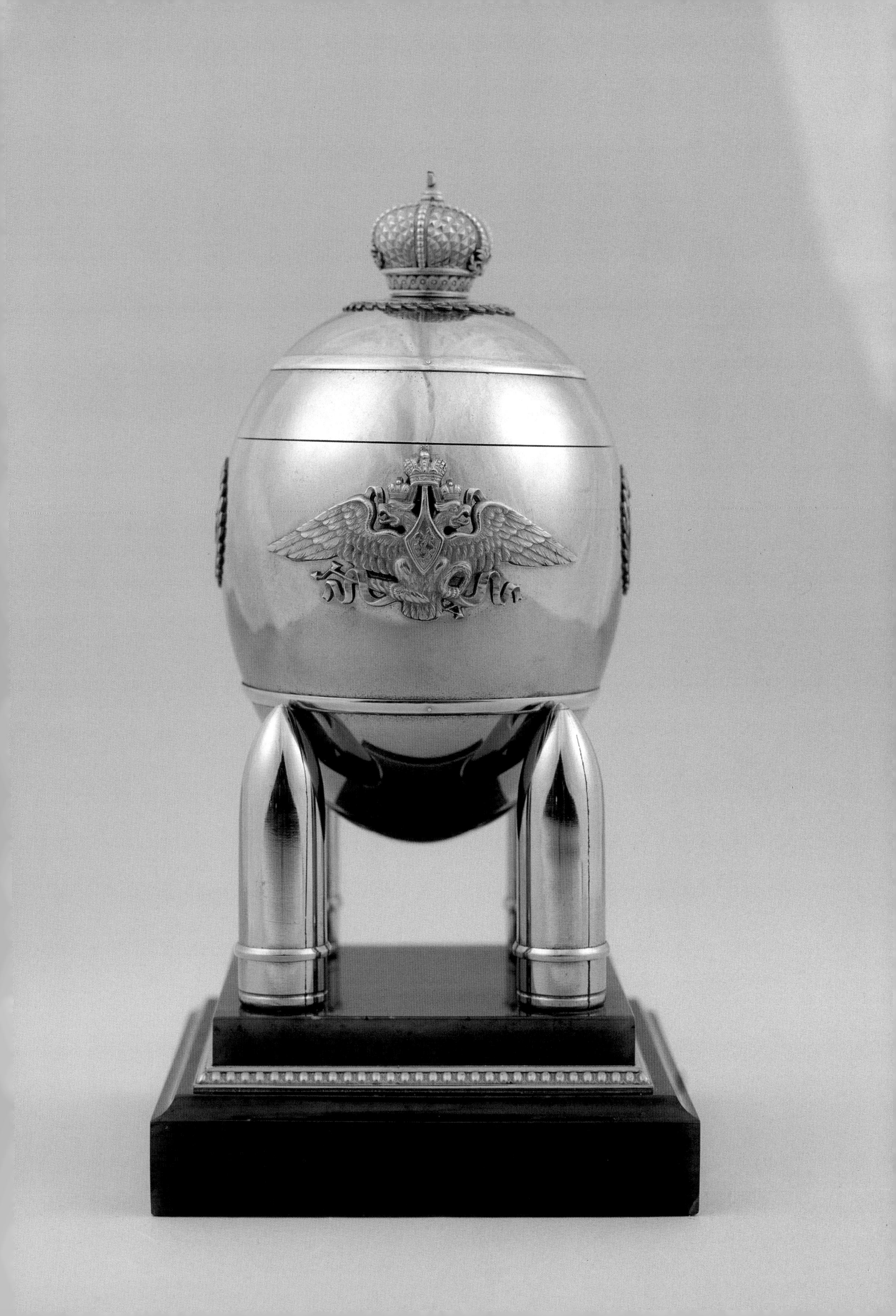

HISTORY

1916–1917 Kept in the study of Her Imperial Majesty Alexandra Fedorovna at the Winter Palace.

The following is a description from a Fabergé album of the Imperial Easter eggs presented to Alexandra Fedorovna between 1907 and 1916.[281]

Easter egg presented to Alexandra Fedorovna in 1916. Steel egg mounted on four steel artillery shells on a nephrite base. The egg is surmounted by an Imperial crown and contains a miniature painting of the Emperor visiting the front lines.

The following telegram was sent by Alexandra to Nicholas while he was visiting the Stavka at the front:

Tsarskoie Selo - General Staff Headquarters, 9 April 1916

Christ is Risen! We all embrace you tenderly. Fabergé has just brought your delightful egg for which I thank you a thousand times. The miniature group is marvellous and all the portraits are excellent. My thoughts and prayers are with you in your dreary solitude. Words cannot describe how sad and empty everything is without you in this great holiday time. All the children are coming to church with me. My heartfelt greetings to all.

Alix[282]

1917 Confiscated by Kerensky's provisional government, along with other treasures, and taken from the Anichkov Palace to the Moscow Kremlin Armoury.

1 metal egg on silver stand, containing easel with frame.[283]

The Steel Military egg was never sold by Antikvariat to the West and has remained in Russia.

Tsar Nicholas II with Grand Duke Nicholas Nicolaievich, the Supreme Commander of the Russian Armed Forces, in early 1915

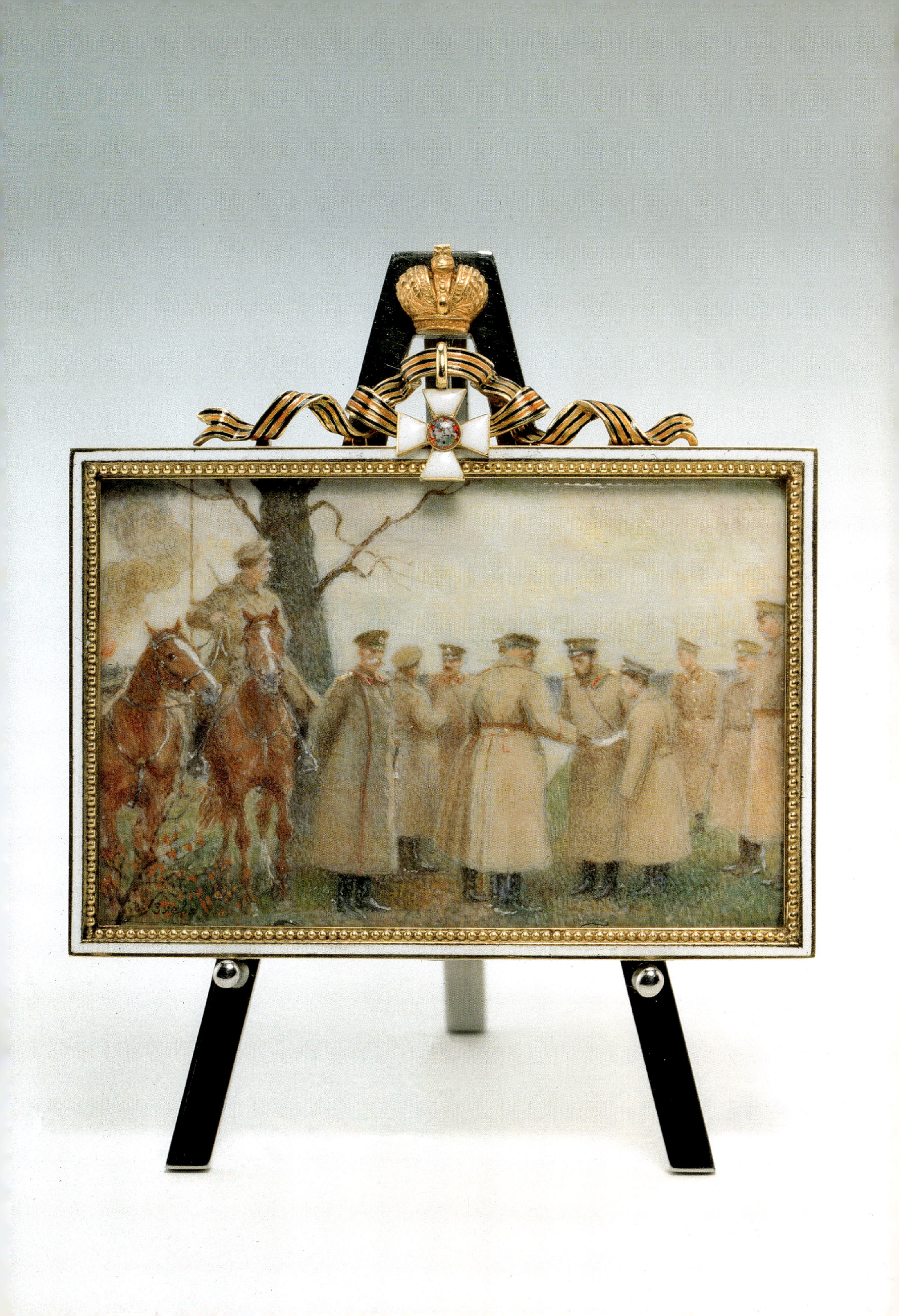

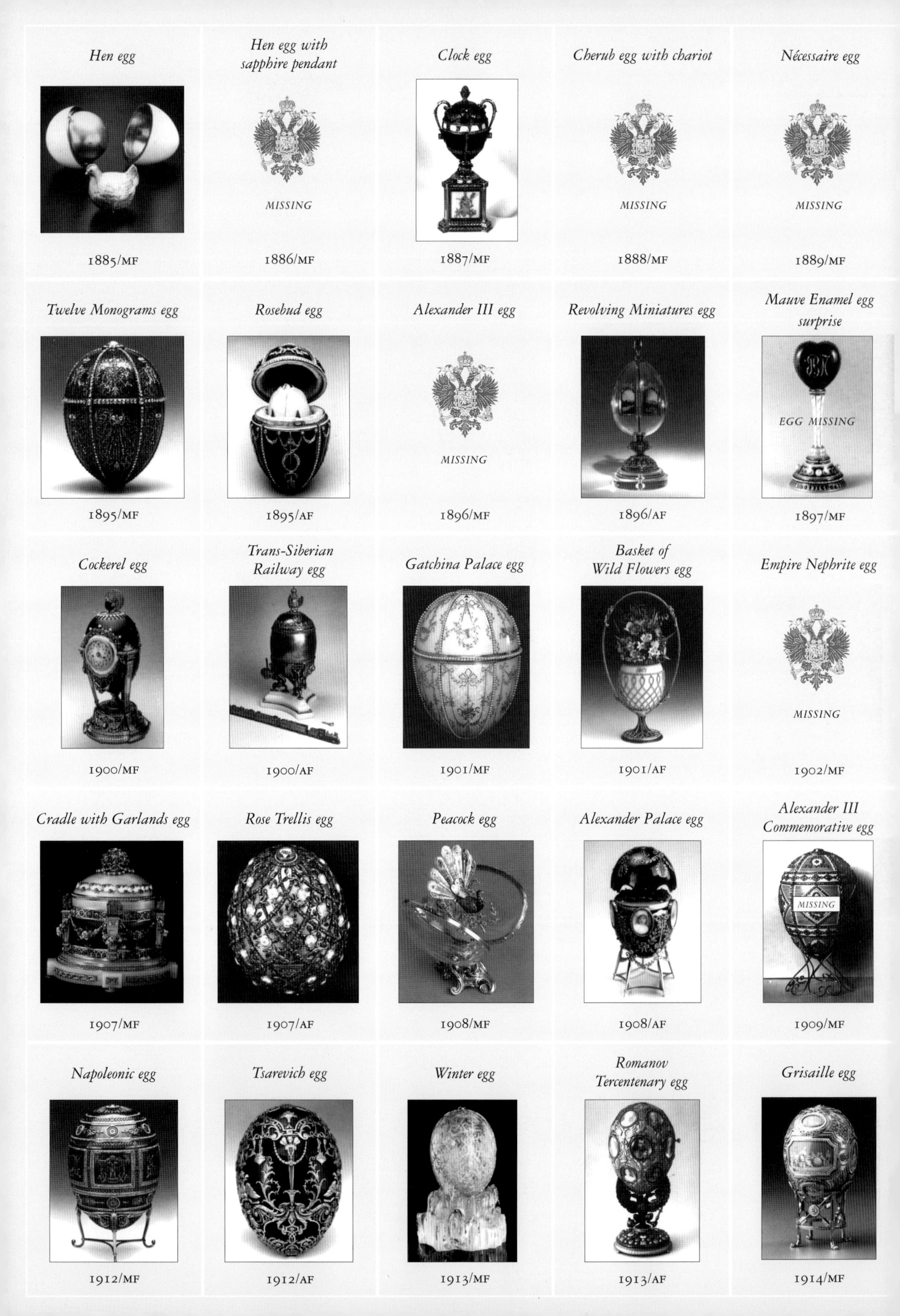

Hen egg 1885/MF	Hen egg with sapphire pendant MISSING 1886/MF	Clock egg 1887/MF	Cherub egg with chariot MISSING 1888/MF	Nécessaire egg MISSING 1889/MF
Twelve Monograms egg 1895/MF	Rosebud egg 1895/AF	Alexander III egg MISSING 1896/MF	Revolving Miniatures egg 1896/AF	Mauve Enamel egg surprise EGG MISSING 1897/MF
Cockerel egg 1900/MF	Trans-Siberian Railway egg 1900/AF	Gatchina Palace egg 1901/MF	Basket of Wild Flowers egg 1901/AF	Empire Nephrite egg MISSING 1902/MF
Cradle with Garlands egg 1907/MF	Rose Trellis egg 1907/AF	Peacock egg 1908/MF	Alexander Palace egg 1908/AF	Alexander III Commemorative egg MISSING 1909/MF
Napoleonic egg 1912/MF	Tsarevich egg 1912/AF	Winter egg 1913/MF	Romanov Tercentenary egg 1913/AF	Grisaille egg 1914/MF

Danish Palaces egg 1890/MF	Memory of Azov egg 1891/MF	Diamond Trellis egg 1892/MF	Caucasus egg 1893/MF	Renaissance egg 1894/MF
Coronation egg 1897/AF	Pelican egg 1898/MF	Lilies of the Valley egg 1898/AF	Pansy egg 1899/MF	Bouquet of Lilies Clock egg 1899/AF
Clover egg 1902/AF	Danish Jubilee egg 1903/MF	Peter the Great egg 1903/AF	Swan egg 1906/MF	Moscow Kremlin egg 1906/AF
Standard egg 1909/AF	Alexander III Equestrian egg 1910/MF	Colonnade egg 1910/AF	Bay Tree egg 1911/MF	Fifteenth Anniversary egg 1911/AF
Mosaic egg 1914/AF	Red Cross egg with Imperial Portraits 1915/MF	Red Cross egg with Triptych 1915/MF	Order of St George egg 1916/MF	Steel Military egg 1916/AF

The original Fabergé invoices translated

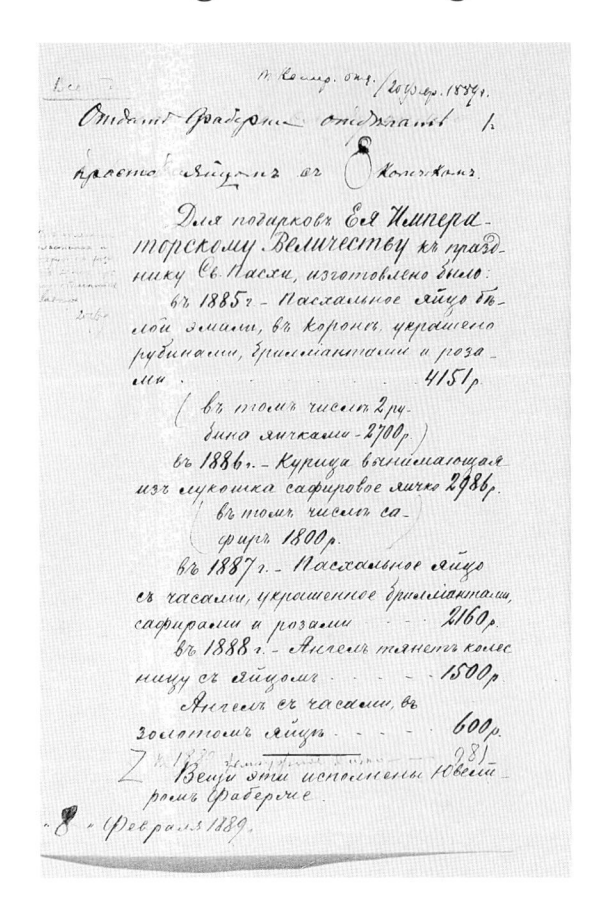

Hen egg (1), Clock egg (3), Cherub egg with chariot (4)

20 February 1889

Give to Fabergé to make a simple pendant egg with a small ring.

For presentation to Her Imperial Majesty on the occasion of the Holy Feast of Easter, the following articles have been prepared:

In 1885 – white enamel Easter egg, with crown, decorated with rubies, diamonds and rose-cut diamonds (including 2 ruby pendant eggs – 2700 roubles)	4151 r.
In 1886 – hen picking a sapphire egg out of a basket (including a sapphire – 1800 r.)	2986 r.
In 1887 – Easter egg with clock, decorated with sapphires and rose-cut diamonds	2160 r.
In 1888 – Cupid drawing a chariot containing an egg	1500 r.
Cupid with clock in gold egg	600 r.

[added in pencil]: *In 1889 pearl pendant egg 981.*

These articles have been executed by the jeweller Fabergé.

8 February 1889

[Note pencilled in the margin]
Under the small ring there is a plate with rose-cut diamonds round it. I shall ask for an explanation of this tomorrow.

Hen egg with sapphire pendant (2)

No. 1461/222	2 April 1886
K. Fabergé	C. Fabergé
Jeweller	Joaillier
St Petersburg	St Petersbourg
Bolshaia Morskaia No.18	rue Grande Morskaia No.18

Invoice for the Cabinet of His Imperial Majesty

<u>Hen</u>

1 sapphire pendant egg		1800
50 rose-cut diamonds	8/32	25
60 -"-	14/32	35
400 -"-	5 1/4	341.25
gold and labour		750
2 cases		35
		2986.25

2 April 1886   [signed] C. Fabergé

Pay
14 Apr 1886   Vorontsov-Dashkov

[In the margin]

*Issue 2986 roub. 25 kop(eks)
22 April 1886
N. Petrov
from the credit of 100,000 roub.*

Receipt No 428

236

Cherub egg with chariot (4)

| 49/770 | Received from His Imperial | 16 |
| To H.I.M. Cabinet | Majesty on 19 May 1888 | 14 |

K. Fabergé	C. Fabergé
Supplier to the Imperial Court	Fournisseur de la Cour Impériale
Jeweller	Joaillier
Moscow St Petersburg	St Petersbourg Moscou

Invoice for His Imperial Majesty

Cherub pulling a chariot containing an egg	1500 s.r.
Cherub with clock in gold egg	600
	s.r. 2100

St Petersburg, 12 May 1888

TO BE PAID

"To be paid" written in H.I.M.'s own hand

19 May 1888	Pay from credit of 100,000 roubles
	2100 r.
	20 May 1888
Give assignation	N. Petrov
20,000	(State Secretary)

s.r. = silver roubles

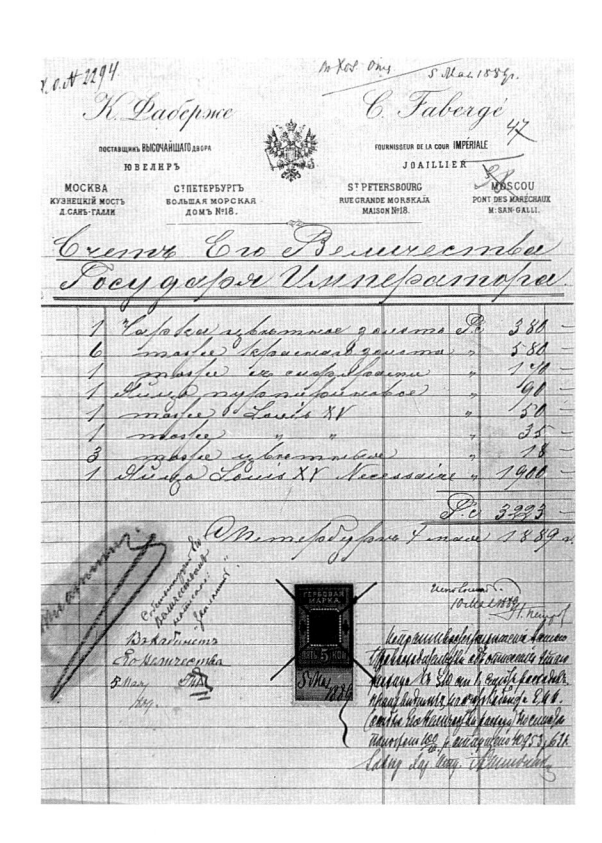

Nécessaire egg (5)

| Household Dept   No. 2294 | To Household Dept   8 May 1889 |

K. Fabergé	C. Fabergé 47 38
Supplier to the Imperial Court	Fournisseur de la Cour Impériale
Jeweller	Joaillier
Moscow St Petersburg	St Petersbourg Moscou

Invoice for His Imperial Majesty

1	Charka in colour gold	380 s.r.
6	" red gold	580
1	" with sapphires	170
1	Purpurine egg	90
1	Louis XV egg	50
1	"	35
3	Multicoloured egg	18
1	Louis XV Nécessaire egg	1900
		s.r. 3223

St Petersburg 4 May 1889

TO BE PAID

"To be paid" written in H.I.M.'s own hand

To be carried out
10 May 1889
N. Petrov

To H.I.M. Cabinet
5 May 1889

Permission is requested from Your Excellency to assign this expenditure to para. 10, article No 1, the expense account relating to the account of H.I.M. Cabinet (special expense account of H.I.M.). From the current account of 100,000 roubles, released 40,953 roubles 63 kopeks.

Head of the Household Dept.

Danish Palaces egg (6)

Household Dept. No. 2633	To the Cabinet of H.I.M.
11 May 90	Vorontsov-Dashkov 6
K. FABERGÉ	C. FABERGÉ
Supplier to the Imperial Court	Fournisseur de la Cour Impériale
Moscow St Petersburg	St Petersbourg Moscou
For assignation No. 1429	TO BE PAID 10 May 90

Invoice for His Imperial Majesty

March 30   Gold egg with pink enamel,
           Louis XVI style   s.r. 4260

St Petersburg 9 May 1890

TO BE PAID

4260 r. 12 May 1890

N. Petrov

<u>Note</u> The sum of 59.922 r. 35 k. remains unspent in the credit balance of the budget of H.I.M. Cabinet for 1890, para. 10, article 1, H.I.M. special expenses. Permission is requested to pay Fabergé 4260 r. from the said credit
Head of the Household Dept.
12 May 1890   Klimchenko

Memory of Azov egg (7)

File No. 1664	To Household Dept. 26 May 1891
No. 3/66	Vorontsov-Dashkov 90
K. FABERGÉ	C. FABERGÉ
Supplier to the Imperial Court	Fournisseur de la Cour Impériale
Moscow St Petersburg	St Petersbourg Moscou

Invoice for His Imperial Majesty

April 19   Engraving of a coat of arms -
           seal with red enamel   200
April 24   Jasper egg with diamonds, Louis XV style,
           and model of the "Memory of Azov"   4500

                                              s.r.   4700

St Petersburg 24 May 1891

TO BE PAID   In H.I.M. Cabinet

"To be paid" written in   *Count Vorontsov*
H.I.M.'s own hand
26 May 1891
N. Petrov   Note on reverse
State Secretary   (note about credit) [in pencil]

Diamond Trellis egg (8)

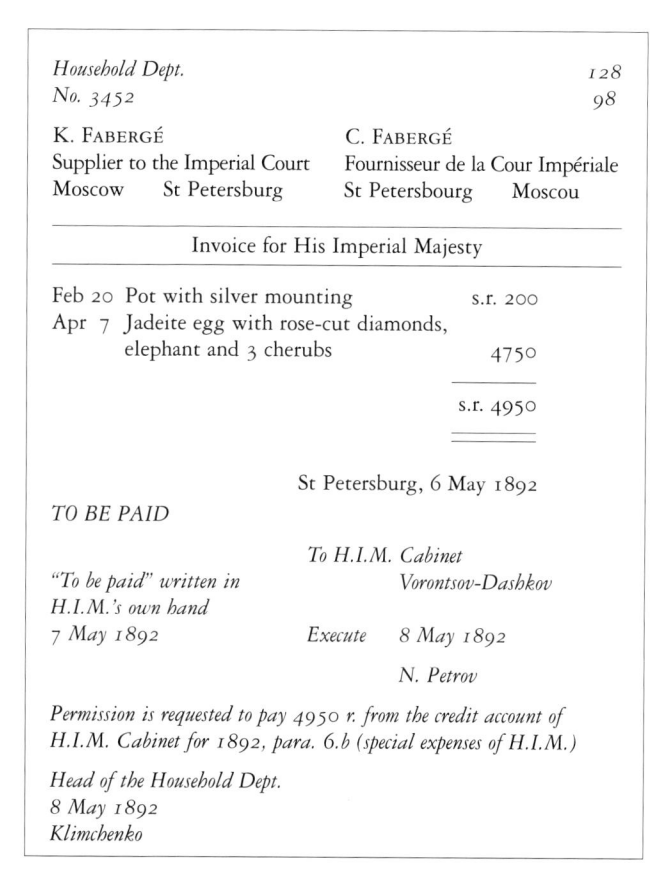

> Household Dept.   *128*
> No. 3452   *98*
>
> K. Fabergé   C. Fabergé
> Supplier to the Imperial Court   Fournisseur de la Cour Impériale
> Moscow   St Petersburg   St Petersbourg   Moscou
>
> Invoice for His Imperial Majesty
>
> Feb 20   Pot with silver mounting   s.r. 200
> Apr 7   Jadeite egg with rose-cut diamonds,
>   elephant and 3 cherubs   4750
>
>   s.r. 4950
>
>   St Petersburg, 6 May 1892
> TO BE PAID
>   To H.I.M. Cabinet
> "To be paid" written in   Vorontsov-Dashkov
> H.I.M.'s own hand
> 7 May 1892   Execute   8 May 1892
>   N. Petrov
>
> Permission is requested to pay 4950 r. from the credit account of
> H.I.M. Cabinet for 1892, para. 6.b (special expenses of H.I.M.)
>
> Head of the Household Dept.
> 8 May 1892
> Klimchenko

Caucasus egg (9)

> No. 3145   Received in the Household Dept.
>   25 May 1893
>
> K. Fabergé   160/125   C. Fabergé   For No. 1757
> Supplier to the Imperial Court   Fournisseur de la Cour Impériale
> Moscow   St Petersburg   St Petersbourg   Moscou
>
> Invoice for His Imperial Majesty
>
> 1   Egg in the Louis XVI style,
>   red enamel, with portrait, diamonds
>   and four miniatures   5200
>
>   s.r. 5200
>
>   St Petersburg 22 May 1893
>
> TO BE PAID
>   To H.I.M. Cabinet
> 24 May 1893
>   Count Vorontsov-Dashkov
>
> *Make copy of invoice*
> *and give original to me*
> *[in pencil]*
>
>   Issue payment from the credit account of
>   H.I.M. personal expenses
>   Head of the Household Dept.
>   Klimchenko

Renaissance egg (10)

Twelve Monograms egg (11), Rosebud egg (12)

Household Dept. No.2524	43 28
K. FABERGÉ	C. FABERGÉ
Supplier to the Imperial Court	Fournisseur de la Cour Impériale
Moscow St Petersburg	St Petersbourg Moscou

Invoice for His Imperial Majesty

1 Agate egg, gold mounting, enamelled in the Renaissance style, with diamonds, rose-cut diamonds, pearls and rubies 4750

s.r. 4750

St Petersburg 6 May 1894

TO BE PAID

To H.I.M. Cabinet
7 *May* 1894

Household Department
For execution
7/V

For payment, No. 1627
[in pencil]

No.1094   Account book of H.I.M 1895   Upon receipt
from H.I.M. account
TO BE PAID

To be paid from H.I.M. personal account 9293 r.

The remainder amounting to 3025 r. to be paid from the account of H.I.M. Empress Alexandra Fedorovna

K. FABERGÉ	C. FABERGÉ
Supplier to the Imperial Court	Fournisseur de la Cour Impériale
Moscow St Petersburg	St Petersbourg Moscou

Invoice for His Imperial Majesty

1895
Feb 13	Engraving of seal	130
Feb 24	Engraving of facsimile in a cigarette case with white enamel	3
	Cigarette case of green enamel Louis XV	750
	Jadeite egg with sapphires	40
	Rhodonite egg, Louis XV style	20
Mar 31	Grey enamel buttons with diamonds	140
	Enamel buttons	70
	Blue enamel egg, Louis XVI style	4500
	Red enamel egg with crown	3250
	Dolphin electric lamp	800
Apr 18	Rhodonite buffalo	110
	Cachalong polecat	90
	Rhodonite polecat	75
	Obsidian sable	80
Apr 24	Large fan	1600
	Jadeite clock with cherubs	425
May 5	Crystal umbrella handle	215

s.r. 12318

correct [in pencil]
St Petersburg 9 May 1895

The underlined items to be shared between the Empress Aθ and myself

Alexander III egg (13),
Revolving Miniatures egg (14)

69	TO BE PAID		135

K. FABERGÉ   C. FABERGÉ
Supplier to the Imperial Court   Fournisseur de la Cour Impériale
Moscow   St Petersburg   St Petersbourg   Moscou

[Stamped] *H.I.M. Office*
17 April 1896

Expenditures to the amount of 17465 r.

For book No.55

Invoice for His Imperial Majesty

Jan	22	Crystal handle for cane with enamel and rose-cut diamond s.r.	130
Feb	10	Toast rack with initials AΘ	35
	12	Orletz electric bell with diamond emerald and moonstone	315
		Topaz brooch with diamonds and rose-cut diamonds	1675
	16	Square jadeite electric bell, Louis XVI style, with garnet and moonstone	110
		Triangular jadeite electric bell, gilt border, Louis XVI style	60
	22	Blue Ural topaz, 18th century polishing	250
	24	Open-work egg, 2 sapphires, 82 rose-cut diamonds	150
	29	Medallion, gold heart with diamond	30
Mar	23	Porte-chaise, Louis XVI style, show-case for precious items	900
Apr	3	Rock crystal egg with rock crystal pedestal, 12 miniatures, with emerald and rose-cut diamonds and mounting	6750
		Blue enamel egg, 6 portraits of H.I.M. Emperor Alexander III, with 10 sapphires, rose-cut diamonds and mounting	3575
Apr	4	Diamond necklace chain, 3/4 part	3000
	5	Brooch with moonstone, with diamonds and mounting	485
		s.r.	17465

St Petersburg, 12 April 1896

"To be paid" written in H.I.M.'s own hand
Count Lamsdorff
Executed 19 April 1896

Mauve Enamel egg (15), Coronation egg (16)

7654/	To H.I.M. Cabinet	TO BE PAID	
1714	Baron Fredericks	24 May 1897	8

K. FABERGÉ C. FABERGÉ
Supplier to the Imperial Court Fournisseur de la Cour Impériale
Moscow   St Petersburg St.Petersbourg   Moscou

Invoice for His Imperial Majesty

Apr 18	Yellow enamel egg and carriage	s.r. 5500
	Emerald pendant egg with diamonds	1000
	Bevelled glass case with jadeite stand	150
	Mauve enamel egg, with 3 miniatures	3250
May 8	Brooch XXV 1 diamond	6000
	1 pendant emerald	3200
	small diamonds and mounting	2300
		s.r. 21400

1st Sector St Petersburg 17 May 1897
Checked for the sum
of 21400 r.
   M.A. G.....
Household Dept.
Transfer to the personal account of H.I.M.
For payment No.1961   24/V

Pelican egg (17), Lilies of the Valley egg (18)

5240/1845 63
K. FABERGÉ C. FABERGÉ
Supplier to the Imperial Court Fournisseur de la Cour Impériale
Moscow   St Petersburg St Petersbourg   Moscou
113/04

Invoice for His Imperial Majesty

Apr 10	Pink enamel egg with three portraits, leaves of green enamel and lilies of the valley of pearls and rose-cut diamonds	s.r. 6700
	Gold egg, Empire style, 9 miniatures	3600
		s.r. 10300

St Petersburg 7 May 1898

[signed] C. Fabergé

TO BE PAID
"To be paid" written in
H.I.M's own hand *Baron Fredericks*
22 May 1898

For Household Dept.
Transfer to the personal account of H.I.M.
22 May 1898
Klimchenko
Household Dept. For payment No.1921

Pansy egg (19), Bouquet of Lilies Clock egg (20)

K. FABERGÉ	C. FABERGÉ	98
Supplier to the Imperial Court	Fournisseur de la Cour Impériale	140
Moscow St Petersburg	St Petersbourg Moscou	

Invoice for His Imperial Majesty

1   Easter egg, with pansies, containing a heart with the monogram "M" and crown of rose-cut diamonds, 11 miniatures, diamonds and rose-cut diamonds   s.r. 5600

1   Easter egg, Louis XVI clock, yellow enamel with rose-cut diamonds, bouquet of lilies of white chalcedony and pendant ruby egg with rose-cut diamonds   6750

s.r. 12350

St Petersburg 17 July 1899

TO BE PAID

"To be paid" written in
H.I.M.'s own hand   Baron Fredericks
28 July 1899
Household Dept.

Cockerel egg (21), Trans-Siberian Railway egg (22)

K. FABERGÉ	C. FABERGÉ	1
Supplier to the Imperial Court	Fournisseur de la Cour Impériale	
Moscow St Petersburg	St Petersbourg Moscou	

Invoice for His Imperial Majesty

1900
April   Easter egg of violet enamel, with cockerel and clock; with one lozenge diamond, 188 rose-cut diamonds, 2 rubies   r. 6500
Easter egg of green enamel, with Siberian train, ruby, pearls and rose-cut diamonds   7000

r. 13500

St Petersburg, 13 January 1901

TO BE PAID

"To be paid" written in
H.I.M.'s own hand   Baron Fredericks

19 January 1901
Household Dept.

Gatchina Palace egg (23), Basket of Wild Flowers egg (24)

		45
K. FABERGÉ	C. FABERGÉ	31
Supplier to the Imperial Court	Fournisseur de la Cour Impériale	
Moscow St Petersburg	St Petersbourg Moscou	

Invoice for His Imperial Majesty

1	Easter egg, white enamel, 1 large rose-cut diamond, 1 lozenge diamond and pearls, with Gatchina Palace	r. 5000
1	Easter egg, white enamel; basket with bouquet of wild flowers. with 4176 rose-cut diamonds and 10 pearls	6850
		r. 11850

correct

St Petersburg, 16 April 1901

TO BE PAID

"To be paid" written in
H.I.M.'s own hand   Baron Fredericks
25 April 1901

Household Dept.

Empire Nephrite egg (25), Clover egg (26)

Allocation No. 1938		35
K. FABERGÉ	C. FABERGÉ	64
Supplier to the Imperial Court	Fournisseur de la Cour Impériale	
Moscow St Petersburg	St Petersbourg Moscou	

Invoice for His Imperial Majesty

Apr 12	Enamel clover egg with rubies and rose-cut diamonds, with large four-leaf clover, 23 diamonds with rose-cut diamonds and 4 miniatures	r. 8750
	Nephrite and gold Empire egg, with 2 diamonds and miniature	6000
		r. 14750

St Petersburg, 10 May 1902

TO BE PAID

"To be paid" written in
H.I.M.'s own hand   Baron Fredericks
28 May 1902

Household Dept.

Danish Jubilee egg (27), Peter the Great egg (28)

5983		
1623		42
K. FABERGÉ	C. FABERGÉ	81
Supplier to the Imperial Court	Fournisseur de la Cour Impériale	
St Petersburg Moscow Odessa	St Petersbourg Moscou Odessa	

[Stamped] *H.I.M. Cabinet*
1 May 1903

Invoice for His Imperial Majesty

Gold egg with monument to Emperor Peter I   r. 9760
Gold egg, in the Louis XIV style,
with two miniatures   7535

                                              r. 17295

St Petersburg 29 April 1903

Total 17295 correct

                                Assistant Executive
                                Secretary
TO BE PAID   Grigor...

"To be paid" written in
H.I.M.'s own hand   Baron Fredericks
30 April 1903

Household Dept.
[in the margin] *Payment issued on 8 May No. 1948*

Swan egg (29), Moscow Kremlin egg (30)

1980		103
K. FABERGÉ	C. FABERGÉ	49
Supplier to the Imperial Court	Fournisseur de la Cour Impériale	
St Petersburg Moscow Odessa	St Petersbourg Moscou Odessa	

Invoice for His Imperial Majesty

1906
1 April 1 Egg, in the Louis XVI style, opaque
            mauve enamel, with bows of rose-cut
            diamonds and 2 diamonds, containing
            a mechanical gold 72° silver-plated
            swan on an aquamarine pediment   r. 7200
         1 Egg, "Moscow Kremlin", of different
            coloured gold and enamel, with white
            enamel egg representing the Uspenski
            Cathedral, with music, on a white
            onyx pediment   11800

                                                 r. 19000

[in margin]
To be executed
according to para. 5
12/VII   *H.I.M. Cabinet*
          Ryudzinski   St Petersburg 7 June 1906
                                per pro C. Fabergé
                                [signed] A. Fabergé
TO BE PAID

"To be paid" written in
H.I.M.'s own hand   Baron Fredericks
12 June 1906

Household Dept.

Cradle with Garlands egg (31), Rose Trellis egg (32)

		58
K. Fabergé	C. Fabergé	37
By Appointment to the Court	Joaillier de la Cour	
St Petersburg Moscow Kiev	St Petersbourg Moscou Kiev	
Odessa Nizhnii Novgorod Fair	Odessa Foire de Nijny-Novgorod	
London	Londres	

Invoice for His Imperial Majesty

21 April Blue and opalescent enamel egg, on white onyx stand, basket with enamel bouquet, garlands of various enamels, mountings of coloured golds with rose-cut diamonds, containing a white enamel easel with one ruby, pearls and rose-cut diamonds, one miniature of the Imperial children   r. 9700

Green enamel egg with branches of roses and enamel leaves, 1 diamond and rose-cut diamonds, containing a diamond chain with medallion and miniature of H.I.H. the Grand Duke Tsarevich Alexei Nikolaievich   8300

r. 18000

St Petersburg 30 April 1907

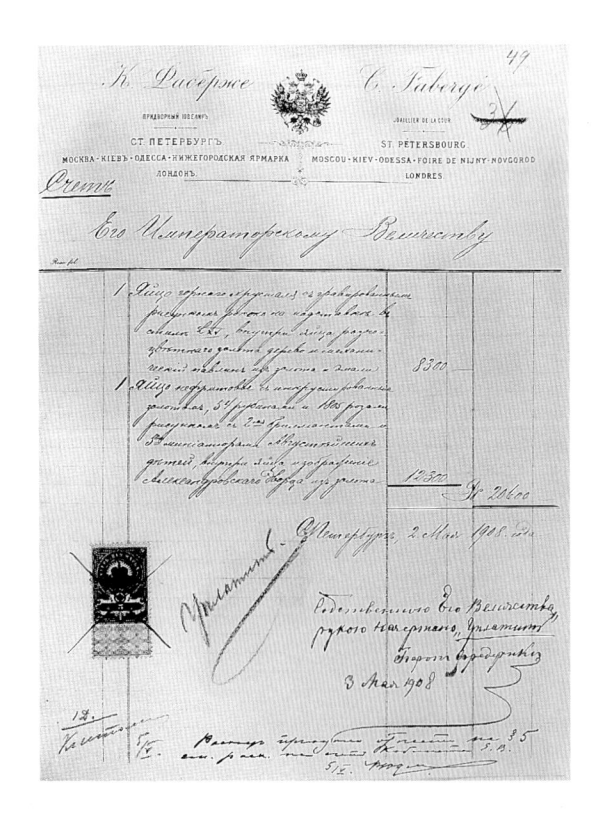

TO BE PAID
"To be paid" written in H.I.M.'s own hand

Baron Fredericks
11 May 1907

Peacock egg (33), Alexander Palace egg (34)

		49
K. Fabergé	C. Fabergé	36
By Appointment to the Court	Joaillier de la Cour	
St Petersburg Moscow Kiev	St Petersbourg Moscou Kiev	
Odessa Nizhnii Novgorod Fair	Odessa Foire de Nijny-Novgorod	
London	Londres	

Invoice for His Imperial Majesty

1 Rock crystal egg with rococo engraved design on a Louis XV style pediment; inside the egg a tree of various kinds of gold and an enamelled mechanical peacock in gold and enamel   r. 8300

1 Nephrite egg with gold incrustations, 54 rubies, 1805 rose-cut diamonds, with 2 diamonds and 5 miniatures of the Imperial children; inside the egg a representation of the Alexander Palace in gold   12300

r. 20600

St Petersburg 2 May 1908

TO BE PAID
"To be paid" written in H.I.M.'s own hand

Baron Fredericks
3 May 1908

To 1st Sector for execution

5/V   *Expenditures to be assigned to para. 5 of H.I.M. Cabinet expenses*
5/V   Ryudman

Alexander III Commemorative egg (35),
Standard egg (36)

2802 *43 48*

K. FABERGÉ C. FABERGÉ
Supplier to the Imperial Court Fournisseur de la Cour Impériale
Jeweller Joaillier
St Petersburg Moscow Odessa St Petersbourg Moscou Odessa

Invoice for His Imperial Majesty

1	Rock crystal egg on rock crystal pediment, with 2 lapis dolphins, decorations of gold and enamel with 2 pearls, 4 diamonds and 1029 rose-cut diamonds; inside the egg a model of the yacht "Standard" in gold, platinum and enamel	12400
1	Egg of opaque white enamel with gold stripes, decorated with 2 diamonds and 3467 rose-cut diamonds; inside a gold bust of Alexander III on a lapis lazuli pediment decorated with rose-cut diamonds	11200
		r. 23600

St Petersburg 9 July 1909

[signed] K. Fabergé

H.I.M. Cabinet is ordered to pay the
sum of roubles 23,600
                Baron Fredericks
                9 July 1909

Allocation No. 3209

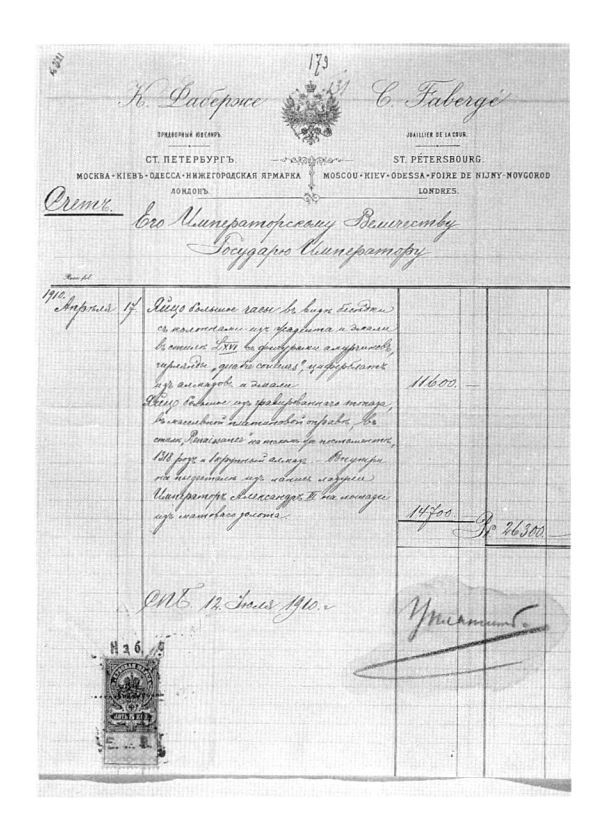

Alexander III Equestrian egg (37),
Colonnade egg (38)

Household Dept.
2621 *179*
            131 [in pencil]

K. FABERGÉ C. FABERGÉ
By Appointment to the Court Joaillier de la Cour
St Petersburg Moscow Kiev St Petersbourg Moscou Kiev
Odessa Nizhnii Novgorod Fair Odessa Foire de Nijny- Novgorod
London Londres

Invoice for His Imperial Majesty

1910
Apr 17 Large clock egg in the form of a summer-house with jadeite and enamel colonnades, in the Louis XVI style, with figures of cherubs, "quatre couleurs" garlands and clock face of diamonds and enamel   11600
Large egg of engraved topaz, in massive platinum mounting, in the Renaissance style, on a similar pediment of the same topaz, 1318 rose-cut diamonds and 1 large diamond. Inside on a lapis-lazuli pedestal a matt gold equestrian figure of the Emperor Alexander III   14700

r. 26300

St Petersburg, 12 July 1910

TO BE PAID

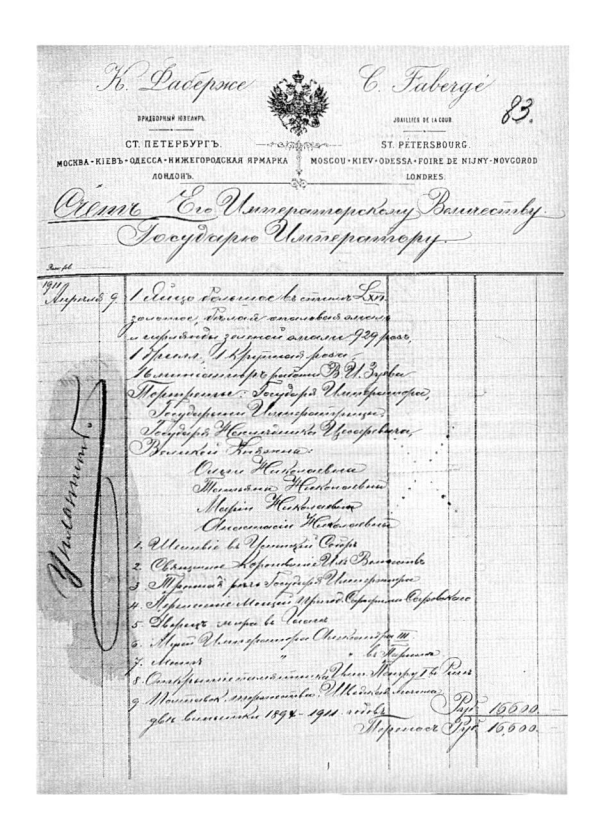

Fifteenth Anniversary egg (40)

K. FABERGÉ	C. FABERGÉ	83
By Appointment to the Court	Joaillier de la Cour	
St Petersburg Moscow Kiev	St Petersburg Moscou Kiev	
Odessa Nizhnii Novgorod Fair	Odessa Foire de Nijny-Novgorod,	
London	Londres	

Invoice for His Imperial Majesty

1911

Apr 9   1 large gold egg, in the Louis XVI style, opalescent white enamel and green enamel, garlands, 929 rose-cut diamonds, 1 diamond, 1 large rose-cut diamond. 16 miniatures by V.I. Zuiev:

portraits: His Majesty the Emperor
            Her Majesty the Empress
            His Highness the Heir-Tsarevich
            The Grand Duchesses:
               Olga Nikolaievna
               Tatiana Nikolaievna
               Maria Nikolaievna
               Anastasia Nikolaievna

TO BE PAID

1. Procession in the Cathedral of the Dormition
2. The Holy Coronation of Their Majesties
3. The Emperor's Speech from the Throne
4. Transfer of the Relics of Saint Seraphim of Sarov
5. The Peace Palace at The Hague
6. The Emperor Alexander III Museum
7. The Emperor Alexander III Bridge in Paris
8. Unveiling of the monument to Peter I in Riga
9. The Poltava Celebrations (Swedish Grave)

Two vignettes "1894" and "1911"   r. 16600

1911

Apr 9   1 large egg in the form of a bay tree in gold, with 325 nephrite leaves, 110 opalescent white enamel flowerets, 25 diamonds, 20 rubies, 53 pearls, 219 rose-cut diamonds, 1 large rose-cut diamond. Inside the tree is a mechanical songbird; a rectangular planter of white Mexican onyx on a nephrite pediment, with 4 nephrite columns at the corners supporting green enamel garlands with pearls   12800

                             r. 29400

St Petersburg, 13 June 1911

"To be paid" written in
H.I.M.'s own hand   *Adjutant-General
Baron Fredericks*

                           TO BE PAID

Bay Tree egg (39)

Winter egg (43)

Romanov Tercentenary egg (44)

2625 63

K. FABERGÉ C. FABERGÉ
By Appointment to the Joaillier de la Cour
Imperial Court Impériale
St Petersburg Moscow St Petersbourg Moscou
Odessa London Odessa Londres

TO BE PAID

Invoice for His Imperial Majesty

1913

Feb	5	Repair of gold paper-knife	4.50
	13	Transform screw into pin	10
	28	Repair of platinum double cuff-links; provide new clasp	4
Mar	6	Repair of three enamelled decorations, two chains with decorations, four clasps added	30
Apr	13	Large egg made of white topaz decorated with frost motifs set with 1508 rose-cut diamonds and incrusted in the topaz with borders set with 360 diamonds, on a topaz base shaped like a rock of ice with icicles set with rose-cut diamonds. Inside the egg is a small platinum basket decorated with 1378 rose-cut diamonds containing snowdrops with nephrite leaves.	24600

TO BE PAID
Written in H.I.M.'s own hand

Carried over r. 24648.50

For the Minister of H.I.M. Court Major-General A.Z.....
7 July 1913

Apr 13 24648.50

Large egg covered inside and out with white enamel. On the outside 18 miniatures of members of the Romanov Dynasty by Zuiev, framed with 1115 rose-cut diamonds, under topazes. Between the miniatures, gold chased and engraved designs with Imperial crowns and fur hats. At each end of the egg, lozenge diamonds with HER MAJESTY'S cipher and the dates of the jubilee year. Inside a blue steel globe with representation of two northern hemispheres. The continents are presented in relief, in different coloured gold, on one hemisphere is represented Russia in 1613, and on the other Russia in 1913. The egg rests on a pediment consisting of a three-sided eagle standing on the Imperial shield made of purpurine and enamel 21300

[copy from the original shield kept at the Armoury in Moscow]

	26	Repair of table calendar	3
	27	Gold seal with initials A.H. and crown	115
Jun	11	Diamond brooch with 1 yellow sapphire	925

r. 46991.50

St Petersburg 24 June 1913

249

Appendix 1

DESCRIPTIONS FROM A FABERGÉ ALBUM OF THE IMPERIAL EASTER EGGS PRESENTED TO ALEXANDRA FEDOROVNA BETWEEN 1907 AND 1916

These captions, found in a Fabergé album, give detailed descriptions of the Easter eggs from the House of Fabergé presented to Alexandra Fedorovna between 1907 and 1916, which makes it possible to identify those made for Maria Fedorovna and for Alexandra Fedorovna over that period. Unfortunately, all the relevant photographs have disappeared. The album is in a private collection.

(32) Easter egg presented to Alexandra Fedorovna in 1907. Green enamel egg covered with a network of diamonds, intertwined with garlands of roses. Contains a portrait of the Heir on ivory, in the form of a medallion surrounded with diamonds, on a similar chain.

(34) Easter egg presented to Alexandra Fedorovna in 1908, of nephrite inlaid with a pattern of diamond wreaths and garlands. The egg bears five medallions with portraits of Their Majesties' august children painted on ivory. The egg contains a miniature gold and enamel model of the Alexander Palace at Tsarskoie Selo.

(36) Easter egg presented to Alexandra Fedorovna in 1909, of rock crystal in gold and enamel setting. At both ends of the egg, double-headed eagles of lapis lazuli with pearl pendants. The egg is placed horizontally on a lapis lazuli dolphin and is completed by a pedestal of rock crystal in a gold setting with white and green enamel. Contains a miniature model of the new Imperial yacht, 'Standard'.

(38) Easter egg presented to Alexandra Fedorovna in 1910. Clock-egg of pink enamel with rotating clock face, surmounted by a cupid pointing to the hour with a rod. The egg is placed on a colonnade of light green serpentine and the columns are entwined with garlands of roses of different colours of gold. In the centre there are two white platinum doves. The colonnade ends with a pedestal of serpentine, gold and pink enamel. At the corners of the pedestal, four cherubs (the Imperial children) hold garlands of roses.

(40) Easter egg presented to Alexandra Fedorovna in 1911. Made of opalescent enamel, divided into thyrsi by green enamel garlands. The thyrsi contain miniature paintings depicting the main events of the reign of Nicholas II, alternating with portraits of members of the Imperial family.

(42) Easter egg presented to Alexandra Fedorovna in 1912. Made of lapis lazuli in Louis XVI style, covered with open-work chased gold ornamentation. Contains a double-headed eagle of diamonds, on whose breast is a two-faceted portrait of Tsarevich Alexei (recto and verso).

(44) Easter egg presented to Alexandra Fedorovna in 1913, commemorating the tercentenary of the rule of the House of Romanov. White enamel egg, covered with chased gold eagles and crowns, among them portraits of Tsars, Emperors and Empresses of the House of Romanov. The egg rests on a double-headed eagle on a pedestal representing the Imperial coat of arms. The egg contains a revolving globe, one half showing a relief map of Russia at the time of Mikhail Fedorovich [founder of the Romanov dynasty] and the other, a similar map of contemporary Russia (1913).

(46) Easter egg presented to Alexandra Fedorovna in 1914. Louis XVI style, open-work of different-coloured precious stones, pearls and white enamel. Contains a medallion with an Imperial crown on a gold and enamel pedestal. On one side of the medallion are portraits of Their Majesties' five children, painted on ivory in cameo style, and on the other side, a basket of flowers and the children's names.

(48) Easter egg presented to Alexandra Fedorovna in 1915 to commemorate the Imperial family's participation in the work of the Red Cross. White enamel egg with two red crosses, between them portraits of Olga Nikolaievna and Tatiana Nikolaievna wearing nurses' head-dresses. Contains a triptych icon of the Resurrection in the 17th-century style, flanked by smaller icons of Saint Olga and Saint Tatiana.

(50) Easter egg presented to Alexandra Fedorovna in 1916. Steel egg mounted on four steel artillery shells on a nephrite base. The egg is surmounted by an Imperial crown and contains a miniature painting of the Emperor visiting the front lines.

Appendix 2

Newspaper accounts of the 1902 exhibition at the von Dervis mansion

Exhibition of artefacts and miniatures

Newspaper *Novoie Vremia*, St Petersburg, 9 March 1902

(Author : P.)

Today, on Friday 8 March, at three o'clock in the afternoon, Her Imperial Majesty the Empress Alexandra Fedorovna and Their Imperial Highnesses the Grand Duchesses Maria Pavlovna, Elizaveta Fedorovna and Maria Georgievna, Grand Duchess Elena Vladimirovna and Grand Duke Georgii Mikhailovich inspected the arrangements for the exhibition of Fabergé artefacts and antique miniatures and snuffboxes to be opened tomorrow at the von Dervis mansion on the Angliskaia Naberezhnaia [English Embankment].

Their Majesties the Tsar Emperor and the Tsaritsa Empress and august members of the Imperial Family contributed precious artefacts in their possession to this exhibition, organized for the benefit of schools of the Imperial Ladies' Patriotic Society.

The exhibition has been accepted under the High Patronage of Her Majesty the Empress Alexandra Fedorovna. The articles shown here are of great interest, if only because these artistic masterpieces are not exhibited publicly at any other time. One room is entirely taken up with objects belonging to Their Majesties.

Among the exhibits are the silver swan presented by members of the Imperial family to Their Majesties on the day of their marriage, a rare collection of miniature portraits of Russian Emperors and members of the Imperial Family, the silver mantelpiece clock with diamond hands presented to the late lamented Emperor Alexander III and the Empress Maria Fedorovna by members of the Imperial Family on the day of Their Majesties' 25th wedding anniversary and collections of Easter eggs belonging to the Empresses Maria Fedorovna and Alexandra Fedorovna. The Empress Alexandra Fedorovna's collection includes an egg with a bouquet of lilies of the valley, surrounded by moss: the flowers are made of pearls, the leaves of nephrite, and the moss of finest gold strands. Another egg contains a whole miniature train of the Great Siberian Railway (22), one of the carriages being an identical replica of the church-carriage. Another noteworthy item is the portrait of the Tsar Emperor by Count Benckendorff. An outstanding item among the artefacts belonging to the Empress Maria Fedorovna is a statuette, carved from nephrite, of a Chinaman with a ruby-studded belt and ruby eyes.

Some noteworthy items are those made for the Imperial Hermitage and shown at the World Fair in Paris, and also the basket of flowers of pearls and precious stones, the pink egg with pearls, the album in a gold cover with an emerald, the clock with a fan, miniatures of Their Majesties' crowns and the Cap of Monomakh – replicas of the Tsars' regalia. Another room and part of the main hall are full of treasures belonging to the Grand Duchesses Maria Pavlovna, Elizaveta Fedorovna, Alexandra Iosifovna, Elizaveta Mavrikievna, Maria Georgievna, Xenia Alexandrovna, Olga Alexandrovna and Duchess Elena Georgievna of Sachsen-Altenburg, and *objets de vertu* belonging to the Grand Dukes Vladimir Alexandrovich, Kiril Vladimirovich, Alexei Alexandrovich, Sergei Alexandrovich, Konstantin Konstantinovich, Nikolai Nikolaievich and Georgii Mikhailovich.

Among the many exhibitors from high society are the Vice-President of the Ladies' Patriotic Society, Lady of the Bedchamber of the Empress Alexandra Fedorovna, Princess Galitzine (collection of miniatures); ladies in waiting Countess Vorontsov-Dashkov, Princess Yusupov, Countess Sumarokov-Elston; the spouses of the High Court Marshal, Princess Dolgorukaia, and of the High Court Master, Madame Vsevolodskaia; Countesses Heyden and Cheremetev; the wife of the French Ambassador, Marquise de Montebello; Mesdames Durnovo, Polovtseva, Gall and von Etter; Countesses Orlov-Davidov and Benckendorff; Princesses Kurakin and Vassilchikov; Princes Orlov and Odoievskii-Maslov and others.

The exhibition will open on the 9th at 3.30 p.m.

Opening of an exhibition of treasures

Newspaper *Novoie Vremia*, St Petersburg, 10 March 1902

(Author : V.P.R.)

The ceremonial opening of the exhibition of Fabergé artefacts, antique miniatures and snuffboxes belonging to members of the Imperial Family and other individuals took place today at half past two in the afternoon at the von Dervis mansion (Angliskaia Naberezhnaia) in aid of the schools of the Imperial Ladies' Patriotic Society.

The exhibition was visited by Their Majesties the Emperor and the Empresses Maria Fedorovna and Alexandra Fedorovna, Their Imperial Highnesses, the Heir to the Throne, Grand Dukes Vladimir Alexandrovich, with his daughter, Grand Duchess Elena Vladimirovna, Andrei Vladimirovich, Alexei Alexandrovich, Sergei Alexandrovich, with his august wife Grand Duchess Elizaveta Fedorovna, Grand Duchess Elizaveta Mavrikievna, Grand Dukes Nikolai Nikolaievich, Mikhail Nikolaievich, Georgii Mikhailovich, with his august wife Grand Duchess Maria Georgievna, Grand Duchesses Xenia Alexandrovna and Olga Alexandrovna, with her august husband Prince Piotr Alexandrovich of Oldenburg, and Duchess Elena Georgievna of Sachsen-Altenburg. The exhibition was also attended by a number of foreign ambassadors and members of the diplomatic corps and of the highest society and Court circles of St Petersburg.

After inspecting all the exhibits, Their Majesties and Their Highnesses proceeded to the buffet, run for charity by Princesses Orlova, Cantacuzène and Beloselskaia-Belozerskaia, Madame Voieikova, Countess Kleinmichel, Mr Voieikov and Mr Knorring. Here the august guests drank a glass of champagne and left the exhibition at about four o'clock.

The most important exhibits, belonging to Their Majesties, have already been mentioned in yesterday's issue. It may be added that among them are miniature gold models of the coronation coach and a steam yacht, and that the exhibits belonging to the Empress Maria Fedorovna include a group of family portraits (miniatures) of the Emperor, the Empress Alexandra Fedorovna and the august son, daughters and grand-children of Her Majesty the Empress Maria Fedorovna. The miniatures are arranged in a precious heart-shaped frame, placed on an easel (19). Each portrait, no bigger than a silver five-kopek piece, is surmounted by a ruby. The splendid collection of Easter eggs included one with miniature portraits of the Imperial Family, another surmounted by a diamond pelican (17) – the Empress Maria's personal symbol – and containing small screens with miniature views of all the Institutes of which Her Majesty is a patron and a third, of gold, containing a picture of Her Majesty's winter residence, the Gatchina Palace (23). A compass and a clock are outstanding among the items lent by the Heir to the Throne. A noteworthy article in the showcase of Grand Duke Vladimir Alexandrovich and Grand Duchess Maria Pavlovna is a gold loving cup in the form of a dipper with representations of various animals and precious stones. The exhibits belonging to Grand Duchess Elizaveta Fedorovna include a beautiful gold fan decorated with an artistically painted spring scene and a splendid vase with flowers of precious stones. An outstanding item belonging to Grand Duchess Alexandra Iosefovna is a pearl and diamond swan. Miniature enamel screens with portraits of the Imperial Family owned by Grand Duchess Elizaveta Mavrikievna are sprinkled with precious stones.

The showcase of Grand Duke Georgii Mikhailovich and Grand Duchess Maria Georgievna contains a miniature portrait of a head by Greuze. The articles lent by Grand Duchess Xenia Alexandrovna have been placed in the first room, and include a splendid silver service in the form of Empire vases. A fan artistically painted by Solomko is an outstanding item of the collection of Grand Duchess Olga Alexandrovna.

Also in the first room is a showcase containing miniatures owned by Duchess Elena Georgievna of Sachsen-Altenburg. The room is full of treasures belonging to the Grand Dukes. Princess Yusupov's collection of snuffboxes and miniatures is wonderful; among her treasures is an animal carved from a single sapphire, with ruby eyes and a diamond tail.

Many beautiful articles are exhibited by Duke N.M. of Leuchtenberg, General Durnovo, Count Fersen and others.

The great success of the exhibition became evident from the first day: 3,000 roubles in entrance fees were collected today. As from tomorrow and until 15 March, the entrance fee will be 1 rouble 10 kopeks.

Exhibition of artefacts, antique miniatures and snuffboxes organized in aid of the schools of the Imperial Ladies' Patriotic Society

Journal *Niva*, Nº 12, 1902

The charity exhibition of Fabergé artefacts, antique miniatures and snuffboxes, organized in aid of the schools of the Imperial Ladies' Patriotic Society under the august patronage of Her Majesty the Empress Alexandra Fedorovna, is of great interest because of its originality and the richness of the exhibits.

The exhibition does not take up a great deal of space, but it contains such riches, so many wonderful and rare objects, that it is truly dazzling. The most interesting are undoubtedly the treasures belonging to the Emperor and Empresses and the Grand Dukes and Grand Duchesses. The last room of the exhibition and part of the last room but one are full of artefacts owned by members of the Imperial Family. It is hard to imagine anything more dazzling and at the same time more exquisite in their workmanship.

Most of the treasures are exhibited in glass showcases, but some large articles are shown separately, on tables and pedestals. Two showcases containing articles belonging to Their Majesties the Empresses Maria Fedorovna and Alexandra Fedorovna are of special interest. Most of these exhibits are precious Easter eggs made by the jeweller Fabergé: one of them contains a superbly fashioned gold model of the Gatchina Palace (23) no more than an inch high.

Some original items are the folding eggs, in the form of albums containing miniature portraits of the Imperial Family and pictures of the Patriotic and Pavlovsk Institutes. Another interesting article is the gold miniature of the Trans-Siberian railway – 'Direct line to Siberia' – which has been taken out of its special egg (22) and is shown separately. The train consists of several carriages attached to one another, each no more than two thirds of an inch long, the last being a model of the church-carriage used on the Siberian railway. The workmanship of this exquisite little object is so fine that it gives an accurate idea of the composition of the Siberian express train, down to the carriages labelled 'Smokers' and 'Non-smokers'.

In the showcase with articles belonging to Her Majesty the Empress Maria Fedorovna, one's special attention is attracted to a heart-shaped silver portrait frame, decorated with precious stones (19). This frame, not more than an inch and half high, contains a multitude of miniature portraits of members of the Imperial Family, each no bigger than a split-pea, but so exquisitely painted that it is in no way inferior to a full-size detailed portrait. The impression is that these miniatures were painted by some Lilliputian artist.

In the same room with these showcases, there are also some large objects belonging to members of the Imperial Family, such as an enormous silver swan and a stone and silver clock, surmounted by a diamond cipher, with diamond hands and surrounded by beautifully cast silver cupids.

Many of the delightful exhibits belong to the Grand Duchesses – for instance, the charming little animals carved from semi-precious stones lent by Her Highness Grand Duchess Xenia Alexandrovna and the lovely fan painted by the artist Solomko belonging to Her Highness Grand Duchess Olga Alexandrovna.

The antique snuffboxes with miniature pictures and individual cameo-miniatures (mostly portraits of historical personages) are of special artistic and at the same time historic interest. The majority of these exhibits have been lent by members of high society – Princess Yusupov Countess Sumarokov-Elston, Countess Benckendorff and others. It is almost unbelievable that a whole hunting scene or a village fair with a multitude of characters can be represented on an area of about a square inch! And represented artistically, in every sense of the word! Here again, we get the impression that these pictures have been painted, not by an ordinary person, but by a pygmy, a Lilliputian, whose eye can adapt itself to all this unfathomable, minute detail of workmanship!

A very large number of historical personages are depicted on cameos, some of which are amazingly small. Particularly noteworthy are the portraits of Russian Tsars and also of Napoleon and the Empress Josephine.

Mention has already been made of the wonderful miniature portraits of members of the Imperial Family. It is hard to imagine anything more attractive than these tiny, beautifully painted portraits.

This interesting and unique exhibition was unfortunately of very short duration, and closed on 15 March after less than two weeks.

Appendix 3

DESCRIPTION OF IMPERIAL EASTER EGGS FROM INVENTORIES: GATCHINA PALACE (1891), THE WINTER PALACE (1909)

Easter eggs at the Gatchina Palace in 1891/92

Russian State Historical Archive – stock 491 (Gatchina Palace Administration), inv. 3, file 1224 (concerning the transfer of pictures to the Hermitage).

p.67
28 March 1891. Her Imperial Majesty arranged the following item in the main study:
'One cupid pushing a two-wheeled chariot containing an egg [the 1888 Cherub with Chariot egg, 4]. Taken on 16 May by the valet Ivoshkin when Their Majesties travelled to Moscow. Issued by Mikhailov. Their Majesties returned it on 18 March 1892.'

p.67 (verso)
'One item in the form of an egg, decorated with stones, containing ladies' toilet articles, 13 pieces [possibly the Nécessaire egg of 1889, 5]. Taken on 16 May by the valet Ivoshkin, when their Majesties travelled to Moscow. Issued by Mikhailov.'

p.175
'One item in the form of an egg, decorated with stones, containing a small folding screen with 10 panels.' [The Danish Palaces egg of 1890, 6]

p.175
Description of objects in the drawing room of His Imperial Majesty, 31 January 1893.
'... Egg consisting of 10 pieces (small folding screen), His Majesty took it to Petersburg on 31 December 1891 [The Danish Palaces egg of 1890, 6]. His Majesty returned it on 28 March 1892.'

p.68
27 November 1891. Deposited the following item in the main study:
'One item in the form of a dark coloured egg, decorated with stones and containing a model of a ship [The Memory of Azov egg of 1891, 7]. Taken to Petersburg on 31 December 1891 [signed] Valet Dinne. His Majesty returned it on 28 March 1892.'

p.182, N° 43
'One egg of pale-green stone, opening into two halves, set in gold, decorated with small rose-cut diamonds.' [The Diamond Trellis egg of 1892, 8]

p.182, N° 44
'Silver group on a round pale-green stone slab representing three little boys holding an egg of pale-green stone, opening into two parts, decorated outside by a trellis of small rose-cut diamonds. This egg is lined with white satin with a space for the figure of an elephant and a key for winding it.' [The Diamond Trellis egg of 1892, 8]

p.182 (verso), N° 45
'Ivory figure of an elephant, clockwork, with a small gold tower, partly enamelled and decorated with rose-cut diamonds, on its back; the sides of the figure bear gold decorations in the form of two crosses, each with five white precious stones. The elephant's forehead is decorated with the same kind of stone. The tusks, the trunk and the harness are decorated with small rose-cut diamonds, and a black mahout is seated on its head.' [The Diamond Trellis egg, 27]

Easter eggs at the Winter Palace in 1909

The following document shows that in 1909 ten eggs belonging to Alexandra Fedorovna were preserved in the Winter Palace. They were the eggs for 1895 (12), 1896 (14), 1897 (16), 1898 (18), 1899 (20), 1900 (22), 1901 (24), 1902 (26), 1903 (28), and 1907 (32). Archive of the State Hermitage. Stock 1, inventory VIII - G, file 7b.

'Inventory of articles belonging to Their Imperial Majesties and preserved in the Private Apartments of the Winter Palace. Cabinet of His Imperial Majesty, Inventory of articles compiled by Her Imperial Majesty's Inspector of Premises of the Imperial Winter Palace, N. Dementiev, on the 10th of April 1909.'

Sheet 47, [verso]: Corner showcase between the door leading into the bedroom and the window.

First shelf from the top:

188. Silver egg on a triangular white onyx pedestal, the rim of the pedestal of ribbed silver gilt. The pedestal bears three gilded gryphons supporting an egg on their wings. The central part of the egg is made of silvered metal engraved with a map of Siberia, in the middle of which appears an engraved coat of arms surmounted by a crown and bearing the inscription 'The Great Siberian Railway, 1900'. The lower part of the egg and its lid are covered with green enamel and blue and orange enamel decorations. The lower rims of the lid and of the middle part of the egg are bordered with green and red gold. The lid is surmounted by the silver-gilt figure of a three-sided eagle under a crown. Inside the egg is a velvet case containing models of five carriages and a locomotive with tender. The carriages and the tender are made of gold, and the locomotive of platinum. The overhead light of the locomotive is represented by a ruby and the model is accompanied by a gold key. (22)

['Consigned to the Office of H.I.M. Cabinet, 17 May 1917'. This note applies to all the following items on the list.]

189. Egg covered with pink enamel, on a four-legged gold stand, the legs representing leaves of lilies of the valley, which are decorated with rose-cut diamonds; a pearl is placed at the tip of each leg. Green enamel lily of the valley leaves cover the body of the egg, and the whole is decorated with lilies of the valley made of pearls and rose-cut diamonds. The egg is surmounted by an Imperial crown made entirely of rose-cut diamonds and containing two cabochon rubies. At the side of the egg there is a button with a single pearl which, when pressed, causes the crown to rise and disclose three miniature medallions framed in rose-cut diamonds. The frames contain portraits of the Emperor Nicholas II and the Imperial children. The reverse side of the medallion is engraved with the figures '5–IV–98'. (18)

190. Small gold model of a State carriage, decorated with red enamel, with eagles made of rose-cut diamonds on the doors and surmounted by an Imperial crown of rose-cut diamonds. The whole carriage is decorated with rose-cut diamonds. The carriage contains a yellow diamond pendant egg (Briolet). It is placed on a rectangular jadeite pediment with a silver-gilt rim and is contained in a rectangular glass case with silver-gilt edging. Silver-gilt Imperial crowns are placed at each of the four corners of the case. [This is the surprise from egg 16]

191. One gold egg covered with a transparent green enamel

trefoil and trefoils of rose-cut diamonds. In some places the trefoils are intertwined with ribbons made of tiny rubies. At the top of the egg is an engraved ruby surrounded with rose-cut diamonds. The egg opens, and on the upper edge of its lower part runs a gold openwork rim along which the initials AΘ and five crowns are repeated and the date 1902 appears once. The egg is mounted on a gold stand representing clumps of clover. (26)

192. Egg made of white rock crystal banded with green enamel containing rose-cut diamonds. The upper edge of the band is connected by a rosette of rose-cut diamonds, in the middle of which is a gold neck with white and red enamel; under the neck is a row of rose-cut diamonds, and above it a gold rosette with its top decorated with tiny rose-cut diamonds and an egg-shaped emerald in the middle. The egg stands on a gold neck, the upper part of which represents the letters A in alternating red and blue, with a crown of rose-cut diamonds under each letter. The lower part of the neck consists of repetitions of the initials AΘ, the letters A made of white enamel and the letters Θ of red enamel, with a crown of rose-cut diamonds under each set of initials. There are four rows of rose-cut diamonds between the patterns on the neck, which ends with a gold-ridged rim attached to a rock crystal pediment. In the middle of the crystal egg is an engraved gold column to which six tiny frames are attached, in the form of a little screen. The frames contain different miniature landscapes on both sides, and revolve round the column, which is set in motion by the emerald at the top of the egg. (14)

Second shelf from the top:

193. The Clock egg consists of a vase of flowers in Louis XVI style. The egg is covered with orange enamel with 12 vertical strips of rose-cut diamonds. The clock face is a horizontal band of white enamel between two strips of rose-cut diamonds, and the figures are made of rose-cut diamonds. The top of the egg bears a rosette of laurel leaves made of green gold; above this rosette is a collar of smooth red gold, surmounted by a wreath of red and yellow gold and platinum roses with green gold leaves. Above this wreath is a bouquet with green gold stems and leaves and flowers of light-coloured agate with hearts of gold and roses. The egg is supported on both sides by ornamental handles of green and red gold studded with rose-cut diamonds. The clock hand is fastened with rose-cut diamonds. The lower part of the egg is placed on a green gold rosette resting on an orange enamel neck decorated with one band of rose-cut diamonds and six vertical rose-cut diamond strips; the neck in turn rests on a wreath of green gold leaves intertwined with rose-cut diamond ribbons. The neck is placed on a square pediment, the sides of which are studded with 12 rose-cut diamonds. The clock-egg is mounted on a rectangular pedestal made of gold and covered with orange enamel, with decorations of red and green gold. The base pediment of enamel is studded with 16 rose-cut diamonds. One side of the pedestal bears the date 1899 picked out in rose-cut diamonds and surmounted by a star consisting of one rose-cut diamond. The pedestal rests on four short legs of green and red gold. (20)

194. Gold egg, chased in Louis XV style, the design decorated in places with rose-cut diamonds and rubies. On the top of the lid are the initials NII and A under a crown made of rose-cut diamonds and surrounded by a wreath of green and red enamel intertwined with a white enamel ribbon. Four watercolour medallions are set in the body of the egg, representing Their Imperial Majesties Nicholas II and Peter the Great, the Winter Palace and Peter the Great's little house. At the bottom of the egg is a black enamel eagle, with a flat diamond in the middle and two rose-cut diamonds in the crown. The egg bears the inscriptions, 'The Emperor Nicholas II, born in 1868, came to the Throne in 1894' and 'The Emperor Peter the Great, born in 1672, founded St Petersburg in 1703'. Two dates made of rose-cut diamonds are inserted between these inscriptions, '1703' on one side and '1903' on the other. The lower part of the egg also bears the inscriptions. 'The first little house of the Emperor Peter the Great in 1703' and 'The Winter Palace of His Imperial Majesty in 1903'. The inside of the lid is lined with yellow enamel and contains a gold plate on which a model of the monument to the Emperor Peter the Great is mounted. The platform supporting the monument, the railing, columns, posts and chains are all made of gold; the rock is of black stone, and the figures of the Emperor and his steed are also made of chased gold. The inscription engraved on the rock reads: 'To Peter the First from Catherine the Second, 1782' - 'Petro Primo Catherina Secunda MDCCLXXXII'. The egg rests on a stand made of red silver-gilt wire. (28)

195. Egg, Louis XVI style, covered with red enamel and decorated with green gold wreaths and garlands and bows and arrows of rose-cut diamonds. The egg is entwined with four bands of rose-cut diamonds. The top is encircled by a strip of rose-cut diamonds and a band of white enamel, containing a flat diamond covering a portrait of the Emperor Nicholas II. The lower part of the egg is similarly encircled by a strip of rose-cut diamonds and a band of white enamel containing a flat diamond, covering the date '1895'. The egg contains a rosebud of yellow enamel with a green enamel stem. The flower opens into two halves, containing an Imperial crown entirely made of rose-cut diamonds, with two cabochon rubies. (12)

198. Egg covered with yellow enamel and a lattice-work of green gold strips, with a black enamel eagle and a single rose diamond at each intersection. The base of the egg is encircled with a smooth gold band. The upper part of the egg contains a small, round gold frame surrounded by 10 diamonds and surmounted by the initials AΘ, the letter A made of rose-cut diamonds and Θ of rubies, under a crown made of rose-cut diamonds and one ruby. The lower part of the egg holds a chased rosette of green gold, with a circle of rose-cut diamonds surmounting a flat diamond covering the date '1897'. The egg is lined with white velvet which serves as a nest for the model State carriage described in this inventory under N°190. The egg rests on a silver-gilt wire stand. (16)

199. Vase in the form of a basket-egg, entirely covered with white enamel. The egg, stand and pediment are decorated with a trellis pattern made entirely of rose-cut diamonds. The base has a horseshoe-shaped handle decorated with bows, the whole made of rose-cut diamonds. The vase is filled with moss of green gold, in which there is a bouquet of wild flowers made of different-coloured enamel. The vase bears the date '1901' picked out in rose-cut diamonds. (24)

Bottom shelf:

204. Egg covered with pale green enamel. The body of the egg is covered with a trellis of rose-cut diamonds and pink enamel rose-cut diamonds with green enamel leaves. At the top of the egg there is a rosette of small rose-cut diamonds with a large diamond in the centre. The bottom of the egg also contains a rosette of small diamonds, with a flat diamond in the middle, covering the inscription '1907'. The egg rests on a stand of silver gilt wire. (32)

Other Easter eggs belonging to the Empress were kept in the Alexander Palace. A photograph of the 'Lilac Drawing-Room of the Empress Alexandra Fedorovna in the Alexander Palace', evidently taken in 1913, gives a clear view of a small corner cupboard containing the Easter eggs for 1906 (30), 1908 (34), 1909 (36), 1910 (38), 1911 (40) and 1913 (44). Only one of the seven eggs displayed in the cupboard (the one on the right-hand side of the lower shelf) is impossible to identify, as it is half-hidden.

Appendix 4

Documents certifying the transfer of confiscated treasures from the Anichkov Palace to the Moscow Kremlin Armoury (1917) and their later transfer to the Sovnarkom (1922)

List of Treasures and Other Items from the Anichkov Palace. Moscow Kremlin Armoury archive, stock 20, inv. 1917, file 5.
Started: 14 Sept. 1917   Closed : 20 Sept. 1917

Items belonging to Her Imperial Majesty Maria Fedorovna:

1. Gold egg in the shape of a bird, covered with red enamel

2. Green jasper egg, sprinkled with pearls, with four images

3. Nephrite egg on gold stand, with medallion portrait of the Emperor Alexander III (25)

4. Large silver egg, gilt-lined

5. Gold egg, covered with pink enamel, with diamonds and emeralds, containing a small mother-of-pearl screen with landscapes in gold frames (6)

6. Gold egg with pink enamel medallions, decorated with pearls and diamonds (45)

7. Gold egg, covered with red enamel and diamond decorations representing the date '*1983*' in medallions with pearls and diamonds (9)

8. Jasper egg, in gold mounting, decorated with diamonds, containing a gold model of a vessel (7)

9. Gold nécessaire egg, decorated with multicoloured precious stones (5)

10. Silver-gilt egg with enamel, containing a small flask

11. Jasper egg, with gold mounting, decorated with diamonds; containing a small heart-shaped gold screen under a crown, decorated with diamond monograms in red enamel medallions (19)

12. Crystal egg in silver mounting, decorated with diamonds, on pediment, containing a statue of Alexander III (37)

13. Gold egg, covered with mauve enamel and decorated with diamonds, containing a small stone vase with a silver swan (29)

14. Gold folding screen egg with medallions, decorated with pearls and surmounted by an enamelled swan [should read pelican], four-legged gold pediment (17)

15. Gold egg, decorated with small diamonds and a sapphire, and pediment consisting of a two-wheeled chariot with cupid (4)

16. Gold egg, covered with white enamel and red cross, on small stand, containing a small mother-of-pearl white-enamel screen and with portraits of Imperial personages in a gold setting (47)

17. Crystal egg, on pediment with bronze mounting, containing a peacock (33)

18. Nephrite egg in gold mounting with diamond trellis; nephrite pediment with three silver cupids (8)

19. Silver-gilt purse, in the form of an egg, covered with red enamel and containing a surprise

20. Silver egg, painted white, containing gilt egg and hen (1)

21. Jasper egg with stone and metal pendants

22. Stone egg in form of pug dog with amethyst head and ruby eyes

23. Red stone egg

24. Stone egg in the shape of a bird's head with ruby eyes

25. Stone egg in silver-gilt mounting with enamel

26. Gold egg in rococo style, covered with green enamel and decorated with diamonds, on pediment

27. Nephrite egg in gold mounting

28. Leather egg with 7 gold discs

29. Stone egg, open in gold mounting

30. Silver-gilt egg with enamel containing a small icon of St Alexander Nevski

31. Ivory egg in silver mounting, on four legs

32. Clock in the form of an egg of violet enamel, on tripod, decorated with pearls and diamonds (21)

33. Gold egg with portrait of the Emperor Alexander II and the Empress Maria Alexandrovna

34. Nephrite bay tree on pediment, gold-mounted with multi-coloured precious stones and with song-bird (39)

This list has been signed by the Managing Director of the Anichkov Palace, Major-General Yerekhovich [?] on 14 September 1917, Petrograd

Total of 84 crates. Received at the Armoury on 19/20 September 1917

Moscow Kremlin Armoury archive, stock 20, file 23.
Started: 26 January 1922   Closed: 22 August 1922

Act of transfer N° 7, sheet 27

On… February, 1922, the undersigned, the President of the College of Armoury Curators and President of the Glavmuzei Expert Commission, M.S. Sergeiev, and the representative of the Special Plenipotentiary of the SNK [Sovnarkom] for the collection and conservation of treasures and Gokhran Expert I.G. Chikarev, in the presence of Chief Inspector of the Educational Branch of the WPI [Workers' and Peasants' Inspectorate] V.A. Nikolskii, have drawn up the present act of transfer by the Glavmuzei to the Special Plenipotentiary of the SNK of the following articles, evacuated to Moscow from the Anichkov Palace and kept in the Armoury, in strongbox N° 19:

Article N°

672/1561   1 gold egg-shaped flask with 1 sapphire and diamonds, on stand in the form of a chariot (4)

676/1545   Gold egg-clock with 3 diamonds, rose-cut diamonds and pearls

677/1555   Jasper egg in silver setting with rose-cut diamonds, containing gold easel with rose-cut diamonds and 1 diamond

678/1551   Gold egg with diamonds, two diamonds and pearls

679/1549   Gold egg with enamel and rose-cut diamonds, containing mother-of-pearl folding icon in gold setting

680/1552   Jasper egg in gold setting with diamonds, containing gold model of a ship (7)

681/1584 Gold egg with enamel, containing phial

682/1548 Gold egg with clock on diamond stand (?) on gold pedestal with 3 sapphires and rose-cut diamonds (3)

683/1575 Gold medallion on stand with rose-cut diamonds and pearls

684/1569 Ivory model of an elephant in gold setting with rose-cut diamonds and diamonds [surprise for 8]

686/1568 1 silver hen, speckled with rose-cut diamonds, on gold stand (2?)

Act of transfer N° 10, sheet 33

... articles stored in an unnumbered strongbox:

701/1563 1 crystal egg in silver setting, containing a peacock (33)

702/1646 1 nephrite tree with songbird, gold ornamentation, rose-cut diamonds, diamonds, topazes, pearls and rubies (39)

703/1558 1 crystal egg in silver setting with 7 diamonds and rose-cut diamonds, containing a gold model of the Alexander III monument (37)

704/1557 1 crystal egg in silver setting with diamonds and rose-cut diamonds on stand

705/1557 1 stone egg with enamel and rose-cut diamonds

706/1550 1 gold egg with 2 diamonds and rose-cut diamonds

707/1660 1 nephrite egg in gold settling with lattice of 2 diamonds and rose-cut diamonds, on stand with 3 silver figures (8)

708/1554 1 gold egg with 2 diamonds and rose-cut diamonds, containing a silver swan on a stone stand, gold handle broken off (29)

711/1560 1 gold screen-egg with rose-cut diamonds and pearls on gold stand (6?)

Sheet 35

23/1459 1 silver bust of Nicholas II on lapis-lazuli stand

Sheet 50

612/1299 1 gold egg with rose-cut diamonds and large diamonds on gold stand, containing gold six-sided folding frame (41)

613/1293 1 gold clock in the form of a vase with rose-cut diamonds (20?)

615/.... 1 crystal egg containing figures on a gold stand with 8 diamonds, rose-cut diamonds and pearls

618/1553 1 gold egg nécessaire, with diamonds, rubies, emeralds and 1 sapphire (5)

619/1601 1 gold and enamel sedan chair with 2 blackamoor bearers (surprise for 45)

Sheet 52

639/1562 1 silver egg with enamel on silver stand containing folding frame

Sheet 53

35/1533 1 silver bust of Alexander III

Sheet 70

48/.... Desk clock in the form of a summer-house, in gold setting with rose-cut diamonds (38)

49/.... 1 egg in the form of the Kremlin, gold, with music (30)

Sheet 71

66/.... 1 gold egg with enamel and 2 crosses (47 or 48)

67/.... 1 nephrite (egg) with gold ornamentation, 2 diamonds and rose-cut diamonds, containing a model of the Tsarskoselsko [Alexander] Palace (34)

68/.... 1 gold egg as though embroidered on canvas, with diamonds, rose-cut diamonds and coloured gemstones, containing a portrait screen with rose-cut diamonds and pearls (46)

63/222 1 silver desk clock with cupid

69/.... lapis lazuli egg in gold setting, 2 cupids, containing cross of rose-cut diamonds and portrait

72/.... 1 gold egg with 2 diamonds and rose-cut diamonds, containing globe on gold stand with enamel (silver eagle) (44)

73/.... 1 metal egg on silver stand, containing easel with frame (50)

74/.... 1 gold egg with 2 diamonds and rose-cut diamonds, covered with portraits and landscapes (9)

75/.... 1 crystal egg in gold setting, with 4 brilliants and rose-cut diamonds, containing a model of a ship (36)

Sheet 73

117/113 1 nephrite egg with rose-cut diamonds (25)

Sheet 93, verso

318/.... 1 silver egg with gold model of a railway train (22)

319/.... 1 gold clock-egg with rose-cut diamonds

320/.... 1 crystal egg with 1 emerald, containing gold folding frame (14)

321/.... 1 gold and enamel egg with rose-cut diamonds, in the form of a vase with flowers (24)

322/.... 1 gold egg with rose-cut diamonds, containing a model of the Peter I monument (28)

323/.... 1 gold egg with rubies and rose-cut diamonds, on stand

324/.... 1 gold egg with rose-cut diamonds and pearls, containing portrait (32)

326/.... 1 gold egg with diamonds and rose-cut diamonds

Sheet 94

327/.... 1 gold egg with diamonds and rose-cut diamonds, containing a gold carriage with a pear-shaped diamond (16)

329/.... 1 gold clock in the form of a vase, with pearls

330/.... 1 gold egg with diamonds and rose-cut diamonds, containing a flower and a crown of rose-cut diamonds (12)

Appendix 5

Correspondence, certificates and inventories relating to the transfer of museum treasures from the Foreign Exchange Fund of the Narkomfin, the Moscow Jewellers' Community (MJC) and other sources, to the Moscow Kremlin Armoury

Archive of the Moscow Kremlin Armoury, stock 20, 1927, file 20. Opened: 14 February 1927 Closed: 30 December 1927

Sheet 18
On 27 June 1927, we the undersigned, I.I. Rabinovich, Head of the Central Depot of the MJC (Moscow Jewellers' Community) and V.I. Dronkin, diamond valuer of the sub-department, on the one hand, and D.D. Ivanov, Director of the Armoury, on the other hand, have delivered and accepted, respectively, museum valuables consisting of 30 items to the value of 9,325 roub. 61 kop. in accordance with inventories N° 2, …

Sheet 20
INVENTORY N° 2
Easter eggs belonging to Nicholas II and his family (held in the MJC)

MJC N°/Armoury N°		Weight in grams	Value in roubles
666/17554 (20) *not sold*	Yellow enamel clock-egg on gold and silver stand, surmounted by a bouquet of onyx flowers, approx. 1,230 rose-cut diamonds	1135.5	700
667/17555 (24) *sold*	White enamel egg on gold and silver stand, surmounted by a bunch of wild flowers, approx. 4,000 rose-cut diamonds, 12 pearls	712	1100
668/17556 (26) *not sold*	Gold egg with green transparent enamel, approx. 1,178 rose-cut diamonds, approx. 232 rubies. 1 large ruby, gold and platinum	150.5	600
669/17557 (41) *sold*	Gold egg, green enamel, on gold stand containing pictures of various regiments in folding gold frames, approx. 4,500 rose-cut diamonds, 2 diamonds	968.5	2400
670/17558 (45) *sold*	Gold egg with pink enamel, painting by Zuiev, 1914, with gold decorations on silver stand, approx. 937 rose-cut diamonds, 2 flat diamonds, approx. 500 half-pearls, empty inside, gold and platinum	677	1036
673/17559 (48) *sold*	Silver folding icon egg, with white enamel and 2 enamel crosses and miniatures of Tatiana and Olga	389.6	125
671/17552 (10) *sold*	Agate egg, nothing inside, with gold decorations and enamel, approx. 550 rose-cut diamonds	472.5	400
672/17553 (6) *sold*	Pink enamel and gold egg, containing folding frame with 10 miniatures by Kryzhitskii, approx. 460 rose-cut diamonds, 21 diamonds, 18 emeralds and 1 sapphire	435.5	500

INVENTORY 188, FILE 2156
Total 8 articles   6861
Head of the Diamond Subdivision Mikh. Tarasov (?Tararov)

Sheets 2-14: Valuation of articles in first category 'M' Easter eggs by a Commission consisting of:
Director of the State Hermitage S.N. Troinitskii
Academician A.E. Fersman
Gemologist/expert assessor A.F. Kotler
Diamond assessor Dmitriev
Weighed by jeweller Krivtsov. Supervisor – Bedrit

1. (19) *sold*
Nephrite egg on 88 proof silver stand, decorated with enamel and rose-cut diamonds, containing tripod with heart bearing 11 miniature portraits of the former house of Romanov, in gold and silver with rose-cut diamonds, enamel, pearls, coloured gold, 1899.
Weight: 634 g.
Contents:
  nephrite egg   1   80 roub.
  diamonds   2   0.3 car. at 100 roub. per carat,   total   30 roub.

pearls	2	at 3 roub.,	total	6 roub.
mother of pearl	1	at 1 roub.,	total	1 roub.
miniatures	11	at 100 roub.,	total	1100 roub.
rose-cut diamonds, approx. 951		at 1 roub.,	total	951 roub.
platinum, gold and silver,				100 roub.
Total cost of materials				2268 roub.
Percentage of increment	70 %			
Material value of article				3855 roub. 60 kop.
Multiplication factor	4			
Minimum price at category 1 valuation				15422 roub. 40 kop.

NB: Stamped 'Fabergé'. Edges of two miniatures damaged. Lid torn off one, enamel chipped on the other.
Total weight: 1 pound 52 zolotniks 76 dolias. Diameter of nephrite egg: 7.5 x 14.1 x 9.8 cm. Armoury N° 17539

2.
(9)
sold

Gold and red enamel egg with diamond rose-cut diamonds and pearls, with 4 miniatures of different views of Abastuman on ivory, signed 'Krizhitskii'. Contains miniature of George, 1893.
Weight: 325.25 g.
Dimensions: 9 x 6.9 cm.
Contents:

portrait diamond	1	approx. 6 car. at 150 roub.,	total	900 roub.
flat diamond	1	approx. 1.75 car. at 120 roub.,	total	210 roub.
diamonds, approx.	53	approx. 1.25 car. at 60 roub.,	total	75 roub.
rose-cut diamonds, approx. 659		at 50 kop.,	total	329 roub. 50 kop.
miniatures	4	at 10 roub.,	total	40 roub.
pearl halves, approx.	175	at 30 kop.,	total	52 roub. 50 kop.
whole pearls, pierced	16	at 3 roub.,	total	48 roub.
gold and silver				250 roub.
Total cost of materials				1905 roub.
Percentage of increment	30 %			
Material value of article				2476 roub. 50 kop
Multiplication factor	4			
Minimum price at category 1 valuation				9906 roub.

NB: Damage: enamel chipped in three places, one rose setting empty. Total weight: 76 zolotniks 25 dolias. Armoury N° 17537

3.
(37)
not sold

Rock crystal egg on rock crystal and platinum stand, decorated with 1 diamond and rose-cut diamonds. Contains gold model of Alexander III monument on lapis lazuli pediment decorated with rose-cut diamonds 1910.
Weight: 1040.42 g.
Dimensions: 15.6 x 11.7 cm.
Contents:

diamond	1	3.5 car. at 220 roub.,	total	770 roub.
rose-cut diamonds, approx. 1250		at 75 kop.,	total	937 roub. 50 kop
lapis lazuli				50 roub.
rock crystal				100 roub.
platinum and gold				3150 roub.
Total cost of materials				5007 roub. 50 kop
Percentage of increment	40 %			
Material value of article				7010 roub. 50 kop
Multiplication factor	4			
Minimum price at category 1 valuation				28042 roub.

NB: Damage: one corner of lapis lazuli pediment knocked off. Total weight: 2 pounds 51 zolotniks 90 dolias. Armoury N° 17545

4.
(17)
sold

Gold egg with pelican on stand, engraved folding frame with 8 views of institutes, decorated with pearls and rose-cut diamonds. Miniatures are signed. Dates: 1797-1897.
Weight: 420.55 g.
Dimensions of stand: 6 x 4 x 7 x 4 cm. Dimensions of egg: 10 x 3 x 5 x 4 cm.
Contents:

rose-cut diamonds	83	at 40 kop.,	total	33 roub. 20 kop.
rubies	2	at 10 kop.,	total	20 kop.
pearls	approx. 803	at 5 kop.,	total	40 roub. 15 kop.
miniatures	8	at 10 roub.,	total	80 roub.
gold				285 roub. 45 kop.
Total cost of materials				439 roub.
Percentage of increment	160 %			
Material value of article				1141 roub. 40 kop.
Multiplication factor	4			
Minimum price at category 1 valuation				4565 roub. 60 kop.

NB: Damage: 2 rose-cut diamonds missing, miniatures and hinges loose, enamel on pelican damaged.
Total weight: 1 pound 2 zolotniks 60 dolias. Armoury N° 17538

5.
(47)
sold

Gold egg with white enamel and red cross on stand, containing folding frame with 5 miniatures of nurses of the former house of Romanov. Fabergé stamp. Dated 1915-1914.
Weight: 316.7 g.
Dimensions of egg: 9.3 x 6.1 cm. Dimensions of folding frame: 19 x 4.8 cm.
Contents:

miniatures	5	at 5 roub.,	total	25 roub.
mother of pearl	5	at 50 kop.,	total	2 roub. 50 kop.
gold and silver				40 roub. 50 kop.
Total cost of materials				68 roub.
Percentage of increment	500 %			
Material value of article				408 roub.
Multiplication factor	4			
Minimum price at category 1 valuation				1632 roub.

Total weight: 74 zolotniks 24 dolias. Armoury N° 17550

6.
(7)
not sold

Jasper (heliotrope) egg with applied chased gold ornamentation and diamonds. Contains a gold model of the ship 'Azov' on an aquamarine base, with platinum.
Weight: 466.42 g.
Dimensions: egg, 9.3 x 7.6 cm.; ship, 4.9 x 7.8 x 4.8 cm.
Contents:

Jasper egg				100 roub.
diamonds	approx. 243	total weight 10 car. at 40 roub.,	total	400 roub.
rose-cut diamonds	approx. 31	at 30 kop.,	total	9 roub. 30 kop.
faceted ruby	1	approx. 1 car. at 20 roub.,	total	20 roub.
aquamarine				10 roub.
platinum, gold and silver				200 roub. 70 kop.
Total cost of materials				740 roub.
Percentage of increment	200 %			
Material value of article				2220 roub.
Multiplication factor	4			
Minimum price at category 1 valuation				8880 roub.

NB: Damage: mast damaged, one rose missing, noticeable crack in the jasper. Total weight: 1 pound 13 zolotniks 36 dolias. Armoury N° 17536

7.
(22)
not sold

The 'Great Siberian Railway' egg, 1900, silver with coloured enamel, on marble stand with silver dragons. The egg contains a gold clockwork train.
Weight: 2099.7 g.
Dimensions: egg and stand, 27.2 x 12.8 cm.; train, 39.8 x 1.4 cm.
Contents:

ruby	1			20 kop.
rose-cut diamonds	2	at 75 kop.,	total	1 roub. 50 kop.
marble				5 roub.
gold and silver				420 roub. 30 kop.
Total cost of materials				427 roub.
Percentage of increment	1000 %			
Material value of article				4697 roub.
Multiplication factor	4			
Minimum price at category 1 valuation				18788 roub.

NB: The article is accompanied by a key. Damage: enamel is chipped in one place. Total weight: 5 pounds 12 zolotniks 33 dolias. Armoury N° 17540

8.
(14)
sold

Rock crystal egg, on silver stand, decorated with rose-cut diamonds, enamel and 1 emerald. Contains 12 miniatures in gold frames, signed
Weight: 1092.2 g.
Dimensions: 24.8 x 9.7 cm.
Contents:

miniatures	12	at 8 roub.,	total	96 roub.
rose-cut diamonds, approx. 830		at 1 roub.,	total	830 roub.
emerald	1	approx. 15 car. at 100 roub.,	total	1500 roub.
rock crystal				100 roub.
gold and silver				200 roub.
Total cost of materials				2726 roub.
Percentage of increment	75 %			
Material value of article				4770 roub. 50 kop.
Multiplication factor	4			
Minimum price at category 1 valuation				19082 roub.

NB: Damage: inside the egg, a corner of the crystal above a miniature is chipped off. Total weight: 2 pounds 64 zolotniks 8 dolias. Armoury N° 17546

9. Kremlin egg, gilded, multicoloured gilding with enamel, on marble pediment with clockwork musical
(30) mechanism. Contains a panorama of the Cathedral of the Dormition. House of Fabergé, 1904.
not sold Weight: 5152.8 g.
Dimensions: 36.2 x 17.5 cm.
Contents:

mechanism		10 roub.
marble pediment		10 roub.
gold and silver		1580 roub.
Total cost of materials		1600 roub.
Percentage of increment	625 %	
Material value of article		11600 roub.
Multiplication factor	4	
Minimum price at category 1 valuation		46400 roub.

NB: The article is badly damaged, many domes broken, two chains missing from the cross. Cupola dented, one window broken, another missing. One eagle and two flags missing. Various small parts dented. Key broken. Total weight: 12 pounds 56 zolotniks 8 dolias. Armoury N° 17542

10. Gold egg with enamel, rose-cut diamonds and miniature portraits of the former House of Romanov,
(44) on purpurine stand. Contains globe. Date: 1613-1913, 300th anniversary of the House of Romanov.
not sold Weight: 1127.52 g.
Dimensions: 18.5 x 11.5 x 8.4 cm.
Contents:

miniatures	18	at 5 roub.,	total	90 roub.
diamond	1	2.25 car. at 120 roub.,	total	270 roub.
diamond	1	0.80 car. at 60 roub.,	total	48 roub.
rose-cut diamonds approx. 1113		at 75 kop.,	total	834 roub. 75 kop.
turquoises	19	at 10 kop.,	total	1 roub. 90 kop.
topaz-crystal	18	at 50 kop.,	total	9 roub.
purpurine				3 roub.
gold and silver				200 roub. 35 kop.
Total cost of materials				1457 roub.
Percentage of increment		200 %		
Material cost of article				4371 roub.
Multiplication factor		4		
Minimum price at category 1 valuation				17484 roub.

NB: House of Fabergé. Total weight: 2 pounds 72 zolotniks 3 dolias. Armoury N° 17548

11. Crystal egg on crystal stand, parts of lazurite (lapis lazuli) and gold of different colours, chased with enamel
(36) and gems: diamonds, rose-cut diamonds and pearls. Contains a gold model of the yacht 'Standard' 1909.
not sold Weight: 887.47 g.
Dimensions: 15.5 x 9.6 x 8.3 cm.
Contents:

diamonds	4	approx. 2.15 car. at 100 roub.,	total	215 roub.
pearl pendants	2	approx. 7 car. at 40 roub.,	total	280 roub.
rose-cut diamonds approx. 915		at 50 kop.,	total	457 roub. 50 kop.
crystal egg and stand				100 roub.
lapis lazuli eagles and dolphins				150 roub.
platinum, gold and silver				200 roub. 50 kop.
Total cost of materials				1403 roub.
Percentage of increment		200 %		
Material value of article				4209 roub.
Multiplication factor		4		
Minimum price at category 1 valuation				16836 roub.

NB: House of Fabergé. Damage: ship clock broken, head of lazurite eagle stuck back, crown loose, and one small separate part wrapped in paper. Ten missing rose-cut diamonds. Total weight: 2 pounds 16 zolotniks 10 dolias. Armoury N° 17544

12. Steel egg with gold ornamentation on filigree stand with steel artillery shells, decorated with gold.
(50) Contains easel with miniature of a military subject.
not sold Weight: 955.7 g.
Dimensions: egg, 10.2 x 7.4 cm.; stand, 9 x 8.1 cm.; easel, 7.1 x 6 cm.
Contents:

nephrite		20 roub.
gold		55 roub.
miniature on ivory		20 roub.
Total cost of materials		95 roub.
Percentage of increment	300 %	
Material value of article		380 roub.
Multiplication factor	4	
Minimum price at category 1 valuation		1520 roub.

NB: Made at the Putilovskii factory (according to Borisov), Fabergé stamp. Artillery shells rusty. Total weight: 2 pounds 32 zolotniks 11 dolias. Armoury N° 17551

13.
(42)
sold

Lapis lazuli egg with chased gold ornamentation. Contains a gold eagle with diamond rose-cut diamonds and portrait of Alexei on lazurite (lapis lazuli) stand. Inscription: AΘ (Alexandra Fedorovna), 1912. Composite lazurite.
Weight: 574.2 g.
Dimensions: egg, 12.1 x 8.7 cm.; eagle with stand, 9.8 x 5.7 cm.
Contents:

flat portrait diamond	1	approx. 1 car. at 60 roub.,	total	60 roub.
diamond	1	approx. at 0.8 car.at 100 roub.,	total	80 roub.
lazurite				200 roub.
gold				200 roub.
rose-cut diamonds approx. 1835		at 1 roub. 25 kop.,	total	2293 roub. 75 kop.
crystal				1 roub. 25 kop.
miniature				6 roub.
Total cost of materials				2841 roub.
Percentage of increment		25 %		
Material value of article				3551 roub. 25 kop.
Multiplication factor		4		
Minimum price at category 1 valuation				14205 roub.

NB: One rose missing. Total weight: 1 pound 38 zolotniks 62 dolias. Armoury N° 17457

14.
(46)
sold

Platinum egg with gold, diamonds, coloured gemstones and pearls. Contains stand with miniatures of the former ruling family. 1914. House of Fabergé.
Weight: 288.7 g.
Dimensions: egg, 9.4 x 7 cm.; stand, 7.7 x 5.5 x 3 x 3.8 cm.
Contents:

miniature	1			15 roub.
diamonds	5	approx. 2.25 car. at 180 roub.,	total	405 roub.
diamonds	approx. 320	approx. 2.75 car., at 150 roub.,	total	412 roub. 50 kop.
rose-cut diamonds, approx. 1368		at 50 kop.,	total	684 roub.
gems, approx.	3567	at 20 kop.,	total	713 roub. 40 kop.
pearl halves,	670	approx.at 20 kop.,	total	134 roub.
whole pearls	18	at 3 roub.,	total	54 roub.
moonstone	1			30 kop.
platinum and gold				1000 roub. 80 kop.
rock crystal				1 roub.
Total cost of materials				3420 roub.
Percentage of increment		120 %		
Material value of article				7524 roub.
Multiplication factor		4		
Minimum price at category 1 valuation				30096 roub.

Total weight: 62 zolotniks 84 dolias. Armoury N° 17549

15.
(34)
not sold

Nephrite egg with gold incrustation and 5 miniatures, diamonds, rubies and rose-cut diamonds. Contains model of Tsarskoie Selo Palace. 1908.
Weight: 436.05 g.
Dimensions: 10.9 x 8.1 cm.
Contents:

miniatures	5	at 3 roub.,	total	15 roub.
diamonds	2	1.6 car. at 60 roub.,	total	96 roub.
rose-cut diamonds, approx. 1782		at 75 kop.,	total	1336 roub. 50 kop.
rubies	59	at 30 kop.,	total	17 roub. 70 kop.
nephrite egg				100 roub.
gold and silver				160 roub. 80 kop.
Total cost of materials				1726 roub.
Percentage of increment		200 %		
Material value of article				5178 roub.
Multiplication factor		4		
Minimum price at category 1 valuation				20712 roub.

NB: 3 rose-cut diamonds missing. Total weight: 1 pound 6 zolotniks 23 dolias. Armoury N° 17543

16.
(28)
sold

Gold egg, decorated with rubies, rose-cut diamonds and chased coloured gold with 2 miniature portraits, of Peter I and Nicholas II, and two views, of the Winter Palace and Peter I's little house. Contains model of the Peter I monument on pediment with sapphire. Date:1703-1903.
Weight: 619.7 g.

Dimensions: egg, 11.3 x 8.4 cm. monument, 4.3 x 7 cm.
Contents:

rose-cut diamonds, approx. 899	at 75 kop.,	total	674 roub. 25 kop.
rubies	86 at 25 kop.,	total	16 roub. 50 kop.
portrait diamond	1 0.35 car. at 80 roub.,	total	28 roub.
miniatures	4		40 roub.
pediment with sapphire			25 roub.
gold and silver			550 roub. 25 kop.
Total cost of materials			1334 roub.
Percentage of increment	200 %		
Material value of article			4002 roub.
Multiplication factor	4		
Minimum price at category 1 valuation			16008 roub.

NB: One rose setting empty. Total weight: 1 pound 49 zolotniks 29 dolias. Armoury N° 17541

Total minimum price: 269579 roubles

Price 'C' (minimum) was determined by a Commission consisting of Director of the State Hermitage S.N. Troinitskii and Academician A.E. Fersman.

14 of the eggs were officially sold
10 remained in the Moscow Kremlin Armoury Museum

Appendix 6

Information on the sales of Imperial Easter eggs from the Moscow Kremlin Armoury in 1930 and 1933

stock 20, file 21, 1930   stock 20, file 21, 1933

In 1930 11 eggs were sold for a total of 46,000 roubles, as follows:

Danish Palaces egg, 1890 (6). Sold in 1930 for 1,500 roubles. Armoury N° 1753.

Caucasus egg, 1893 (9). Sold in 1930 for 5,000 roubles. N° 17537.

Renaissance egg, 1894 (10). Sold in 1930 for 1,000 roubles. Armoury N° 17552.

Revolving Miniatures egg, 1896 (14). Sold in 1930 for 8,000 roubles. Armoury N° 17547. At the time of the sale, it was indicated that the year of presentation was 1895.

Pelican egg, 1898 (17). Sold in 1930 for 1,000 roubles. Armoury N° 17538. At the time of the sale, it was indicated that the year of presentation was 1897.

Pansy egg, 1899 (19). Sold in 1930 for 7,500 roubles. Armoury N° 17539. At the time of the sale it was said to contain 'miniature portraits of members of the Imperial family covered with enamel lids opening simultaneously on pressure of a button (one lid detached, enamel on some lids chipped)'.

Napoleonic egg, 1912 (41). Sold in 1930 for 5,000 roubles. Armoury N° 17557.

Tsarevich egg, 1912 (42). Sold in 1930 for 8,000 roubles. Armoury N° 17547.

Grisaille egg, 1914 (45). Sold in 1930 for 8,000 roubles. Armoury N° 17558.

Red Cross Portraits egg, 1915 (47). Sold in 1930 for 500 roubles. Armoury N° 17550.

Red Cross Triptych egg, 1915 (48). Sold in 1930 for 500 roubles. Armoury N° 17559.

In 1933 a further 3 eggs were sold for a total of 11,000 roubles, as follows:

Wild Flowers egg, 1901 (24). Sold in 1933 for 2,000 roubles, on the basis of the Antikvariat valuation. The Armoury valuation was 15,000 roubles. Armoury N° 17555.

Peter the Great egg, 1903 (28). Sold in 1933 for 4,000 roubles on the basis of the Antikvariat valuation. The Armoury valuation was 20,000 roubles. Armoury N° 17511.

Mosaic egg, 1914 (46). Sold in 1933 for 5,000 roubles on the basis of the Antikvariat valuation. The Armoury valuation was 20,000 roubles. Armoury N° 17549.

Thus, a total of 14 eggs were sold officially in 1930 and 1933 for 57,000 roubles.

Notes

1. H.C. Bainbridge, *Peter Carl Fabergé:. His Life and Work*, B.T. Batsford Ltd, London, 1949, p.66.
2. *Fabergé: Imperial Jeweller,* St Petersburg-Paris-London exhibition catalogue,1993, p.35.
3. Lynette G. Proler archives.
4. Christel Ludewig McCanless. *Fabergé and His Works: An Annotated Bibliography of the First Century of His Art*, The Scarecrow Press, Inc. Metuchen, N.J. & London, 1994
5. Tatiana Fabergé archives.
6. *Fabergé in America*, exhibition catalogue, Thames and Hudson Inc., New York, 1996, p.23.
7. *Fabergé: Imperial Jeweller*, St Petersburg-Paris-London exhibition catalogue, 1993, p.71.
8. E.B. Gusarova, M.N. Larchenko, V.F. Petrov, N.V. Rashkovan, eds, *The World of Fabergé* catalogue, Moscow 1996, p.12.
9. SARF, stock 652, inv. 1, file 380, p.16.
10. SARF, stock 677, inv. 1, file 738, p.34.
11. SARF, stock 652, inv. 1, file 380, p.21.
12. SARF, stock 642, inv. 1, file 650 (translated from Danish).
13. *Novoie Vremia*, St Petersburg, 9 April 1914.
14. Tatiana Fabergé archives.
15. Tatiana F. Fabergé and Valentin V. Skurlov, *The History of the House of Fabergé* , St Petersburg, 1992, pp.24-25.
16. ibid., pp.4-5.
17. T.N. Muntian in *The World of Fabergé* exhibition catalogue, Moscow-Vienna, 1992, p.26. (in Russian).
18. Report of the General Commissioner of the Russian Section, St Petersburg, (1901), pp.33-34.
19. Henry Charles Bainbridge, *Peter Carl Fabergé: His Life and Work*, B.T. Batsford Ltd, London, 1949, p.34.
20. Tatiana Fabergé archives.
21. H.C. Bainbridge, *Peter Carl Fabergé: His Life and Work*, B.T. Batsford Ltd, London, 1949, p.33.
22. Tatiana Fabergé archives. Agathon Carlovich's reference to working at the Postal Museum can be put into context as he was one of the most respected philatelists in Russia.
23. Tatiana Fabergé archives.
24. Robert K. Massie and Jeffrey Finestone II, *The Last Courts of Europe*, The Vendome Press, New York, 1981, p.24.
25. ibid, p.24.
26. ibid, p.26.
27. Diaries of Emperor Nicholas II, 1882-1918. CSAOR, stock 601, inv.1, file 217-266.
28. ibid.
29. Ian Vorres, *The Last Grand Duchess - Her Imperial Highness Grand Duchess Olga Alexandrovna, 1 June 1882-24 November 1960*, Hutchinson, London, 1964, pp.29-31.
30. Diaries of Emperor Nicholas II, 1882-1918.CSAOR, stock 601, inv. 1, file 217-266.
31. RSHA, stock 1340, inv. 1, file 358, p.175..
32. Ian Vorres, *The Last Grand Duchess - Her Imperial Highness Grand Duchess Olga Alexandrovna, 1 June 1882-24 November 1960*, Hutchinson, London, 1964, p.81.
33. Mademoiselle de L'Escaille Collection, Hoover Institution Archives.
34. Tatiana Fabergé archives.
35. *Fabergé in America*, exhibition catalogue, Thames and Hudson Inc., New York, 1996, p.23, (56 eggs, produced from 1884 to 1916).
36. Tatiana F. Fabergé and Valentin V. Skurlov, *The History of the House of Fabergé,* St Petersburg, 1992, p.24.
37. ibid., pp.26-27.
38. Tatiana Fabergé archives.
39. The exchange rate in 1887 was approximately 10 roubles to the pound, and allowing for inflation £1 would be worth approximately £40 in 1993. *The Lost Fortune of the Tsars*, William Clark, Weidenfeld and Nicholson, London, 1994.
40. T.A. Solovieva, *The von Dervises Houses*, Beloe i Chernoe, St Petersburg, 1995, p.68 (in Russian).
41. Diaries of Emperor Nicholas II, 1882-1918. TSGAORR SSSR, file 601, inv. 1, file 217-266.
42. Diaries of S.R. Mintslov, St Petersburg 1903-1910, Riga, 1931, p.77.
43. ibid, p.66.
44. ibid., p.148.
45. RSHA, stock 468, inv. 32, file 1650.
46. RSHA, stock 468, inv. 32, file 1652.
47. CSAOD, stock 1468, inv. 2, file 508.
48. RSHA, stock 472, inv. 66, file 120.
49. Tatiana Fabergé archives.
50. Tatiana F. Fabergé and Valentin V. Skurlov, *The History of the House of Fabergé*, St Petersburg, 1992, p.26.
51. Tatiana Fabergé archives.
52. A. Kenneth Snowman, *The Art of Carl Fabergé,* Faber and Faber Ltd, London, 1953, p.386.
53. RSHA, stock 528, inv. 1, file 2271, pp.10,12.
54. Marie, Grand Duchess of Russia, *Education of a Princess – a Memoir,* New York, The Viking Press, 1930, pp.271-272.
55. Robert C. Williams, *Russian Art and American Money - 1900-1940*, Cambridge: Harvard University Press, 1980, p.6 and pp.191-260.
56. Carl Blumay and Henry Edwards, *The Dark Side of Power: The Real Armand Hammer*, Simon and Schuster, New York, 1992, p.103.
57. *Masterpieces from the House of Fabergé*, ed. A. von Solodkoff, Harry N. Abrams, Inc., New York, 1984. pp.123-129. His chapter entitled 'Wartski and Fabergé'.
58. Tradition has it that the Kelkh family owned 7 Easter eggs. This information is based upon past and present research.
59. The sources for facts that are used here were obtained from: All St Petersburg 1860-1916; All Moscow 1880-1917.
60. A.E. Fersman, notes for *Essay on the History of Stone.*
61. State Central Historical Archive, stock 1102, inv. 2, file 599.
62. Leningrad KGB archives, partly available.
63. RSHA, stock 472, inv. 43, file 16.
64. 615/...Transfer N° 10, sheet 50, from Anichkov Palace to Moscow Kremlin Armoury – unnumbered strongbox. Begun 26 January 1922. Completed 22 August 1922.
65. Tatiana Fabergé archives.
66. ibid.
67. ibid.
68. A.Kenneth Snowman, *The Art of Carl Fabergé*, Faber and Faber Ltd, London, 1953, p.286.
69. Geza von Habsburg, *Fabergé*, (English book edition of Munich 1986/87 catalogue). Geneva, 1987, p.267.
70. Geza von Habsburg and Marina Lopato, *Fabergé: Imperial Jeweller*, exhibition catalogue, St Petersburg, 1993, p.73.
71. H. Waterfield and C. Forbes, *C. Fabergé: Imperial Easter Eggs and Other Fantasies*, New York, 1978, p.19.
72. Department of Manuscript, Graphical, Printed and Photo-graphic Documents of the Moscow Kremlin Historical and Cultural Museum and Monument, stock. 20, arch. 4, 1917, p.1.
73. ibid., stock 10, arch. 2, 1923, p.6.
74. ibid., p.3.
75. ibid., stock 20, chr. 21, inv. 1929/1930, p.104.
76. CSHA, stock 1343, inv. 40, file 5243, 1890, pp.3-4.
77. CSHA, stock 468, inv. 13, file 2548, p.29.

78 T.N. Muntian, 'Some new information on the Fabergé collection in the Kremlin' in *The Brilliant Age of Fabergé* (exhibition catalogue), 1992, p.65 (in Russian).
79 T.N. Muntian, 'Artefacts of Russian factories and firms of the late XIXth and early XXth centuries' in *The World of Fabergé* (exhibition catalogue), Moscow-Vienna, 1992, p.29.
80 N.M. Ambodik, *Selected Emblems and Symbols*, St Petersburg, 1811, p.XLIX.
81 SARF, stock 652, inv. 1, file 380, p.16.
82 RSHA, stock 468, inv. 7, file 372, p.1.
83 RSHA, stock 482, inv. 3 (799/1976), file 30, p.505/506.
84 RSHA, stock 468, inv. 7, file 372, p.1.
85 N° 20. Moscow Kremlin Armoury archive (hereafter called MKA), stock 20, inv. 1917, file 5, p.117.
86 Tatiana Fabergé archives.
87 RSHA, stock 468, inv. 7, file 270, p.4
88 RSHA, stock 468, inv. 7, file 372, p.1.
89 686/1568. Transfer N° 7, sheet 27, from Anichkov to Moscow Kremlin Armoury, strongbox N° 19. MKA archive, stock 20, file 23, 1922.
90 RSHA, stock 468, inv. 7, file 270.
91 RSHA, stock 468, inv. 7, file 372, p.1.
92 RSHA, stock 482, inv. 3 (799/1976), file 296, pp.430/431.
93 682/1548. Transfer N° 7, sheet 27, from Anichkov to Moscow Kremlin Armoury, strongbox N° 19. MKA archive, stock 20, file 23, 1922.
94 RSHA, stock 468, inv. 32, file 1619, p.16.
95 RSHA, stock 468, inv. 7, file 372, p.1.
96 RSHA, stock 491 (Gatchina Palace Administration), inv. 3, file 1224, p.67 (concerning the transfer of pictures to the Hermitage).
97 N° 15. From list of treasures and other items from the Anichkov Palace, MKA archive, stock 20, inv. 1917, file 5, p.116.
98 672/1561. Transfer N° 7, sheet 27, from Anichkov to Moscow Kremlin Armoury, strongbox N° 19. MKA archive, stock 20, file 23, 1922.
99 Lord and Taylor catalogue 4524, 1933, p.11.
100 RSHA, stock 468, inv. 32, file 1619, p. 47
101 RSHA, stock 491, (Gatchina Palace Administration), inv. 3, file 1224, p.67 verso (concerning the transfer of pictures to the Hermitage).
102 N° 9. From the list of treasures and other items from the Anichkov Palace, 1917. MKA archive, stock 20, inv. 1917, file 5.
103 618/1553 Transfer N° 10, sheet 50, from Anichkov to Kremlin Armoury, unnumbered strongbox. MKA archive, stock 20, file 23, 1992.
104 Wartski, *Fabergé: A Loan Exhibition of the Works of Carl Fabergé*, London, November 8 - 25th, 1949, p.10. [see also note 284]
105 Discovered by Rifat Gafifullin.
106 RSHA, stock 468, inv. 32, file 1619, p.90.
107 RSHA, stock 491 (Gatchina Palace), inv. 3, file 1224, p.175.
108 N° 5. From the list of treasures and other items from the Anichkov Palace, 1917. MKA archive, stock 20, inv. 1917. file 5, p.116.
109 711/1560. Transfer N° 10, sheet 33, from Anichkov to Moscow Kremlin Armoury, unnumbered strongbox. MKA archive, stock 20, file, 1922.
110 Moscow Kremlin Armoury number 17553. From information on sales of Imperial Easter eggs from the Moscow Kremlin Armoury in 1930 and 1933, stock 20, file 21, 1930.
111 Tatiana Fabergé archives. Letter from Eugène Fabergé to H.C. Bainbridge.
112 RSHA, stock 468, inv. 13, file 781, p.6.
113 RSHA, stock 491 (Gatchina Palace Administration), inv. 3, file 1224 (concerning the transfer of pictures to the Hermitage). N° 68.
114 N° 8. From the list of treasures and other items from the Anichkov Palace. MKA archive, stock 20, inv. 1917, p.116.
115 680/1552. Transfer N° 7, sheet 27, from Anichkov to Moscow Kremlin Armoury, strongbox N° 19. MKA archive, stock 20, file 23, 1922. Begun 26 January 1922. Completed 22 August 1922.
116 RSHA, stock 468, inv. 32, file 1619, p.128.
117 RSHA, stock 491 (Gatchina Palace Administration), inv. 3, file 1224 (concerning the transfer of pictures to the Hermitage), p.182, N° 43.
118 ibid., p.182, N° 44.
119 ibid., p.182, verso N° 45.
120 N° 18. From the list of treasures and other items from the Anichkov Palace. Moscow Kremlin Armoury archive, stock 20, inv. 1917, file 5, p.116.
121 684/1569. Transfer N° 7, sheet 27, from Anichkov to Moscow Kremlin Armoury, strongbox N° 19. MKA archive, stock 20, file 23, 1922.
122 707/1660. Sheet N° 33. Transfer N° 10 from Anichkov to Moscow Kremlin Armoury, unnumbered strongbox. MKA archive, stock 20, file 23, 1922.
123 RSHA, stock 468, inv. 32, file 1619, p.160.
124 The information on the letter from Vorontsov-Dashkov was kindly contributed by Doctor of History, D.I. Ismail-Zadé. SARF, stock 919, inv. 2, file 1214, p. 122.
125 N° 7. From the list of treasures and other items from the Anichkov Palace. MKA archive, stock 20, inv. 1917, file 5, p.116.
126 74/... Transfer N° 10, sheet 71, from Anichkov to Moscow Kremlin Armoury, unnumbered strongbox. MKA archive, stock 20, file 23, 1922.
127 Moscow Kremlin Armoury inventory number 17537, stock 20, file 21, 1930.
128 RSHA, stock 468, inv. 32, file 1623, p.43
129 Moscow Kremlin Armoury inventory N° 17552, stock 20, file 21, 1930.
130 RSHA, stock 1340, inv. 1, file 358, p.175.
131 ibid. Nicholas II paid for the eggs bought from Fabergé from his personal funds, although there is this one case, in 1895, when he paid only half the cost of the egg intended for his mother, the Dowager Empress Maria Fedorovna.
132 Letter to Tatiana Fabergé from Anne Odom, Chief Curator, Hillwood Museum, Washington D.C. 19 December 1995.
133 RSHA, stock 1340, inv. 1, file 358, p.175.
134 Consigned to the Office of H.I.M. Cabinet, 17 May 1917.
135 Easter Eggs at the Winter Palace in 1909. Archive of the State Hermitage. Stock 1, inventory VIII - G, file 7b, N° 195.
136 330/... Transfer N° 10, sheet 94, from Anichkov to Moscow Kremlin Armoury, unnumbered strongbox. MKA archive, stock 20, file 23, 1922.
137 RSHA, stock 525, inv. 3, file 8, p.135.
138 RSHA, stock 525, inv. 3, file 8, p.135.
139 Consigned to the Office of H.I.M. Cabinet, 17 May 1917.
140 Easter Eggs at the Winter Palace in 1909. Archive of the State Hermitage. Stock 1, inventory VIII - G, file 7b, N° 192.
141 320/... Transfer N° 10, sheet 93, verso, from Anichkov to Moscow Kremlin Armoury, strongbox N° 19. MKA archive, stock 20, file 23, 1922.
142 Moscow Kremlin Armoury inventory N° 17547. Stock 20, file 21, 1930.
143 RSHA, stock 468, inv.13, file 1843, p.8
144 A. Kenneth Snowman, *The Art of Carl Fabergé*, Faber and Faber Ltd, London, 1953, p.81
145 RSHA, stock 468, inv. 13, file 1843, p.8.
146 Consigned to the Office of H.I.M. Cabinet, 17 May 1917.
147 Easter Eggs at the Winter Palace in 1909. N° 198. Archive of the State Hermitage. Stock 1, inventory VIII - G, file 7b. Sheet 47, verso, N° 198.
148 ibid. N° 190.
149 327/...Transfer N° 10, sheet 94, from Anichkov to Moscow Kremlin Armoury, unnumbered strongbox. MKA archive, stock 20, file 23, 1922.
150 Christel Ludewig McCanless, *Fabergé and His Works*, The Scarecrow Press Inc., 1994, p.258
151 RSHA, stock 468, inv. 32, file 1635, p.113.

152 *Novoie Vremia*, 10 March 1902. 'Opening of an Exhibition of Treasures'. This information is very important and has also helped us to distinguish between eggs presented to Maria Fedorovna and to Alexandra Fedorovna.
153 N° 14. From the list of treasures and other items from the Anichkov Palace. MKA archive, stock 20, inv. 1917, file 5, p.116.
154 Moscow Kremlin Armoury inventory number 17538. Stock 20, file 21, 1930.
155 Letter to Madame Sidonie de L'Escaille, Hoover Institution.
156 RSHA, stock 468, inv. 32, file 1635, p.113.
157 Consigned to the Office of H.I.M. Cabinet, 17 May 1917.
158 Easter Eggs at the Winter Palace in 1909. Archive of the State Hermitage. Stock 1, inventory VIII - G, file 7b. N° 189.
159 Newspaper *Novoie Vremia*, St Petersburg, 9 March 1902. 'Exhibition of Artefacts and Miniatures.'
160 RSHA, stock 468, inv. 32, file 1637, p.140.
161 Newspaper *Novoie Vremia*, 10 March 1902.
162 Journal *Niva*, N°.12, 1902, Photo K. Bulla, St Petersburg.
163 N°.11. From the list of treasures and other items from the Anichkov Palace. MKA archive, stock 20, inv. 1917, file 5, p.116.
164 Moscow Kremlin Armoury inventory number 17539. Stock 20, file 21, 1930.
165 RSHA, stock 468, inv. 32, file 1637, p.140.
166 Consigned to the Office of H.I.M. Cabinet, 17 May 1917.
167 Easter Eggs at the Winter Palace in 1909. Archive of the State Hermitage. Stock 1, inventory VIII - G, file 7b. N° 193.
168 613/1293. Transfer N° 10, sheet 50, from Anichkov to Moscow Kremlin Armoury, unnumbered strongbox. MKA archive, stock 20, file, 1922. Begun 26 January 1922. Completed 22 August 1922.
169 RSHA, stock 468, inv. 32, file 1643, p.1.
170 N° 32. From the list of treasures and other items from the Anichkov Palace. MKA archive, stock 20, inv. 1917, file 5, p.117.
171 'Golden Egg', *USA Today*, Wednesday, June 12, 1985.
172 RSHA, stock 468, inv. 32, file 1643, p.1.
173 Consigned to the Office of H.I.M. Cabinet, 17 May 1917.
174 Easter Eggs at the Winter Palace in 1909. Archive of the State Hermitage. Stock 1, inventory VIII - G, file 7b. N° 188.
175 Journal *Niva*, N° 12, 1902 St Petersburg. 'Exhibition of artifacts, antique miniatures and snuffboxes organized in aid of schools of the Imperial Ladies' Patriotic Society.'
176 Newspaper *Novoie Vremia*, St Petersburg, 9 March 1902. 'Exhibition of Artefacts and Miniatures.'
177 318/... Transfer N° 10, sheet 93 verso, from Anichkov to Moscow Kremlin Armoury, unnumbered strongbox. MKA archive, stock 20, file 23, 1922. Begun 26 January 1922. Completed 22 August 1922.
178 RSHA, stock 468, inv. 32, file 1643, p.45.
179 Newspaper *Novoie Vremia*, 10 March 1902. 'Opening of an Exhibition of Treasures.'
180 Journal *Niva*, N° 12, 1902.
181 Moscow Kremlin Armoury inventory number 17555. Stock 20, file 21, 1933.
182 RSHA, stock 468, inv. 32, file 1643, p. 45.
183 Henry Charles Bainbridge, *Peter Carl Fabergé: Goldsmith and Jeweller to the Russian Imperial Court*, B.T. Batsford Ltd, 1949, subsequent editions, 1966, 1968, ill. pl. 35.
184 Consigned to the Office of H.I.M. Cabinet, 17 May 1917.
185 Easter Eggs at the Winter Palace in 1909. Archive of the State Hermitage. Stock 1, inv. VIII - G, file 7b. N° 199.
186 321/.. Transfer N° 10, sheet 93 verso, from Anichkov to Moscow Kremlin Armoury, unnumbered strongbox. MKA archive, stock 20, file 23, 1922.
187 Moscow Kremlin Armoury inventory number 17555. Stock 20, file 21, 1933.
188 Lynette G. Proler archives.
189 Tatiana Fabergé archives.
190 RSHA, stock 468, inv. 32, file 1644, p.64.
191 N° 3. From the list of treasures and other items from the Anichkov Palace. MKA archive, stock 20, inv. 1917, file 5.
192 117/113. Transfer N° 10, sheet 73, from Anichkov to Moscow Kremlin Armoury, unnumbered strongbox. MKA archive, stock 20, file 23, 1922. Begun 26 January 1922. Completed 22 August 1922.
193 RSHA, stock 468, inv. 32, file 1644, p.64.
194 Consigned to the Office of H.I.M. Cabinet, 17 May 1917.
195 Easter Eggs at the Winter Palace in 1909. Archive of the State Hermitage. Stock 1, inv. VIII - G, file 7b. N° 191.
196 668/17556. MKA archive, stock 20, 1927, file 20, begun 14 February 1927, completed 30 December 1927, inv. N° 2, sheet 20.
197 H.C. Bainbridge, 'Russian Imperial Easter Gifts. The Work of Carl Fabergé'. *The Connoisseur*, Vol. 93 (1934), pp.299-306.
198 H.C. Bainbridge, 'Russian Imperial Easter Gifts. The Work of Carl Fabergé'. *The Connoisseur*, p. 387, 1934, July.
199 RSHA, stock 468, inv. 32, file 1648, p.81.
200 SARF, stock 642, inv. 1, file 2327.
201 RSHA, stock 468, inv. 32, file 1648, p.81.
202 Consigned to the Office of H.I.M. Cabinet, 17 May 1917.
203 Easter Eggs at the Winter Palace in 1909. Archive of the State Hermitage. Stock 1, inv. VIII- G, file 7b. N° 194.
204 322/... Transfer N° 10, sheet 93 verso, from Anichkov to Moscow Kremlin Armoury, unnumbered strongbox, MKA archive, stock 20, file 23, 1922. Begun 26 January 1922. Completed 22 August 1922.
205 Moscow Kremlin Armoury inventory number 17511. Stock 20, file 21, 1933.
206 RSHA, stock 468, inv. 32, file 1655, p.103.
207 N° 13. From the list of treasures and other items from the Anichkov Palace. MKA archive, stock 20, inv. 1917, file 5.
208 708/1554. Transfer N° 10, sheet 33, from Anichkov Palace to Moscow Kremlin Armoury, unnumbered strongbox. MKA archive, stock 20, file 23, 1922. Begun 26 January 1922. Completed 22 August 1922.
209 *Education of a Princess - a Memoir*, Marie, Grand Duchess of Russia. New York, The Viking Press, 1930, p.16.
210 RSHA, stock 468, inv. 32, file 1655, p.103.
211 49/... Transfer N° 10, Sheet 70, from Anichkov Palace to Moscow Kremlin Armoury, unnumbered strongbox. MKA archive, stock 20, file 23, 1922. Begun 26 January 1922. Completed 22 August 1922.
212 Tatiana F. Fabergé and Valentin V. Skurlov, *The History of the House of Fabergé*, St Petersburg, 1992, p.26.
213 RSHA, stock 468, inv. 32 file 1656, p.58.
214 Tatiana F. Fabergé and Valentin V. Skurlov, *The History of the House of Fabergé*, St Petersburg, 1992, p.34.
215 RSHA, stock 468, inv. 32 file 1656, p.58.
216 Consigned to the Office of H.I.M. Cabinet, 17 May 1917.
217 Private collection.
218 324/... Transfer N° 10, sheet 93 verso, from Anichkov Palace to Moscow Kremlin Armoury. MKA archive, stock 20, file 23, 1922. Begun 26 January 1922. Completed 22 August 1922.
219 Anonymous, *The Russian Diary of an Englishman*. William Heinemann, London, 1919.
220 RSHA, stock 472, inv.43 (471/2420), file 146.
221 RSHA, stock 468, inv. 32. File 1657, p.49.
222 N° 17. List of treasures and other items from the Anichkov Palace. MKA archive, stock 20, inv. 1917, file 5.
223 701/1563. Transfer N° 10, sheet 33, from Anichkov Palace to Moscow Kremlin Armoury, unnumbered strongbox. MKA archive, stock 20, file 23, 1922. Begun 26 January 1922. Completed 22 August 1922.
224 RSHA, stock 468, inv. 32. file 1657, p.49.
225 Private collection.
226 67/... Transfer N° 10, sheet 71, from Anichkov Palace to Moscow Kremlin Armoury, unnumbered strongbox. MKA archive, stock 20, file 23, 1922. Begun 26 January 1922. Completed 22 August 1922.

227 H.C. Bainbridge, *The Connoisseur*, p.386, 1934, July.
228 RSHA, stock 468, inv. 17, file 1212, p.48.
229 Tatiana Fabergé archives.
230 RSHA, stock 468, inv. 17, file 1212, p.48.
231 Private collection.
232 75/... Transfer N° 10, sheet 71, from Anichkov Palace to Moscow Kremlin Armoury, unnumbered strongbox, MKA archive, stock 20, file 23, 1922. Begun 26 January 1922. Completed 22 August 1922.
233 RSHA, stock 468, inv. 32, file 1661, p. 179.
234 N° 12. From the list of treasures and other items from the Anichkov Palace. MKA archive, stock 20, inv. 1917, file 5.
235 703/1558. Transfer N° 10, sheet 33, from Anichkov Palace to Moscow Kremlin Armoury, unnumbered strongbox. MKA archive, stock 20, file 23, 1922. Begun 26 January 1922. Completed 22 August 1922.
236 RSHA, stock 468, inv. 32, file 1661, p.179.
237 Private collection.
238 48/... Transfer N° 10, sheet 70, from Anichkov Palace to the Moscow Kremlin Armoury, unnumbered strongbox. MKA archive, stock 20, file 23, 1922. Begun 26 January 1922. Completed 22 August 1922.
239 Lynette G. Proler archives.
240 RSHA, stock 468, inv. 32, file 1663, p. 83 (verso).
241 N° 34. From the list of treasures and other items from the Anichkov Palace. MKA archive, stock 20, inv. 1917, file 5.
242 702/1646. Transfer N° 10 - sheet 33, from Anichkov Palace to Moscow Kremlin Armoury, unnumbered strong box. MKA archive, stock 20, file 23, 1922. Begun 26 January 1922. Completed 22 August 1922.
243 Rita Reif, 'Glittering Baubles Made for a Czar', *New York Times*. Sunday, April 16, 1978: Sec D (II), p.24, col.1.
244 RSHA, stock 468, inv. 32, file 1663, p.83.
245 Private collection.
246 RSHA, stock 525, inv. 2 (215/2713), file 2.
247 612/1299. Transfer N° 10, sheet 50, from Anichkov Palace to Moscow Kremlin Armoury, unnumbered strongbox. MKA archive, stock 20, file 23, 1922. Begun 26 January 1922. Completed 22 August 1922.
248 Moscow Kremlin Armoury inventory N° 17557. Stock 20, file 21, 1930.
249 Tatiana Fabergé archives.
250 Private collection.
251 Moscow Kremlin Armoury inventory number 17547. Stock 20, file 21, 1930.
252 RSHA, stock 468, inv. 44, file 1178, p. 63.
253 704/1557. Transfer N° 10, sheet 33, from Anichkov Palace to Moscow Kremlin Armoury, unnumbered strongbox. MKA archive, stock 20, file 23, 1922. Begun 26 January 1922. Completed 22 August 1922.
254 RSHA, stock 468, inv. 44, file 1178, p.63 (verso).
255 Private collection.
256 72/... Transfer N° 10, sheet 71, from Anichkov Palace to the Moscow Kremlin Armoury, unnumbered strongbox. MKA archive, stock 20, file 23, 1022. Begun 26 January 1922. Completed 22 August 1922.
257 Alexander von Solodkoff archives.
258 RSHA, stock 525, inv. 2 (217/2715), file 5.
259 N° 6. From the list of treasures and other items from the Anichkov Palace. MKA archive, stock 20, inv. 1917, file 5.
260 619/1601. Transfer N° 10, sheet 50, from Anichkov Palace to Moscow Kremlin Armoury, unnumbered strongbox. MKA archive, stock 20, file 23, 1922. Begun 26 January 1922. Completed 22 August 1922.
261 Moscow Kremlin Armoury inventory number 17558, stock 20, file 21, 1930
262 In 1949 the sedan chair was exhibited at Wartski, London and was later sold at Christie's, Geneva 13 November. 1985 for $662,037 - ex collection of Sir Charles Clore.
263 H.C. Bainbridge, *Peter Carl Fabergé, His Life and Work*, New York (1949), pp.76 and 142. A.K. Snowman, *The Art of Carl Fabergé*, Faber and Faber Ltd, London (1953), p.101.
264 Private collection.
265 68/... Transfer N° 10, sheet 71, from Anichkov Palace to Moscow Kremlin Armoury, unnumbered strongbox. MKA archive, stock 20, file 23, 1922. Begun 26 January. Completed 22 August 1922.
266 Moscow Kremlin Armoury inventory number 17549. Stock 20, file 21, 1933.
267 Lynette G. Proler archives.
268 Tatiana F. Fabergé and Valentin V. Skurlov, *The History of the House of Fabergé*, St Petersburg, 1992, p.26.
269 RSHA, stock 525, inv. 2 (217/2715), file 331.
270 N° 16. From the list of Treasures from Anichkov Palace. MKA archive, stock 20, inv. 1917, file 5.
271 639/1562. Transfer N° 10, sheet 52, from Anichkov Palace to Moscow Kremlin Armoury, unnumbered strongbox. MKA archive, stock 20 file 23, 1922. Begun 26 January 1922. Completed 22 August 1922.
272 Moscow Kremlin Armoury inventory number 17550. Stock 20, file 21, 1930.
273 Private collection.
274 Marie, Grand Duchess of Russia, *Education of a Princess - a Memoir*, New York, The Viking Press, 1930, p.196.
275 66/.... Transfer N° 10, sheet 71, from Anichkov Palace to Moscow Kremlin Armoury, unnumbered strongbox. MKA archive, stock 20, file 23, 1922. Begun 26 January 1922. Completed 22 August 1922.
276 Moscow Kremlin Armoury inventory number 17559. Stock 20, file 21, 1930.
277 Lynette G. Proler archive.
278 A.E. Fersman. *Remarks on the History of Stone*, vol. 2, Moscow Academy of Sciences, 1961 (in Russian), p.298.
279 Stock 525, inv. 2 (217/2715), file 158.
280 Tatiana Fabergé archives.
281 Private collection.
282 Gosizdat, M.-L., *Correspondence between Nicholas and Alexandra Romanov*, Vol. IV, 1926, p.210.
283 73/... Transfer N° 10, sheet 71, from Anichkov Palace to Moscow Kremlin Armoury, unnumbered strongbox. MKA archive, stock 20, file 23, 1922. Begun 26 January 1922. Completed 22 August 1922.
284 Entry in the Wartski catalogue (cf p.101) reads as follows: '*Lent* ANONYMOUSLY:
20. A Fine Gold Egg, richly set with diamonds, cabochon rubies, emeralds, a large coloured diamond at topand a cabochon saphire at point. The interior is designed as an Etui with thirteen gold and diamond set implements.'

Note:
TSGAORR SSSR: USSR Central State Archive of the October Revolution, Moscow.
SARF: State Archive of the Russian Federation
RSHA: Russian State Historical Archive.
CSHA: Central State Historical Archive
CSAOD: Central State Archive of Old Documents.

Select Bibliography

EXHIBITION CATALOGUES

A Loan Exhibition of the Works of Carl Fabergé. Wartski, London, 1949.

Peter Carl Fabergé: An Exhibition of His Works. A La Vieille Russie, New York, 1949.

Peter Carl Fabergé – Imperial Court Jeweller. Hammer Galleries, New York, 1951.

Fabergé, Hofjuwelier der Zaren. Hypo-Kulturstiftung, Munich, 1986.

The Great Fabergé. Elagin Palace Museum, Leningrad, 1989.

Fabergé, The Imperial Easter Eggs (in English and Russian). San Diego-Moscow Kremlin, 1989-1990.

The World of Fabergé (in Russian). Moscow-Vienna, 1992.

Fabergé: Imperial Jeweller. St Petersburg-Paris-London, 1993.

The World of Fabergé. Perth-Melbourne-Sydney, 1996.

Fabergé in America. New York-San Francisco-Richmond-New Orleans-Cleveland, 1996.

BOOKS AND ARTICLES

Anonymous. *The Russian Diary of an Englishman*, William Heinemann, London, 1919.

Bainbridge, Henry Charles. *Twice Seven*, George Routledge & Sons, Ltd, London, 1933.

Bainbridge, Henry Charles. 'The Workmasters of Fabergé'. *The Connoisseur*, August 1935, p.85 ff.

Bainbridge, Henry Charles. *Peter Carl Fabergé, His Life and Work*, B.T. Batsford Ltd, London, 1949 (with revised reissues in 1966 and 1974).

Blumay C. and Edwards H. *The Dark Side of Power: The Real Armand Hammer*, Simon and Schuster, London, 1992.

Booth, John. *The Art of Fabergé*, Bloomsbury, London, 1990.

Botkine, Tatiana. *Au Temps des Tsars*, Grasset & Fasquelle, 1980.

Chapuis, Alfred and Droz, Edmond. *Automata, a Historical and Technological Study* (translated by Alec Reid), B.T. Batsford Ltd, London, 1958.

Clarke, William. *The Lost Fortune of the Tsars*, Weidenfeld & Nicolson, London, 1994.

Curry, David Park. *Fabergé: Virginia Museum of Fine Arts*, Virginia Museum of Fine Arts, 1995.

Fabergé, Tatiana F. and Skurlov, Valentin V. *The History of the House of Fabergé*, St Petersburg, 1992.

Fitzlyon, Kyril and Browning, Tatiana. *Before the Revolution*, The Overlook Press, New York, 1978.

Glenny, Michael and Stone, Norman. *The Other Russia, the Experience of Exile.* Viking Penguin, Harmondsworth, 1991.

Hill, Gerard, Smorodinova G.G., and Ulyanova B.L. *Fabergé and the Russian Master Goldsmiths*, Hugh Lauter Levin Associates, Inc., New York, 1989.

Keefe, John Webster. *Masterpieces of Fabergé*, The Matilda Geddings Gray Foundation Collection, New Orleans Museum of Art, 1993.

Lopato, Marina. 'New Light on Fabergé', *Apollo*, 1984, pp.43-49.

Lopato, Marina. 'Fabergé Eggs. Re-dating from new evidence', *Apollo*, February 1991, pp.91-94.

Marie, Grand Duchess of Russia. *Education of a Princess – à Memoir*, The Viking Press, New York, 1930.

Massie, Robert K. *Nicholas and Alexandra*, London, 1969.

Massie, Robert K. *The Romanovs, the Final Chapter*, Jonathan Cape, London, 1995.

Massie, Robert K. and Jeffrey Finestone II. *The Last Courts of Europe*, The Vendome Press, New York, 1981.

McCanless, Christel Ludewig. *Fabergé and His Works,* The Scarecrow Press, Inc. Metuchen, N.J. & London, 1994.

Paleologue, Maurice. *An Ambassador's Memoirs*, Hutchinson & Co., London 1925.

Poliakoff, Vladimir. *The Empress Marie of Russia and Her Times*, Thornton Butterworth, Ltd, London, 1926.

Pfeffer, Susanna. *Fabergé Eggs: Masterpieces from Czarist Russia*, Hugh Lauter Levin Associates, Inc., New York, 1990.

Proler, Lynette G. 'Fabergé, From Fake to Fabric', *Villages* Magazine, October 1994, pp.24-26.

Radzinsky, Edvard. *The Last Tsar, the Life and Death of Nicholas II*, Doubleday, New York, 1992.

Ross, Marvin C. *The Art of Karl Fabergé*, University of Oklahoma Press, 1965.

Skurlov, Valentin V., and Smorodinova, Galina S. *Fabergé and Russian Court Jewellers* (in Russian), Terra, Moscow, 1992.

Snowman, A. Kenneth. *The Art of Carl Fabergé*, Faber and Faber Ltd, London, 1953.

Snowman, A. Kenneth. *Carl Fabergé, Goldsmith to the Imperial Court of Russia*, Debrett's Peerage, London, 1979.

Solodkoff, Alexander von. *Masterpieces from the House of Fabergé*, Harry N. Abrams, New York, 1984.

Solovieva, T.A. *The von Dervises Houses*, Beloe I. Chernoe, St Petersburg, 1995.

Vorres, Ian. *The Last Grand-Duchess, Her Imperial Highness Grand Duchess Olga Alexandrovna*, Hutchinson Ltd, London, 1964.

Waterfield, Hermione. and Forbes, Christopher. *Fabergé: Imperial Eggs and Other Fantasies*, Bramhall House, New York, 1978.

Williams, Robert C. *Russian Art and American Money, 1900-1940*, Harvard University Press, Cambridge, Mass., 1980.

Index

Italics = illustrations
Bold = main catalogue raisonné entry

A

abdication, Nicholas II, 43
after the Revolution, 64, 69
A La Vieille Russie, 77, 226
Alexander II, 34, 35, 36, 41, 92
Alexander III, Tsar, 7, 8, 15, *16*, 18, 23, 34, 36, 37, 38, 39, 42, 92
Alexander III Commemorative egg, 11, 69, 90, **186**, *234,* 247
Alexander III egg, 10, 69, 90, *123, 234,* 241
Alexander III Equestrian egg, 11, 69, 83, 90, **191**, *235,* 247, 255, 256, 258
Alexander III, gifts to Maria Fedorovna (*see* Maria Fedorovna, eggs from ~)
Alexander Palace, 40, 87
  (*see also* Tsarskoie Selo)
Alexander Palace egg, 11, 69, 82, 83, 87, 90, **182**, *234,* 246, 250, 254, 256, 261
Alexandra Fedorovna, Empress, 15, 17, 18, *34,* 37, 38, 39, 40, 41, *43*
Alexandra Fedorovna, eggs from, 18, 41, 47, 49, 65, 70, 120, 124, 130, 136, 142, 150, 156, 160, 164, 170, 176, 182, 188, 194, 200, 207, 212, 219, 225, 230
Alexandra, Queen of England, 41
Alexei Alexandrovich, Grand Duke, 60
Alexei Nikolaievich, Tsarevich, 42, 59, 87
Anatra, A.A., 77
Anichkov Palace, *18,* 36, 37, 38, 40, 44, 47, 82
Anichkov Palace, storage and removal of eggs, 64, 82, 255
Antikvariat, 67, 69, 84, 114, 117, 124, 135, 140, 144, 152, 158, 160, 166, 172, 185, 190, 192, 206, 208, 214, 218, 221, 224, 226, 232
Apple Blossom egg, 77
Armoury (*see* Moscow Kremlin Armoury)
Azov, 84

B

Bad Homburg, 28
Bainbridge, Henry Charles, 7, 27, 45, 46, 49, 79
Baletta, Elisabeth, 59
Baron von Steiglitz School, 26, 33, 87
Basket of Wild Flowers egg, 10, 55, 69, 84, 90, **156**, *234,* 244, 254, 256, 257, 262
Bay Tree egg, 8, 11, 68, 69, 90, **197**, *235,* 248, 255, 256
Bazanov family, 72-77
Bazanov, Ivan (*see* Kelkh family)
Bazanova, Yulia Ivanovna, (*see* Kelkh family)
Bazanova, Varvara (*see* Kelkh family)
Belishova, Nina, 28
Benois, Alexander N., 58
Birbaum, Franz Petrovich, 8, 24, 27, 32, 33, 44, 59, 61, 62, 87
blue diamond, 74
Blue Enamel Louis XVI egg, 41 (*see also* Twelve Monograms egg)
Blue Serpent Clock egg, 10, 55, 69, 90, 98, *234,* 236, 256
Blue Striped Enamel egg, 11, 80
Blue Tsarevich Constellation egg, 11, 62, *63*
Blumay, Carl, 67
Bolshaia Morskaia, 21, 23, 31, 71
Bolsheviks, 27, 28, 37, 47, 64, 65, 66, 79
Bonbonnière egg, 77
Bouquet of Lilies Clock egg, 10, 55, 69, 84, 86, 90, **142**, *235,* 243, 254, 256, 257
Bourdier, 78
Bowe, Allan, 60
branches of Fabergé, 24, 27, *30* (*see also* St Petersburg, Kiev, London, Moscow, Odessa)

C

Cabinet, His Imperial Majesty's, 8
Cacheux, 26
Cameo corner, 7, 221
Cathedral of the Dormition (*see* Uspenski Cathedral)
Catherine the Great, 35
Catherine the Great egg (*see* Grisaille egg)
Catherine Palace, 40
Caucasus egg, 10, 32, 55, 69, 83, 90, **112**, *234,* 239, 255, 256, 258, 262
Chanticleer egg, 77
Cherub egg with Chariot, 10, 69, 90, **100**, *234,* 236, 237, 253, 255
Chicago World Fair, 67
Chinariov, Ivan Gavrilovich, 83
Christian IX, King of Denmark, 36, 38
Christie, Lansdell K., 80
Christie's, 67, 77, 79, 80, 81, 126, 149, 211, 218
Christmas, 17
Clover egg, 10, 27, 69, 84, 86, 90 **160**, *235,* 244, 254, 257
Cockerel egg, 8, 10, 69, 90, **146**, *234,* 243, 255
Colonnade egg, 11, 69, 90, **194**, *235,* 247, 250, 254, 256
Commission of the Plenipotentiary, 83
coronation carriage, 47
Coronation egg, 10, 32, 47, 55, 69, 90, **130** , *235,* 242, 254, 256
coronation, Nicholas II, 39-41
Cottage Palace (*see* Peterhof)
Cradle with Garlands egg, 11, 59, 69, 90, **174**, *234,* 246
craftsmen, 31-33, 47, 59
Crimea, 18, 38, 63, 65
Crimean War, 36
Crystal egg, 79, 82
Cuckoo egg, 8 (*see also* Cockerel egg)

D

Dagmar, Princess of Denmark, 36
Danish gold Easter egg, *17*
Danish Jubilee egg, 10, 69, 90, **162**, *235,* 245
Danish Palaces egg, 10, 32, 83, 90, **102**, *235,* 238, 253, 255, 256, 257, 262
dates of eggs (*see* individual eggs)
Davies, Joseph E., US Ambassador, 67
Deterding, Lady, 126
Derbyshev, Piotr, 28, 32
von Dervis
  family, 53-57
  exhibition, 26, 52-57, 98, 110, 118, 135, 138, 139, 152, 158
von Dervis, Baron Pavel Pavlovich, 53
design, designers, 27, 31-33, 44
Diamond Trellis egg, 10, 31, 55, 69, 90, **109**, *235,* 239, 253, 255, 256
Drager, 109
Duchess of Marlborough egg, 81

E

Easter ritual, 17, 18
Edward VII, King, 41
Ekaterinburg School of Art, 32
Elizabeth II, Queen, collection, 7, 77, 156, 194, 219
Empire Nephrite egg, 10, 69, 82, 90, **159**, *234,* 244, 245, 255, 256
Empress Alexandra (*see* Alexandra Fedorovna)
Empress Maria (*see* Maria Fedorovna)
enamellers, 33
Escaille, Sidonie de l', 42
evaluation of eggs, 1920s, 66
exhibition, 1902 von Dervis, 52, 53, 54, 55, 56, 57
exhibition, 1996 Fabergé in America, 8
exhibition, Moscow Pan-Russian, 23, 29
exhibition, Paris Universal, 26, 29, 251

F

Fabergé, Agathon Carlovich, 26, 28, 64, 66, 83
Fabergé, Agathon Gustavovich, 21, 25, 85
Fabergé, Alexander, 24, 26 , 28
Fabergé, Augusta Bogdanovna, 27, 28
Fabergé, Carl, 22, 25, 27, 28
  death of, 28
  departure from Russia, 28
  mentor of, 21
  personality, 26, 27
  watercolours of, 8, 62-63
  as designer, 26
  Legion of Honour, 26, 29
  150th anniversary of death, 9
Fabergé, Eugène, 8, 24, 25, 27, 45, 61, 62, 79, 85
Fabergé, family, 22, 25-26
Fabergé family tree, 22
Fabergé, Gustav, 21
Fabergé, Nicholas, 24, 26
Fabergé, Tatiana, 22, 61, 62, 65
Farouk, King of Egypt, collection 77, 169
Fifteenth Anniversary egg, 2, 11, 33, 68, 69, 90, **200**, *235,* 248, 250, 254

268

Fine Arts Society, London, 122
first Imperial egg, 8, 15, 44, 92
First World War, 28, 43, 57
Flask egg, 65
FORBES magazine collection, 72, 77, 79, 80, 81, 92, 94, 116, 117, 120, 122, 126, 130, 136, 146, 197, 200, 227
Foreign Currency Fund, 83

G

Gatchina Palace 36, 47, 64, 65
   description of eggs at the, 253
Gatchina Palace egg, 10, 55, 69, 90, 154, *234*, 244, 252, 253
Geddings Gray, Mrs Matilda 67, 103, 114, 140
Geddings Gray collection, Matilda, 102, 112, 202, 206
gem cutters, setters, 47
gemstones, Kelkh, 74
George V, King, 7, 221
glassworks, Imperial, 89
Glavmuseum, 83
Glinka street, 75
Gokhran, 83
Gold pendant egg, 82
Gorky, Maxim, 60
Grand Duchess Elizabeth Fedorovna, 43
Grand Duke Michael Alexandrovich, 43
Grantchester, Lady, 94
Grisaille egg, 11, 69, 84, 90, **216**, *234*, 255, 256, 257, 262

H

Hammer, Armand, 67, 69, 80, 100, 114, 135
Hammer Galleries Inc., 114, 124, 206
Hanau, Academy of, 25
Hen egg, first Imperial egg, 7, 10, *14*, 44, 69, 79, 90, *92*, *234*, 236, 255
Hen egg, red enamel, 72, 77
Hen egg with sapphire pendant, 10, 44, 69, 90, **95**, *234*, 236, 256
Herbette, Ambassador of France, 67
Hermitage, The, 23, 67
Hesse and the Rhine, princess of, 37, 38
Hollming, August, 24, 31
Holmström, Albert, 24, 32, 209
Holmström, August, 31, 106, 109, 219
Holmström, Fanny, 31, 32
House of Fabergé, 15, 20, 21-23, 28, 29 37, 44, 61, 72
Huguenots, 21

I

Imperial archives, 7
Imperial court, 39
Imperial Easter egg(s), 7, 9-11, 41, 44-47, 67, 69, 92-233, *234-235*
   album, Alexandra Fedorovna, 250
   chronology, 8
   cost of, 47 (*see also* invoices)
   current location of, 90
   descriptions of (1891, 1909), 253-254
   evaluation, 1920s, 66

the first, 15-19, 44, 92
the last, 61-63, 87
missing, 47, 65
presented to Alexandra Fedorovna, 250
sale from Soviets to first owner, 69
themes, 46, 47
Imperial family, 34-43
   (*see also* Romanov Dynasty)
Imperial palaces, 35
   (*see also* Alexander Palace, Anichkov Palace, Gatchina Palace, Livadia Palace, Peterhof Palace, Tauride Palace and Winter Palace)
industrial revolution, 42
inventory, Armoury, 66, 78, 79
invoices, 47, 65, 234-249
Iossilevich, Commissar, 28
Ivashev, Alexander Ivanovich, 27, 33, 61

J

Jacobs, Augusta, 85
Jacobs, Gottlieb, 85
Jacobson, E.E., *33*
Jarke, Otto-Gustav, 60

K

Karelian Birch egg, 11, 63
Kelkh family, 70-77
Kelkh Apple Blossom egg, *74*
Kelkh Bonbonnière egg, *75*
Kelkh Chanticleer egg, *76*
Kelkh Easter eggs, 70-77
Kelkh Hen egg, *72*
Kelkh Pine Cone egg, *73*
Kelkh Rocaille egg, *74*
Kelkh Twelve Panel egg, *73*
Kharkov, 39
Kiev, Fabergé branch in, 24
Kitson, T.B., 109
Klein, V.K., 84
Kollin, Erik August, 31
Krasovskii, Alexander Fedorovich, 56
Kremlev, Piotr Mikhailovich, 32
Kremlin, the, 40, 67
Kremlin Armoury, 9, 66
Kremlin Collection, 82-88
Kryzhitski, Konstantin Yakovlevich, 32, 102, 112
Kshesinskaia, Mathilde, 37
Kuprin, Alexander Ivanovich, 65

L

Lausanne, 28
Lena Gold Fields, 76
Lenin, 37, 43, 62, 67
Lilies of the Valley egg, 10, 32, 55, 69, 86, 90, **136**, *235*, 242, 251, 253
Linsky, 117
Livadia Palace, 18, 38, 46
London, Fabergé branch in, 24, 26
Lord and Taylor, 67, 208, 244
Lopato, Marina, 80
Louise, Queen of Denmark, 17, *19*
Love Trophy egg
   (*see* Cradle with Garlands egg)
Ludwig, Nicholas H., 103

M

Malyshev, Georgii, 164
Manchuria, invasion of, 58
Maria Fedorovna, Empress, 15, *16*, 17, 18, *19*, 36, 38, *40*, 42, 63, 65
Maria Fedorovna, Empress, eggs, 18, 44, 47, 98, **100**, **101**, **102**, **106**, **109**, **112**, **116**
Maria Fedorovna, Dowager Empress, eggs, **118**, **123**, **126**, **133**, **139**, **146**, **154**, **159**, **162**, **168**, **174**, **179**, **186**, **191**, **197**, **202**, **209**, **216**, **222**, **227**
Mary, Queen, 67, 158, 196, 221
Mauve Enamel egg, 10, 69, 90, **126**, *234*, 242
Mellon, Andrew, 65
Memory of Azov egg, 10, 69, 83, 84, 86, 90, **106**, *235*, 238, 253, 255, 259
Merchant of the Second Guild, 21
Merriweather Post, Marjorie, 118
miniature Easter eggs, 41
miniatures, 49, 52
miniaturists, 32
Minshall, India Early, 226
Mintslov, S.R., diaries of, 59, 78
Monakhtin, S.I., 84
Mosaic egg, 7, 11, 27, 32, 33, 68, 69, 83, 90, *91*, **219**, *235*, 250, 256, 261, 262
Moscow, Fabergé branch in, 24, 26, 29
Moscow Kremlin Armoury, 9, 64-67, 69
Moscow Kremlin Armoury, storage of eggs, 64, 82-89
Moscow Kremlin egg, 11, 58, 60, 68, 69, 83, 86, 87, 90, **170**, *235*, 245, 254, 256, 260
Moscow, Pan-Russian Exhibition, 23, 29, 37
Museum of Art, Cleveland, 225
Museum, Hillwood, 118, 216
Museum, The Hermitage, 23, 67
Museum of Fine Arts, Virginia, 124, 133, 164, 207, 222
Museum, Moscow Kremlin Armoury, 106, 142, 150, 160, 170, 182, 188, 191, 212, 230 (*see also* Moscow Kremlin Armoury)
Museum, Postal, 28
Museum, Victoria & Albert, 81

N

Napoleonic egg, 11, 69, 84, 90, **202**, *234*, 256, 257, 262
Narkomfin, transfer of treasures, 257
Narkompros, 84
Nécessaire egg, 10, 47, 69, 90, **101**, *234*, 236, 253, 255, 256
Newspaper articles, 251, 252
   (*see also* Novoie Vremia *and* Niva)
Nicholas II, Tsar, 7, 15, *34*, 37-40, 42, 43, *46*, 58, 59
Nicholas II Equestrian egg, 11, 80
Nijnii Novgorod Fair, 29, 30
Nikolai, Fedor, 85
Nikolai, Wilhelmina, 85
Nikolai, Yurii, 85
Niva, 252
Nobel Ice egg, 81

269

Nobel, Dr Emmanuel, 81
Novoie Vremia, 18, 251

O

October Revolution, 8, 64
Odessa, Fabergé branch in, 24, 27, 29
Orange Tree egg, (*see* Bay Tree egg)
Order of St George egg, 11, 65, 69, 90, **227**, *235*
Orlov, 87
Osinovaia Roshcha, 72

P

Pan-Russian movement, 36
Pansy egg, 10, 55, 69, 83, 86, 88, 90, **139**, *235, 243,* 252, 253, 255, 257, 262
Paris Universal Exhibition, 26, 29, 31
Parsons, Charles, 122
Pavlova-Kaufman, Natalia, 272
Peacock egg, 11, 68, 69, 90, **179**, *234, 246,* 255, 256
Pelican egg, 10, 83, 90, **133**, *235,* 242, 252, 258, 262
Pendin, Hiskias, 21, 31
Perkhin, Mikhail, 23, 26, *31*, 79, 84, 85, 86, 102, 106, 112, 116, 118, 120, 124, 130, 133, 136, 139, 142, 146, 150, 160, 164
Peter the Great, 35
Peter the Great egg, 10, 69, 83, 90, **164**, *235, 245,* 254, 256, 261, 262
Peterhof Palace, 35, 38
Petrograd, 43, 82
Petrokommuna, 27
Petropavlovsk, 59
Petrov, Alexander Fedorovich, 8, 33
Petrov, Dimitrii Alexandrovich, 33
Petrov, N., 8, *33,* 92, 95, 96, 97, 98, 100
Petukhov, 89
Pihl, Alma Theresia, 27, 31, 32, 81, 209, 219
Pihl, Knut Oscar, 31, 32
Pine Cone egg, 73, 77
Polovtsov, Alexander, 154, 178
Popov, Peter Nikolaievich, 33
Post, Marjorie Merriweather, 67, 218
Prat, Lillian Thomas, 124, 135, 208, 224
pricing, 47
Promyshlennosty Company, 75, 76
Putilovskii Steel Plant, 33

R

Rainier III, Prince of Monaco, collection, 98
Rasputin, Grigorii, 42, 43
Red Cross, 65
Red Cross egg with Imperial portraits, 11, 84, 69, 90, **222**, *235,* 255, 256, 259, 262
Red Cross egg with Triptych, 11, 69, 83, 90, **225**, *235,* 250, 256, 257, 262
Renaissance egg, 55, 69, 83 90, **118**, *235, 240,* 257, 262
Renaissance style, 10, 88

Resurrection egg, 11, 79
Revolving Miniatures egg, 10, 55, 68, 69, 83, **124**, *234, 241,* 254, 256, 259, 262
Riga, 28
Rimsky-Korsakov, 60
Rocaille egg, 77
Romanov Dynasty, 28, 41, 43, 44, 63, 67
Romanov Tercentenary egg, 11, 68, 69, 83, 90, **212**, *234,* 249, 250, 254, 256, 260
Rose Trellis egg, 11, 69, 90, **176**, *234,* 246, 250, 254, 256
Rosebud egg, 10, 55, 69, 90, **120**, *234, 240,* 254, 256
Russian Church, 17, 18
Russian Crown Jewels, 66
Russian Empire, 43
Russian Revolution, 8, 28, 43, 61, 64, 66
Russkiye Samotsvety, 32
Russo-Japanese War, 43, 58-60, 75, 76, 86
Rynnanen, Lauri, 32

S

St Olga, 86
St Petersburg, 35, 37, 43
sale of eggs, 67-69
Sandoz, Edouard and Maurice Foundation Collection, 81, 168, 179
Schmidt, Carl Carlovich, 23, 72
sculptors, 32
Sergei Alexandrovich, Grand Duke, 38, 60, 87
Sergeiev, Mikail Sergeievich, 83
Serov, Valentin, 60
Shkilter, Gustav, 33
Sibiriakov, Konstantin, 70
Sibiriakov, Mikhail, 70
Silver egg with red enamel, 82
Snowman, A.K., 67
Snowman, Emanuel, 7, 67, 69
Sotheby's, 67, 77, 81, 149, 169, 174, 198, 211, 227
Soviet Republic, 83
Sovnarkom, 255
Spala, Imperial lodge at, 38
Spring Flowers egg, 11, 80
Stalin, Josef, 57, 67
Standard, Imperial yacht, 38, 85, 88
Standard egg, 11, 68, 69, 83, 90, **188**, *235,* 247, 250, 254, 256, 260
State Depository for valuables, 83
state treasures, 67
Steel Military egg, 11, 68, 69, 83, 90, **230**, *235,* 250, 256, 260
Stein, George, 32, 47, 130
stone carvers, 32
Stone egg, 82
Swan egg, 10, 60, 69, 90, **168**, *235, 245,* 255, 256

T

Talbot de Vere Clifton, Henry, 117, 122
Tauride Palace, 43
Taylor, R.S., 79
Temple of Love egg (*see* Colonnade egg)

Tolstoy, Leo, 60
Trans-Siberian Railway egg, 10, 55, 68, 69, 83, 85, 86, 90, **150**, *234, 243,* 251, 253, 256, 259
Trepov, 60
Tsarevich (*see* Alexei Nikolaievich)
Tsarevich egg, 11, 46, 69, 83, 90, **207**, *234,* 250, 261, 262
Tsarskoie Selo, 35, 38, 40, 43, 88 (*see also* Alexander Palace)
Twelve Monograms egg, 10, 69, 90, **118**, *234, 240*
Twelve-panel egg, 77
Twilight egg, 11, 81

U

undocumented Easter eggs, 78-81
Uspenski Cathederal, 49, 86, 87

V

Vanderbilt, Consuelo, Duchess of Malborough, 81
Victoria, Queen, 36, 38, 42
Vladimir Alexandrovich, Grand Duke, 15, *19,* 63, 92

W

Walters, Henry C., 154, 176, 178
Wartski, 7, 101, 122, 132, 138
Wiesbaden, 28
Wigstrom, Henrik Emanuel, 23, 31, 62, 84, 88, 174, 179, 182, 188, 194, 202, 207, 212, 216, 222, 225, 230
Winter egg, 7, 11, 27, 32, 33, 47, 68, 69, 90, **209**, *234,*
Winter Palace, 35, *36,* 39, 40, 43, 64
description of eggs at the, 253
Woerffel, Karl Feodorovich, 32
wooden egg (*see* Karelian Birch egg)
workmasters, 31
Wyazemski, Prince, 27

Y

Yudenich, General, 65
Yusupov egg, 81
Yusupov, Prince Felix, 81

Z

Zehngraf, Johannes, 32, 124, 133, 136
Zolotnitzky, Jacques, 77
Zuiev, Vassilii Ivanovich, 33, 89, 202, 216

Photographic credits

All photographs not credited below are from the Tatiana Fabergé archives and the Valentin V. Skurlov archives.

Reproduced by gracious permission of Her Majesty the Queen. © Royal Collection Enterprises Ltd: pp.73 top, 91, 157, 158 bottom, 195, 220. Photos Steven Chapman.

Reproduced by gracious permission of Her Majesty the Queen of Denmark Collection: p.17.

Courtesy Prince Rainier III of Monaco Collection: p.99.

Courtesy Armory Museum, State Museums of the Moscow Kremlin: pp.54-56, 107, 143, 145, 151, 153, 161, 183, 184, 185, 189, 190, 192 bottom right, 193, 213-215, 231, 233.

Courtesy Cleveland Museum of Art, the India Early Minshall Collection: p.225.

Courtesy Edouard and Maurice Sandoz Foundation, Switzerland: pp.81 bottom right, 169, 181.

Courtesy FORBES Magazine Collection: pp.72, 76, 79, 80, 81 top right, 93, 117, 121, 122, 127, 129, 147, 148, 198, 199, 201, 228, 229.

The FORBES Magazine Collection, © Metropolitan Museum of Art: pp.131, 137. Photos Joseph Coscia.

Courtesy Hillwood Museum, Washington DC: p.119, 217. Photo E. Owen.

Courtesy Kunsthistorisches Museum, Vienna: p.116.

Courtesy Pavlovsk Museum: p.45.

Courtesy Matilda Geddings Gray Foundation Collection, New Orleans: pp.103-105, 113, 115, 141, 203-206. Photos Owen F. Murphy Jr.

© 1996, Courtesy Virginia Museum of Fine Arts, bequest of Lillian Thomas Pratt, Richmond: pp.125, 133, 134, 165, 167, 207, 223, 224. Photos Katherine Wetzel.

Courtesy Walters Art Gallery, Baltimore: pp.155, 177.

Courtesy Christie's: pp.73 bottom, 74 bottom, 75, 81 top left, 210, 211, 218.

Courtesy Tatiana Fabergé: pp. 22, 23, 24, 25, 27, 28, 32 (bottom), 62, 63, 108, 144, 149, 163, 172, 179, 187, 196, 208.

Courtesy M. Jacques Ferrand: pp.19, 191.

Courtesy Gérard Gorokhoff Collection: pp.15, 37, 38, 41, 40, 42.

Courtesy Slavia Interbook, S.P. Khval': pp.34, 180.

Courtesy Alexander von Solodkoff: pp.71, 216.

Courtesy Sotheby's, London: pp.74 top, 81 bottom left, 111, 175.

Courtesy Victor Szabo, Studio Milar, Vienna: pp.171, 173.

Courtesy Alexis de Tiesenhausen: p. 232.

Courtesy Ulla Tillander-Godenhielm for the drawing of the Napoleonic egg: p.31 middle and bottom, 32 top, 202.

Copyright Maurice Aeschiman: p.22 lower right.

Photo Maya Brashmane: p.33 middle.

Photo V.N. Guseva: pp.25 bottom, 33 bottom left, 98, 110 top, 158 top.

We gratefully acknowledge the work of the following photographers in the Catalogue of the FORBES Magazine Collection: Joseph Coscia, Eric Landsberg, Steven Mays, Larry Stein, Robert Wharton.

We gratefully acknowledge the work of P. Demidov, A.V. Sidorenkov and O. Trubski for the photographs of various palaces in Russia: pp.18, 20, 53, 57, 65, 192 left.

Acknowledgements

In 1991, Mr Rifat Gaffifulin and an expert on Alexander III's art collection discovered among the Emperor's papers correspondence that enabled the authors to end all speculation about the date on which the first Imperial Easter egg was made by Fabergé. We are extremely grateful to Mr Gaffifulin for sharing this important discovery with us.

The authors wish to thank Natalia Heseltine-Galitzine for her painstaking translations, Natalia Pavlova-Kaufman for the in-depth research she conducted on the Kelkh family, and Virginia Llewellyn Smith and Jacqueline Bradshaw-Price for their help and contribution. The generous support of the Igor Carl Fabergé Foundation, Geneva, is gratefully acknowledged both for obtaining authorization to publish photographs of the Imperial Easter eggs and for underwriting some of the costs.

Valuable help and support extended to the authors by the directors, curators and staff of the following institutions in Russia are gratefully acknowledged: Director of the State Hermitage, M.V. Piotrovskii; Director of the Moscow Kremlin Museums, Irina A. Rodimtseva; Director of the Pavlovsk Museum, Yu. N. Mudrov, Chief Curator, A.N. Gusanov; Director of the Marriages Palace (ex von Dervis Mansion), N.A. Grishina; Head of RSHA Reading Room, S.I. Varekhova; Russkyie Samotsvety General Director, A.S. Gorynia, Member of Directorate, I.P. Melsitov, Director of NIYuvelirprom, V.O. Bakharev; Editor of Slavia Interbook, S.P. Khval'; translator, I.N. Orlova; photographers, A.V. Sidorenkov, P. Demidov, O. Trubski; Master Ltd, J. Killedjan. Tatiana Muntian, the learned curator of the Fabergé collection in the Moscow Armoury Museum, has contributed an illuminating essay on the fate of the Imperial Easter eggs during and after the Russian Revolution.

The authors wish to thank the curators and staff of the following institutions for their assistance and cooperation: Henry Hawley, Chief Curator, Later Western Art, the Cleveland Museum of Art; Margaret Kelly, Director, Robyn Tromeur, Assistant Curator, and Catherine S. Thomas, Registrar, The FORBES Magazine Collection, New York; Anne Odom, Chief Curator, Hillwood Museum, Washington, DC; John Webster Keefe, Curator of Decorative Arts, New Orleans Museum of Art; David Park Curry, Curator of American Arts, Virginia Museum of Fine Arts, Richmond; William R. Johnston, Curator of 18th and 19th Century Art, Walters Art Gallery, Baltimore; and Lady Sheila de Bellaigue, Registrar, The Royal Archives, Windsor Castle.

Gerard Hill and Hayden E. Williams of Sotheby's generously supplied photographs. Valuable help from Maurice Aeschimann, Geneva, in producing photographs of documents in Tatiana Fabergé's archives is gratefully appreciated.

Urs Oeggerli, husband of Lynette G. Proler, is to be warmly thanked for his valuable assistance in organizing the complicated materials for this book.

Many thanks to our publishers, Christie's, and a special acknowledgement to Alexis de Tiesenhausen, Head of the Russian department in Europe and America, to whom we owe a debt of gratitude. Though only scant and tantalizing information was afforded him by the authors, he recognized the importance of this project, brought it immediately to the attention of Christie's, and then unfailingly gave much of his time and expertise. Shaunagh Money-Coutts, undaunted by the overwhelming complexities of publishing this work, goodnaturedly prodded and nudged from all sides throughout the manuscript's progress.

The authors had the good fortune of receiving guidance from Stanley Kekwick, Managing Director of Art Books International, into whose hands the manuscript was placed with the simple request to produce an extraordinarily handsome book in the shortest time possible. This was no small feat given the complexity of the material and photographs, but was admirably accomplished with the tireless commitment of Cathy Muscat, our unflappable and most competent editor. The beautiful presentation of the book is due to the creativity of Simon Bell and Martin Richards.